TRAVELS IN THE GREAT WESTERN PRAIRIES

A Da Capo Press Reprint Series

THE AMERICAN SCENE
Comments and Commentators

GENERAL EDITOR: WALLACE D. FARNHAM
University of Illinois

Travels in the Great Western Prairies, the Anahuac and Rocky Mountains, and in the Oregon Territory

By Thomas J. Farnham

Two Volumes in One

DA CAPO PRESS · NEW YORK · 1973

Library of Congress Cataloging in Publication Data

Farnham, Thomas Jefferson, 1804-1848.
  Travels in the great western prairies, the Anahuac
and Rocky Mountains, and in the Oregon Territory.

  (The American scene: comments and commentators)
  Reprint of the 1843 ed.
  1. The West—Description and travel—To 1848.
2. Oregon—Description and travel. 3. Overland
journeys to the Pacific. 4. Rocky Mountains.
5. Indians of North America—The West. I. Title.
F592.F23   1973   917.8   68-16231
ISBN 0-306-71012-9

This Da Capo Press edition of *Travels in the
Great Western Prairies* is an unabridged republication
in one volume of the two-volume
edition published in London in 1843.

Da Capo Press, Inc.
A Subsidiary of Plenum Publishing Corporation
227 West 17th Street, New York, New York 10011

Manufactured in the United States of America

TRAVELS

IN THE

GREAT WESTERN PRAIRIES.

—

VOL. I.

TRAVELS

IN THE

GREAT WESTERN PRAIRIES,

THE ANAHUAC AND ROCKY MOUNTAINS,

AND IN

THE OREGON TERRITORY.

BY THOMAS J. FARNHAM.

IN TWO VOLUMES.

VOL. I.

LONDON:

RICHARD BENTLEY, NEW BURLINGTON STREET,

Publisher in Ordinary to Her Majesty.

1843.

LONDON
PRINTED BY SCHULZE AND CO., 13, POLAND STREET.

PREFACE BY THE EDITOR.

THIS authentic account of the Great Western Prairies and Oregon Territory supplies a deficiency which has been felt for a long time. The author, by his own personal observations, has been enabled to furnish a very interesting narrative of travel; and whether he treats of the Prairies, or of the Oregon region, the various incidents related by him cannot fail to give entertainment and instruction.

With respect to the Introduction, in which the Author asserts the claims of the United States to the Oregon Territory little need be said here : the subject will no doubt receive the full consideration of the Governments interested in the decision of the question.

London, 1843.

PREFACE.

It was customary in old times for all Authors to enter the world of letters on their knees, and with uncovered head, and a bow of charming meekness write themselves some brainless dolt's "most humble and obedient servant." In later days, the same feigned subserviency has shown itself in other forms. One desires that some will kindly pardon the weakness and imbecility of his production ; for, although these faults may exist in his book, he wrote under "most adverse circumstances," as the crying of a hopeful child, the quarrels of his poultry, and other disasters of the season.

Another, clothed with the mantle of the sweetest self-complacency, looks out from his Preface, like a sun-dog on the morning sky, and merely *shines out* the query, "Am I not a Sun?" while he secures a retreat for his self-love, in case anybody should suppose he ever indulged such a singular sentiment.

A few others of our literary shades make no pretensions to modesty. They hold out to the world no need of aid in laying the foundations of their fame; and, however adverse the opinions of the times may be to their claims to renown, they are sure of living hereafter, and only regret they should have lived a hundred years before the world was prepared to receive them.

There is another class, who, confident that they understand the subjects they treat of, if nothing else, and that, speaking plain truth for the information of plain men, they cannot fail to narrate matter of interest concerning scenes or incidents they have witnessed, and sensations they have experienced—trouble not themselves with the qualms of inability, or lack of polish, but speak from the heart. These write their names on their title-pages, and leave their readers at leisure to judge of their merits as they develope themselves in the work itself, without any special pleading or any deprecatory prayers to the reviews, by

THE AUTHOR.

INTRODUCTION.

The Oregon Territory forms the terminus of these Travels ; and, as that country is an object of much interest on both sides of the Atlantic, I have thought proper to preface my wanderings there by a brief discussion of the question as to whom it belongs.

By treaties between the United States and Spain and Mexico and Russia, the southern boundary of Oregon is fixed on the 42nd parallel of north latitude ; and the northern on an east and west line, at 54° 40′ north. Its natural boundary on the east is the main ridge of the Rocky Mountains, situated about four hundred miles east of the Pacific Ocean, which washes it on the west. From these data the reader will observe that it is about six hundred miles in length, and four hundred in breadth.

According to the well-established laws of nations applicable to the premises, the title to the sovereignty over it depends upon the prior discovery and occupancy of it, and upon cessions by treaty from the first discoverer and occupant. These several important matters I proceed to examine, with Greenough's History of the North-west Coast of America, and the works therein named, before me as sources of reference.

From the year 1532 to 1540, the Spanish government sent four expeditions to explore the north-west coast of America, in search of what did not exist—a water communication from the Pacific to the Atlantic. These fleets were severally commanded by Mazuela, Grijalva, Becera, and Ulloa. They visited the coast of California, and the south-western shore of Oregon.

The next naval expedition, under the same Power, commanded by Bartoleme Ferrello, penetrated to the north as far as latitude 43°, and discovered Cape Blanco.

Juan de Fuca discovered and entered the Straits that bear his name in the year 1592. He spent twenty days within the Straits in making himself acquainted with the surrounding country, trading with the natives, and in taking possession of the adjacent territories in the name of the Spanish Crown. The Straits de Fuca enter the land in latitude 49° north, and, running one hundred miles in a south-easterly direction, change their course north-westwardly, and enter the ocean again under latitude 51° north. Thus it appears that Spain discovered the Oregon Coast from latitude 42° to 49° north two hundred and fifty-one years ago ; and, as will appear by reference to dates, one hundred and eighty-four years prior to the celebrated English Expedition under Captain Cook.

In 1602, and subsequent years, Corran and Viscaino, in the employment of Spain, surveyed many parts of the Oregon Coast, and in the following year Aguiler, in the same service, discovered the mouth of the Umpqua River in latitude 44° north.

In August, 1774, Parez and Martinez, under the Spanish flag, discovered and anchored in Nootka Sound. It lies between 49° and 50° of north latitude.

In 1774 and 1775 the north-west coast was explored by Parez and Martinez of the Spanish service, as far north as the 58th parallel of latitude.

On the 6th day of May, 1789, the Spanish Captain Martinez, commanding two national armed vessels, took possession of Nootka Sound and the adjoining country.

Previous to this event, say the authorities
referred to, no jurisdiction had been exercised by the subjects of any civilized power
on any part of the north-west coast of
America between 37° and 60° of north latitude.

Thus is it shown on how firm and incon-
trovertible data the Spanish claims rest to
the prior discovery and occupancy of the
Oregon Territory.

But as against England this claim was
rendered if possible more certain by the treaty
of February 10th, 1763, between Spain,
England and France—by which England
was confirmed in her Canadian possessions,
and Spain in her discoveries and purchased
possessions west of the Mississippi. If,
then, England has any claim to Oregon as
derived from Spain, it must rest on treaty
stipulations entered into subsequently to the
10th of February, 1763.

We accordingly find her to have formed
a treaty with Spain in the year 1800, settling the difficulties between the two powers
in relation to Nootka Sound. By the first
article of the convention, Spain agreed to
restore to England those portions of the
country around Nootka Sound which En-

gland had so occupied in regard to time and manner as to have acquired a right to them. The 5th article stipulates as follows :

" 5th. As well in the places which are to be restored to the British subjects by virtue of the first article as in all other ports of the North-West Coast of North America, or of the Island, adjacent, situate to the north of the coast already occupied by Spain wherein the subjects of either of the two Powers shall have made settlements since the month of April 1789, or shall hereafter make any. The subjects of the other shall have free access and shall carry on their trade without any disturbance or molestation."

The inquiries that naturally arise here are, on what places or parts of the North-West Coast did this article operate ; what rights were granted by it, and to what extent the United States, as the successors of Spain, in the ownership of Oregon, are bound by this treaty ?

These will be considered in their order.

Clearly the old Spanish settlements of the Californias were not included among the places or parts of the North-West Coast on which this article was intended to operate, for the reason that England, the party in interest, has never claimed that they were. But on the contrary, in all her diplomatic and commercial intercourse with Spain since 1800, she has treated the soil of the Californias with the same consideration that she has any portion of the Spanish territories in Europe.—And since that country has formed a department of the Mexican Republic, England has set up no claims within its limits under this treaty.

Was Nootka Sound embraced among the places referred to in this article ? That was the only settlement on the North West Coast, of the subjects of Spain or England, made between the month of April, 1787, and the date of the treaty, and was undoubtedly embraced in the Fifth Article. And so was the remainder of the coast, lying northward of Nootka, on which Spain had claims. It did not extend south of Nootka Sound. Not an inch of soil in the valley of the Columbia and its tributaries was included in the provisions of the treaty of 1763.

Our next inquiry relates to the nature and extent of the rights at Nootka, and northward, which England acquired by this treaty. They are defined in the concluding phrase of the article before cited. The subjects of both the contracting Powers "shall have free access, and shall carry on their trade without disturbance or molestation." In other words the subjects of England shall have the same right to establish trading posts and carry on a trade with the Indians, as were, or should be enjoyed by Spanish subjects in those regions. Does this stipulation abrogate the sovereignty of Spain over those territories? England herself can scarcely urge with seriousness a proposition so ridiculously absurd. A grant of an equal right to settle in a country for purposes of trade, and a guarantee against "disturbance" and "molestation," does not, in any vocabulary, imply a cession of the sovereignty of the territory in which these acts are to be done.

The number and nature of the rights granted to England by this treaty, are simply a right to the joint occupancy of Nootka and the Spanish territories to the northward, for purposes of trade with the Indians; a joint tenancy, subject to be terminated at the will of the owner of the title to the fee and the sovereignty; and, if not thus terminated, to be terminated by the operations of the necessity of things—the annihilation of the trade

—the destruction of the Indians themselves as they should fall before the march of civilisation. It could not have been a perpetual right, in the contemplation of either of the contracting parties.

But there are reasons why the provisions of the treaty of 1763 never had been, and never can be binding on the United States as the successors of Spain in the Oregon territory.

There is the evidence of private gentlemen of the most undoubted character to show, that Spain neither surrendered to England any portion of Nootka, or other parts of the north-west coast ; for that if she offered to do so, the offer was not acted upon by England ; and testimony to the same effect in the debates of the times in the Parliament of Britain, in which this important fact is distinctly asserted, authorise us to declare that the treaty of 1763 was annulled by Spain, and so considered by England herself. And if England did not mean to show the world that she acquiesced in the non-fulfilment of Spain, she should have re-asserted her right, if she thought she had any, and not left third parties to infer that she had quietly abandoned them. The United States had every reason to infer such abandonment; and in view of it, thus manifested, purchased Oregon of Spain. Under these circumstances, with what justice can England, after the lapse of nearly half a century, come forward and demand of the successor of Spain rights in Oregon which she thus virtually abandoned—which were refused by Spain, and to which she never had the shadow of a right on the score of prior discovery, occupancy or purchase? The perpetually controlling and selfishness of her policy is the only plea that history will assign to her in accounting for her pretensions in this matter.

England also places her claim to Oregon upon the right of discovery. Let us examine this:—

The first English vessel which visited that coast was commanded by Francis Drake. He entered the Pacific in 1770* and sailed up the coast to the 45th parallel of north latitude, and then returned to the 38th degree; accepted the crown of the native Prince in the name of his Queen— called the country New Albion, returned to England and was knighted.

---

* This date is incorrect. It was in 157/; and he sailed to the 48th parallel of north latitude.— D.

The portions of Oregon seen by Drake had been seen and explored by the Spaniards several times within the previous thirty years.

Sir Thomas Cavendish next came upon the coast ; but did not see so much of it as Drake had seen.

The celebrated Captain Cook followed Cavendish. He saw the coast in latitude 43 and 48 degrees. He passed the Straits de Fuca without seeing them, and anchored in Nootka Sound on the 16th February, 1779.* In trading with the Indians there, he found that they had weapons of iron, ornaments of brass, and spoons of Spanish manufacture. Nootka had been discovered and occupied by the Spaniards four years before Cook arrived.

The subsequent English navigators— Mesrs. Vancouver, and others, so far as the Oregon coast was the field of their labours, were followers in the tracks pointed out by the previous discoveries of the Spaniards.

So ends the claim of England to Oregon, on the right of prior discovery. As opposed to England, Spain's rights on this principle were incontestible.

* He was killed on the 14th February, 1779.—Ed.

By the treaty of Florida, ratified February 22d, 1819, Spain ceded to the United States her right in the Oregon territory, in the following words: " His Catholic Majesty cedes to the said United States all his rights, claims, and pretensions to any territories east and north of said line;" meaning the 42d parallel of north latitude, commencing at the head waters of the Arkansas, and running west to the Pacific ; " and for himself, his heirs and successors, renounces all claim to the said territories for ever."

But the United States have rights to Oregon which of themselves annihilate the pretensions not only of England but the world. Her citizens first discovered that the country on which Nootka Sound is situated was an island ; they first navigated that part of the Straits of Fuca lying between Puget's Sound and Queen Charlotte's Island, and discovered the main coast of north-west America, from latitude 48° to 50° north. American citizens also discovered Queen Charlotte's Island, sailed around it, and discovered the main land to the east of it, as far north as latitude 55°.

England can show no discoveries between these latitudes so important as these ; and consequently has not equal rights with the

Americans as a discoverer, to that part of Oregon north of the 49th degree of latitude. We also discovered the Columbia River ; and its whole valley, in virtue of that discovery, accrues to us under the laws of nations. One of these laws is that the nation which discovers the mouth of a river, by implication discovers the whole country watered by it. We discovered the mouth of the Columbia and most of its branches ; and that valley is ours against the world—ours, also, by purchase from Spain, the first discoverer and occupant of the coast — ours by prior occupancy of its great river and valley, and by that law which gives us, in virtue of such discovery and occupancy, the territories naturally dependent upon such valley. We are the rightful and sole owner of all those parts of Oregon, which are not watered by the Columbia, lying on its northern and southern border, and which, in the language of the law, are naturally dependent upon it. Oregon territory, for all these reasons is the rightful property of the United States.

CONTENTS

TO

THE FIRST VOLUME.

CHAPTER I.

The Rendezvous—The Destination—The Education of
Mules—The Santa Fé Traders—The Mormons—The
Holy War—Entrance upon the Indian Territory—A
Scene—An Encampment—A Loss—A Hunt—The
Osage River—A Meeting and Parting—Kauzaus In-
dians—An Indian Encampment—Council Grove—
Ruins—An Indian and his Wants—Elk—A Tempest
—Captain Kelly—A comfortless Night .   . 1—38

CHAPTER II.

Scarcity of Food—An Incident—Looing and Bleating—
Messrs. Bents—Trade—Little Arkansas—A Nauseous
Meal—A Flood—An Onset—A Hard Ride—The De-
liverance—The Arkansas—An Attack—The Simili-
tude of Death—The Feast and a bit of Philosophy—
The Traders Walworth and Alvarez's Teams—A
Fright—A Nation of Indians—Their Camp and Hunts
—A Treaty—A Tempest—Indian Butchering—A
Hunt among the Buffalo—A Wounded Man—A
Drive—A Storm and its Enemy—Night among the
Buffalo—The Country and the Heavens—The Ford
—A Mutiny and its Consequences—Blistered Fingers
—Liberty—Bent's Fort—Disbanding.   . 39—100

CHAPTER III.

The Great Prairie Wilderness—Its Rivers and Soil—
Its People and their Territories—Choctaws—Chickasaws—Cherokees—Creeks—Senecas and Shawnees
—Seminoles—Pottawatamies—Weas—Pionkashas—
Peorias and Kaskaskias—Ottowas—Shawnees or Shawanoes—Delawares—Kausaus—Kickapoos—Sauks
and Foxes—Iowas—Otoes—Omehas—Puncahs—
Pawnees, remnants—Carankauas—Cumanche, remnants—Knistineaux—Naudowisses or Sioux—Chippeways, and their traditions   .   .   . 101—172

CHAPTER IV.

Fort William—its Structure, Owners, People, Animals,
Business, Adventures, and Hazards—A Division—A
March—Fort el Puebla—Trappers and Whisky—A
Genius—An Adventurous Iroquois—A Kentuckian—
Horses and Servant—A Trade—A Start—Arkansas
and Country—Wolfano Mountains—Creeks—Rio
Wolfano—A Plague of Egypt—Cordilleras—James'
Peak—Pike's Peak—A Bath—The Prison of the Ar-
kansas—Entrance of the Rocky Mountains—A
Vale   173-252

CHAPTER V.

An Ascent—A Misfortune—A Death—The Mountain
of the Holy Cross—Leaping Pines—Killing a Buffalo

—Asses and Tyrants—Panther, &c.—Geography—
Something about descending the Colorado of the
West — Dividing Ridges — A Scene — Tumbleton's
Park — A War Whoop — Meeting of Old Fellow
Trappers—A Notable Tramp—My Mare—The eti-
quette of the Mountains—Kelly's Old Camp, &c.—
A Great Heart—Little Bear River—Vegetables and
Bitterness—Two White Men, a Squaw and Child—
A Dead Shot—What is Tasteful—Trapping—Black-
foot and Sioux—A Bloody Incident—A Cave—Hot
Spring—The Country—A Surprise—American and
Canadian Trappers—The Grand River—Old Park—
Death before us—The Mule—Despair   253—297

TRAVELS

IN THE

GREAT WESTERN PRAIRIES,

&c. &c.

CHAPTER I.

The Rendezvous—The Destination—The Education of
Mules—The Santa Fé Traders—The Mormons—The
Holy War—Entrance upon the Indian Territory—A
Scene—An Encampment—A Loss—A Hunt—The
Osage River—A Meeting and Parting—Kauzaus In-
dians—An Indian Encampment—Council Grove—
Ruins—An Indian and his Wants—Elk—A Tempest
—Captain Kelly—A comfortless Night.

On the 21st of May, 1839, the author
and sixteen others arrived in the town of Independence, Missouri. Our destination was
the Oregon Territory. Some of our number sought health in the wilderness—others
sought the wilderness for its own sake—
and others sought a residence among the
ancient forests and lofty heights of the
valley of the Columbia; and each actuated
by his own peculiar reasons, or interest,
began his preparations for leaving the fron-

VOL. I.   B

tier. Pack mules and horses and pack-saddles were purchased and prepared for service. Bacon and flour, salt and pepper, sufficient for four hundred miles, were secured in sacks; our powder-casks were wrapt in painted canvas, and large oil-cloths were purchased to protect these and our sacks of clothing from the rains; our arms were thoroughly repaired; bullets were moulded; powder-horns and cap-boxes filled; and all else done that was deemed needful, before we struck our tent for the Indian territory.

But before leaving this little woodland town, it will be interesting to remember that it is the usual place of rendezvous and " outfit " for the overland traders to Santa Fé and other Mexican states. In the month of May of each year, these traders congregate here, and buy large Pennsylvania waggons, and teams of mules to convey their calicoes, cottons, cloths, boots, shoes, etc, over the plains to that distant and hazardous market. It is quite amusing to greenhorns, as those are called who have never been engaged in the trade, to see the mules make their first attempt at practical pulling They are harnessed in a team, two upon the shaft, and the remainder two abreast in long swinging iron traces; and then, by way of initiatory intimation that they have passed from a life of monotonous contemplation, in the seclusion of their nursery pastures, to the bustling duties of the "Santa Fé trade," a hot iron is applied to the thigh or shoulder of each, with an embrace so cordially warm, as to leave there, in blistered perfection, the initials of their last owner's name. This done, a Mexican Spaniard, as chief muleteer, mounts the right-hand wheel mule, and another, the left hand one of the span next the leaders, while four or five others, as foot-guard, stand on either side, armed with whips and thongs. The team is straightened—and now comes the trial of passive obedience. The chief muleteer gives the shout of march, and drives his long spurs into the sides of the animal that bears him ; his companion before follows his example ; but there is no movement. A leer—an unearthly bray, is the only response of these martyrs to human supremacy. Again the team is straightened, again the rowel is applied, the body-guard on foot raise the shout, and all apply the lash at the same moment. The untutored animals kick and leap, rear and plunge, and fall in their harness. In fine, they act the mule, and generally succeed in breaking neck or limb of some one of their number, and in raising a tumult that would do credit to any order of animals accustomed to long ears.

After a few trainings, however, of this description, they move off in fine style. And, although some luckless animal may at intervals brace himself up to an uncompromising resistance of such encroachment upon his freedom, still, the majority preferring passive obedience to active pelting, drag him onward, till, like themselves, he submits to the discipline of the traces.

' Independence' was the first location of the *Mormons* west of the Mississippi. Here they laid out grounds for their temple, built the ' Lord's store,' and in other ways prepared the place for the permanent establishment of their community. But, becoming obnoxious to their neighbours, they crossed the Missouri, and founded the town of ' Far West.' In 1838 they recommenced certain practices of their faith in their new abode, and were ejected from the state by its military forces.

The misfortunes of these people seem to have arisen from proceeding upon certain rules of action peculiar to themselves. The basis of these rules is the assumption that

they are the " Saints of the Most High," to
whom the Lord promised of old the inheri-
tance of the earth; and that as such they
have the right to take possession of whatever they may be inspired to desire. Any
means are justifiable, in their belief, to bring
about the restoration to the " Children of
God" of that which He has bequeathed to
them. In obedience to these rules of action,
any Mormon or "Latter-Day Saint" labouring for hire on a " worldly" man's plantation, claimed the right to direct what improvements should be made on the premises; what trees should be felled, and
what grounds should, from time to time, be
cultivated. If this prerogative of saintship
were questioned by the warm-blooded Missourians, they were with great coolness and
gravity informed that their godly servants
expected in a short time to be in comfortable possession of their employers' premises;
for that the Latter-Days had come, and with
them the Saints; that wars and carnage
were to be expected; and that the Latter-
Day Prophet had learned, in his communi-
cations with the Court of Heaven, that the
Missourians were to be exterminated on the
first enlargement of the borders of " Zion;"
and that over the graves of those " enemies

of all righteousness" would spring that vast spiritual temple which was "to fill the earth."

The prospect of being thus immolated upon the altar of Mormonism, did not produce so much humility and trembling among these hardy frontiersmen as the prophet Joe had benevolently desired. On the contrary, the pious intimation that their throats would be cut to glorify God, was resisted by some ruthless and sinful act of self-defence; and all the denunciations of the holy brotherhood were impiously scorned as idle words. However, in spite of the irreligious wrath of these deluded, benighted Missourians, the Saints cut timber wherever they listed on the domains which were claimed by the people of the world. And if the "Lord's hogs or horses" wanted corn, the farms in the hands of the wicked were resorted to at a convenient hour of the night for a supply. In all these cases, the "Saints" manifested a kind regard to the happiness even of the enemies of their faith. For whenever they took corn from fields in possession of the world's people, they not only avoided exciting unholy wrath by allowing themselves to be seen in the act, but, in order that peace might reign in the bosoms of the wicked, even, the longest possible time, they stripped that portion of the harvest field which would be last seen by the ungodly owner.

The "Church militant," however, being inefficient and weak, the Prophet Joe declared that it was their duty to use whatever means the Lord might furnish to strengthen themselves. And as one powerful means would be the keeping its doings as much as possible from the world, it was he said, the will of Heaven, revealed to him in proper form, that in no case, when called before the ungodly tribunals of this perverse and blind generation, should they reveal, for any cause, any matter or thing which might, in its consequences, bring upon the brotherhood the infliction of those pretended rules of Justice, by the world called Laws. Under the protection of this prophecy, a band of the brethren was organized, called the "Tribe of Dan," whose duty it was to take and bring to the "Lord's store," in the far West, any of the Lord's personal estate which they might find in the possession of the world, and which might be useful to the "Saints," in advancing their kingdom. Great good is said to have been done by this Tribe of Dan;

for the Lord's store was soon filled, and
the Saints praised the name of Joe. The
Prophet's face shone with the light of an
all-subduing delight at the increase of
" Zion," and the efficiency of his administration.

The Missourians, however, were destitute of the Latter-Day Faith, and of just
views of the rights devised to those, who,
in the Lord's name, should destroy his
adversaries, and restore the earth to the
dominion of millennial righteousness. Poor
mortals and deluded sinners! They believed that the vain and worldly enactments
of legislative bodies were to prevail against
the inspirations of the Latter-Day Prophet
Joe; and in their unsanctified zeal, declared the Saints to be thieves, and unjust,
and murderous; and the Tribe of Dan to
be a pest to the constitutional and acknowledged inherent and natural right to acquire,
possess, and enjoy property. From this
honest difference of opinion arose the "Mormon War," whose great events are recorded
in the narrative of the " Latter-Day
Saints ?" Some events, there were, however, not worthy to find record there, which
may be related here.

The Governor of the Missouri ordered

out the State troops to fight and subdue
the Mormons, and take from them the
property which the "Tribe of Dan" had
deposited in the "Lord's brick store" in
the "citadel of Zion," called "Far West."
It was in 1838 they appeared before the
camp of the "Saints" and commanded them
to surrender. It was done in the manner
hereafter described. But before this event
transpired, I am informed that the Prophet
Joe opened his mouth in the name of the
Lord, and said it had been revealed to him
that the scenes of Jericho were to be re-
enacted in Far West; that the angelic host
would appear on the day of battle, and
by their power give victory to the "Saints."

To this end he ordered a breast-work
of inch pine boards to be raised around the
camp, to show by this feeble protection
against the artillery of their foes, that their
strength was in the "breast-plate of
righteousness," and that they were the soldiers of the militant portion of the Kingdom of Heaven. There were moments of
awful suspense in the camp of the "Saints."
The Missouri bayonets bristled brightly
near their ranks, and an occasional bullet
carelessly penetrated the pine-board rampart, regardless of the inhibition of the

Prophet. The Heavens were gazed upon
for the shining host, and listening ears
turned to catch the rushing of wings
through the upper air. The demand of
surrender was again and again repeated;
but Faith had seized on Hope, and Delay
was the offspring.

At this juncture of affairs, a sturdy old
Missourian approached the brick store,
pickaxe in hand, apparently determined to
do violence to the sacred depository. One
of the sisters in robes of white accosted
him, and with proper solemnity made
known that the " Lord of the Faithful" had
revealed to Joe, the Prophet, that every
hand raised against that "holy structure"
would instantly be withered. The fron-
tiersman hesitated, but the hardihood characteristic of these men of the rifle returning, he replied, " Well, old gal, I'll go it
on one hand any how." The awful blow
was struck ; the hand did not wither !   " I
doubles up now," said the daring man, and
with both hands inflicted a heavy blow
upon a corner brick. It tumbled to the
ground, and the building quickly fell under
the weight of a thousand vigorous arms.
The confidence of the Saints in their
Prophet waned, and a surrender followed.

Some of the principal men were put in custody, but the main body were permitted to leave the State without farther molestation. We afterwards met many of them with their herds, &c., on the road from Far West to Quincy, Illinois. It was strongly intimated by the planters in that section of country, that these emigrating " saints" found large quantities of the "Lord's corn" on their way, which they appropriated as need suggested to their own and their animals' wants.

The origin of the " Book of Mormon" was for some time a mystery. But recent developements prove it to have been written in 1812 by the Rev. Solomon Spaulding, of New Salem, in the state, Ohio. It was composed by that gentleman as a historical romance of the long extinct race who built the mounds and forts which are scattered over the valley States. Mr. Spaulding read the work while composing it to some of his friends, who, on the appearance of the book in print, were so thoroughly convinced of its identity with the romance of their deceased pastor, that search was made, and the original manuscript found among his papers. But there was yet a marvel how the work could have got into the hands of Joe

Smith. On further investigation, however, it appeared that the reverend author had entertained thoughts of publishing it; and, in pursuance of his intention, had permitted it to lie a long time in the printing office in which Sidney Rigdon, who has figured so prominently in the history of the Mormons, was at the time employed. Rigdon, doubtless, copied poor Spaulding's novel, and with it, and the aid of Joe Smith, has succeeded in building up a system of superstition, which, in vileness and falsehood, is scarcely equalled by that of Mahomet.

Solomon Spaulding was a graduate of Dartmouth College.

On the 30th of May, we found ourselves prepared to move for the Indian Territory. Our pack-saddles being girded upon the animals, our sacks of provisions, &c. snugly lashed upon them, and protected from the rain that had begun to fall, and ourselves well mounted and armed, we took the road that leads off southwest from Independence in the direction of Santa Fé. But the rains which had accompanied us daily since we left Peoria, seemed determined to escort us still, our ill-natured scowls to the contrary notwithstanding : for we had travelled only three miles when

such torrents fell, that we found it necessary
to take shelter in a neighbouring school-
house for the night. It was dismal enough ;
but a blazing fire within, and a merry
song from a jovial member of our company
imparted as much consolation as our circumstances seemed to demand, till we responded to the howling storm the sonorous
evidence of sweet and quiet slumber.

The following morning was clear and
pleasant, and we were early on our route.
We crossed the stream called Big Blue, a
tributary of the Missouri, about twelve
o'clock, and approached the border of the
Indian domains. All were anxious now to
see and linger over every object which reminded us we were still on the confines of
that civilization which we had inherited
from a thousand generations ; a vast and
imperishable legacy of civil and social happiness. It was, therefore, painful to approach the last frontier enclosure—the last
habitation of the white man—the last semblance of home. At length the last cabin was
approached. We drank at the well and travelled on. It was now behind us. All, indeed
was behind us with which the sympathies of
our young days had mingled their holy
memories. Before us were the treeless

plains of green, as they had been since the flood—beautiful, unbroken by bush or rock ; unsoiled by plough or spade ; sweetly scented with the first blossomings of the spring. They had been, since time commenced, the theatre of the Indian's prowess —of his hopes, joys, and sorrows. Here, nations, as the eve of deadly battle closed around them, had knelt and raised the votive offering to Heaven, and implored the favour and protection of the Great Spirit who had fostered their fathers upon the wintry mountains of the North, and when bravely dying, had borne them to the islands of light beneath the setting sun. A lovely landscape this, for an Indian's meditation ! He could almost behold in the distance where the plain and sky met, the holy portals of his after-state—so mazy and beautiful was the scene !

Having travelled about twenty-five miles over this beautiful prairie, we halted on the banks of a small stream at a place called Elm Grove. Here we pitched our tent, tied our horses to stakes, carried for that purpose, and after considerable difficulty having obtained fuel for a fire, cooked and ate for the first time in the Indian Territory.

At this encampment final arrangements were made for our journey over the Prairies. To this end provisions, arms, ammunition, packs and pack-saddles, were overhauled, and an account taken of our common stock of goods for trade with the Indians. The result of this examination was, that we determined to remain here a while, and send back to the Kauzaus Indian mill for two hundred pounds of flour. We were induced to take this step by assurances received from certain traders whom we met coming from the mountains, that the buffalo had not advanced so far north as to furnish us with their fine hump-ribs so early by a week or fortnight as we had expected. Officers were also chosen and their powers defined ; and whatever leisure we found from these duties during a stay of two days, was spent in regaling ourselves with strawberries and gooseberries, which grew in great abundance near our camp.

Our friends having returned from the mill with the flour for which they had been despatched, we left Elm Grove on the 3d of June, travelled along the Santa Fé trail about fifteen miles, and encamped upon a high knoll, from which we had an extensive view of the surrounding plains. The grass was now about four inches in height, and

bent and rose in most sprightly beauty
under the gusts of wind which at intervals
swept over it. We remained here a day
and a half, waiting for two of our number
who had gone in search of a horse that had
left our encampment at Elm Grove. The
time, however, passed agreeably. We
were, indeed, beyond the sanctuaries of
society, and severed from the kind pulsa-
tions of friendship; but the spirit of the
Red Man, wild and careless as the storms
he buffets, began to come over us; and we
shouldered our rifles and galloped away
for a deer in the lines of timber that threaded the western horizon. Our first hunt in
the depths of the beautiful and dreadful
wilderness! It was attended with no success, however, but was worth the effort.
We had begun to hunt our food.

In the afternoon of the 4th, our friends
returned with the strayed animals. The
keepers immediately fired the signal-guns,
and all were soon in camp. Our road on
the 5th was through a rich, level prairie,
clothed with the wild grass common to the
plains of the West. A skirt of black oak
timber occasionally lined the horizon or
strayed up a deep ravine near the trail.
The extreme care of the pioneers in the

overland Santa Fé trade was every where noticeable, in the fact that the track of their richly-loaded waggons never approached within musket-shot of these points of timber. Fifteen miles' march brought us to our place of encampment. A certain portion of the company allotted to that labour, unpacked the company's mules of the common-stock property, provisions, ammunitions, &c.; another portion pitched the tent; another gathered wood and kindled a fire; whilst others brought water, and still others again put seething-pots and frying-pans to their appropriate duties. So that at this, as at many a time before and after, a few minutes transposed our little cavalcade from a moving troop into an eating, drinking, and joyous camp. A thunder-storm visited us during the night. The lightning was intensely vivid, and the explosions were singularly frequent and loud. The sides of the heavens appeared to war like contending batteries in deadly conflict. The rain came in floods; and our tent, not being ditched around, was flooded soon after the commencement of the storm, and ourselves and baggage thoroughly drenched.

The next day we made about fifteen miles through the mud and rain, and stopped for

the night near a solitary tree upon the
bank of a small tributary of the Konzas
river. Here fortune favoured our fast decreasing larder. One of the company killed
a turtle, which furnished us all with an excellent supper. This was the only description of game that we had seen since leaving
the frontier.

On the 7th, as the sun was setting, we
reached Osage River—a stream which
flows into the Missouri below Jefferson
City. The point where we struck it, was
one hundred miles south-west of Independence. We pitched our tent snugly by a
copse of wood within a few yards of it ;
staked down our animals near at hand, and
prepared, and ate in the usual form, our
evening repast. Our company was divided
into two messes, seven in one, and eight in
the other. On the ground, each with a tin
pint cup and a small round plate of the
same material, the first filled with coffee,
tea, or water, the last with fried bacon
and dough fried in fat ; each with a butcher-
knife in hand, and each mess sitting, tailor-
like, around its own frying-pan, eating with
the appetite of tigers formed the *coup-d'œil*
of our company at supper on the banks of
the Osage.

Near us were encamped some waggoners on their return to Missouri, who
had been out to Council Grove with the
provisions and that part of the goods of the
Santa Fé traders which the teams of untrained mules had been unable to draw when
they left Independence. With these men
we passed a very agreeable evening; they
amused us with yarns of mountain-life,
which from time to time had floated in, and
formed the fireside legends of that wild
border. In the morning, while we were saddling our animals, two of the Kauzaus Indians came within a few rods of our camp,
and waited for an invitation to approach.
They were armed with muskets and knives.
The manner of carrying their fire-arms was
peculiar, and strongly characteristic of Indian caution. The breech was held in the
right hand, and the barrel rested on the left
arm ; thus they are always prepared to fire.
They watched us narrowly, as if to ascertain
whether we were friends or foes, and upon
our making signs to them to approach, they
took seats near the fire, and with most im-
perturbable calmness, commenced smoking
the compound of willow-bark and tobacco
with which they are wont to regale themselves. When we left the ground, one of

the men threw away a pair of old boots, the soles of which were fastened with iron nails. Our savage visitors seized upon them with the greatest eagerness, and in their panto-mimic language, aided by harsh, guttural grunts, congratulated themselves upon be-coming the possessors of so much wealth. At eight o'clock we were on march.

The morning breezes were bland, and a thousand young flowers gemmed the grassy plains. It seemed as if the tints of a brighter sky and the increasing beauty of the earth were lifting the clouds from the future, and shedding vigour upon our hopes. But this illusion lasted but a moment. Three of my valuable men had determined to accompany the waggoners to the States; and as they filed off and bade adieu to the enterprise in which they had embarked, and blighted many cheering expectations of social inter-course along our weary way-faring to Ore-gon, an expression of deep discouragement shaded every face. This was of short du-ration. The determination to penetrate the valleys of Oregon soon swept away every feeling of depression, and two hunters being sent forward to replenish our larder, we travelled happily onward.

The Osage River at this place is one

hundred yards wide, with about two-and-a-half feet of water. Its banks are clothed with timber of cotton-wood, ash and hickory. We crossed it at eight o'clock in the morning, passed through the groves which border it, and continued to follow the Santa Fé trail. The portion of country over which it ran was undulating and truly beautiful; the soil rich, very deep, and intersected by three small streams, which appeared from their courses to be tributaries of the Osage.

At night-fall, we found ourselves upon a height overlooking a beautiful grove. This we supposed to be Council Grove. On the swell of the hill were the remains of an old Kauzaus' encampment; a beautiful clear spring gushed out from the rock below. The whole was so inviting to us, weary and hungry as we were, that we determined to make our bed there for the night. Accordingly, we fired signal-guns for the hunters, pitched our tents, broke up the boughs which had been used by the Indians in building their wigwams, for fuel, and proceeded to cook our supper. This encampment had been made by the Kauzaus six years ago, when on their way south to their annual buffalo-hunt. A semi-circular piece of ground was enclosed by the outer lodges.

The area was filled with wigwams, built in straight lines, running from the diameter to the circumference. They were constructed in the following manner. Boughs of about two inches in diameter were inserted by their butts into the ground, and withed together at the top in an arched form ; over these were spread blankets, skins of the buffalo, etc. Fires were built in front of each: the grass beneath, covered with skins, made a delightful couch, and the Indian's home was complete. Several yards from the outer semi-circular row of lodges and parallel to it, we found large stakes driven firmly into the earth, for the purpose of securing their horses during the night. We appropriated to ourselves, without hesitation, whatever we found here of earth, wood or water, which could be useful to us, and were soon very comfortable. About nine o'clock, our signal-guns were answered by the return of our hunters. They had scoured the country all day in quest of game, but found none. Our hopes were somewhat depressed by this result. We had but one hundred pounds of flour and one side of bacon left ; and the buffalo, by the best estimates we could make, were still three hundred miles distant ; the country between

us and these animals, too, being constantly
scoured by Indian hunters, afforded us but
little prospect of obtaining other game.
However, we did not dwell very minutely
upon the evils that might await us, but
having put ourselves upon short allowance,
and looked at our horses as the means of
venting starvation, we sought rest for the
fatigues of the next day's march.

In the morning we moved down the hill.
Our way lay directly through the little grove
already referred to ; and, however we might
have admired its freshness and beauty, we
were deterred from entering into the full
enjoyment of the scene by the necessity,
which we supposed existed of keeping, a
sharp look-out among its green recesses for
the lurking savage. The grove is the northern limit of the wanderings of the Cumanches—a tribe of Indians who make their
home on the rich plains along the western
borders of the republic of Texas. Their ten
thousand warriors, their incomparable horse-
manship, their terrible charge, the unequalled rapidity with which they load and
discharge their fire-arms, and their insatiable
hatred, make the enmity of these Indians
more dreadful than that of any other tribe
of aborigines. Fortunately for us, however,

these Spartans of the plains did not appear,
and right merrily did we cross the little savannah between it and Council Grove, a
beautiful lawn of the wilderness, some of
the men hoping for the sweets of the bee-
tree, others for a shot at a turkey or a deer,
and others again that among the drooping
boughs and silent glades might be found the
panting loins of a stately elk.

Council Grove derives its name from the
practice among the traders, from the commencement of the overland commerce with
the Mexican dominions, of assembling there
for the appointment of officers and the establishment of rules and regulations to
govern their march through the dangerous
country south of it. They first elect their
commander-in-chief. His duty is to appoint subordinate leaders, and to divide the
owners and men into watches, and to assign
them their several hours of duty in guarding the camp during the remainder of their
perilous journey. He also divides the caravan into two parts, each of which forms
a column when on march. In these lines
he assigns each team the place in which it
must always be found. Having arranged
these several matters, the council breaks
up ; and the commander, with the guard on

duty, moves off in advance to select the track and anticipate approaching danger. After this guard the head teams of each column lead off about thirty feet apart, and the others follow in regular lines, rising and dipping gloriously; two hundred men, one hundred waggons, eight hundred mules; shoutings and whippings, and whistlings and cheerings, are all there; and, amidst them all, the hardy Yankee move happily onward to the siege of the mines of Montezuma. Several objects are gained by this arrangement of the waggons. If they are attacked on march by the Cumanche cavalry or other foes, the leading teams file to the right and left, and close the front; and the hindermost, by a similar movement, close the rear; and thus they form an oblong rampart of waggons laden with cotton goods that effectually shields teams and men from the small arms of the Indians. The same arrangement is made when they halt for the night.

Within the area thus formed are put, after they are fed, many of the more valuable horses and oxen. The remainder of the animals are ' staked'—that is, tied to stakes, at a distance of twenty or thirty yards, around the line. The ropes by which

they are fastened are from thirty to forty
feet in length, and the stakes to which they
are attached are carefully driven, at such
distances apart, as shall prevent their being
entangled one with another.

Among these animals the guard on duty
is stationed, standing motionless near them,
or crouching so as to discover every moving
spot upon the horizon of night. The reasons assigned for this, are, that a guard in
motion would be discovered and fired upon
by the cautious savage before his presence
could be known ; and farther, that it is impossible to discern the approach of an Indian creeping among the grass in the dark,
unless the eye of the observer be so close to
the ground as to bring the whole surface
lying within the range of vision between it
and the line of light around the lower
edge of the horizon. If the camp be attacked, the guard fire and retreat to the
waggons. The whole body then take positions for defence ; at one time sallying out,
rescue their animals from the grasp of the
Indians ; and at another, concealed behind
their waggons, load and fire upon the iu-
truders with all possible skill and rapidity.
Many were the bloody battles fought on
the ' trail,' and such were some of the anxie-

ties and dangers that attended and still attend the 'Santa Fé Trade.' Many are the graves, along the track, of those who have fallen before the terrible cavalry of the Cumanches. They slumber alone in this ocean of plains : no tears bedew their graves ; no lament of affection breaks the stillness of their tomb. The tramp of savage horsemen—the deep bellowing of the buffalo—the nightly howl of the hungry wolf—the storms that sweep down at midnight from the groaning caverns of the 'shining heights ;' or, when Nature is in a tender mood, the sweet breeze that seems to whisper among the wild flowers that nod over his dust in the spring—say to the dead, "You are alone ; no kindred bones moulder at your side."

We traversed Council Grove with the same caution and in the same manner as we had the other ; a platoon of four persons in advance to mark the first appearance of an ambuscade ; behind these the pack animals and their drivers ; on each side an unincumbered horseman ; in the rear a platoon of four men, all on the look-out, silent, with rifles lying on the saddles in front, steadily winding along the path that the heavy waggons of the traders had made among the matted under-brush. In this manner we marched half a mile, and emerged from the Grove at a place where the traders had, a few days before, held their council. The grass in the vicinity had been gnawed to the earth by their numerous animals ; their fires were still smouldering and smoking ; and the ruts in the road were fresh. These indications of our vicinity to the great body of the traders produced an exhilarating effect on our spirits ; and we drove merrily away along the trail, cheered with renewed hopes that we should overtake our countrymen, and be saved from starvation.

The grove that we were now leaving was the largest and most beautiful we had passed since leaving the frontier of the States. The trees, maple, ash, hickory, black walnut, oaks of several kinds, butternut, and a great variety of shrubs clothed with the sweet foliage of June—a pure stream of water murmuring along a gravelly bottom, and the songs of the robin and thrush, made Council Grove a source of delight to us, akin to those that warm the hearts of pilgrims in the great deserts of the East, when they behold, from the hills of scorching sands, the green thorn-tree, and the waters of the bubbling spring. For we also were pilgrims in a land destitute of the means of subsistence, with a morsel only of meat and bread per day, lonely and hungry ; and although we were among the grassy plains instead of a sandy waste, we had freezing storms, tempests, lightning and hail, which, if not similar in the means, were certainly equal in the amount of discomfort they produced, to the sand-storms of the Great Sahara.

But we were leaving the Grove and the protection it might yield to us in such disagreeable circumstances. On the shrubless plain again ! To our right the prairie rose gradually, and stretched away for ten miles, forming a beautiful horizon. The whole was covered with a fine coat of grass a foot in height, which was at this season of the deepest and richest green. Behind us lay a dark line of timber, reaching from the Grove far into the eastern limits of sight, till the leafy tops seemed to wave and mingle among the grass of the wild swelling meadows. The eyes ached as we endeavoured to embrace the view. A sense of vastness was the single and sole conception of the mind !

Near this grove are some interesting Indian ruins. They consist of a collection of dilapidated mounds, seeming to indicate the truth of the legend of the tribes, which says, that formerly this was the Holy ground of the nations, where they were accustomed to meet to adjust their difficulties, exchange the salutations of peace, and cement the bonds of union with smoking, and dancing, and prayers, to the Great Spirit.

We had advanced a few miles in the open country when we discovered, on the summit to the right, a small band of Indians. They proved to be a party of Caws or Kauzaus. As soon as they discovered our approach, two of them started in different directions at the top of their speed, to spread the news of our arrival among the remote members of the party. The remainder urged on with the utmost velocity their pack-horses laden with meat, skins, blankets, and other paraphernalia of a hunting excursion. We pursued our way, making no demonstrations of any kind, until one old brave left his party, and came towards us, stationing himself beside our path, and awaiting our near approach. He stood quite upright and motionless. As we advanced, we noted closely his appearance and position. He had no clothing, except a blanket tied over the left shoulder and drawn under the right arm. His head was shaven entirely bare, with the exception of a tuft of hair about two inches in width, extending from the centre of the occiput over the middle of the head to the forehead. It was short and coarse, and stood erect, like the comb of a cock. His figure was the perfection of physical beauty. It was five feet nine or ten inches in height, and looked the Indian in every respect. He stood by the road-side, apparently perfectly at ease ; and seemed to regard all surrounding objects, with as much interest as he did us. This is a distinguishing characteristic of the Indian. If a thunderbolt could be embodied and put in living form before their eyes, it would not startle them from their gravity. So stood our savage friend, to all appearance unaware of our approach. Not a muscle of his body or face moved, until I rode up and proffered him a friendly hand. This he seized eagerly and continued to shake it very warmly, uttering meanwhile with great emphasis and rapidity, the words " How de," " how," " how." As soon as one individual had withdrawn his hand from his grasp, he

passed to another, repeating the same process and the same words. From the careful watch we had kept upon his movements
since he took his station, we had noticed
that a very delicate operation had been
performed upon the lock of his gun. Something had been warily removed therefrom,
and slipped into the leathern pouch worn
at his side. We expected, therefore, that
the never-failing appeal to our charity
would be made for something ; and in this
we were not disappointed. As soon as the
greetings were over, he showed us, with the
most solicitous gestures, that his piece had
no flint. We furnished him with one ; and
he then signified to us that he would
like something to put in the pan and barrel ; and having given him something of
all, he departed at the rapid swinging gait
so peculiar to his race.

As we advanced, the prairie became more
gently undulating. The heaving ridges
which had made our trail thus far appear
to pass over an immense sea, the billows of
which had been changed to waving meadows the instant they had escaped from
the embraces of the tempest, gave place to
wide and gentle swells, scarcely perceptible
over the increased expanse in sight. Ten

miles on the day's march ; the animals were tugging lustily through the mud, when the advance guard shouted " Elk ! Elk !" and " steaks broiled," and " ribs boiled," and " marrow bones," and " no more hunger !" " Oregon for ever, starve or live," as an appointed number of my companions filed off to the chase.

The hunters circled around the point of the sharp ridge on which the Elk were feeding, in order to bring them between themselves and the wind ; and laying closely to their horses' necks, they rode slowly and silently up the ravine towards them. While these movements were making, the cavalcade moved quietly along the trail for the purpose of diverting the attention of the Elk from the hunters. And thus the latter were enabled to approach within three hundred yards of the game before they were discovered. But the instant—that anxious instant to our gnawing appetites—the instant that they perceived the crouching forms of their pursuers approaching them, tossing their heads in the air, and snuffing disdainfully at such attempt to deceive their wakeful senses, they put hoof to turf in fine style. The hunters attempted pursuit ; but having to ascend one side of the ridge,

while the Elk in their flight descended the
other, they were at least four hundred yards
distant, before the first bullet whistled after
them. None were killed. And we were
obliged to console our hunger with the hope
that three hunters, who had been despatched
ahead this morning, would meet with more
success. We encamped soon after this
tourney of ill luck—ate one of the last
morsels of food that remained—pitched our
tent, stationed the night-guard, &c., and,
fatigued and famished, stretched ourselves
within it.

On the following day we made twenty-
five miles over a prairie nearly level, and
occasionally marshy. In the afternoon we
were favoured with what we had scarcely
failed, for a single day, to receive since the
commencement of our journey, viz: all
several and singular, the numerous benefits
of a thunder-storm. As we went into camp
at night, the fresh ruts along the trail indicated the near vicinity of some of the
Santa Fé teams. No sleep ; spent the
night in drying our drenched bodies and
clothes.

On the 12th under weigh very early : and
travelled briskly along, intending to overtake the traders before nightfall. But

another thunder-storm for a while arrested the prosecution of our desires.—
It was about three o'clock when a black cloud arose in the south-east, another in the south-west, and another in the north-east; and involving and evolving themselves like those that accompany tornadoes of other countries, they rose with awful rapidity towards the zenith. Having mingled their dreadful masses over our heads, for a moment they struggled so terrifically that the winds appeared hushed at the voice of their dread artillery—a moment of direful battle; and yet not a breath of wind. We looked up for the coming catastrophe indicated by the awful stillness; and beheld the cloud rent in fragments, by the most terrific explosion of electricity we had ever witnessed. Then, as if every energy of the destroying elements had been roused by this mighty effort, peal upon peal of thunder rolled around, and up and down the heavens; and the burning bolts appeared to leap from cloud to cloud across the sky, and from heaven to earth, in such fearful rapidity, that the lurid glare of one had scarcely fallen on the sight, when another followed of still greater intensity. The senses were abso-

lutely stunned by the conflict. Our animals, partaking of the stupifying horror
of the scene, madly huddled themselves
together and became immovable. They
heeded neither whip nor spur ; but with
backs to the tempest drooped their heads,
as if awaiting their doom. The hail and rain
came down in torrents. The plains were
converted into a sea ; the sky, overflowing
with floods, lighted by a continual blaze
of electric fire ! It was such a scene as
no pen can adequately describe.

After the violence of the storm had in
some degree abated, we pursued our way,
weary, cold and hungry. About six o'clock
we overtook a company of Santa Fé traders,
commanded by Captain Kelly. The gloom
of the atmosphere was such, that when
we approached his camp, Captain Kelly supposed us to be Indians, and took measures
accordingly to defend himself. Having
stationed his twenty-nine men within the
barricade formed by his waggons, he himself, accompanied by a single man, came
out to reconnoitre. He was not less
agreeably affected, to find us whites and
friends, than were we at the prospect of
society and food. Traders always carry
a supply of wood over these naked plains,

and it may be supposed that, drenched and
pelted as we had been by the storm, we
did not hesitate to accept the offer of their
fire to cook our supper, and warm ourselves.
But the rain continued to fall in cold
shivering floods; and, fire excepted, we
might as well have been elsewhere as in
company with our countrymen, who were
as badly sheltered and fed, as ourselves.
We, therefore, cast about for our own
means of comfort. While some were cooking our morsel of supper, others staked out
the animals, others pitched our tent; and all,
when their tasks were done, huddled under
its shelter. We now numbered thirteen.

We ate our scanty suppers, drank the
water from the puddles, and sought rest.
But all our packs being wet, we had no
change of wardrobe, that would have enabled us to have done so with a hope of
success. We, however, spread our wet
blankets upon the mud, put our saddles
under our heads, had a song from our
jolly Joe, and mused and shivered until
morning.

As the sun of the 13th rose, we drove
our animals through Cottonwood creek.
It had been very much swollen by the
rains of the previous day; and our packs

and ourselves, were again thoroughly wet. But, once out of the mire and the dangers of the flood, our hearts beat merrily as we lessened, step by step, the distance from Oregon.

CHAPTER II.

Scarcity of Food—An Incident—Looing and Bleating—
Messrs. Bents—Trade—Little Arkansas—A Nauseous
Meal—A Flood—An Onset—A Hard Ride—The De-
liverance—The Arkansas—An Attack—The Simili-
tude of Death—The Feast and a bit of Philosophy—
The Traders Walworth and Alvarez's Teams—A
Fright—A Nation of Indians—Their Camp and Hunts
—A Treaty—A Tempest—Indian Butchering—A
Hunt among the Buffalo—A Wounded Man—A
Drive—A Storm and its Enemy—Night among the
Buffalo—The Country and the Heavens—The Ford
—A Mutiny and its Consequences—Blistered Fingers
—Liberty—Beat's Fort—Disbanding.

OUR hunters, who had been despatched
from Council Grove in search of game, had
rejoined us in Kelly's camp. And as our
larder had not been improved by the hunt,
another party was sent out, under orders
to advance to the buffalo with all possible
dispatch, and send back to the main body
a portion of the first meat that should be
taken. This was a day of mud and discomfort. Our pack and riding animals,
constantly annoyed by the slippery clay

beneath them, became restive, and not unfrequently relieved themselves of riders or packs, with little apparent respect for the wishes of their masters. And yet, as if a thousand thorns should hatchel out at least one rose, we had one incident of lively interest. For, while halting to secure the load of a pack-mule, whose obstinacy would have entitled him to that name, whatever had been his form, we espied upon the side of a neighbouring ravine several elk and antelope. The men uttered pleas for their stomachs at the sight of so much fine meat, and with teeth shut in the agony of expectation, primed anew their rifles, and rushed away for the prize.

Hope is very delusive, when it hunts elk upon the open plain. This fact was never more painfully true, than in the present instance. They were approached against the wind—the ravines that were deepest, and ran nearest the elk, were traversed in such a manner that the huntsmen were within three hundred yards of them before they were discovered; and then never did horses run nearest their topmost speed for a stake in dollars than did ours for a steak of meat. But, alas! the little advantage gained at the start, from the bewildered inaction of the game, began to diminish as soon as those fleet coursers of the prairie laid their nimble hoofs to the sward, and pledged life upon speed. In this exigency a few balls were sent whistling after them, but they soon slept in the earth, instead of the panting hearts they were designed to render pulseless ; and we returned to our lonely and hungry march.

At sunset we encamped on the banks of a branch of the Arkansas. Our rations were now reduced to one-eighth of a pint of flour to each man. This, as our custom was, was kneaded with water, and baked or rather dried in our frying-pan, over a fire sufficiently destitute of combustibles to have satisfied the most fastidious miser in that line.—Thus refreshed, and our clothing dried in the wind during the day, we hugged our rifles to our hearts, and slept soundly.

The sun of the following morning was unusually bright, the sky cloudless and delightfully blue. These were new pleasures ; for the heavens and the earth had, till that morning, since our departure from home, scourged us with every discouragement which the laws of matter could produce. Now all around us smiled. Dame

Nature, a prude though she be, seemed pleased that she had belaboured our courage with so little success. To add to our joy, a herd of oxen and mules were feeding and lowing upon the opposite bank of the stream. They belonged to the Messrs. Bents, who have a trading post upon the Arkansas. One of the partners and thirty odd men were on their way to St. Louis, with ten waggons laden with peltries. They were also driving down two hundred Santa Fé sheep, for the Missouri market. These animals are usually purchased from the Spaniards; and if the Indians prove far enough from the track so as to permit the purchaser to drive them into the States, his investment is unusually profitable. The Indians, too, residing along the Mexican frontier, not infrequently find it convenient to steal large numbers of mules, &c., from their no less swarthy neighbours; and from the ease with which they acquire them, find themselves able and willing to sell them to traders for a very easily arranged compensation.

Of these several sources of gain, it would seem the Messrs. Bents avail themselves; since, on meeting the gentleman in charge of the waggons before spoken of, he informed us that he had lost thirty Mexican mules and seven horses ; and desired us, as we intended to pass his post, to recover and take them back. A request of any kind from a white face in the wilderness is never denied. Accordingly, we agreed to do as he desired, if within our power.

We made little progress to-day. Our packs, that had been soaked by storm and stream, required drying, and for that purpose we went early into camp. The country in which we now were, was by no means sacred to safety of life, limb or property. The Pawnee and Cumanche war-parties roam through it during the spring and summer months, for plunder and scalps. The guards, which we had had on the alert since leaving Council Grove, were therefore carefully stationed at night-fall among the animals around the tent, and urged to the most careful watchfulness. But no foe molested us. In the expressive language of the giant of our band, prefaced always with an appropriate sigh and arms akimbo, " We were not murdered yet."

About twelve o'clock of the 14th, we passed the Little Arkansas. Our hunters had been there the previous night, and had succeeded in taking a dozen cat-fish. Their

own keen hunger had devoured a part of
them without pepper, or salt, or bread, or
vegetable.   The remainder we found attached to a bush in the stream, in an un-
wholesome state of decomposition. They
were, however, taken up and examined by
the senses of sight and smell alternately;
and viewed and smelt again in reference to
our ravenous palates ; and although some
doubt may have existed in regard to the
Hebrew principle of devouring so unclean
a thing, our appetites allowed of no demur.
We roasted and ate, as our companions
had done.

I had an opportunity at this place to
observe the great extent of the rise and
fall of these streams of the plains in a
single day or night. It would readily be
presumed, by those who have a correct idea
of the floods of water that the thunder-
storms of this region pour upon the rolling
prairies, that a few miles of the channels of
a number of the creeks over which the
storms pass may be filled to the brim in an
hour; and that there are phenomena of
floods and fails of water occurring in this
vast den of tempests, such as are found
nowhere else. Still, bearing this evidently
true explanation in mind, it was with some

difficulty that I yielded to the evidences on the banks of the Little Arkansas, that that stream had fallen fifteen feet during the last twelve hours. It was still too deep for the safety of the pack animals to attempt to ford it in the usual way. The banks, also, at the fording-place were left by the retiring flood, a quagmire ; so soft, that a horse without burthen could, with the greatest difficulty, drag himself through it to the water below. In our extremity, however, we tied our lashing-lines together, and, attaching one end to a strong stake on the side we occupied, sent the other across the stream, and tied it firmly to a tree. Our baggage, saddles and clothing suspended to hooks running to and fro on this line, were securely passed over. The horses being then driven across at the ill-omened ford, and ourselves over by swimming and other means, we saddled and loaded our animals with their several burthens, and recommenced our march.

The 14th, 15th and 16th, were days of more than ordinary hardships. With barely food enough to support life, drenched daily by thunder-storms and by swimming and fording the numerous drains of this alluvial

region, and wearied by the continual packing and unpacking of our animals, and enfeebled by the dampness of my couch at
night, I was so much reduced when I dismounted from my horse on the evening of
the 16th, that I was unable to loosen the
girth of my saddle or spread my blanket for
repose.

The soil thus far from the frontier appeared to be from three to six feet in depth;
generally undulating, and occasionally,
far on the western horizon, broken into
ragged and picturesque bluffs.   Between
the swells, we occasionally met small tracts
of marshy ground saturated with brackish
water.

On the night of the 16th, near the hour
of eight o'clock, we were suddenly roused
by the rapid trampling of animals near our
camp.   " Indians !" was the cry of the
guard, " Indians !"   We had expected an
encounter with them as we approached the
buffalo, and were consequently not unpre-
pared for it.   Each man seized his rifle,
and was instantly in position to give the intruders a proper reception.   On they came,
rushing furiously in a dense column till
within thirty yards of our tent; and then
wheeling short to the left, abruptly halted.

Not a rifle-ball or an arrow had yet cleft the air. Nor was it so necessary that they should; for we discovered that, instead of bipeds of bloody memory, they were the quadrupeds that had eloped from the fatherly care of Mr. Bent, making a call of ceremony upon their compatriot mules, &c., tied to stakes within our camp.

17th. We were on the trail at seven o'clock. The sun of a fine morning shone upon our ranks of beasts and men. Were I able to sketch the woe-shrivelled visages of my starving men, with occasional bursts of wrath upon Mr. Bent's mules as they displayed their ungrateful heels to us, who had restored them from the indecencies of savage life to the dominion of civilized beings, my readers would say that the sun never looked upon a more determined disregard of the usages of social life. A long march before us—the Arkansas and its fish before us, the buffalo with all the delicate bits of tender loin and marrow bones, (even the remembrance of them inspires me)—with all these before us, who that has the sympathies of the palate sensibilities within him, can suppose that we did not use the spur, whip and goad with a right good will on that memorable day?

Thirty or forty miles, none but the vexed
plains can tell which, were travelled over
by one o'clock. The afternoon hours, too,
were counted slowly. High bluffs, and
butes, and rolls, and salt marshes alternately
appearing and falling behind us, with here
and there a plat of the thick short grass of the
upper plains and the stray bunches of the
branching columnar and foliated prickly
pear, indicated that we were approaching
some more important course of the mountain waters than we had yet seen since leaving the majestic Missouri. " On, merrily
on," rang from our parched and hungry
mouths ; and if the cheerful shout did not
allay our appetites or thirst, it quickened
the pace of our mules, and satisfied each
other of our determined purpose to behold
the Arkansas by the light of that day.

During the hurried drive of the afternoon
we became separated from one another
among the swells over which our track ran.
Two of the advanced platoon took the liberty, in the absence of their commander, to
give chace to an antelope which seemed
to tantalize their forbearance by exhibiting
his fine sirloins to their view. Never
did men better earn forgiveness for disobe-
dience of orders. One of them crept as I

learned half a mile upon his hands and knees to get within rifle shot of his game;—shot at three hundred yards' distance and brought him down! And now, who, in the tameness of an enough-and-to-spare state of existence, in which every emotion of the mind is surfeited and gouty, can estimate our pleasure at seeing these men gallop into our ranks with this antelope? You may "guess," reader, you may " reckon," you may " calculate," or if learned in the demi-semi-quavers of modern exquisiteness, you may thrust rudely aside all these wholesome and fat old words of the heart, and "shrewdly imagine," and still you cannot comprehend the feelings of that moment! Did we shout? were we silent? no, neither. Did we gather quickly around the horse which bore the slaughtered animal? No, nor this. An involuntary murmur of relief from the most fearful forebodings, and the sudden halt of the riding animals in their tracks were the only movements, the only acts that indicated our grateful joy at this deliverance.

Our intention of seeing the Arkansas that night, however, soon banished every other thought from the mind. Whips and spurs therefore were freely used upon our animals as they ascended tediously a long roll of prairies covered with the wild grasses and stinted stalks of the sun-flower. We rightly conceived this to be the bordering ridge of the valley of the Arkansas. For on attaining its summit we saw ten miles of that stream lying in the sunset like a beautiful lake among the windings of the hills. It was six miles distant—the sun was setting. The road lay over sharp rolls of land that rendered it nearly impossible for us to keep our jaded animals on a trot. But the sweet water of that American Nile, and a copse of timber upon its banks that offered us the means of cooking the antelope to satisfy our intolerable hunger, gave us new energy; and on we went at a rapid pace while sufficient light remained to show us the trail.

When within about a mile and a half of the river a most annoying circumstance crossed our path. A swarm of the most gigantic and persevering musquitoes that ever gathered tribute from human kind, lighted on us and demanded blood. Not in the least scrupulous as to the manner in which they urged their claims, they fixed themselves boldly and without ceremony upon our organs of sight, smell, and whip-

ping, in such numbers, that in consequence
of the employment they gave us in keeping
them at the distance, and the pain which
they inflicted upon our restive animals, we
lost the trail. And now came quagmires,
flounderings, and mud, such as would have
taught the most hardened rebel in morals
that deviations from the path of duty lead
sometimes to pain, sometimes to swamps.
Long perseverance at length enabled us to
reach the great " River of the Plains."

We tarried for a moment upon the banks
of the stream, and cast about to extricate
ourselves from the Egyptian plagues around
us. To regain our track in the darkness of
night, now mingled with a dense fog, was no
easy task. We, however, took the lead of a
swell of land that ran across it, and in thirty
minutes entered a path so well marked that
we could thread our way onward till we
should find wood sufficient to cook our supper. This was a dreary ride. The stars
gave a little light among the mist, which
enabled us to discern, on the even line of the
horizon, a small speck that after three hours'
travel we found to be a small grove of cotton
wood upon an island. We encamped near
it ; and after our baggage was piled up so

as to form a circle of breastworks for defence, our weariness was such that we sank
among it supperless, and slept with nothing
but the heavens over us. And although we
were in the range of the Cumanche hunting
as well as war-parties, the guard slept in
spite of the savage eyes that might be gloat-
ing vengeance on our little band. No fear
or war-whoop could have broken the slumbers of that night. It was a temporary
death. Nature had made its extreme effort,
and sunk in helplessness till its ebbing
energies should reflow.

On the morning of the 18th of June we
were up early—early around among our
animals to pull up the stakes to which
they were tied, and drive them fast again,
where they might graze while we should
eat. Then to the care of ourselves. We
wrestled manfully with the frying-pan and
roasting-stick ; and anon in the very manner that one sublime act always follows its
predecessor, tore bone from bone the antelope ribs, with so strong a grip and with
such unrestrained delight that a truly phi-
losophic observer might have discovered in
the flash of our eyes and the quick energetic motion of the nether portions of our

physiognomies, that eating, though an un-
common, was nevertheless our favourite
occupation. — Then " catch up," " saddles on," "packs on," " mount," "march,"
were heard on all sides, and we were on the
route, hurry-scurry, with forty loose mules
and horses leering, kicking and braying,
and some six or eight pack animals making
every honourable effort to free themselves
from servitude, while we were applying to
their heads and ears certain gentle intima-
tions that such ambitious views accorded
not with their master's wishes.

In the course of the day we crossed
several tributaries of the Arkansas. At one
of these, called by the traders Big Turkey
Creek, we were forced to resort again to
our Chilian bridge.   In consequence of the
spongy nature of the soil and the scarcity
of timber, we here found more difficulty in
procuring fastenings for our ropes, than
in any previous instance. At length,
however, we obtained pieces of flood-
wood, and drove them into the soft banks
" at an inclination," said he of the axe,
" of precisely 45° to the plane of the
horizon." Thus supported, the stakes
stood sufficiently firm for our purposes ;

and our bags, packs, selves, and beasts were over in a trice, and in the half of that mathematical fraction of time, we were repacked, remounted, and trotting off at a generous pace, up the Arkansas. The river appeared quite unlike the streams of the East, and South, and Southwest portion of the States in all its qualities. Its banks were low—one and a half feet above the medium stage of water, composed of an alluvium of sand and loam as hard as a public highway, and generally covered with a species of wiry grass that seldom grows to more than one and a half or two inches in height. The sun-flower of stinted growth, and a lonely bush of willow, or an ill-shaped sapless, cotton-wood tree, whose decayed trunk trembled under the weight of years, together with occasional bluffs of clay and sand-stone, formed the only alleviating features of the landscape. The stream itself was generally three-quarters of a mile in width, with a current of five miles per hour, water three and a half to four feet, and of a chalky whiteness. It was extremely sweet, so delicious that some of my men declared it an excellent substitute for milk.

Camped on the bank of the river where
the common tall grass of the prairie grew
plentifully; posted our night-guard, and
made a part of our meat into soup for
supper. I will here give a description of
the manner of making this soup. It was
indeed a rare dish; and my friends of the
trencher—ye who have been spiced, and
peppered, and salted, from your youth up,
do not sneer when I declare that of all the
innovations upon kitchen science which
civilization has engrafted upon the good
old style of the patriarchs, nothing has
produced so depraving an effect upon taste,
as these self-same condiments of salt, pepper, &c. But to our soup. It was made
of simple meat and water—of pure water,
such as kings drank from the streams of the
good old land of pyramids and flies, and of
the wild meat of the wilderness, untainted
with any of the aforesaid condiments—
simply boiled, and then eaten with strong,
durable iron spoons and butcher-knives.
Here I cannot restrain from penning one
strong and irrepressible emotion that I
well remember to have experienced while
stretched upon my couch after our repast.
The exceeding comfort of body and mind

at that moment undoubtedly gave it being.
It was an emotion of condolence for those
of my fellow mortals who are engaged in
the manufacture of rheumatisms and gout.
Could they only for an hour enter the
portals of prairie life—for one hour breathe
the inspiration of a hunter's transcendentalism—for one hour feed upon the milk and
honey and marrow of life's pure unpeppered
and unsalted viands, how soon would they
forsake that ignoble employment—how soon
would their hissing and vulgar laboratories
of disease and graves be forsaken, and the
crutch and Brandreth's pills be gathered to
the tombs of our fathers!

Our next day's march terminated in
an encampment with the hunters whom
I had sent forward for game. They had
fared even worse than ourselves. Four of
the seven days they had been absent from
the company, and had been without food.
Many of the streams, too, that were forded
easily by us, were, when they passed, wide
and angry floods. These they were obliged
to swim, to the great danger of their
lives.

On the 18th, however, they overtook
Messrs. Walworth and Alvarez's teams,

and were treated with great hospitality by those gentlemen. On the same day they killed a buffalo bull, pulled off the flesh from the back, and commenced drying it over a slow fire preparatory to packing. On the morning of the 19th, two of them started off for us with some strips of meat dangling over the shoulders of their horses. They met us about four o'clock, and with us returned to the place of drying the meat. Our horses were turned loose to eat the dry grass, while we feasted ourselves upon roasted tongue and liver. After this we " caught up" and went on with the intention of encamping with the Santa Féäns; after travelling briskly onward for two hours, we came upon the brow of a hill that overlooks the valley of Pawnee Fork, the largest branch of the Arkansas on its northern side. The Santa Fé traders had encamped on the east bank of the stream. The waggons surrounded an oval piece of ground, their shafts or tongues outside, and the forward wheel of each abreast of the hind wheel of the one before it. This arrangement gave them a fine aspect, when viewed from the hill, over which we were passing.

But we had scarcely time to see the

little I described, when a terrific scream of
" Pawnee! Pawnee!" arose from a thousand tongues on the farther bank of the
river ; and Indian women and children ran
and shrieked horribly, "Pawnee! Pawnee!"
as they sought the glens and bushes of the
neighbourhood. We were puzzled to know
the object of such an outburst of savage delight, as we deemed it to be, and for a time
thought that we might well expect our blood
to slumber with the buffalo, whose bones
lay bleaching around us. The camp of the
traders also was in motion ; arms were
seized and horses saddled with " hot haste."
A moment more, and two whites were galloping warily near us ; a moment more
brought twenty savage warriors in full paint
and plume around us. A quick reconnoitre,
and the principal chief rode briskly up to
me, shook me warmly by the hand, and with
a clearly apparent friendship said " Sacre
fœdus " (holy league,) "Kauzaus," " Caw."
His warriors followed his example. As
soon as our friendly greetings were discovered by some of the minor chiefs, they galloped their fleet horses at full speed over
the river, and the women and children issued
from their concealments, and lined the bank
with their dusky forms. The chiefs rode

with us to our camping ground, and remained till dark, examining with great interest the various articles of our travelling
equipage; and particularly our tent as it
unfolded its broadsides like magic, and assumed the form of a solid white cone.
Every arrangement being made to prevent
these accomplished thieves from stealing
our horses, &c., we supped, and went to
make calls upon our neighbours.

The owners of the Santa Fé waggons
were men who had seen much of life. Ur-
bane and hospitable, they received us in the
kindest manner, and gave us much information in regard to the mountains, the best
mode of defence, &c., that proved in our
experience remarkably correct. During the
afternoon, the chiefs of the Kauzaus sent
me a number of buffalo tongues, and other
choice bits of meat. But the filth disco-
verable on their persons generally deterred
us from using them. For this they cared
little. If their presents were accepted, an
obligation was by their laws incurred on
our part, from which we could only be relieved by presents in return. To this rule
of Indian etiquette we submitted; and a
council was accordingly held between myself
and the principal chief through an inter-

preter, to determine upon the amount and quality of my indebtedness in this regard. The final arrangement was, that in consideration of the small amount of property I had then in possession, I would give him two pounds of tobacco, a side-knife, and a few papers of vermillion ; but that, on my return, which would be in fourteen months, I should be very rich, and give him more. To all these obligations and pleasant prophecies, I of course gave my most hearty concurrence.

The Caws, or Kauzaus, are notorious thieves. We therefore put out a double guard at night, to watch their predatory operations, with instructions to fire upon them, if they attempted to take our animals. Neither guard nor instructions, however, proved of use ; for the tempest, which the experienced old Santa Féans had seen in the heavens, thunder-cloud in the northwest at sunset, proved a more efficient protection than the arm of man. The cloud rose slowly during the early part of the night, and appeared to hang in suspense of executing its awful purpose. The lightning and heavy rumbling of the thunder were frightful. It came to the zenith about twelve o'clock. When in that position, the cloud covered one-half the heavens, and for

some minutes was nearly stationary. After
this, the wind broke forth upon it at the
horizon, and rolled up the dark masses over
our heads—now swelling, now rending to
shreds its immense folds. But as yet not
a breath of air moved over the plains. The
animals stood motionless and silent at the
spectacle. The nucleus of electricity was at
the zenith, and thence large bolts at last
leaped in every direction, and lighted for an
instant the earth and skies so intensely, that
the eye could not endure the brightness.
The report which followed was appalling.
The ground trembled—the horses and mules
shook with fear, and attempted to escape.
But where could they or ourselves have
found shelter ? The clouds at the next moment appeared in the wildest commotion,
struggling with the wind. " Where shall
we fly ? " could scarcely have been spoken,
before the wind struck our tent, tore the
stakes from the ground, snapped the centre
pole, and buried us in its enraged folds.
Every man, we were thirteen in number, immediately seized some portion and held it
with all his might. Our opinion at the time
was, that the absence of the weight of a
single man would have given the storm the
victory—our tent would have eloped in the

iron embraces of the tempest. We attempted to fit it up again after the violence
of the storm had in some degree passed over,
but were unable so to do. The remainder
of the night was consequently spent in gathering up our loose animals, and in shivering
under the cold peltings of the rain.

The Santa Féäns, when on march through
these plains, are in constant expectation of
these tornadoes. Accordingly, when the sky
at night indicates their approach, they chain
the wheels of adjacent waggons strongly
together to prevent them from being upset
—an accident that has often happened, when
this precaution was not taken. It may well
be conceived, too, that to prevent their
goods from being wet in such cases, requires
a covering of no ordinary powers of protection. Bows in the usual form, except that
they are higher, are raised over long sunken
Pennsylvania waggons, over which are
spread two or three thicknesses of woollen
blankets ; and over these, and extended to
the lower edge of the body, is drawn a
strong canvas covering, well guarded with
cords and leather straps. Through this
covering these tempests seldom penetrate.

At seven o'clock on the morning of the
27th, " Catch up, catch up," rang round

the waggons of the Santa Féäns. Immediately each man had his hand upon a horse
or mule ; and ere we, in attempting to follow their example, had our horses by the
halter, the teams were harnessed and ready
for the " march." A noble sight those
teams were, about forty in number, their immense waggons still unmoved, forming an
oval breastwork of wealth, girded by an
impatient mass of near four hundred mules,
harnessed and ready to move again along
their solitary way. But the interest of the
scene was much increased when, at the call
of the commander, the two lines, team after
team, straightened themselves into the
trail, and rode majestically away over the
undulating plain. We crossed the Pawnee
Fork, and visited the Caw Camp. Their
wigwams were constructed of bushes inserted into the ground, twisted together at
the top, and covered with the buffalo hides
which they had been gathering for their
winter lodges. Meat was drying in every
direction. It had been cut in long narrow
strips, wound around sticks standing upright in the ground, or laid over a rick of
wicker-work, under which slow fires are
kept burning. The stench, and the squalid
appearance of the women and children,

were not sufficiently interesting to detain us long ; and we travelled on for the buffalo which were bellowing over the hills in advance of us. There appeared to be about one thousand five hundred souls, almost in a state of nudity, and filthy as swine. They make a yearly hunt to this region in the spring, lay in a large quantity of dried meat, return to their own territory in harvest time, gather their beans and corn, make the buffalo hides, (taken before the hair is long enough for robes), into conical tents, and thus prepare for a long and merry winter.

They take with them, on these hunting excursions, all the horses and mules belonging to the tribe, which can be spared from the labour of their fields upon the Konzas River, go south till they meet the buffalo, build their distant wigwams, and commence their labour. This is divided in the following manner between the males, females, and children :—The men kill the game. The women dress and dry the meat, and tan the hides. The instruments used in killing vary with the rank and wealth of each individual. The high chief has a lance, with a handle six feet and blade three feet in length. This in hand, mounted upon a fleet horse, he rides boldly to the side of the flying buffalo, and thrusts it again and again through the liver or heart of one, and then another of the affrighted herd till his horse is no longer able to keep near them. He is thus able to kill five or six, more or less, at a single heat. Some of the inferior chiefs also have these lances; but they must all be shorter than that of his Royal Darkness. The common Indians use muskets and pistols. Rifles are an abomination to them. The twisting motion of the ball as it enters, the sharp crack when discharged, and the direful singing of the lead as it cuts the air, are considered symptoms of witchcraft that are unsafe for the Red Man to meddle with. They call them medicines—inscrutable and irresistible sources of evil. The poorer classes still use the bow and arrow. Nor is this, in the well-trained hand of the Indian, a less effective weapon than those already mentioned. Astride a good horse, beside a bellowing band of wild beef, leaning forward upon the neck, and drawing his limbs close to the sides of his horse, the naked hunter uses his national weapon with astonishing dexterity and success. Not unfrequently, when hitting no bones, does he throw his arrows quite through the buffalo. Twenty or thirty thus variously armed, advance upon a herd. The chief leads the chase, and by the time they come alongside the band, the different speed of the horses has brought them into a single file or line. Thus they run until every individual has a buffalo at his side. Then the whole line fire guns, throw arrows or drive lances, as often and as long as the speed of the horses will allow ; and seldom do they fail in encounters of this kind, to lay upon the dusty plain numbers of these noble animals.

A cloud of squaws who had been hovering in the neighbourhood, now hurry up, astride of pack-animals, strip off hides, cut off the best flesh, load their pack-saddles, mount themselves on the top, and move slowly away to the camp. The lords of creation have finished their day's labour. The *ladies* cure the meat in the manner described above, stretch the hides upon the ground, and with a blunt wooden adze hew them into leather. The younger shoots of the tribe during the day are engaged in watering and guarding the horses and mules that have been used in the hunt—changing their stakes from one spot to another of fresh grass, and crouching along the heights around the camp to notice the approach of

foes, and sound the alarm. Thus the Konzas, Kausaus, or Caws, lay in their annual
stores. Unless driven from their game by
the Pawnees, or some other tribe at enmity
with them, they load every animal with
meat and hides about the first of August,
and commence the march back to their
fields, fathers, and wigwams, on the Konzas
River.

This return-march must present a most
interesting scene in savage life — seven
hundred or eight hundred horses or mules
loaded with the spoils of the chase, and
the children of the tribe holding on to
the pack with might and main, naked as
eels, and shining with buffalo grease, their
fathers and mothers loaping on foot behind,
with their guns poised on the left arm, or
their bows and arrows swung at their back
ready for action, and turning their heads
rapidly and anxiously for lurking enemies—
the attack, the screams of women and
children, each man seizing an animal for a
breastwork, and surrounding thus their
wives and children, the firing, the dying,
the conquest, the whoop of victory and
rejoicings of one party, and the dogged, sullen submission of the other—all this and
more has occurred a thousand times upon

these plains, and is still occurring. But if victory declare for the Caws, or they march to their home without molestation, how many warm affections spring up in their untamed bosoms, as they see again their parents and children, and the ripened harvest, the woods, the streams, and bubbling springs, among which the gleeful days of childhood were spent! And when greetings are over, and welcomes are said, embraces exchanged, and their homes seen and smiled upon; in fine, when all the holy feelings of remembrance, and their present good fortune, find vent in the wild night-dance, who, that wears a white skin and ponders upon the better lot of civilized men, will not believe that the Indian too, returned from the hunt and from war, has not as much happiness, if not in kind the same, and as many sentiments that do honour to our nature, as are wrapped in the stays and tights of a fantastic, mawkish civilization—that flattering, pluming, gormandizing, unthinking, gilded life, which is beginning to measure mental and moral worth by the amount of wealth possessed, and the adornment of a slip or pew in church.

We travelled eight miles and encamped.

A band of buffalo cows were near us. In other words, we were determined upon a hunt—a determination the consequences of which, as will hereafter appear were highly disastrous. Our tent having been pitched, and baggage piled up, the fleetest horses selected, and the best marksmen best mounted, we trotted slowly along a circling depression of the plain, that wound around near the herd on the leeward side. When we emerged in sight of them, we put the horses into a slow gallop till within three hundred yards of our game ; and then for the nimblest heel ! Each was at his utmost speed. We all gained upon the herd. But two of the horses were by the side of the lubbers before the rest were within rifle-reach ; and the rifles and pistols of their riders discharged into the sleek, well-larded body of a noble bull. The wounded animal did not drop ; the balls had entered neither liver nor heart ; and away he ran for his life. But his unwieldy form moved slower and slower, as the dripping blood oozed from the bullet-holes in his loins. He ran towards our tent ; and we followed him in that direction, till within a fourth of a mile of it, when our heroes of the rifle laid him wallowing in his blood, a mountain of flesh weighing at least three thousand pounds. We butchered him in the following manner : Having turned him upon his brisket, split the skin above the spine, and pared it off as far down the sides as his position would allow, we cut off the flesh that lay outside the ribs as far back as the loins. This the hunters call " the fleece." We next took the ribs that rise perpendicularly from the spine between the shoulders, and support what is termed the " hump." Then we laid our heavy wood-axes upon the enormous side-ribs, opened the cavity, and took out the tender-loins, tallow, &c.,—all this a load for two mules to carry into camp.

It was prepared for packing as follows : the fleece was cut across the grain into slices an eighth of an inch in thickness, and spread upon a scaffolding of poles, and dried and smoked over a slow fire. While we were engaged in this process, information came that three of Mr. Bent's mules had escaped. The probability was that they had gone to the guardianship of our neighbours, the Caws. This was a misfortune to our honourable intention of restoring them to their lawful owners. Search was immediately ordered in the Indian camp and elsewhere for them. It was

fruitless. The men returned with no very
favourable account of their reception by the
Caws, and were of opinion that farther
search would be in vain. Being disposed to try my influence with the principal
chief, I gave orders to raise the camp and
follow the Santa Féans, without reference to
my return, and mounting my horse, in
company with three men, sought his lodge.
The wigwams were deserted, save by a few
old women and squalid children, who were
wallowing in dirt and grease, and regaling
themselves upon the roasted intestines of
the buffalo. I inquired for the chiefs, for
the mules, whether they themselves were
human or bestial; for, on this point, there
was room for doubt: to all which inquiries,
they gave an appropriate grunt. But no
chief or other person could be found, on
whom any responsibility could be thrown in
regard to the lost mules. And after climbing
the heights to view the plains, and riding
from band to band of His Darkness's quadrupeds for three hours in vain, we returned
to our camp sufficiently vexed for all purposes of comfort.

Yet this was only the beginning of the
misfortunes of the day. During my absence,
one of those petty bickerings, so common

among men released from the restraints of
society and law, had arisen between two of
the most quarrelsome of the company, ter-
minating in the accidental wounding of one
of them.   It occurred, as I learned in the
following manner : a dispute arose between
the parties as to their relative moral honesty in some matter, thing, or act in the
past.   And as this was a question of great
perplexity in their own minds, and doubt
in those of others, words ran high and abu-
sive, till some of the men, more regardful
of their duty than these warriors, began
preparations to strike the tent.   The re-
doubtable combatants were within it ; and
as the cords were loosed, and its folds
began to swing upon the centre pole, the
younger of the braves, filled with wrath at
his opponent, attempted to show how terrible his ire would be if once let loose among
his muscles.   For this purpose, it would
seem he seized the muzzle of his rifle
with every demonstration of might, &c.,
and attempted to drag it from among the
baggage.   The hammer of the lock caught,
and sent the contents of the barrel into his
side.   Every thing was done for the wounded man that his condition required, and
our circumstances permitted.   Doctor Wal-

worth, of the Santa Fé caravan, then eight
miles in advance, returned, examined, and
dressed the wound, and furnished a carriage for the invalid. During the afternoon the high chief of the Caws also visited us ; and by introducing discoloured
water into the upper orifice, and watching
its progress through, ascertained that the
ball had not entered the cavity. But notwithstanding that our anxieties about the
life of Smith were much lessened by the
assurances of Dr. Walworth, and our friend
the Chief, yet we had others of no less ur-
gent nature, on which we were called to
act. We were on the hunting-grounds of
the Caws. They were thieves ; and after
the Santa Fé traders should have left the
neighbourhood, they would without scruple
use their superior force in appropriating
to themselves our animals, and other means
of continuing our journey. The Pawnees,
too, were daily expected. The Cumanches were prowling about the neighbourhood. To remain, therefore, in our present encampment, until Smith could travel
without pain and danger, was deemed certain death to all. To travel on in a manner as comfortable to the invalid, as our

condition would permit—painful to him
and tedious to us though it should be—
appeared therefore the only means of
safety to all, or any of us. We accordingly covered the bottom of the carriole
with grass and blankets, laid Smith upon
them, and with other blankets bolstered
him in such manner that the jolting of the
carriage would not roll him. Other arrangements necessary to raising camp being
made, I gave the company in charge of my
lieutenant; and ordering him to lead on
after me as fast as possible, took the reins
of the carriage and drove slowly along the
trail of the Santa Féans.

The trail was continually crossed by deep
paths made by the buffalo, as a thousand generations of them had in single file followed
their leaders from point to point through
the plains. These, and other obstructions,
jolted the carriage at every step, and caused
the wounded man to groan pitiably. I drove
on till the stars indicated the hour of midnight ; and had hoped by this time to have
overtaken the traders, but was disappointed. In vain I looked through the darkness
for the white embankment of their waggons.
The soil over which they had passed was

now so hard, that the man in advance of
the carriage could no longer find the trail;
and another storm was crowding its dark
pall up the western sky. The thunder
aroused and enraged the buffalo bulls. They
pawed the earth and bellowed, and gathered
around the carriage madly, as if they considered it a huge animal of their own species, uttering thunder in defiance of them.
It became dangerous to move. It was useless also; for the darkness thickened so
rapidly that we could not keep the track.
My men, too, had not come up; they had
doubtless lost the trail—or, if not, might
join me if I waited there till the morning.
I therefore halted in a deep ravine, which
would partially protect me from the mad-
dened buffalo and the storm, tied down my
animals head to foot, and sought rest.
Smith was in great pain. His groans were
sufficient to prevent sleep. But had he
been comfortable and silent, the storm
poured such torrents of rain and hail, with
terrible wind and lightning, around us, that
life instead of repose became the object
of our solicitude. The horseman who had
accompanied me, had spread his blankets
on the ground under the carriage, and,

with his head upon his saddle, attempted
to disregard the tempest as an old-fashion-
ed stoic would the tooth-ache. But it beat
too heavy for his philosophy. His Macki-
naw blankets and slouched hat, for a time
protected his ungainly body from the effects of the tumbling flood. But when the
water began to stream through the bottom
of the carriage upon him, the ire of the
animal burst from his lank cheeks like the
coming of a rival tempest. He cursed his
stars, and the stars behind the storm, his
garters, and the garters of some female
progenitor, consigned to purgatory the
thunder, lightning, and rain, and waggon,
alias poor Smith; and gathering up the
shambling timbers of his mortal frame,
raised them bolt upright in the storm, and
thus stood, quoted Shakspeare, and ground
his teeth till day-light.

As soon as day dawned I found the trail
again, and at seven o'clock overtook the Santa
Féäns. Having changed Smith's bedding,
I drove on in the somewhat beaten track
that forty odd waggons made. Still every
small jolt caused the unfortunate man to
scream with pain. The face of the country
around Pawnee Fork was, when we saw it,

a picture of beauty. The stream winds silently among bluffs covered with woods, while from an occasional ravine, long groves stretch out at right angles with its main course into the bosom of the plains. The thousand hills that swelled on the horizon, were covered with dark masses of buffalo peacefully grazing, or quenching their thirst at the sweet streams among them. But the scene had now changed. No timber, not a shrub was seen to-day. The soft rich soil had given place to one of flint and sand, as hard as M'Adam's pavements; the green, tall prairie grass, to a dry, wiry species, two inches in height. The water, too, disgusting remembrance! There was none, save what we scooped from the puddles, thick and yellow with buffalo offal.

We travelled fifteen miles, and halted for the night. Smith was extremely unwell. His wound was much inflamed and painful. Dr. Walworth dressed it, and encouraged me to suppose that no danger of life was to be apprehended. My company joined me at twelve o'clock, on the 22d, and we followed in the rear of the cavalcade. After supper was over, and Smith made comfort-

able, I sought from some of them a relation
of their fortunes during the past night.　It
appeared they had found the buffalo troublesome as soon as night came on ; that the
bands of bulls not unfrequently advanced
in great numbers within a few feet of them,
pawing and bellowing in the most threatening manner ; that they also lost the trail
after midnight, and spent the remainder of
the night in firing upon the buffalo, to keep
them from running over them. Their situation
was dangerous in the extreme ; for when
buffalo become enraged, or frightened in
any considerable number, and commence
running, the whole herd start simultane-
ously, and pursue nearly a right-line course,
regardless of obstacles.　So that, had they
been frightened by the Santa Féans, or
myself, or any other cause, in the direction
of my companions, they must have trampled
them to death.　The danger to be apprehended from such an event, was rendered
certain in the morning, when we perceived
that the whole circle of vision was one black
mass of these animals.　What a sea of life
—of muscular power—of animal appetite—
of bestial enjoyment !　And if lashed to
rage by some pervading cause, how fear-

ful the ebbing and flowing of its mighty
wrath !

On the 23d the buffalo were more numerous than ever. They were arranged in long
lines from the eastern to the western
horizon. The bulls were forty or fifty yards
in advance of the bands of cows to which
they severally intended to give protection.
And as the moving embankment of waggons, led by the advanced guard, and
flanked by horsemen riding slowly from
front to rear, and guarded in the rear by my
men, made its majestic way along, these
fiery cavaliers would march each to his own
band of dames and misses, with an air that
seemed to say " we are here ;" and then
back again to their lines, with great apparent satisfaction, that they were able to do
battle for their sweet ones and their native
plains. We travelled fifteen or sixteen
miles ; distance usually made in a day by
the traders. Smith's wound was more inflamed and painful ; the wash and salve of
the Indian chief, however, kept it soft, and
prevented to a great extent the natural in-
flammation of the case.

The face of the country was still an arid
plain—the water as on the 22d—fuel, dried

buffalo offal—not a shrub of any kind in sight. Another storm occurred to-night. Its movements were more rapid than that of any preceding one which we had experienced. In a few moments after it showed its dark outline above the earth, it rolled its pall over the whole sky, as if to build a wall of wrath between us and the mercies of heaven. The flash of the lightning, as it bounded upon the firmament, and mingled its thunder with the blast, that came groaning down from the mountains; the masses of inky darkness crowding in wild tumult along, as if anxious to lead the leaping bolt upon us—the wild world of buffalo, bellowing and starting in myriads, as the drapery of this funeral scene of nature, a vast cavern of fire was lighted up; the rain roaring and foaming like a cataract—all this, a reeling world tottering under the great arm of its Maker, no eye could see and be unblenched; no mind conceive, and keep its clayey tenement erect.

I drew the carriole in which Smith and myself were attempting to sleep, close to the Santa Fé waggons, secured the curtains as firmly as I was able to do, spread blankets over the top and around the sides, and lashed them firmly with ropes passing over, under, and around the carriage in every direction; but to little use. The penetrating powers of that storm were not resisted by such means. Again we were thoroughly drenched. The men in the tent fared still worse than ourselves. It was blown down with the first blast; and the poor fellows were obliged to lie closely and hold on strongly to prevent it and themselves from a flight less safe than parachuting.

On the morning of the 24th, having given Smith in charge of my excellent Lieutenant, with assurance that I would join him at the " Crossings," I left them with the traders, and started with the remainder of my company for the Arkansas.

The buffalo during the last three days had covered the whole country so completely, that it appeared oftentimes extremely dangerous even for the immense cavalcade of the Santa Fé traders to attempt to break its way through them. We travelled at the rate of fifteen miles a day. The length of sight on either side of the trail, 15 miles; on both sides, 30 miles:—
$15 \times 3 = 45 \times 30 = 1,350$ square miles of

country, so thickly covered with these noble animals, that when viewed from a
height, it scarcely afforded a sight of a
square league of its surface.   What a quantity of food for the sustenance of the Indian
and the white pilgrim of these plains!   It
would have been gratifying to have seen
the beam kick over the immense frames of
some of those bulls.   But all that any of us
could do, was to ' guess' or 'reckon' their
weight, and contend about the indubitable
certainty of our several suppositions.   In
these disputes, two butchers took the lead ;
and the substance of their discussions that
could interest the reader is, " that many of
the large bulls would weigh 3,000 pounds
and upwards ; and that, as a general rule,
the buffalo were much larger and heavier
than the domesticated cattle of the States."
We were in view of the Arkansas at
four o'clock. P.M. The face of the earth was
visible again ; for the buffalo were now
seen in small herds only, fording the river,
or feeding upon the bluffs. Near nightfall
we killed a young bull, and went into camp
for the night.

On the 25th we moved slowly along up
the bank of the river. Having travelled

ten miles, one of the men shot an antelope, and we went into camp, to avoid if possible another storm that was lowering upon us from the north-west; but in spite of this precaution, we were again most uncomfortably drenched.

On the 26th we struck across a southern bend in the river, and made the Santa Fé "Crossings" at four o'clock, P.M.; 27th. we lay at the "Crossings," waiting for the Santa Féäns, and our wounded companion. On this day a mutiny, which had been ripening ever since Smith was wounded, assumed a clear aspect. It now appeared that certain individuals of my company had determined to leave Smith to perish in the encampment where he was shot; but failing in supporters of so barbarous a proposition, they now endeavoured to accomplish their design by less objectionable means. They said it was evident, if Smith remained in the company, it must be divided; for that they, pure creatures, could no longer associate with so impure a man. And that, in order to preserve the unity of the company, they would propose that arrangements should be made with the Santa Féäns to take him along with them.

In this wish a majority of the company, induced by a laudable desire for peace, and the preservation of our small force entire, in a country filled with Indian foes, readily united. I was desired to make the arrangement; but my efforts proved fruitless. The traders were of opinion that it would be hazardous for Smith, destitute of the means of support, to trust himself among a people of whose language he was ignorant, and among whom he could consequently get no employment; farther, that Smith had a right to expect protection from his comrades; and they would not, by any act of theirs, relieve them from so sacred a duty. I reported to my company this reply, and dwelt at length upon the reasons assigned by the traders.

The mutineers were highly displeased with the strong condemnation contained in them, of their intention to desert him; and boldly proposed to leave Smith in the carriole, and secretly depart for the mountains. Had we done this inhuman act, I have no doubt that he would have been treated with great humanity and kindness, till he should have recovered from his wound. But the meanness of the proposition to leave a sick com-

panion on the hands of those who had
shown us unbounded kindness, and in vio-
lation of the solemn agreement we had all
entered into on the frontier of Missouri —
" to protect each other to the last extremity" — was so manifest, as to cause
C. Wood, Jourdan, Oakley, J. Wood, and
Blair, to take open and strong grounds
against it. They declared, that " however
unworthy Smith might be, we could neither
leave him to be eaten by wolves, nor to the
mercy of strangers; and that neither should
be done while they had life to prevent
it."

Having thus ascertained that I could rely
upon the co-operation of these men, two of
the company made a litter, on which the
unfortunate man might be borne between
two mules. In the afternoon of the 28th, I
went down to the traders, five miles below
us, to bring him up to my camp. The
traders generously refused to receive anything for the use of their carriage, and
furnished Smith, when he left them, with
every little comfort in their power for his
future use. It was past sunset when we left
their camp. Deep darkness soon set in, and
we lost our course among the winding bluffs.

But as I had reason to suppose that my
presence in the camp the next morning with
Smith was necessary to his welfare, I drove
on till three o'clock in the morning. It
was of no avail : the darkness hid heaven
and earth from view. We therefore halted,
tied the mules to the wheels of the carriage,
and waited for the sight of morning. When
it came, we found that we had travelled
during the night at one time up and at another time down the stream, and were then
within a mile and a half of the trader's
camp.

On reaching my encampment, I found
every thing ready for marching, sent back
the carriole to its owners, and attempted to
swing Smith in his litter for the march ; but
to our great disappointment, it would not
answer the purpose. How it was possible
to convey him, appeared an inquiry of the
most painful importance. We deliberated
long ; but an impossibility barred every
attempt to remove its difficulties. We had
no carriage ; we could not carry him upon
our shoulders; it seemed impossible for him
to ride on horseback ; the mutineers were
mounted ; the company was afraid to stay
longer in the vicinity of the Cumanche In-

dians, with so many animals to tempt them
to take our lives ; the Santa Fé waggons were
moving over the hills ten miles away on the
other side of the river ; I had abjured the
command, and had no control over the
movements of the company ; two of the individuals who had declared for mercy towards
Smith had gone with the traders ; there was
but one course left—one effort that could
be made ; he must attempt to ride an easy,
gentle mule. If that failed, those who had
befriended him would not then forsake him.
About eleven o'clock, therefore, on the 29th,
Smith being carefully mounted on a pacing
mule, our faces were turned to Bent's trading post, one hundred and sixty miles up the
Arkansas. One of the principal mutineers,
a hard-faced villain of no honest memory
among the traders upon the Platte, assumed to guide and command. His malice towards Smith was of the bitterest
character, and he had an opportunity
now of making it felt. With a grin upon
his long and withered physiognomy, that
shadowed out the fiendish delight of a heart
long incapable of better emotions, he drove
off at a rate which none but a man in
health could have long endured. His mo-

tive for this was easily understood. If we fell behind, he would get rid of the wounded man, whose presence seemed to be a living evidence of his murderous intentions, thwarted and cast back blistering upon his already sufficiently foul character. He would, also, if rid of those persons who had devoted themselves to saving him, be able to induce a large number of the remainder of the company to put themselves under his especial guardianship in their journey through the mountains ; and if we should be destroyed by the Cumanche Indians who were prowling around our way, the blackness of his heart might be hidden, awhile at least, from the world.

The rapid riding, and the extreme warmth, well-nigh prostrated the remaining strength of the invalid. He fainted once, and had nearly fallen headlong to the ground ; but all this was delight to the self-constituted leader ; and on he drove, belabouring his own horse unmercifully to keep up the pace ; and quoting Richard's soliloquy with a satisfaction and emphasis, which seemed to say " the winter" of *his* discontent had passed away, as well as that of his ancient prototype in villany.

The buffalo were seldom seen during the day : the herds now becoming fewer and smaller. Some of the men, when it was near night, gave chase to a small band near the track, and succeeded in killing a young bull. A fine fresh steak, and night's rest, cheered the invalid for the fatigues of a long ride the following day. And a long one it was. Twenty-five miles under a burning sun, with a high fever, and three broken ribs, required the greatest attention from his friends, and the exertion of the utmost remaining energies of the unfortunate man. Base though he was in everything that makes a man estimable and valuable to himself and others, Smith was really an object of pity and the most assiduous care. His couch was spread—his cup of water fresh from the stream, was always by his side—and his food prepared in the most palatable manner which our circumstances permitted. Everything indeed that his friends (no, not his friends, for he was incapacitated to attach either the good or the bad to his person, but those who commiserated his condition), could do, was done to make him comfortable.

In connexion with this kindness bestowed

on Smith, should be repeated the name of
Blair, an old mechanic from Missouri, who
joined my company at the Crossings of the
Arkansas. A man of a kinder heart never
existed. From the place where he joined
us to Oregon Territory, when I or others
where worn with fatigue, or disease, or
starvation, he was always ready to administer whatever relief was in his power.
But towards Smith in his helpless condition
he was especially obliging. He dressed his
wound daily. He slept near him at night,
and rose to supply his least want. And in
all the trying difficulties that occurred along
our perilous journey, it was his greatest delight to diffuse peace, comfort, and content-
ment, to the extent of his influence. I can
never forget the good old man. He had
been cheated out of his property by a near
relative of pretended piety, and had left the
chosen scenes of his toils and hopes in
search of a residence in the wilderness
beyond the mountains. For the purpose of
getting to the Oregon Territory, he had
hired himself to a gentleman of the traders'
caravan, with the intention of going to the
country by the way of New Mexico and
California. An honest man—an honourable

man—a benevolent, kind, sympathizing friend—he deserves well of those who may have the good fortune to become acquainted with his unpretending worth.

On the 30th, twenty-five miles up the river.—This morning the miscreant who acted as leader exchanged horses, that he might render it more difficult for Smith to keep in company. During the entire day's march, Shakspeare was on the tapis. If there be ears of him about the ugly world, to hear his name bandied by boobies, and his immortal verse mangled by barbarians in civilized clothing, those ears stood erect, and his dust crawled with indignation, as this savage in nature and practice discharged from his polluted mouth the inspirations of his genius.

The face of the country was such as that found ever since we struck the river. Long sweeping bluffs swelled away from the water's edge into the boundless plains. The soil was a composition of sand, clay, and gravel — the only vegetation — the short furzy grass, several kinds of prickly pear, a stinted growth of sun-flower, and a few decrepid cotton-wood trees on the margin of the stream. The south side of the river was blackened by the noisy buffalo. It was amusing when our trail led us near the bank, to observe the rising wrath of the bulls. They would walk with a stately tread upon the verge of the bank, at times almost yelling out their rage, and tramping, pawing, falling upon their knees, and tearing the earth with their horns ; till, as if unable to keep down the safety-valve of their courage any longer, they would tumble into the stream, and thunder, and wade, and swim, and whip the waters with their tails, and thus throw off a quantity of their bravery. But, like the wrath and courage of certain members of the biped race, these manifestations were not bullet proof, for the crack of a rifle, and the snug fit of a bullet about their ribs operated instantaneously as an anodyne to all such like nervous excitation.

We pitched our tent at night near the river. There was no timber near ; but after a long and tedious search we gathered fire-wood enough to make our evening fire.

The fast riding of the day had wearied Smith exceedingly. An hour's rest in camp however, had restored him, to such an ex-

tent, that our anxiety as to his ability to ride
to Bent's was much diminished.   His noble
mule proved too nimble and easy to gratify
the malice of the vagabond leader.   The
night brought us its usual tribute—a storm.
It was as severe as any we had experienced.
If we may distinguish between the severities
of these awful tumults of nature, the thunder was heavier, deeper.   The wind also
was very severe.   It came in long gusts,
loaded with large drops of rain, which struck
through the canvas of our tent, as if it had
been gauze.

The last day of June gave us a lovely
morning.   The grass looked green upon the
flinty plains.   Nor did the apparent fact that
they were doomed to the constant recurrence
of long draughts take from them some of the
interest which gathers around the hills and
dales within the lines of the States.   There
is indeed a wide difference in the outline of
the surface and the productions of these
regions.   In the plains are none of the
evergreen ridges, the cold clear springs, and
snug flowering valleys of New England;
none of the pulse of busy men that beats
from the Atlantic through the great body of
human industry to the western border of the

republic ; none of the sweet villages and
homes of the old Saxon race ; but there
are the vast savannahs, resembling molten
seas of emerald sparkling with flowers,
arrested while stormy and heaving, and fixed
in eternal repose. Nor are lowing herds
to be found there, and bleating flocks, which
dependance on man has rendered subser-
vient to his will ; but there are thousands of
fleet and silent antelope, myriads of the bellowing buffalo, the perpetual patrimony of
the wild, uncultivated red man. And however other races may prefer the haunts of
their childhood, the well-fenced domain and
the stall-pampered beast—still, even they
cannot fail to perceive the same fitness of
things in the beautiful adaptation of these
conditions of nature to the wants and pleasures of her uncultivated lords.

We made fifteen miles on the 1st of July.
The bluffs along the river began now to be
striped with strata of lime and sand-stone.
No trees that could claim the denomination of
timber appeared in sight. Willows of various
kinds, a cotton-wood tree, at intervals of
miles, were all; and so utterly sterile was the
whole country that, as night approached,
we were obliged carefully to search along

the river's bends for a plat of grass of sufficient size to feed our animals: Our encampment was twelve miles above Choteau's
Island. Here was repeated, for the twentieth
time, the quarrel about the relative and
moral merits of the company. This was
always a question of deep interest with
the mutineers ; and many were the amusing
arguments adduced and insisted upon as incontestible, to prove themselves great men,
pure men, and saints. But as there was much
difference of opinion, I shall not be expected to remember all the important judg-
ments rendered in the premises. If, however,
my recollection serves me, it was adjudged,
that our distinguished leader was the only
man among us that ever saw the plains or
mountains, the only one of us that ever
drove an ox-waggon up the Platte, stole a
horse and rifle from his employers, opened
and plundered a " cache" of goods, and ran
back to the States with well-founded pretensions to an " honest character."

Matters of this kind being thus satisfactorily settled, we gave ourselves to the
musquitoes for the night. These companions of our sleeping hours were much
attached to us—an amiable quality which

"runs in the blood;" and not unlike the birthright virtues of another race in its effect upon our happiness.

It can scarcely be imparting information to my readers to say that we passed a sleepless night. But it is due to the guards outside the tent, to remark, that each and every of them manifested the most praiseworthy vigilance, and industry, during the entire night. So keen a sense of duty did musquito beaks impart.

The next day we travelled twelve miles, and fell in with a band of buffalo. There being a quantity of wood near at hand wherewithal to cure meat, we determined to dry, in this place, what might be needed, till we should fall in with buffalo again beyond the hunting-grounds of the Messrs. Bents. Some of the men, for this purpose, filed off to the game, while the remainder formed the encampment. The chase was spirited and long. They succeeded, however, in bringing down two noble bullocks: and led their horses in, loaded with the choicest meat.

In preparing and jerking our meat, our man of the stolen rifle here assumed extraordinary powers in the management of

affairs.   Like other braves, arm in hand, he
recounted the exploits of his past life, consisting of the entertainment of serious
intentions to have killed some of the men
who had left, had they remained with us ;
and also, of *how dangerous his wrath would*
have been in the settlements and elsewhere,
had any indignity been offered to his honourable person, or his plantation ; of which
latter he held the fee simple title of a
" squatter."   On this point, " let any man,
or Government even," said he, " attempt to
deprive me of my inborn rights, and my
rifle shall be the judge between us.
Government and laws ! what are they but
impositions upon the freeman."   With this
ebullition of wrath at the possibility that
the institutions of society might demand of
him a rifle, or the Government a price of a
portion of the public lands in his possession,
he appeared satisfied that he had convinced
us of his moral acumen, and sat himself
down, with his well-fed and corpulent coad-
jutor, to slice the meat for drying.   While
thus engaged, he again raised the voice of
wisdom.   " These democratic parties for
the plains, what are they? what is equa-
lity any where ?   A fudge.   One must

rule ; the rest obey, and no grumbling, by
G* * * !"

The mutineers were vastly edified by these
timely instructions ; and the man of parts
ceasing to speak, directed his attention to
drying the meat. He, however, soon broke
forth again, found fault with every arrange‑
ment which had been made, and with his
own mighty arm wrought the changes he
desired.

Meanwhile, he was rousing the fire,
already burning fiercely, to more and more
activity, till the dropping grease blazed,
and our scaffold of meat was wrapped in
flames.

" Take that meat off," roared he. No
one obeyed, and he stood still. " Take
that meat off," he cried again, with the
emphasis and mien of an Emperor ; not
deigning himself to soil his rags, by obey-
ing his own command. No one obeyed.
The meat burned rapidly. His ire waxed
high ; yet, no one was so much frightened
as to heed his command. At length his
sublime forbearance had an end. The great
man seized the blazing meat, dashed it
upon the ground, raised the temperature
of his fingers to the blistering point, and
rested from his labours.

Three days more fatiguing travel along the bank of the Arkansas brought us to the trading-post of the Messrs. Bents. It was about two o'clock in the afternoon of the 5th of July, when we came in sight of its noble battlements, and struck our caravan into a lively pace down the swell of the neighbouring plain. The stray mules that we had in charge belonging to the Bents, scented their old grazing ground, and galloped cheerfully onward. And our hearts, relieved from the anxieties which had made our camp for weeks past a travelling Babel, leaped for joy as the gates of the fort were thrown open; and " welcome to Fort William" — the hearty welcome of fellow-countrymen in the wild wilderness, greeted us. Peace again—roofs again—safety again from the winged arrows of the savage; relief again from the depraved suggestions of inhumanity; bread, ah! bread again: and a prospect of a delightful tramp over the snowy heights between me and Oregon, with a few men of true and generous spirit, were some of the many sources of pleasure which struggled with my slumbers on the first night's tarry among the hospitalities of " Fort William."

My company was to disband here; the property held in common to be divided; and each individual to be left to his own resources. And while these and other things are being done, the reader will allow me to introduce him to the Great Prairie Wilderness, and the beings and matters therein contained.

CHAPTER III.

The Great Prairie Wilderness—Its Rivers and Soil—
Its People and their Territories—Choctaws—Chickasaws—Cherokees—Creeks—Senecas and Shawnees
—Seminoles—Pottawotamies — Weas— Pionkashas—
Peorias and Kaskaskias—Ottowas—Shawnees or Shawanoes—Delawares — Kausaus — Kickapoos — Sauks
and Foxes — Iowas — Otoes — Omehas—Puncahs—
Pawnees, remnants—Carankauas—Cumanche, remnants—Knistineaux—Naudowisses or Sioux—Chippeways, and their traditions.

THE tract of country to which I have
thought it fitting to apply the name of the
" Great Prairie Wilderness," embraces the
territory lying between the States of Louisiana, Arkansas, and Missouri, and the
Upper Mississippi on the east, and the
Black Hills, and the eastern range of the
Rocky and the Cordilleras mountains on
the west. One thousand miles of longitude, and two thousand miles of latitude, 2,000,000 square miles, equal to
1,280,000,000 acres of an almost unbroken
plain ! The sublime Prairie Wilderness !

The portion of this vast region, two

hundred miles in width, along the coast of
Texas and the frontier of the States of
Louisiana, Arkansas, and Missouri, and
that lying within the same distance of the
Upper Mississippi in the Iowa Territory,
possess a rich, deep, alluvial soil, capable
of producing the most abundant crops of
grains, vegetables, &c., that grow in such
latitudes.

Another portion lying west of the irregular western line of that just described,
five hundred miles in width, extending
from the mouth of St. Peter's River to the
Rio del Norte, is an almost unbroken plain,
destitute of trees, except here and there one
scattered at intervals for many miles along
the banks of the streams. The soil, except
the intervals of some of the rivers, is composed of coarse sand and clay, so thin and
hard that it is difficult for travellers to
penetrate it with the stakes they carry with
them wherewithal to fasten their animals or
spread their tents. Nevertheless it is covered thickly with an extremely nutritious
grass peculiar to this region of country, the
blades of which are wiry and about two
inches in height.

The remainder of this Great Wilderness,
lying three hundred miles in width along

the eastern radices of the Black Hills and
that part of the Rocky Mountains between
the Platte and the Cordilleras-range east of
the Rio del Norte, is the arid waste usually
called the " Great American Desert." Its
soil is composed of dark gravel mixed with
the sand. Some small portions of it, on
the banks of the streams, are covered with
tall prairie and bunch grass ; others, with
wild wormwood ; but even these kinds of
vegetation decrease and finally disappear
as you approach the mountains. It is a
scene of desolation scarcely equalled on
the continent, when viewed in the dearth of
midsummer from the base of the hills.
Above, rise in sublime confusion, mass
upon mass, shattered cliffs through which
is struggling the dark foliage of stinted
shrub-cedars ; while below you spreads far
and wide the burnt and arid desert, whose
solemn silence is seldom broken by the
tread of any other animal than the wolf
or the starved and thirsty horse which bears
the traveller across its wastes.

The principal streams that intersect the
Great Prairie wilderness are the Colorado,
the Brasos, Trinity, Red, Arkansas, Great
Platte and the Missouri. The latter is in
many respects a noble stream ; not so

much so indeed for the intercourse it opens
between the States and the plains, as the
theatre of agriculture and the other pursuits
of a densely populated and distant interior;
for these plains are too barren for general
cultivation. As a channel for the transportation of heavy artillery, military stores,
troops, &c. to posts that must ultimately be
established along our northern frontier, it
will be of the highest use.

In the months of April, May, and June
it is navigable for steam-boats to the Great
Falls ; but the scarcity of water during
the remainder of the year, as well as
the scarcity of wood and coal along its
banks, its steadily rapid current, its tortuous course, its falling banks, timber imbedded in the mud of its channel, and its
constantly shifting sand bars, will ever
prevent its waters from being extensively
navigated, how great soever may be the
demand for it. In that part of it which
lies above the mouth of the Little Missouri
and the tributaries flowing into it on either
side, are said to be many charming and
productive valleys, separated from each other
by secondary rocky ridges sparsely covered
with evergreen trees ; and high over all, far in
south-west, west and north-west, tower into

view, the ridges of the Rocky Mountains, whose inexhaustible magazines of ice and snow have, from age to age, supplied these valleys with refreshing springs—and the Missouri—the Great Platte—the Columbia —and Western Colorado rivers with their tribute to the seas.

Lewis and Clark, on their way to Oregon in 1805, made the Portage at the Great Falls eighteen miles. In this distance the water descends three hundred and sixty-two feet. The first great pitch is ninety-eight feet, the second nineteen, the third forty-eight, and the fourth twenty-six. Smaller rapids make up the remainder of the descent. After passing over the Portage with their boats and baggage, they again entrusted themselves to the turbulent stream—entered the chasms of the Rocky Mountains seventy-one miles above the upper rapids of the Falls, penetrated them one hundred and eighty miles, with the mere force of their oars against the current, to Gallatin, Madison and Jefferson's Forks— and in the same manner ascended Jefferson's River two hundred and forty-eight miles to the extreme head of navigation, making from the mouth of the Missouri, whence they started, three thousand and ninety-six miles; four hundred and twenty-nine of which lay among the sublime crags and cliffs of the mountains.

The Great Platte has a course by its northern fork of about one thousand five hundred miles; and by its southern fork somewhat more than that distance; from its entrance into the Missouri to the junction of these forks about four hundred miles. The north fork rises in Wind River Mountain, north of the Great Pass through Long's range of the Rocky Mountains, in latitude 42° north. The south fork rises one hundred miles west of James Peak, and within fifteen miles of the point where the Arkansas escapes from the chasms of the mountains, in latitude 39° north. This river is not navigable for steamboats at any season of the year. In the spring floods, the batteaux of the American fur traders descend it from the forts on its forks. But even this is so hazardous that they are beginning to prefer taking down their furs in waggons by the way of the Konsas River to Westport, Missouri, thence by steamboat to St. Louis. During the summer and autumn months its waters are too shallow to float a canoe. In the winter it is bound in ice. Useless as it is for purposes of navigation, it is destined to be of great value in another respect.

The overland travel from the States to Oregon and California will find its great highway along its banks.   So that in years to come, when the Federal Government shall take possession of its Territory West of the Mountains, the banks of this stream will be studded with fortified posts for the protection of countless caravans of American citizens emigrating thither to establish their abode ; or of those that are willing to endure or destroy the petty tyranny of the Californian Government, for a residence in that most beautiful, productive country.   Even now, loaded waggons can pass without serious interruption from the mouth of the Platte to navigable waters on the Columbia River in Oregon, and the Bay of San Francisco, in California.

As it may interest my readers to peruse a description of these routes given me by different individuals who had often travelled them, I will insert it: "Land on the north side of the mouth of the Platte ; follow up that stream to the Forks, four hundred miles ; in this distance only one stream where a raft will be needed, and that near the Missouri ; all the rest fordable.   At the Forks, take the north side of

the North one ; fourteen days' travel to the
Black Hills ; thence leaving the river's bank,
strike off in a North West direction to the
Sweet-water branch, at "Independence
Rock," (a large rock in the plain on which
the old trappers many years ago carved the
word "Independence" and their own
names ; oval in form ;) follow up the sweet-
water three days ; cross it and go to its
head ; eight or ten days travel this ; then
cross over westward to the head waters of a
small creek running southwardly into the
Platte, thence westward to Big Sandy creek
two days, (this creek is a large stream coming from Wind river Mountains in the
North ;) thence one day to Little Sandy
creek—thence westward over three or four
creeks to Green River, (Indian name Sheetskadee,) strike it at the mouth of Horse
creek—follow it down three days to Pilot
Bute ; thence strike westward one day to
Ham's Fork of Green River—two days up
Ham's Fork—thence West one day to
Muddy Branch of Great Bear River—down
it one day to Great Bear River—down this
four days to Soda Springs ; turn to the right
up a valley a quarter of a mile below the
Soda Springs ; follow it up a north west
direction two days to its head ; there take
the left hand valley leading over the dividing

ridge ; one day over to the waters of Snake
River at Fort Hall; thence down Snake
River twenty days to the junction of the
Lewis and Clark Rivers—or twenty days
travel westwardly by the Mary's River—
thence through a natural and easy passage
in the California Mountains to the navigable waters of the San Joiquin—a noble
stream emptying into the Bay of San Francisco."

The Platte therefore when considered in
relation to our intercourse with the habitable countries on the Western Ocean as-
sumes an unequal importance among the
streams of the Great Prairie Wilderness !
But for it, it would be impossible for man or
beast to travel those arid plains, destitute
alike, of wood, water and grass, save what
of each is found along its course. Upon
the head waters of its North Fork, too, is the
only way or opening in the Rocky mountains
at all practicable for a carriage road through
them. That traversed by Lewis and Clark,
is covered with perpetual snow ; that near
the debouchure of the South Fork of the
river is over high and nearly impassable
precipices ; that travelled by myself farther
south, is, and ever will be impassable for
wheel carriages. But the Great Cap, nearly

on a right line between the mouth of Missouri and Fort Hall on Clark's River—the point where the trails to California and Oregon diverge—seems designed by nature as the great gateway between the nations on the Atlantic and Pacific seas.

The Red River has a course of about one thousand five hundred miles. It derives its name from a reddish colour of its water, produced by a rich red earth or marl in its banks, far up in the Prairie Wilderness. So abundantly is this mingled with its waters during the spring freshets, that as the floods retire, they leave upon the lands they have overflowed a deposit of half an inch in thickness. Three hundred miles from its mouth commences what is called " The Raft," a covering formed by drift-wood, which conceals the whole river for an extent of about forty miles. And so deeply is this immense bridge covered with the sediment of the stream, that all kinds of vegetable common in its neighbourhood, even trees of a considerable size, are growing upon it. The annual inundations are said to be cutting a new channel near the hill. Steamboats ascend the river to the Raft, and might go fifty leagues above, if that obstruction were removed. Above this latter point

the river is said to be embarrassed by many
rapids, shallows, falls, and sand-bars. Indeed, for seven hundred miles its broad bed
is represented to be an extensive and perfect
sand-bar ; or rather a series of sand-bars ;
among which during the summer months,
the water stands in ponds. As you approach
the mountains, however, it becomes contracted within narrow limits over a gravelly
bottom, and a swift, clear, and abundant
stream. The waters of the Red River are
so brackish when low, as to be unfit for
common use.

The Trinity River, the Brazos, and the
Rio Colorado, have each a course of about
twelve hundred miles, rising in the plains
and mountains on the north and north-west
side of Texas, and running south south-east
into the Gulf of Mexico.

The Rio Bravo del Norte bounds the Great
Prairie Wilderness on the south and south-
west. It is one thousand six hundred and fifty
miles long. The extent of its navigation is
little known. Lieutenant Pike remarks in
regard to it, that " for the extent of four or
five hundred miles before you arrive near
the mountains, the bed of the river is extensive and a perfect sand-bar, which at a certain season is dry, at least the waters stand

in ponds, not affording sufficient to procure a running course. When you come nearer the mountains, you find the river contracted, a gravelly bottom and a deep navigable stream. From these circumstances it is evident that the sandy soil imbibes all the waters which the sources project from the mountains, and render the river in dry season *less navigable five hundred miles*, than two hundred from its source." Perhaps we should understand the Lieutenant to mean that five hundred miles of sand bar and two hundred miles immediately below its source being taken from its whole course, the remainder, nine hundred and fifty miles, would be the length of its navigable waters.

The Arkansas, after the Missouri, is the most considerable river of the country under consideration. It takes its rise in that cluster of secondary mountains which lie at the eastern base of the Anahuac Ridge, in latitude 41° north—eighty or ninety miles north-west of James Peak. It runs about two hundred miles—first in a southerly and then in a south-easterly direction among these mountains ; at one time along the most charming valleys and at another through the most awful chasms —till it rushes from them with a foaming current in latitude 39° north. From the place of its debouchure to its entrance into the Mississippi is a distance of 1981 miles; its total length 2173 miles. About fifty miles below, a tributary of this stream, called the Grand Saline, a series of sandbars commence and run down the river several hundred miles. Among them, during the dry season, the water stands in isolated pools, with no apparent current. But such is the quantity of water sent down from the mountains by this noble stream at the time of the annual freshets, that there is sufficient depth, even upon these bars, to float large and heavy boats; and having once passed these obstructions, they can be taken up to the place where the river escapes from the crags of the mountains. Boats intended to ascend the river, should start from the mouth about the 1st of February. The Arkansas will be useful in conveying munitions of war to our southern frontier. In the dry season, the waters of this river are strongly impregnated with salt and nitre.

There are about 135,000 Indians inhabiting the Great Prairie Wilderness, of whose social and civil condition, manners and customs, &c. I will give a brief account. It would seem natural to commence with those tribes which reside in what is called "The Indian Territory;" a tract of country bounded south by the Red River, east by the States of Arkansas and Missouri—on the north-east and north by the Missouri and Punch Rivers, and west by the western limit of habitable country on this side of the Rocky Mountains. This the National Government has purchased of the indigenous tribes at specific prices; and under treaty stipulations to pay them certain annuities in cash, and certain others in facilities for learning the useful arts, and for acquiring that knowledge of all kinds of truth which will, as is supposed, in the end excite the wants, create the industry, and confer upon them the happiness of the civilized state.

These benevolent intentions of Government, however, have a still wider reach. Soon after the English power had been extinguished here, the enlightened men who had raised over its ruins the temples of equal justice, began to make efforts to restore to the Indians within the colonies the few remaining rights that British injustice had left within their power to return; and so to exchange property with them, as to secure to the several States the right of sovereignty within their several limits, and to the Indians, the functions of a sovereign power, restricted in this, that the tribes should not sell their lands to other person or body corporate, or civil authority, beside the Government of the United States; and in some other respects restricted, so as to preserve peace among the tribes, prevent tyranny, and lead them to the greatest happiness they are capable of enjoying.*

Various and numerous were the efforts made to raise and ameliorate their condition in their old haunts within the precincts of the States. But a total or partial failure followed them all. In a few cases, indeed, there seemed a certain prospect of final success, if the authorities of the States in which they resided had permitted them to remain where they were. But as all experience tended to prove that their proximity to the whites induced among them more vice than virtue; and as the General Government, before any attempts had been made to elevate them, had become bound to remove them from

* This is a gratuitous remark. The conduct of the British Government will compare most favourably with that of the United States. The English have not thought of hunting Indians with blood-hounds.—ED.

many of the States in which they resided,
both the welfare of the Indians, and the
duty of the Government, urged their colo-
nization in a portion of the western domain, where, freed from all questions of
conflicting sovereignties, and under the
protection of the Union, and their own
municipal regulations, they might find a
refuge from those influences which threatened the annihilation of their race.

The "Indian Territory" has been selected for this purpose. And assuredly if
an inexhaustible soil, producing all the necessaries of life in greater abundance, and
with a third less labour than they are produced in the Atlantic States, with excellent
water, fine groves of timber growing by
the streams, rocky cliffs rising at convenient distances for use among the deep
alluvial plains, mines of iron and lead ore
and coal, lakes and springs and streams of
salt water, and innumerable quantities of
buffalo ranging through their lands, are
sufficient indications that this country is a
suitable dwelling-place for a race of men
which is passing from the savage to the
civilized condition, the Indian Territory has
been well chosen as the home of these unfortunate people. Thither the Government,
or the last thirty years, has been endea-
f

vouring to induce those within the jurisdiction of the States to emigrate.

The Government purchase the land which the emigrating tribes leave—giving them others within the Territory; transport them to their new abode ; erect a portion of their dwellings ; plough and fence a portion of their fields ; furnish them teachers of agriculture, and implements of husbandry, horses, cattle, &c.; erect schoolhouses, and support teachers in them the year round ; make provision for the subsistence of those who, by reason of their recent emigration, are unable to support themselves ; and do every other act of benevolence necessary to put within their ability to enjoy, not only all the physical comforts that they left behind them, but also every requisite, facility, and encouragement to become a reasoning, cultivated, and happy people.

Nor does this spirit of liberality stop here. The great doctrine that Government is formed to confer upon its subjects a greater degree of happiness than they could enjoy in the natural state, has suggested that the system of hereditary chieftaincies, and its dependant evils among the tribes, should yield, as circumstances may permit, to the ordination of nature, the supremacy of intellect and virtue. Accordingly, it is contemplated to use the most efficient means to abolish them, making the rulers elective, establishing a form of government in each tribe, similar in department and duties to our State Governments, and uniting the tribes under a General Government, similar in powers and functions to that at Washington.

It is encouraging to know that some of the tribes have adopted this system ; and that the Government of the Union has been so far encouraged to hope for its adoption by all those in the Indian Territory, that in 1837 orders were issued from the Department of Indian affairs, to the Superintendent of Surveys, to select and report a suitable place for the Central Government. A selection was accordingly made of a charming and valuable tract of land on the Osage river, about seven miles square; which, on account of its equal distance from the northern and southern line of the Territory, and the beauty and excellence of the surrounding country, appears in every way adapted to its contemplated use. It is a little more than sixteen miles from the western line of Missouri. Any member of those tribes which come into the confederation, may own property in the district, and no other.

The indigenous, or native tribes of the Indian Territory, are—the Osages, about 5,510; the Kauzaus or Caws, 1,720; the Omahas, 1,400; the Otoe and Missouri, 1,600; the Pawnee, 10,000; Puncah, 800; Quapaw, 600—making 21,660. The tribes that have emigrated thither from the States, are—the Choctaw, 15,600 (this estimate includes 200 white men, married to Choctaw women, and 600 negro slaves); the Chickasaws, 5,500; the Cherokees, 22,000 (this estimate includes 1,200 negro slaves owned by them); the Cherokees (including 900 slaves), 22,000; the Creeks (including 393 negro slaves) 22,500; the Senecas and Shawnees, 461; the Seminoles, 1,600; the Pottawatamies, 1,650; the Weas, 206; the Piankashas, 157; the Peorias and Kaskaskias, 142; the Ottawas, 240; the Shawnees, 823; the Delawares, 921; the Kickapoos, 400; the Sauks, 600; the Iowas, 1,000. It is to be understood that the numbers assigned to these tribes represent only those portions of them which have actually removed to the Territory. Large numbers of several tribes are still within the borders of the States. It appears from the above tables, then, that 72,200 have had lands assigned them; and, abating the relative effects of births and deaths among them, in increasing or diminishing their numbers, are actually residing in the Territory. These, added to 21,000 of the indigenous tribes, amount to 94,860 under the fostering care of the Federal Government, in a fertile and delightful country, six hundred miles in length from north to south, and east and west from the frontier of the Republic to the deserts of the mountains.

The Choctaw country lies in the extreme south of the Territory. Its boundaries are —on the south, the Red River, which separates it from the Republic of Texas ; on the west, by that line running from the Red River to the Arkansas River, which separates the Indian American Territory from that of Mexico; on the north, by the Arkansas and the Canadian Rivers ; and on the east, by the State of Arkansas. This tract is capable of producing the most abundant crops, the small grains, Indian corn, flax, hemp, tobacco, cotton, &c. The western portion of it is poorly supplied with timber; but all the distance from the Arkansas' frontier westward, two hundred miles, and extending one hundred and sixty miles from its northern to its southern boundary, the country is capable of supporting a population as dense as that of England. 19,200,000 acres of soil suitable for immediate settlement, and a third as much more to the westward that would produce the black locust in ten years after planting, of sufficient size for fencing the very considerable part of it which is rich enough for agricultural purposes, will, doubtless, sustain any increased population of this tribe that can reasonably be looked for during the next five hundred years.

They have suffered much from sickness incident to settlers in a new country. But there appear to be no natural causes existing, which, in the known order of things, will render their location permanently unhealthy. On the other hand, since they have become somewhat inured to the change of climate, they are quite as healthy as the whites near them; and are improving in civilization and comfort; have many large farms; much live stock, such as horses, mules, cattle, sheep, and swine; three flouring-mills, two cotton-gins, eighty-eight looms, and two hundred and twenty spinning-wheels; carts, waggons, and other farming utensils. Three or four thousand Choctaws have not yet settled on the lands assigned to them. A part of these are in

Texas, between the rivers Brazos and Trinity, 300 in number, who located themselves
there in the time of the general emigration ;
and others in divers places in Texas, who
emigrated thither at various times, twenty,
thirty, and forty years ago. Still another
band continues to reside east of the Mississippi.

The Choctaw Nation, as the tribe deno-
minates itself, has adopted a written constitution of Government, similar to the Constitution of the United States. Their De-
claration of Rights secures to all ranks and
sects equal rights, liberty of conscience, and
trial by jury, &c. It may be altered or
amended by a National Council. They
have divided their country into four judicial
districts. Three of them annually elect
nine, and the other thirteen, members of
the National Assembly. They meet on the
first Monday in October annually ; organize
by the election of a Speaker, the necessary
clerks, a light-horseman (sergeant-at-arms),
and door-keeper ; adopt by-laws, or rules
for their governance, while in session ; and
make other regulations requisite for the
systematic transaction of business. The
journals are kept in the English language ;
but in the progress of business are read off

in Choctaw. The preliminary of a law is, " Be it enacted by the General Council of the Choctaw Nation."

By the Constitution, the Government is composed of four departments, viz. : Legislative, Executive, Judicial and Military. Three judges are elected in each district by popular vote, who hold inferior and superior courts within their respective districts. Ten light-horse menin each district perform the duties of sheriffs. An act has been passed for the organization of the militia. Within each judicial district an officer is elected, denominated a chief, who holds his office for the term of four years. These chiefs have honorary seats in the National Council. Their signatures are necessary to the passage of a law. If they veto an act, it may become a law by the concurrence of two-thirds of the Council. Thus have the influences of our institutions begun to tame and change the savages of the western wilderness.

At the time when the lights of religion and science had scarcely begun to dawn upon them—when they had scarcely discovered the clouds of ignorance that had walled every avenue to rational life—even while the dust of antiquated barbarism was still hanging upon their garments—and the night of ages, of sloth, and sin held them in its cold embraces—the fires on the towers of this great temple of civil freedom arrested their slumbering faculties, and they read on all the holy battlements, written with beams of living light, "All men are, and of right ought to be, free and equal." This teaching leads them. It was a pillar of fire moving over the silent grave of the past—enlightening the vista of coming years—and, by its winning brightness, inviting them to rear in the Great Prairie wilderness, a sanctuary of republican liberty—of equal laws—in which to deposit the ark of their own future well-being.

The Chikasaws have become merged in the Choctaws. When they sold to the Government their lands east of the Mississippi, they agreed to furnish themselves with a home. This they have done in the western part of the Choctaw country for the sum of £106,000. It is called the Chickasaw district; and constitutes an integral part of the Choctaw body politic in every respect, except that the Chickasaws, like the Choctaws, received and invest for their own sole use, the annuities and other moneys proceeding from the sale of their lands east of the Mississippi.

The treaty of 1830 provides for keeping forty Choctaw youths at school, under the direction of the President of the United States, for the term of twenty years. Also, the sum of £500 is to be applied to the support of three teachers of schools among them for the same length of time. There is, also, an unexpended balance of former annuities, amounting to about £5,000, which is to be applied to the support of schools, at twelve different places. School-houses have been erected for this purpose, and paid for, out of this fund. Also, by the treaty of 1825, they are entitled to an annuity of £1,200, for the support of schools within the Choctaw District.

The treaty of the 24th of May, 1834, provides that £600 annually, for fifteen years, shall be applied, under the direction of the Secretary of War, to the education of the Chickasaws. These people have become very wealthy, by the cession of their lands east of the Mississippi to the United States. They have a large fund applicable to various objects of civilization; £2,000 of which is, for the present applied to purposes of education.

The country assigned to the Cherokees is bounded as follows: beginning on the north bank of Arkansas River, where the western line of the State of Arkansas crosses the river ; thence north 7° 35′ west, along the line of the State of Arkansas, seventy-seven miles to the south-west corner of the State of Missouri ; thence north along the line of Missouri, eight miles to Seneca River ; thence west along the southern boundary of the Senecas to Neosho River ; thence up said river to the Osage lands ; thence west with the South boundary of the Osage lands, two hundred and eighty-eight and a half miles ; thence south to the Creek lands, and east along the north line of the creeks, to a point about forty-three miles west of the State of Arkansas, and twenty-five miles north of Arkansas River, thence south to Verdigris River, thence down Verdigris to Arkansas River ; thence down Arkansas River to the mouth of Neosho River ; thence South 53° west one mile ; thence south 18° 19′ west thirty-three miles ; thence south four miles, to the junction of the North Fork and Canadian Rivers ; thence down the latter to the Arkansas ; and thence down the Arkansas, to the place of beginning.

They also own a tract, described, by beginning at the south-east corner of the Osage lands, and running north with the Osage line, fifty miles ; thence east twenty-five miles to the west line of Missouri; thence west twenty-five-miles, to the place of beginning.

They own numerous Salt Springs, three of which are worked by Cherokees. The amount of Salt manufactured is probably about 100 bushels per day. They also own two Lead Mines.—Their Salt Works and Lead Mines are in the Eastern portion of their country. All the settlements yet formed are there also. It embraces about 2,500,000 acres. They own about 20,000 head of cattle, 3,000 horses, 15,000 hogs, 600 sheep, 110 waggons, often several ploughs to one farm, several hundred spinning wheels, and one hundred looms. Their fields are enclosed with rail fences. They have erected for themselves good log dwellings, with stone chimneys and plank floors. Their houses are furnished with plain tables, chairs, and bedsteads, and with table and kitchen furniture, nearly or quite equal to the dwellings of white people in new countries.—They have seven native merchants, and one regular physician, beside several " quacks " Houses of entertainment, with neat and comfortable accommodation, are found among them.

Their settlements are divided into four districts, each of which elects for the term of two years, two members of the National Council—the title of which is, " The General Council of the Cherokee Nation." By law, it meets annually on the first Monday in October. They have three chiefs, which till lately have been chosen by the General Council. Hereafter, they are to be elected by the people. The approval of the chiefs is necessary to the passage of a law ; but an act upon which they have fixed their veto, may become a law by a vote of two thirds of the Council. The Council consists of two branches. The lower, is denominated the *Committee*, and the upper, the *Council*. The concurrence of both is necessary to the passage of a law. The chiefs may call a Council at pleasure. In this, and in several other respects, they retain in some degree the authority common to hereditary chiefs. Two Judges belong to each district, who hold courts when necessary. Two officers, denominated Light-horsemen, in each district perform the duties of Sheriffs. A company of six or seven Light-horsemen, the leader of whom is styled captain, constitute a National Corps of Regulators, to prevent infractions of the law, and to bring offenders to justice.

It is stipulated in the treaty of the 6th

of May, 1823, that the United States will pay £400 annually to the Cherokees for ten years, to be expended under the direction of the President of the United States, in the education of their children, *in their own country*, in letters and mechanic arts. Also £200 toward the purchase of a printing-press and types. By the treaty of December 29, 1835, the sum of £30,000 is provided for the support of common schools, and such a literary institution of a higher order as may be established in the Indian country. The above sum is to be added to an education fund of £10,000 that previously existed, making the sum of £40,000 which is to remain a permanent school fund, only the interest of which is to be consumed. The application of this money is to be directed by the Cherokee Nation, under the supervision of the President of the United States. The interest of it will be sufficient constantly to keep in a boarding-school two hundred children ; or eight hundred, if boarded by their parents.

The country of the Creeks joins Canadian river, and the lands of the Choctaws on the south, and the Cherokee lands on the east and north. Their eastern limit is about sixty-two miles from north to south;

their western limit the Mexican boundary.

Their country is fertile, and exhibits a healthy appearance ; but of the latter Creek emigrants who reached Arkansas in the winter and spring of 1837, about two hundred died on the road ; and before the 1st of October succeeding the arrival, about three thousand five hundred more fell victims to bilious fevers. In the same year three hundred of the earlier emigrants died. They own salt springs, cultivate corn, vegetables, &c., spin, weave and sew, and follow other pursuits of civilised people. Many of them have large stocks of cattle. Before the crops of 1837 had been gathered, they had sold corn to the amount of upwards of £7,800 ; and vast quantities still remained unsold. Even the emigrants who arrived in their country during the winter and spring, previous to the cropping season of 1837, broke the turf, fenced their fields, raised their crops for the first time on the soil, and sold their surplus of corn for £2,000. They have two native merchants.

The civil government of this tribe is less perfect than that of the Cherokees. There are two bands ; the one under McIntosh, the other under Little Doctor. That led

by the former, brought with them from
their old home written laws which they enforce as the laws of their band. That under
the latter, made written laws after their
arrival. Each party holds a general council.
The members of each are hereditary chiefs,
and a class of men called councillors. Each
of these great bands is divided into lesser
ones ; which severally may hold courts, try
civil and criminal causes, sentence, and
execute, &c. Laws, however, are made
by the general councils only ; and it is becoming customary to entertain trials of
cases before these bodies, and to detail some
of their members for executioners. The
legislative, judicial, and executive departments of their government are thus becoming strangely united in one.

The treaty of the 6th of March, 1832,
stipulates that an annuity of £600 shall
be expended by the United States, under
the direction of the President, for the term
of twenty years, in the education of their
children. Another £200 by the treaty
of the 14th of February, 1833, is to be
annually expended during the pleasure of
Congress for the same object, under the
direction of the President.

In location and government the Seminoles are merged in the Creeks. In the spring of 1836, about four hundred of them emigrated from the east, and settled on the north fork of Canadian river. In October, 1837, they were reduced by sickness nearly one-half. During these awful times of mortality among them, some of the dead were deposited in the hollows of the standing and fallen trees, and others, for want of these, were placed in a temporary inclosure of boards, on the open plains. Guns and other articles of property were often buried with the dead, according to ancient custom; and so great is said to have been the terror of the time, that, having abandoned themselves awhile to their wailings around the burial-places of their friends, they fled to the western deserts till the pestilence subsided. Of the two thousand and twenty-three emigrants who had reached their new homes prior to October, 1832, not more than one thousand six hundred remained alive.

The Senecas consist of three bands, namely : Senecas two hundred, Senecas and Shawanoes two hundred and eleven, Mohawks fifty; in all four hundred and sixty-one. The lands of the Senecas proper adjoin those of the Cherokees on the south, and, abutting on the Missouri border, the distance of thirteen miles, extend north to Neosho river. The lands of the mixed band of Senecas and Shawanoes, extend north between the State of Missouri and Neosho river, so far as to include sixty-thousand acres.

These people, also, are in some measure civilized. Most of them speak English. They have fields inclosed with rail fences, and raise corn and vegetables sufficient for their own use. They own about eight-hundred horses, twelve hundred cattle, thirteen yoke of oxen, two hundred hogs, five waggons, and sixty-seven ploughs; dwell in neat, hewn log cabins erected by themselves, and furnished with bedsteads, chairs, tables, &c., of their own manu-facture; and own one grist and saw-mill, erected at the expense of the United States.

The country of the Osages lies north of the western portion of the Cherokee lands, commencing twenty-five miles west of the State of Missouri, and thence, in a width of fifty miles, extends westward as far as the country can be inhabited. In 1817, they numbered ten thousand five hundred. Wars with the Sioux, and other causes, have left only five thousand five hundred.

About half the tribe reside on the eastern portion of their lands ; the residue in the Cherokee country, in two villages on Verdigris river.

This tribe has made scarcely any improvement. Their fields are small and badly fenced. Their huts are constructed of poles inserted in the ground, bent together at the top, and covered with bark, mats, &c., and some of them with buffalo and elk skins. The fire is placed in the centre, and the smoke escapes through an aperture at the top. These huts are built in villages, and crowded together without order or arrangement, and destitute of furniture of any kind, except a platform raised about two feet upon stakes set in the ground. This extends along the side of the hut, and may serve for a seat, a table, or a bedstead. The leggings, and mocassins for the feet, are seldom worn except in cold weather, or when they are travelling in the grass. These, with a temporary garment fastened about the loins, and extending downwards, and a buffalo robe or blanket thrown loosely around them, constitute the sole wardrobe of the males and married females. The unmarried females wear also a strip of plain cloth eight or nine inches wide, which they throw over one shoulder, draw it over the breasts, and fasten it under the opposite arm.

The Osages were, when the whites first knew them, brave, warlike, and in the Indian sense of the term, in affluent circumstances. They were the hardiest and fiercest enemies of the terrible Sioux; but their independent spirit is gone, and they have degenerated into the miserable condition of insolent, starving thieves. The government has been, and is making the most generous efforts to elevate them. The treaty of 1825 provides, "that the President of the United States shall employ such persons to aid the Osages in their agricultural pursuits, as to him may seem expedient." Under this stipulation, £240 annually have been expended, for the last fifteen years. This bounty of the government, however, has not been of any permanent benefit to the tribe. The same treaty of 1825, required fifty-four sections of land to be laid off and sold under the direction of the President of the United States, and the proceeds to be applied to the education of Osage children. Early in the year 1838, government made an arrangement by which they were to be paid two dollars per acre, for the whole tract of fifty-four sections,

34,560 acres. This commutation has secured to the Osage tribe, the sum of £13,824
for education ; a princely fund for five thousand five hundred and ten individuals. Government hereditary chieftaincies.

The band of Quapaws was originally connected with the Osages. Their lands lie
immediately north of the Senecas and Shawanoes, and extend north between the state
of Missouri on the east, and Neosho River
on the west, so far as to include 96,000
acres. Their country is south-east of, and
near to the country of the Osages. Their
habits are somewhat more improved, and
their circumstances more comfortable than
those of the last named tribe. They subsist
by industry at home, cultivate fields enclosed with rail fences ; and about three-
fourths of them have erected for themselves
small log dwellings with chimneys. Unfortunately for the Quapaws, they settled on
the lands of the Senecas and Shawanoes,
from which they must soon remove to their
own. A small band of them, forty or fifty
in number, have settled in Texas, and about
thirty others live among the Choctaws.

The Pottawatamies, in emigrating to the
west, have unfortunately been divided into
two bands. One thousand or fifteen hun-

dred have located themselves on the northeast side of the Missouri River, two hundred and forty miles from the country designated by government as their permanent residence. Negotiations have been made to effect their removal to their own lands, but without success. About fifteen hundred others have settled near the Sauks, on the Mississippi, and manifest a desire to remain there. The country designated for them lies on the sources of the Osage and Neosho rivers; it commences sixteen miles and four chains west of the State of Missouri, and in a width of twenty-four miles, extends west two hundred miles. By the treaty of 1833, they are allowed the sum of £14,000 dollars for purposes of education and the encouragement of the useful arts. Also by the same treaty, is secured to them the sum of £30,000 to be applied in the erection of mills, farmhouses, Indian houses, and blacksmiths' shops; to the purchase of agricultural implements and live stock, and for the support of physicians, millers, farmers, and blacksmiths, which the President of the United States shall think proper to appoint to their service.

The Weas and Piankashas are bands of Miamis. Their country lies north of the

Pottawatamies, adjoins the State of Missouri on the east, the Shawanoes on the north, and the Peorias and Kaskaskias on the west—160,000 acres. These people own a few cattle and swine. About one-half of their dwellings are constructed of logs, the remainder of bark, in the old native style. Their fields are enclosed with rails, and they cultivate corn and vegetables sufficient for a comfortable subsistence. The Piankasha band is less improved than the Weas. The former have a field of about fifty acres, made by the government; the latter have made their own improvements.

The Peorias and Kaskaskias are also bands of the Miamis. Their land lies immediately west of the Weas; adjoins the Shawanoes on the north, and the Ottowas on the west. They own 96,000 acres. They are improving, live in log-houses, have small fields generally enclosed with rail-fences, and own considerable numbers of cattle and swine.

The lands of the Ottowas lie immediately west of the Peorias and Kaskaskias, and south of the Shawanoes. The first band of emigrants received 36,000 acres, and one which arrived subsequently, 40,000 acres, adjoining the first. They all live in good

log cabins, have fields enclosed with rail-
fences, raise a comfortable supply of corn
and garden vegetables, are beginning to
raise wheat, have horses, cattle and swine,
a small grist-mill in operation, and many
other conveniences of life, that indicate an
increasing desire among them to seek from
the soil, rather than the chase, the means of
life.   About five thousand Ottowas, residing
in Michigan, are soon to be removed to their
brethren in the Territory.   The country of
the Ottowas lies upon the western verge of
the contemplated Indian settlement, and
consequently opens an unlimited range to
the westward.   Their government is based
on the old system of Indian chieftaincies.

Immediately on the north of the Weas
and Piankashas, the Peorias and Kaskaskias
and Ottowas, lies the country of the Shawnees, or Shawanoes.   It extends along the
line of the State of Missouri, north, twenty-
eight miles to the Missouri River at its
junction with the Konzas, thence to a point
sixty miles on a direct course to the lands
of the Kauzaus, thence south on the
Kauzaus line six miles, and from these lines,
with a breadth of about nineteen miles to a
north and south line, one hundred and
twenty miles west of the State of Missouri,

containing 1,600,000 acres. Their principal settlements are on the north-east corner
of their country, between the Missouri border and the Konzas River. Most of them
live in neatly hewn log-cabins, erected by
themselves, and partially supplied with furniture of their own manufacture. Their
fields are inclosed with rail-fences, and sufficiently large to yield plentiful supplies of
corn and culinary vegetables. They keep
cattle and swine, work oxen, and use horses
for draught, and own some ploughs, waggons and carts. They have a saw and
grist-mill, erected by government at an expense of about £1,600 This, like many
other emigrant tribes, is much scattered.
Besides the two bands on the Neosho,
already mentioned, there is one on Trinity
River, in Texas, and others in divers places.

Under the superintendance of Missionaries of various denominations, these people
are making considerable progress in Education and the Mechanic Arts. They have a
printing press among them, from which is
issued a monthly periodical, entitled the
" Shauwawnoue Kesauthwau"—Shawanoe
Sun.

The lands of the Delawares lie north of
the Shawanots, in the forks of the Konzas

and Missouri Rivers; extending up the former to the Kauzaus lands, thence north twenty-four miles, to the north-east corner of the Kauzaus survey, up the Missouri twenty-three miles, in a direct course to Cantonment Leavenworth, thence with a line westward to a point ten miles north of the north-east corner of the Kauzaus survey, and then a slip not more than ten miles wide, it extends westwardly along the northern boundary of the Kauzaus, two-hundred and ten miles from the State of Missouri.

They live in the eastern portion of their country, near the junction of the Konzas and Missouri Rivers; have good hewn log-houses, and some furniture in them; inclose their fields with rail fences; keep cattle and hogs; apply horses to draught; use oxen and ploughs; cultivate corn and garden vegetables, sufficient for use: have commenced the culture of wheat; and own a grist and saw-mill, erected by the United States. Some of these people remain in the Lake country; a few are in Texas; about one-hundred reside on the Choctaw lands near Arkansas River, one hundred and twenty miles west of the state of Arkansas. These latter have acquired the languages of the Cumanches, Keaways, Pawnees, &c., and are extensively employed as interpreters by traders from the Indian Territory. The Treaty of September, 1829, provides that thirty-six sections of the *best* land within the district at that time ceded to the United States, be selected and sold, and the proceeds applied to the support of Schools for the education of Delaware children. In the year 1838, the Delawares agreed to a commutation of two dollars per acre, which secures to them an Education Fund of £9,000.

The country of the Kauzaus lies on the Konzas River. It commences sixty miles west of the State of Missouri, and thence, in a width of thirty miles, extends westward as far as the plains can be inhabited. It is well watered and timbered; and in every respect delightful. They are a lawless, dissolute race. Formerly they committed many depredations upon their own traders, and other persons ascending the Missouri River. But, being latterly restrained in this regard by the United States, they have turned their predatory operations upon their red neighbours. In language, habits and condition in life, they are in effect the same as the Osages. In

matters of peace and war, the two tribes
are blended. They are virtually one
people.

Like the Osages, the Kauzaus are ignorant and wretched in the extreme; un-
commonly servile, and easily managed by
the white men who reside among them.
Almost all of them live in villages of straw,
bark, flag and earth huts. These latter are
in the form of a cone; wall two feet in
thickness, supported by wooden pillars
within. Like the other huts, these have
no floor except the earth. The fire is
built in the centre of the interior area. The
smoke escapes at an opening in the apex
of the cone. The door is a mere hole,
through which they crawl, closed by the
skin of some animal suspended therein.
They cultivate small patches of corn, beans
and melons. They dig the ground with
hoes and sticks. Their fields generally, are
not fenced. They have one, however,
of three hundred acres, which the United
States six years ago ploughed and fenced
for them. The principal Chiefs have log-
houses built by the Government Agent.

It is encouraging, however, to know that
these miserable creatures are beginning to
yield to the elevating influences around

them. A missionary has induced some of them to leave the villages, make separate settlements, build log-houses, &c. The United States have furnished them with four yoke of oxen, one waggon, and other means of cultivating the soil. They have succeeded in stealing a large number of horses and mules ; own a very few hogs ; no stock cattle. By a treaty formed with them in 1825, thirty-six sections, or 23,040 acres, of good land were to be selected and sold to educate Kauzaus children within their territory. But proper care not having been taken in making the selection, 9,000 acres only have been sold. The remaining 14,040 acres of the tract, it is said, will scarcely sell at any price, so utterly worthless is it. Hence only £2,250 have been realised from this munificent appropriation. By the same treaty, provision was made for the application of £120 per annum, to aid them in agriculture.

The Kickapoo lands lie on the north of the Delawares ; extend up the Missouri river thirty miles direct, thence westward about forty five miles, and thence south twenty miles to the Delaware line, embracing 768,000 acres.

They live on the south-eastern extremity

of their lands, near Cantonment Leaven-worth. In regard to civilization, their condition is similar to that of the Peorias. They are raising a surplus of the grains, &c. have cattle and hogs, £140 worth of the latter, and three hundred and forty head of the former from the United States, in obedience to treaty stipulations ; have about thirty yoke of oxen, fourteen yoke of them purchased chiefly with the produce of their farms ; have a saw and grist mill, erected by the United States. Nearly one-half of the tribe are unsettled and scattered, some in Texas, others with the southern tribes, and still others ranging the mountains. The treaty of October 24th, 1832, provides that the United States shall pay £100 per annum for ten successive years, for the support of a school, purchase of books, &c. for the benefit of the Kickapoo tribe on their own lands. A school-house and teacher have been furnished in conformity with this stipulation. The same treaty provides £200 for labour and improvements on the Kickapoo lands.

The Sauks, and Reynards or Foxes, speak the same language, and are so perfectly consolidated by intermarriages and other ties of interest, as, in fact, to be one nation.

They formerly owned the north-western half of the State of Illinois, and a large part of the State of Missouri. No Indian tribe, except the Sioux, has shown such daring intrepidity, and such implacable hatred towards other tribes. Their enmity, when once excited, was never known to be appeased, till the arrow and tomahawk had for ever prostrated their foes. For centuries the prairies of Illinois and Iowa were the theatre of their exterminating prowess ; and to them is to be attributed the almost entire destruction of the Missouris, the Illinois, Cahokias, Kaskaskias, and Peorias. They were, however, steady and sincere in their friendship to the whites ; and many is the honest old settler on the borders of their old dominion, who mentions with the warmest feelings, the respectful treatment he has received from them, while he cut the logs for his cabin, and ploughed his " potato patch" on that lonely and unprotected frontier.

Like all the tribes, however, this also dwindles away at the approach of the whites. A melancholy fact. The Indians' bones must enrich the soil, before the plough of civilized man can open it. The noble heart, educated by the tempest to endure the last pang of departing life without a cringe of a muscle ; that heart educated by his condition to love with all the powers of being, and to hate with the exasperated malignity of a demon ; that heart, educated by the voice of its own existence —the sweet whisperings of the streams— the holy flowers of spring—to trust in, and adore the Great producing and sustaining Cause of itself, and the broad world and the lights of the upper skies, must fatten the corn hills of a more civilized race ! The sturdy plant of the wilderness droops under the enervating culture of the garden. The Indian is buried with his arrows and bow.

In 1832 their friendly relations with their white neighbours were, I believe, for the first time, seriously interrupted. A treaty had been formed between the chiefs of the tribe and commissioners, representing the United States, containing, among other stipulations, the sale of their lands north of the Rock River, &c. in the State of Illinois. This tract of country contained the old villages and burial-places of the tribe. It was, indeed, the sanctuary of all that was venerable and sacred among them. They wintered and summered there long before the date of their historical legends. And on

these flowering plains the spoils of war—
the loves of early years—every thing that
delights man to remember of the past, clung
closely to the tribe, and made them dis-
satisfied with the sale. Black-Hawk was
the principal chief.   He, too, was unwilling
to leave his village in a charming glen, at
the mouth of Rock River, and increased the
dissatisfaction of his people by declaring
that " the white chiefs had deceived himself and the other contracting chiefs" in
this, " that he had never, and the other
chiefs had never consented to such a sale
as the white chiefs had written, and were
attempting to enforce upon them." They
dug up the painted tomahawk with great
enthusiasm, and fought bravely by their
noble old chief for their beautiful home.
But, in the order of nature, the plough
must bury the hunter.   And so it was with
this truly great chief and his brave tribe.
They were driven over the Mississippi to
make room for the marshalled host of veteran husbandmen, whose strong blows had
levelled the forests of the Atlantic States ;
and yet unwearied with planting the rose
on the brow of the wilderness, demanded
that the Prairies also should yield food to
their hungry sickles.

The country assigned them as their permanent residence, adjoins the southern boundary of the Kickapoos, and on the north and north east the Missouri river. They are but little improved. Under treaty stipulations, they have some few houses and fields made for them by the United States, and are entitled to more. Some live stock has been given them, and more is to be furnished. The main body of the Sauks, usually denominated the Sauks and Foxes, estimated at four thousand six hundred souls, reside on the Iowa river, in Iowa Territory. They will ultimately be removed to unappropriated lands adjoining those already occupied by their kindred within the Indian Territory. Both these bands number twelve thousand four hundred. By the treaty of Prairie du Chien of 1830, the Sauks are entitled to £100 a year for the purposes of education. By treaty of September, 1836, they are entitled to a schoolmaster, a farmer, and blacksmith, as long as the United States shall deem proper. Three comfortable houses are to be erected for them, two hundred acres of prairie land fenced and ploughed, such agricultural implements furnished as they may need for five years, one ferry-boat, two hundred and five head of cattle, one hundred stock hogs, and a flouring mill. These benefits they are receiving, but are making an improvident use of them.

The country of the Iowas contains one hundred and twenty-eight thousand acres adjoining the north eastern boundaries of the Sauks, with the Missouri river on the north east, and the great Nemaha river on the north. Their condition is similar to that of the Sauks. The aid which they have received, and are to receive from the government, is about the same in proportion to their numbers. The village of the Sauks and Iowas, are within two miles of each other.

The Otoes are the descendants of the Missouris, with whom they united after the reduction of the latter tribe by the Sauks and Foxes. They claim a portion of land lying in the fork between Missouri and Great Platte rivers. The government of the United States understand, however, that their lands extend southward from the Platte down the Missouri to Little Nemaha river, a distance of about forty miles; thence their southern boundary extends westward up Little Nemaha to its source, and thence due west. Their western and northern boundaries are not particularly defined. Their southern boundary is about twenty-five miles north of the Iowa's land.

By treaty, such of their tribe as are related to the whites, have an interest in a tract adjoining the Missouri river, and extending from the Little Nemaha to the Great Nemaha, a length of about twenty-eight miles, and ten miles wide. No Indians reside on this tract.

The condition of this people is similar to that of the Osages and Kauzaus. The United States Government has fenced and ploughed for them one hundred and thirty acres of land. In 1838, they cultivated three hundred acres of corn. They own six ploughs, furnished by Government. Their progenitors, the Missouris, were, when the French first knew the country, the most numerous tribe in the vicinity of Saint Louis; and the great stream, on whose banks they reside, and the State which has risen upon their hunting grounds when the race is extinct, will bear their name to the generations of coming time. They are said to have been an energetic and thrifty race before they were visited by the small-pox, and the destroying vengeance of the Sauks and Foxes. The site of their ancient village is to be seen on the north bank of the river, honoured with their name, just below where Grand river now enters it. Their territory embraced the fertile country lying a considerable distance along the Missouri, above their village—and down to the mouth of the Osega, and thence to the Mississippi. The Osegas consider them their inferiors, and treat them oftentimes with great indignity.

The Omahas own the country north of the mouth of the Great Platte. The Missouri river is considered its north-eastern limit ; the northern and western boundary are undefined. This tribe was formerly the terror of their neighbours. They had, in early times, about one thousand warriors, and a proportionate number of women and children. But the small-pox visited them in 1802, and reduced the tribe to about three hundred souls. This so disheartened those who survived, that they burnt their village, and became a wandering people. They have at last taken possession again of their country, and built a village on the south-west bank of the Missouri, at a place chosen for them by the United States. Their huts are constructed of earth, like those of the Otoes. A treaty made with them in July, 1830, provides that an annuity of five hundred dollars shall be paid to them in agricultural implements, for ten years thereafter, and longer if the President of the United States thinks proper. A blacksmith also, is to be furnished them for the same length of time. Another treaty obliges the United States to plough and fence one hundred acres of land for them, and to expend, for the term of ten years, £100 annually, in educating Omaha children.

The Puncahs, or Ponsars, are the remnant of a nation of respectable importance, formerly living upon Red river, of Lake Winnipeg. Having been nearly destroyed by the Sioux, they removed to the west side of the Missouri river, where they built a fortified village, and remained some years; but being pursued by their ancient enemies, the Sioux, and reduced by continual wars, they joined the Omahas, and so far lost their original character as to be undistinguished from them. They, however, after a while, resumed a separate existence, which they continue to maintain. They reside in the northern extremity of the Indian Territory. Their circumstances are similar to those of the Pawnees.

The Pawnees own an extensive country lying west of the Otoes and Omahas, on the Great Platte river. Their villages are upon this stream and its lower tributaries. They are said to have about two thousand five hundred warriors. Among them are still to be found every custom of old Indian life. The earth-hut, the scalping-knife, the tomahawk, and the scalps of their foes dangling from the posts in their smoky dwellings, the wild war cries, the venerated medicine bag, with the calumet of peace, the sacred wampum that records their treaties, the feasts and dances of peace and of war, those of marriage and of sacrifice, the moccasins, and leggings, and war-caps, and horrid paintings ; the moons of the year, as March, the 'worm moon,' April, the ' moon of plants,' May, the ' moon of flowers,' June, the ' hot moon,' July, the ' buck moon,' August, the 'sturgeon moon,' September, the ' corn moon,' October, the ' travelling moon,' November, the ' beaver moon,' December, the ' hunting moon,' January, the ' cold moon,' February, the ' snow moon,' and in reference to its phases, the " dead moon" and " live moon ;" and days are counted by " sleeps," and their years by " snows." In a word, the Pawnees are as yet unchanged by the enlightening influences of knowledge and

religion. The philanthropy of the United
States Government, however, is putting
within their reach every inducement to improvement. By treaty, £400 worth of agricultural implements is to be furnished
them annually for the term of five years,
or longer, at the discretion of the President of the United States ; also, £200
worth of live stock whenever the President shall believe them prepared to profit
thereby ; also, £400 annually are to be
expended to support two smitheries, with
two smiths in each, for supplying iron,
steel, &c., for the term of ten years ; also
four grist mills, propelled by horse power ;
also four farmers during the term of five
years. Also the sum of £200 annually, for
ten years, is to be allowed for the support
of schools among them.

These are the emigrant and native Indians
within the " Indian Territory," and their
several conditions and circumstances, so far
as I have been able to learn them. The
other Indians in the Great Prairie Wilderness will be briefly noticed under two divi-
sions—those living south, and those living
north of the Great Platte river.

There are living on the head waters of
Red river, and between that river and the

Rio Bravo del Norte, the remains of twelve
different tribes—ten of which have an average population of two hundred souls; none of
them number more than four hundred. The
Carankouas and Tetaus, or Cumanches, are
more numerous. The former live about the
Bay of St. Bernard. They were always
inimical to the Mexicans and Spaniards;
never would succumb to their authority, or
receive their religious teachers. And many
hard battles were fought in maintaining
their independence in these respects. In
1817, they amounted to about three thousand, of which six hundred were warriors.

The Cumanches are supposed to be twenty
thousand strong. They are a brave vagrant
tribe, and never reside but a few days in a
place, but travel north with the buffalo in
the summer, and, as winter comes on, return
with them to the plains west of Texas. They
traverse the immense space of country extending from the Trinity and Brazos to the
Red River, and the head waters of the Arkansas, and Colorado to the west, to the
Pacific Ocean, and thence to the head
streams of the Missouri, and thence to their
winter haunts. They have tents made of
neatly dressed skins, in the form of cones.
These, when they stop, are pitched so as to

form streets and squares. They pitch and strike these tents in an astonishingly short space of time. To every tent is attached two pack-horses, the one to carry the tent, and the other the polished cedar poles with which it is spread. These loaded in a trice —the saddle horses harnessed in still less time—twenty thousand savages—men, women, and children, warriors and chiefs—start at a signal whoop, travel the day, again raise their city of tents to rest and feed themselves and animals for another march.

Thus passes life with the Cumanches. Their plains are covered with buffalo, elk, deer, and wild horses. It is said that they drink the blood of the buffalo warm from the veins. They also eat the liver in its raw state, using the gall as sauce. The dress of the women is a long loose robe which reaches from the chin to the ground, made of deer skin dressed very neatly, and painted with figures of different colours and significations. The dress of the men is close pantaloons, and a hunting shirt or frock made of the same beautiful material. They are a warlike and brave race, and stand in the relation of conquerors among the tribes in the south. The Spaniards of New Mexico are all acquainted with the strength of their enemy, and their power to punish those whom they hate. For many are the scalps and death-dances among these Indians, which testify of wars and tomahawks which have dug tombs for that poor apology of European extraction. They are exceedingly fond of stealing the objects of their enemies' affection. Female children are sought with the greatest avidity, and adopted or married. " About sixty years ago," as the tale runs, " the daughter of the Governor-General at Chilhuahua, was stolen by them. The father immediately pursued, and by an agent, after some weeks had elapsed, purchased her ransom. But she refused to return to her parents, and sent them these words : ' That the Indians had tattooed her face according to their style of beauty—had given her to be the wife of a young man by whom she believed herself enceinte—that her husband treated her well, and reconciled her to his mode of life —that she would be made more unhappy by returning to her father under these circumstances, than by remaining where she was.' She continued to live with her husband in the nation, and raised a family of children."

There are the remains of fifteen or twenty tribes in that part of the Great Prairie Wilderness north of the Great Platte, and north and west of the Indian Territory. They average about eight hundred each. The Sioux and the small-pox have reduced them thus.

The Knistineaux chiefly reside in the British possessions along the northern shores of Lake Superior. Some bands of them have established themselves south of latitude 49° north, near the head waters of these branches of Red River of Lake Winnipeg, which rise south of the sources of the Mississippi. They are moderate in stature, well proportioned, and of great activity. Mackenzie remarks that their countenances are frank and agreeable, that the females are well-formed, and their features are more regular and comely than those of any other tribe he saw upon the continent. They are warlike—number about three thousand; but the Sioux are annihilating them.

The Sioux claim a country equal in extent to some of the most powerful empires of Europe. Their boundaries " commence at the Prairie du Chien, and ascend the Mississippi on both sides to the River De

Corbeau, and up that to its source, from thence to the sources of the St. Peter's, thence to the ' Montaigne de la Prairie,' thence to the Missouri, and down that river to the Omahas, thence to the sources of the River Des Moines, and thence to the place of beginning." They also claim a large territory south of the Missouri.

The country from Rum River to the River de Corbeau is claimed by them and the Chippeways, and has been the source of many bloody encounters for the past two hundred years. These Indians have conquered and destroyed immense numbers of their race. They have swept the banks of the Missouri from the Great Falls to the mouth of the Great Platte and the plains that lie north of the latter stream, between the Black Hills and the Mississippi. They are divided into six bands, viz.: the Menowa Kontong, which resides around the falls of St. Anthony, and the lower portion of St. Peter's River; the Washpetong, still higher on that stream; the Sussetong, on its head waters and those of Red River, of Lake Winnipeg; the Yanktons of the north, who rove over the plains on the borders of the Missouri valley south of the sources of the St. Peter's; the Yonktons Ahnah, who

live on the Missouri near the entrance of
James River; the Tetons Brulos; Tetons
Okandandas; Tetons Minnekincazzo, and
Tetons Sahone, who reside along the banks
of the Missouri from the Great Bend northward to the villages of the Riccarees. Theirs
is the country from which is derived the
colouring matter of that river. The plains
are strongly impregnated with Glauber
salts, alum, copperas, and sulphur. In the
spring of the year immense bluffs fall in the
stream; and these, together with the leach-
ings from these medicated prairies, give to
the waters their mud colour, and purgative
qualities.

These bands comprise about twenty-
eight thousand souls. They subsist upon
buffalo meat, and the wild fruits of their
forests. The former is prepared for winter, and for travelling use, in the following manner:—The lean parts of the
buffalo are cut into thin slices, dried over
a slow fire, in the sun, or by exposing it
to frost—pounded fine, and then, with a
portion of berries, mixed with an equal
quantity of fat from the humps and brisket,
or with marrow, in a boiling state, and
sewed up tightly in sacks of green hide, or
packed closely in baskets of wicker work.
This " pemican," as they call it, will keep

for several years.   They also use much of
the wild rice, avena fatua, which grows in
great abundance on the St. Peter's, and
among the lakes and head streams of Red
River, of Winnipeg, and in other parts of
their territory.   It grows in water from
four to seven feet deep with a muddy bottom.   The plant rises from four to eight
feet above the surface of the water, about
the size of the red cane of Tennessee, full
of joints, and of the colour and texture of
bull-rushes : the stalks above the water,
and the branches which bear the grain, resemble oats.

To these strange grain fields the wild
duck and geese resort for food in the
summer.   And to prevent it from being
devoured by them, the Indians tie it, when
the kernel is in the milky state, just below
the head, into large bunches.   This arrangement prevents these birds from pressing
the heads down within their reach.   When
ripe, the Indians pass among it with canoes
lined with blankets, into which they bend
the stalks, and whip off the grain with
sticks ; and so abundant is it, that an expert squaw will soon fill a canoe.   After
being gathered, it is dried and put into
skins or baskets for use.   They boil or
parch it, and eat it in the winter season

with their pemican. This plant is found
no farther south than Illinois, no farther
east than Sandusky Bay, and north nearly
to Hudson's Bay. The rivers and lakes of
the Sioux and Chippeway country are said
to produce annually several million bushels
of it. It is equally as nutritious and palatable as the Carolina rice. Carver also says
that the St. Peter's flows through a country
producing spontaneously all the necessaries
of life in the greatest abundance. Besides
the wild rice, he informs us that every part
of the valley of that river " is filled with
trees bending under their loads of plums,
grapes, and apples ; the meadows with
hops, and many sorts of vegetables, while
the ground is stored with edible roots, and
covered with such amazing quantities of
sugar-maple, that they would produce sugar
enough for any number of inhabitants."

Mr. Carver seems to have been, to say
the least, rather an enthusiastic admirer of
nature ; and although later travellers in the
country of the Naudowessies (Sioux) have
not been able to find grouped within it all
the fruits and flowers of an Eden, yet that
their lands lying on the Mississippi, the St.
Peter's, and the Red Rivers, produce a luxu-
rious vegetation, groves of fine timber sepa-

rated by open plains of the rich wild grasses, and by lakes and streams of pure water well stored with fish; that there are many valuable edible roots there: and the whortleberry, blackberry, wild plumb and crabapple, other and later travellers have seen and declared; so that no doubt can be entertained that this talented and victorious tribe possess a very desirable and beautiful country. A revolted band of the Sioux called Osinipoilles, live near the Rocky Mountains upon the Sascatchiwine river, a pleasant champaign country, abounding in game. They subsist by the chase, and the spoils of war. Their number is estimated to be eight thousand. Their dwellings are neat conical tents of tanned buffalo skins.

The Chippewyans or Chippeways, were supposed by Lewis and Clark to inhabit the country lying between the 60th and 65th parallels of north latitude, and 100° and 110° of west longitude. Other authorities, and I believe more correct, assert that they also occupy the head waters of the Mississippi, Ottertail, and Leach, De Corbeau and Red rivers, and Winnipeg lake. They are a numerous tribe, speak a copious language, are timorous, vagrant, and selfish; stature rather low; features coarse; hair

lank, and not unfrequently a sunburnt
brown ; women more agreeable (and who
can doubt the fact) than the men ; but
have an awkward gait ; which proceeds
from their being accustomed, nine months
in the year, to wear snow shoes, and
drag sledges of a weight from two hundred to four hundred pounds. They are
entirely submissive to their husbands ; and
for very trifling causes are treated with such
cruelty as to produce death ! These people
betroth their children when quite young ;
and when they arrive at puberty the ceremony of marriage is performed ; that is, the
bridegroom pays the market price for his
bride, and takes her to his lodge, not " for
better or for worse," but to put her away and
take another when he pleases. Plurality of
wives is customary among them. They
generally wear the hair long. The braves
sometimes clip it in fantastic forms. The
women always wear it of great length,
braided in two queues, and dangling down
the back. Jealous husbands sometimes
despoil them of these tresses. Both sexes
make from one to four bars of lines upon
the forehead or cheeks, by drawing a thread
dipped in the proper colour beneath the skin
of those parts.

No people are more attentive to comfort in dress than the Chippeways. It is composed of deer and fawn skins, dressed with the hair on, for the winter, and without the hair for the summer wear. The male wardrobe consists of shoes, leggings, frock and cap, &c. The shoes are made in the usual moccassin form, save that they sometimes use the green instead of the tanned hide. The leggings are made like the legs of pantaloons unconnected by a waistband. They reach to the waist; and are supported by a belt. Under the belt a small piece of leather is drawn, which serves as an apron before and behind. The shoes and leggings are sewed together. In the former are put quantities of moose and reindeer hair; and additional pieces of leather as socks. The frock or hunting shirt is in the form of a peasant's frock. When girded around the waist it reaches to the middle of the thigh. The mittens are sewed to the sleeves, or suspended by strings from the shoulders. A kind of tippet surrounds the neck. The skin of the deer's head furnishes a curious covering to the head; and a robe made of several deer or fawn skins sewed together, covers the whole. This dress is worn single or double, as circumstances suggest; but in winter the hair side of the undersuit is worn next the person, and that of the outer one without. Thus arrayed, the Chippeway will lay himself down on the ice, in the middle of a lake, and repose in comfort; and when rested, and disencumbered of the snow-drifts which have covered him while asleep, he mounts his snow shoes, and travels on without fear of frosts or storm. The dress of the women differs from that of the men. Their leggings are tied below the knee; and their frock or chemise extends down to the ankle. Mothers make these garments large enough about the shoulders to hold an infant; and when travelling carry their little ones upon their backs next the skin.

Their arms and domestic apparatus, in addition to guns, &c., obtained from the whites, are bows and arrows, fishing-nets, and lines made of green deer-skin thongs, and nets of the same material for catching the beaver, as he escapes from his lodge into the water; and sledges and snow-shoes. The snow-shoes are of very superior workmanship. The inner part of the frame is straight; the outer one curved; the ends are brought to a point, and in front turned up. This frame done, they are neatly placed with light thongs of deer-skin. Their sledges are made of red fir-tree boards, neatly polished and turned up in front. The means of sustaining life in the country claimed by these Indians are abundant ; and if sufficient forethought were used in laying in food for winter, they might live in comparative comfort. The woodless hills are covered with a moss that sustains the deer and moose and reindeer ; and when boiled, forms a gelatinous substance very acceptable to the human palate. Their streams and lakes are stored with the greatest abundance of valuable fish. But although more provident than any other Indians on the continent, they often suffer severely in the dead of winter, when, to prevent death from cold, they fly from their fishing stations to their scanty woods.

They are superstitious in the extreme. Almost every action of their lives is influenced by some whimsical notion. They believe in the existence of a good and evil spirit, that rule in their several departments over the fortunes of men ; and in a state of future rewards and punishments. They have an order of priests who administer the rites of their religion—offer sacrifices at their solemn feasts, &c. They have conjurors who cure diseases—as rheumatism, flux and consumption.

"The notion which these people entertain of the creation is of a very singular nature. They believe that at first the earth was one vast and entire ocean, inhabited by no living creature except a mighty Bird, whose eyes were fire, whose glances were lightning, and the flapping of whose wings was thunder. On his descent to the ocean, and touching it, the earth instantly arose, and remained on the surface of the waters. This omnipotent Bird then called forth all the variety of animals from the earth except the Chippeways, who were produced from a dog. And this circumstance occasions their aversion to the flesh of that animal, as well as the people who eat it. This extraordinary tradition proceeds to relate that the great Bird, having finished his work, made an arrow, which was to be preserved with great care and to remain untouched; but that the Chippeways were so devoid of understanding as to carry it away; and the sacrilege so enraged the great Bird that he has never since appeared."

"They have also a tradition among them that they originally came from another country, inhabited by very wicked people, and had traversed a great lake, which was narrow, shallow and full of islands, where they had suffered great misery—it being always winter, with ice and deep snow. At the Coppermine River, where they had made the first land, the ground was covered with copper, over which a body of earth had since been collected to the depth of a man's height. They believe, also, that in ancient times, their ancestors lived till their feet were worn out with walking, and their throats with eating. They describe a deluge when the waters spread over the whole earth, except the highest mountains, on the top of which they preserved themselves. They believe that immediately after their death they pass into another world, where they arrive at a large river, on which they embark in a stone canoe ; and that a gentle current bears them on to an extensive lake, in the centre of which is a most beautiful island ; and that in view of this delightful abode they receive that judgement for their conduct during life, which determines their final state and unalterable allotment. If their good actions are declared to predominate, they are landed upon the island, where there is to be no

end to their happiness ; which, however, to
their notion, consists in an eternal enjoyment of sensual pleasure and carnal gratification.   But if there be bad actions to
weigh down the balance, the stone canoe
sinks at once, and leaves them up to their
chins in water, to behold and regret the
reward enjoyed by the good, and eternally
struggling, but with unavailing endeavours,
to reach the blissful island from which they
are excluded for ever."

It would be interesting, in closing this
notice of the Great Prairie wilderness, to
give an account of the devoted Missionaries of the various denominations who are
labouring to cultivate the Indian in a manner which at once bespeaks their good sense
and honest intentions.   But, as it would
require more space and time than can be
devoted to it, merely to present a skeleton
view of their multifarious doings, I shall
only remark, in passing, that they appear
to have adopted, in their plan of operations,
the principle that to civilize these people,
one of the first steps is to create and gratify
those physical wants peculiar to the civilized state ; and also, that the most successful means of civilizing their mental
state, is to teach them a language which is

filled with the learning, sciences, and the religion which has civilized Europe, that they may enter at once, and with the fullest vigour into the immense harvests of knowledge and virtue which past ages and superior races have prepared for them.

CHAPTER IV.

Fort William—its Structure, Owners, People, Animals, Business, Adventures, and Hazards—A Division—A March—Fort el Puebla—Trappers and Whisky—A Genius—An Adventurous Iroquois—A Kentuckian—Horses and Servant—A Trade—A Start—Arkansas and Country—Wolfano Mountains—Creeks—Rio Wolfano—A Plague of Egypt—Cordilleras—James's Peak—Pike's Peak—A Bath—The Prison of the Arkansas—Entrance of the Rocky Mountains—A Vale.

FORT WILLIAM, or Bent's Fort, on the north side of the Arkansas, eighty miles north by east from Taos in the Mexican dominions, and about one hundred and sixty miles from the mountains, was erected by gentlemen owners in 1832, for purposes of trade with the Spaniards of Santa Fé and Taos, and the Eutaw, Cheyenne and Cumanche Indians. It is in the form of a parallelogram, the northern and southern sides of which are about a hundred and fifty feet, and the eastern and western a hundred feet in length. The walls are six or seven feet in thickness at the base, and seventeen or eighteen feet in height. The fort is entered through

a large gateway on the eastern side, in
which swing a pair of immense plank
doors. At the north-west and south-east
corners stand two cylindrical bastions,
about ten feet in diameter and thirty feet
in height.

These are properly perforated for the
use of cannon and small arms; and command the fort and the plains around it.
The interior area is divided into two parts.
The one and the larger of them occupies
the north-eastern portion. It is nearly a
square. A range of two story houses, the
well, and the blacksmith's shop are on the
north side; on the west and south are
ranges of one-story houses; on the east the
blacksmith's shop, the gate and the outer
wall. This is the place of business. Here
the owners and their servants have their
sleeping and cooking apartments, and here
are the storehouses. In this area the Indians in the season of trade gather in large
numbers and barter, and trade, and buy,
under the guardianship of the carronades
of the bastions loaded with grape, and
looking upon them. From this area a passage leads between the eastern outer wall
and the one-story houses, to the caral or
cavy-yard, which occupies the remainder
of the space within the walls. This is the

place for the horses, mules, &c., to repose
in safety from Indian depredations at night.
Beyond the caral to the west and adjoining
the wall, is the waggon-house. It is strongly
built, and large enough to shelter twelve or
fifteen of those large vehicles which are
used in conveying the peltries to St. Louis,
and goods thence to the post. The long
drought of summer renders it necessary to
protect them from the sun.

The walls of the fort, its bastions and
houses, are constructed of adobies or un-
burnt bricks, cemented together with a
mortar of clay. The lower floors of the
building are made of clay, a little moistened
and beaten hard with large wooden mallets;
the upper floors of the two-story houses
and the roofs of all are made in the same
way and of the same material, and are supported by heavy transverse timbers covered
with brush. The tops of the houses being
flat and gravelled, furnish a fine promenade
in the moonlight evenings of that charming
climate. The number of men employed in
the business of this establishment is supposed to be about sixty. Fifteen or twenty
of them in charge of one of the owners, are
employed in taking to market the buffalo
robes, &c., which are gathered at the fort,

and in bringing back with them new stocks
of goods for future purchases. Another
party is employed in hunting buffalo meat
in the neighbouring plains; and another
in guarding the animals while they cut
their daily food on the banks of the
river. Others, under command of an experienced trader, goes into some distant
Indian camp to trade. One or more of the
owners, and one or another of these parties which chances to be at the post, defend
it and trade, keep the books of the company, &c. Each of these parties encounters
dangers and hardships, from which persons
within the borders of civilization would
shrink.

The country in which the fort is situated
is in a manner the common field of several
tribes, unfriendly alike to one another and
the whites. The Eutaws and Cheyennes of
the mountains near Santa Fé, and the Pawnees of the great Platte, come to the Upper
Arkansas to meet the buffalo in their annual
migrations to the north; and on the trail of
these animals follow up the Cumanches.
And thus in the months of June, August,
and September, there are in the neighbourhood of these traders from fifteen to twenty
thousand savages ready and panting for

plunder and blood. If they engage in bat-
tling out old causes of contention among
themselves, the Messrs. Bents feel comparatively safe in their solitary fortress.
But if they spare each other's property and
lives, they occasion great anxieties at
Fort William ; every hour of day and night
is pregnant with danger. These untameable
savages may drive beyond reach the buffalo
on which the garrison subsists ; may begirt
the fort with their legions, and cut off supplies ; may prevent them from feeding their
animals upon the plains ; may bring upon
them starvation and the gnawing their own
flesh at the door of death ! All these are
expectations, which as yet the ignorance
alone of the Indians as to the weakness of
the post, prevents from becoming realities.
But at what moment some chieftain or white
desperado may give them the requisite
knowledge, is an uncertainty which occasions at Fort William many well-grounded
fears for life and property.

Instances of the daring intrepidity of the
Cumanches which occurred just before and
after my arrival here, will serve to show the
hazards and dangers of which I have
spoken. About the middle of June, 1839,
a band of sixty of them, under cover of

night, crossed the river, and concealed themselves among the bushes growing thickly on the bank near the place where the animals of the establishment feed during the day. No sentinel being on duty at the time, their presence was unobserved ; and when morning came the Mexican horse-guard mounted his horse, and with the noise and shoutings usual with that class of servants when so employed, drove his charge out of the fort, and riding rapidly from side to side of the rear of the band, urged them on, and soon had them nibbling the short dry grass in a little vale within grape-shot distance of the guns of the bastions. It is customary for a guard of animals about these trading-posts to take his station beyond his charge ; and if they stray from each other, or attempt to stroll too far, to drive them together, and thus keep them in the best possible situation to be hurried hastily to the caral, should the Indians, or other evil persons, swoop down upon them. As there is constant danger of this, his horse is held by a long rope and grazes around him, that he may be mounted quickly, at the first alarm, for a retreat within the walls. The faithful guard at Bent's, on the morning of the dis-

aster I am relating, had dismounted after
driving out his animals, and sat upon the
ground, watching with the greatest fidelity
for every call of duty, when these fifty or
sixty Indians sprang from their hiding-
places, ran upon the animals, yelling horribly, and attempted to drive them across
the river. The guard, however, nothing
daunted, mounted quickly, and drove his
horse at full speed among them. The mules
and horses hearing his voice amidst the
frightning yells of the savages, immediately
started at a lively pace for the fort ; but the
Indians were on all sides, and bewildered
them. The guard still pressed them onward, and called for help ; and on they
rushed, despite the efforts of the Indians
to the contrary. The battlements were
covered with men. They shouted encouragement to the brave guard—" Onward !
onward !" and the injunction was obeyed.
He spurred his horse to his greatest speed
from side to side, and whipped the hindermost of the band with his leading rope. He
had saved every animal ; he was within
twenty yards of the open gate ; he fell ;
three arrows from the bows of the Cumanches had cloven his heart. Relieved
of him, the lords of the quiver gathered

their prey, and drove them to the borders of Texas, without injury to life or limb. I saw this faithful guard's grave. He had been buried a few days. The wolves had been digging into it. Thus forty or fifty mules and horses, and their best servant's life, were lost to the Messrs. Bents in a single day. I have been informed also that those horses and mules, which my company had taken great pleasure in recovering for them in the plains, were also stolen in a similar manner soon after my departure from the post ; and that gentlemen owners were in hourly expectation of an attack upon the fort itself.

The same liability to the loss of life and property attends the trading expeditions to the encampments of the tribes.

An anecdote of this service was related to me. An old trapper was sent from this fort to the Eutaw camp, with a well-assorted stock of goods, and a body of men to guard it. After a tedious march among the snows and swollen streams and declivities of the mountain, he came in sight of the village. It was situated in a sunken valley, among the hideously dark cliffs of the Eutaw mountains ; and so small was it, and so deep, that the overhanging heights not only protected it from the blasts of approaching winter, but drew to their frozen embrace the falling snows, and left this valley its grasses and flowers, while their own awful heads were glittering with perpetual frosts.

The traders encamped upon a small swell of land that overlooked the smoking wigwams, and sent a deputation to the chiefs to parley for the privilege of opening a trade with the tribe. They were received with great haughtiness by those monarchs of the wilderness, and were asked "why they had dared to enter the Eutaw mountains without their permission." Being answered that they "had travelled from the fort to that place, in order to ask their highnesses' permission to trade with the Eutaws," the principal chief replied, that no permission had been given to them to come there, nor to remain. The interview ended, and the traders returned to their camp with no very pleasant anticipations as to the result of their expedition. Their baggage was placed about for breastworks; their animals drawn in nearer, and tied firmly to stakes; and a patrol guard stationed, as the evening shut in. Every preparation for the attack, which appeared determined upon on the part of the Indians, being

made, they waited for the first ray of day—
a signal of dreadful havoc among all the
tribes—with the determined anxiety which
fills the bosom, sharpens the sight, nerves
the arm, and opens the ear to the slightest
rustle of a leaf, so remarkably, among the
grave, self-possessed, and brave traders of
the Great Prairie and Mountain Wilderness.

During the first part of the night the
Indians hurrying to and fro through the village, their war speeches and war dances, and
the painting their faces with red and black,
in alternate stripes, and an occasional scout
warily approaching the camp of the whites,
indicated an appetite for a conflict that appeared to fix, with prophetic certainty, the
fate of the traders. Eight hundred Indians to
fifty whites, made fearful odds. The morning light streamed faintly up the east at
last. The traders held their rifles with the
grasp of dying men. Another and another
beam kindled on the dark blue vault, and
one by one quenched the stars. The silence
of the tomb rested on the world. They
breathed heavily, with teeth set in terrible
resolution. The hour—the moment—had
arrived ! Behind a projecting ledge, the
dusky forms of three or four hundred Eutaws undulated near the ground, like herds

of bears intent on their prey. They approached the ledge, and for an instant lay
flat on their faces, and motionless.   Two or
three of them gently raised their heads high
enough to look over upon the camp of the
whites.

The day had broken over half the firmament ; the rifles of the traders were levelled
from behind the baggage, and glistened
faintly ; a crack—a whoop—a shout—a
rout ! The scalp of one of the peepers over
the ledge had been bored by the whistling
lead from one of the rifles—the chief warrior had fallen.   The Indians retreated to
their camp, and the whites retained their
position, each watching the others movements.   The position of the traders was
such as could command the country within
long rifle-shot on all sides ; the Indians,
therefore, declined an attack.   The number of their foes, and perhaps some pru-
dential consideration as to having an advantageous location, prevented the traders from
making an assault.   Well would it have
been for them had they continued to be
careful.   About nine o'clock, the warlike
appearance gave place to signs of peace.
Thirty or forty unarmed Indians, denuded
of clothing and of paint, came towards the

camp of the traders, singing and dancing, and bearing the Sacred Calumet, or Great Pipe of Peace. A chief bore it who had acted as lieutenant to the warrior that had been shot. Its red marble bowl, its stem broad and long, and carved into hierogly-phics of various colours and significations, and adorned with feathers of beautiful birds, was soon recognized by the traders, and secured the bearer and his attendants a reception into their camp. Both parties seated themselves in a great circle ; the pipe was filled with tobacco and herbs from the venerated medicine bag ; the well-kindled coal was reverently placed upon the bowl ; its sacred stem was then turned towards the heavens, to invite the Great Spirit to the solemn assembly, and to implore his aid ; it was then turned towards the earth, to avert the influence of malicious demons ; it was then borne in a horizontal position, till it completed a circle, to call to their help in the great smoke, the beneficent, invisible agents which live on the earth, in the waters, and the upper air ; the chief took two whiffs, and blew the smoke first towards heaven, and then round upon the ground ; and so did others, until all had inhaled the smoke—the breath of Indian

fidelity—and blown it to the earth and heaven, loaded with the pious vows that are
supposed to mingle with it while it curls
among the lungs near the heart. The chief
then rose and said, in the Spanish language,
which the Eutaws east of the mountains
speak well, " that he was anxious that
peace might be restored between the parties ; that himself and people were desirous
that the traders should remain with them ;
and that if presents were made to him to
the small amount of £140, no objection
would remain to the proposed proceedings
of the whites; but on no account could
they enter the Eutaw country without paying tribute in some form. They were in
the Eutaw country, the tribute was due,
they had killed a Eutaw chief, and the
blood of a chief was due ; but that the latter
could be compromised by a prompt com-
pliance with his proposition in regard to
the presents."

The chief trader was explicit in his reply. " That he had come into the country to sell goods, not to give them away ;
that no tribute could be paid to him or
to any other Eutaw ; and that if fighting
were a desideratum with the chief and
his people, he would do his part to make

it sufficiently lively to be interesting."
The council broke up tumultuously. The
Indians carried back the wampum belts to
their camp, held war councils, and whipt
and danced around posts painted red, and
recounted their deeds of valour, and showed
high in air, as they leaped in the frenzy of
mimic warfare, the store of scalps that garnished the doors of the family lodges ; and
around their camp-fires the following night
were seen features distorted with the most
ghastly wrath.   Indeed, the savages appeared resolved to destroy the whites. And
as they were able, by their superior numbers
to do so, it was deemed advisable to get beyond their reach, with all practicable haste.

At midnight, therefore, when the fires had
smouldered low, the traders saddled in silent
haste, bound their bales upon their pack-
mules, and departed while the wolves were
howling the hour ; and succeeded by the
dawn of day in reaching a gorge where
they had expected the Indians (if they had
discovered their departure in season to reach
it) would oppose their retreat.   On recon-
noitering, however, it was found clear ; and
with joy they entered the defile, and beheld from its eastern opening, the wide cold
plains, and the sun rising, red and cheerful,

on the distant outline of the morning sky.
A few days after, they reached the post—
not a little glad that their flesh was not rot-
ting with many who had been less successful than themselves, in escaping death at
the hands of the Eutaws.   For the insults,
robberies, and murders, committed by this
and other tribes, the traders Bents have
sought opportunities to take well-measured
vengeance : and liberally and bravely have
they often dealt it out.   But the consequence seems to have been the exciting
of the bitterest enmity between the parties ;
which results in a little more inconvenience
to the traders than to the Indians ; for the
latter, to gratify their propensity to steal,
and their hatred to the former, make an
annual levy upon the cavy-yard of the
fortress, which, as it contains usually from
eighty to one hundred horses, mules, &c.,
furnishes to the men of the tomahawk a
very comfortable and satisfactory retribution
for the inhibition of the owners of them
upon their immemorial right to rob and
murder, in manner and form as prescribed
by the customs of their race.

The business within the walls of the post
is done by clerks and traders.   The former
of these are more commonly young gentle-

men from the cities of the States; their
duty is to keep the books of the establishment. The traders are generally selected
from among those daring individuals who
have traversed the Prairie and Mountain
Wilderness with goods or traps, and understand the best mode of dealing with the
Indians. Their duty is to weigh sugar,
coffee, powder, &c., in a Connecticut pint-
cup; and measure red baize, beads, &c.,
and speak the several Indian languages that
have a name for beaver skins, buffalo robes,
and money. They are as fine fellows as
can anywhere be found.

Fort William is owned by three brothers,
by the name of Bent, from St. Louis. Two
of them were at the post when we arrived.
They seemed to be thoroughly initiated into
Indian life; dressed like chiefs—in moccasins thoroughly garnished with beads and
porcupine quills; in trousers of deer skin,
with long fringes of the same extending
along the outer seam from the angle to the
hip; in the splendid hunting-shirt of the
same material, with sleeves fringed on the
elbow seam from the wrist to the shoulder,
and ornamented with figures of porcupine
quills of various colours, and leathern fringe
around the lower edge of the body. And

chiefs they were in the authority exercised in their wild and lonely fortress.

A trading establishment to be known must be seen. A solitary abode of men, seeking wealth in the teeth of danger and hardship, rearing its towers over the uncultivated wastes of nature, like an old baronial castle that has withstood the wars and desolations of centuries; Indian women tripping around its battlements in their glittering moccasins and long deer skin wrappers; their children, with most perfect forms, and the carnation of the Saxon cheek struggling through the shading of the Indian, and chattering now Indian, and now Spanish or English; the grave owners and their clerks and traders, seated in the shade of the piazza, smoking the long native pipe, passing it from one to another, drawing the precious smoke into the lungs by short hysterical sucks till filled, and then ejecting it through the nostrils; or it may be, seated around their rude table, spread with coffee or tea, jerked buffalo meat, and bread made of unbolted wheaten meal from Taos; or, after eating, laid comfortably upon their pallets of straw and Spanish blankets, and dreaming to the sweet notes of a flute; the old trappers withered with

exposure to the rending elements, the half-
tamed Indian, and half civilized Mexican
servants, seated on the ground around a
large tin pan of dry meat, and a tankard of
water, their only rations, relating adventures about the shores of Hudson's Bay, on
the rivers Columbia and Mackenzie, in the
Great Prairie Wilderness, and among the
snowy heights of the mountains ; and delivering sage opinions about the destination
of certain bands of buffalo ; of the distance
to the Blackfoot country, and whether my
wounded man was hurt as badly as Bill the
mule was, when the " meal party" was fired
upon by the Cumanches—present a tolerable idea of every thing within its walls.

If we add, the opening of the gates on
a winter's morning—the cautious sliding in
and out of the Indians whose tents stand
around the fort, till the whole area is filled
six feet deep with their long hanging black
locks, and dark watchful flashing eyes ; and
traders and clerks busy at their work ; and
the patrols walking the battlements with
loaded muskets ; and the guards in the
bastions standing with burning matches by
the carronades ; and when the sun sets, the
Indians retiring again to their camp outside,
to talk over their newly purchased blankets

and beads, and to sing and drink and dance; and the night sentinel on the fort that treads his weary watch away; we shall present a tolerable view of this post in the season of business.

It was summer time with man and beast when I was there. The fine days spent in the enjoyment of its hospitalities were of great service to ourselves, and in recruiting our jaded animals. The man, too, who had been wounded on the Santa Fé trade, recovered astonishingly.

The mutineers, on the 11th of July, started for Bent's Fort, on the Platte; and myself, with three sound and good men, and one wounded and bad one, strode our animals and took trail again for the mountains and Oregon Territory. Five miles above Fort William, we came to Fort El Puebla. It is constructed of adobies, and consists of a series of one-story houses built around a quadrangle, in the general style of those at Fort William. It belongs to a company of American and Mexican trappers, who, wearied with the service, have retired to this spot to spend the remainder of their days in raising grain, vegetables, horses, mules, &c., for the various

trading establishments in these regions.
And as the Arkansas, some four miles above
the post, can be turned from its course over
large tracts of rich land, these individuals
might realize the happiest results from their
industry ;—for, as it is impossible, from the
looseness of the soil and the scarcity of rain,
to raise any thing thereabout without irrigation ; and, as this is the only spot, for a
long distance up and down the Arkansas,
where any considerable tracts of land can be
watered, they could supply the market with
these articles without any fear of competition.

But these, like the results of many honest
intentions, are wholly crippled by want of
capital and a superabundance of whisky.
The proprietors are poor, and when the keg
is on tap, dream away their existence under
its dangerous fascinations.   Hence it is
that these men, destitute of the means to
carry out their designs in regard to farming,
have found themselves not wholly unemploy-
ed in drunkenness ; a substitute which many
other individuals have before been known to
prefer.   They have, however, a small stock,
consisting of horses and mules, cattle,
sheep, and goats ; and still maintain their
original intention of irrigating and culti-

vating the land in the vicinity of their establishment.

We arrived here about four o'clock in the afternoon ; and, being desirous of purchasing a horse for one of the men, and making some farther arrangements for my journey, I determined to stop for the night. At this place I found a number of independent trappers, who after the spring-hunt had come down from the mountains, taken rooms free of rent, stored their fur, and opened a trade for whisky. One skin, valued at four dollars, buys in that market one pint of whisky ; no more, no less. Unless, indeed, some theorists in the vanity of their dogmas, may consider it less, when plentifully mollified with water ; a process that increases in value, as the faucet falters in the energy of its action ; for the seller knows, that if the pure liquid should so mollify the whisky, as to delay the hopes of merriment too long, another beaver-skin will be taken from the jolly trapper's pack, and another quantity of the joyful mixture obtained. Thus matters will proceed, until the stores of furs, the hardships of the hunt, the toils and exposures of trapping, the icy streams of the wilderness, the bloody fight, foot to foot, with the knife and tomahawk, and the long days and nights of thirst and starvation, are satisfactorily cancelled in the dreamy felicity which whisky, rum, gin, brandy and ipecacuanha, if properly administered, are accustomed to produce.

One of these trappers was from New Hampshire; he had been educated at Dartmouth College, and was altogether one of the most remarkable men I ever knew. A splendid gentleman, a finished scholar, a critic on English and Roman literature, a politician, a trapper, an Indian! His stature was something more than six feet; his shoulders and chest were broad, and his arms and lower limbs well formed, and very muscular. His forehead was high and expansive; Causality, Comparison, Eventuality, and all the perceptive organs, (to use a phrenological description), remarkably large. Locality was, however, larger than any other organ in the frontal region. Benevolence, Wonder, Ideality, Secretiveness, Destructiveness and Adhesiveness, Combativeness, Self-Esteem and Hope were very high. The remaining organs were low. His head was clothed with hair as black as jet, two and a half feet in length, smoothly combed, and hanging down his back. He was dressed in a deer-skin frock, leggings and moccasins; not a shred of cloth about his person. On my first interview with him, he addressed me with the stiff, cold formality of one conscious of his own importance; and, in a manner that he thought unobserved, scrutinized the movement of every muscle of my face, and every word which I uttered. When any thing was said of political events in the States or Europe, he gave silent and intense attention.

I left him without any very good impressions of his character; for I had induced him to open his compressed mouth but once, and then to make the no very agreeable inquiries, "When do you start?" and "What route do you take?" At my second interview, he was more familiar. Having ascertained that he was proud of his learning, I approached him through that medium. He seemed pleased at this compliment to his superiority over those around him, and at once became easy and talkative. His "Alma Mater" was described and redescribed; all the fields, and walks, and rivulets, the beautiful Connecticut, the evergreen primitive ridges lying along its banks, which, he said, "had smiled for a thousand ages on the march of decay;" were successive themes of his vast imagination. His descriptions were minute and exquisite. He saw in every thing all that Science sees, together with all that his capacious intellect, instructed and imbued with the wild fancyings and legends of his race, could see. I inquired the reason of his leaving civilized life for a precarious livelihood in the wilderness. "For reasons found in the nature of my race," he replied. "The Indian's eye cannot be satisfied with a description of things, how beautiful soever may be the style, or the harmonies of verse in which it is conveyed. For neither the periods of burning eloquence, nor the mighty and beautiful creations of the imagination, can unbosom the treasures and realities as they live in their own native magnificence on the eternal mountains, and in the secret, untrodden vale.

"As soon as you thrust the ploughshare under the earth, it teems with worms and useless weeds. It increases population to an unnatural extent; creates the necessity of penal enactments, builds the jail, erects the gallows, spreads over the human face a mask of deception and selfishness, and substitutes villany, love of wealth and power, and the slaughter of millions for the gratification of some individual instead of the single-minded honesty, the hospitality, the honour and the purity of the natural state. Hence, wherever Agriculture appears, the increase of moral and physical wretchedness induces the thousands of necessities, as they are termed, for abridging human liberty ; for fettering down the mind to the principles of right, derived, not from nature, but from a restrained and forced condition of existence. And hence my race, with mental and physical habits as free as the waters which flow from the hills, become restive under the rules of civilized life ; dwindle to their graves under the control of laws, customs, and forms, which have grown out of the endless vices, and the factitious virtue of another race. Red men often acquire and love the Sciences. But with the nature which the Great Spirit has given them, what are all their truths to them? Would an Indian ever measure the height of a mountain that he could climb ? No, never. The legends of his tribe tell him nothing about quadrants, and base lines and angles. Their old braves, however, have for ages watched from the cliffs, the green life in the spring, and the yellow death in the autumn, of their holy forests. Why should he ever calculate an eclipse ? He always knew such occurrences to be the doings of the Great Spirit.

" Science, it is true, can tell the times and seasons of their coming; but the Indian, when they do occur, looks through nature, without the aid of science, up to its cause. Of what use is a Lunar to him? His swift canoe has the green embowered shores, and well-known headlands, to guide its course. In fine, what are the arts of peace, of war, of agriculture, or any thing civilized, to him? His nature and its elements, like the pine which shadows its wigwam, are too mighty, too grand, of too strong a fibre, to form a stock on which to engraft the rose or the violet of polished life. No. I must range the hills, I must always be able to out-travel my horses, I must always be able to strip my own wardrobe from the backs of the deer and buffalo, and to feed upon their rich loins; I must always be able to punish my enemy with my own hand, or I am no longer an Indian. And if I am any thing else, I am a mere imitation of an ape."

The enthusiasm with which these sentiments were uttered, impressed me with an awe I had never previously felt for the unborrowed dignity and independence of the genuine, original cha-

racter of the American Indians. Enfeebled,
and reduced to a state of dependence by
disease and the crowding hosts of civilized
men, we find among them still, too much
of their own, to adopt the character of
another race, too much bravery to feel like
a conquered people, and a preference of
annihilation to the abandonment of that
course of life, consecrated by a thousand
generations of venerated ancestors.

This Indian has been trapping among the
Rocky Mountains for seventeen years.
During that time, he has been often employed as an express to carry news from
one trading post to another, and from the
mountains to Missouri. In these journeys
he has been remarkable for the directness
of his courses, and the exceedingly short
space of time required to accomplish them.
Mountains which neither Indian nor white
man dared attempt to scale, if opposing his
right-line track, he has crossed. Angry
streams, heavy and cold from the snows,
and plunging and roaring among the girding caverns of the hills, he has swum ; he
has met the tempest as it groaned over the
plains, and hung upon the trembling towers
of the everlasting hills ; and without a
horse, or even a dog, traversed often the
terrible and boundless wastes of mountains,

and plains, and desert valleys, through which I am travelling ; and the ruder the blast, the larger the bolts, and the louder the peals of the dreadful tempest, when the earth and the sky seem joined by a moving cataract of flood and flame driven by the wind, the more was it like himself, a free, unmarred manifestation of the sublime energies of nature. He says that he never intends again to visit the States, or any other part of the earth " which has been torn and spoiled by the slaves of agriculture." " I shall live," said he, " and die in the wilderness." And assuredly he should thus live and die. The music of the rushing waters should be his requiem, and the Great Wilderness his tomb.

Another of these peculiar men was an Iroquois from Canada ; a stout, old man, with a flat nose, broad face, small twinkling black eyes, a swarthy, dirty complexion, a mouth that laughed from ear to ear. He was always relating some wonderful tale of a trapper's life, and was particularly fond of describing his escapes from the Sioux and Blackfeet, while in the service of the Hudson's Bay Company. On one occasion he had separated from his fellow-trappers and travelled far up the Missouri

into a particularly beautiful valley. It was
the very spot he had sought in all his wanderings, as a retreat for himself and his
squaw to live in till they should die. It
appeared to him like the gateway to the
Isles of the Blest. The lower mountains
were covered with tall pines, and above and
around, except in the east, where the morning sun sent in his rays, the bright glittering
ridges rose high against the sky, decked in
the garniture of perpetual frosts. Along
the valley lay a clear, pure lake, in the centre of which played a number of fountains,
that threw their waters many feet above its
surface, and sending tiny waves rippling
away to the pebbly shores, made the mountains and groves that were reflected from
its rich bosom seem to leap and clap their
hands for joy, at the sacred quiet that
reigned among them.

The old Indian pitched his skin tent on
the shore, in a little copse of hemlock, and
set his traps. Having done this, he explored carefully every part of the neighbouring mountains for ingress and egress,
" signs," &c. His object in this was to
ascertain if the valley were frequented by
human beings ; and if there were places of
escape, should it be entered by hostile per-

sons through the pass that led himself to
it. He found no other pass, except one
for the waters of the lake through a deep
chasm of the mountain ; and this was such
that no one could descend it alive to the
lower valleys. For as he waded and swam
by turns down its still waters, he soon found
himself drawn by an increasing current,
which sufficiently indicated to him the
cause of the deep roar that resounded from
the caverns beyond. He accordingly made
the shore, and climbed along among the
projecting rocks till he overlooked an abyss
of fallen rocks, into which the stream
poured and foamed and was lost in the
mist. He returned to his camp satisfied.
He had found an undiscovered valley,
stored with beaver and trout, and grass for
his horses, where he could trap and fish and
dream awhile in safety. And every morning,
for three delightful weeks, did he draw the
beaver from the deep pools into which they
had plunged when the quick trap had
seized them, and stringing them two and
two together over his pack-horse, bore them
to his camp ; and with his long side-knife
stripped off the skins of fur, pinned them
to the ground to dry, and in his camp kettle
cooked the much-prized tails for his mid-

day repast. " Was it not a fine hunt that ?" asked he ; " beaver as thick as musquitoes, trout as plenty as water. But the ungodly Blackfeet !" The sun had thrown a few bright rays upon the rim of the eastern firmament, when the Blackfeet war-whoop rang around his tent—a direful " whoop-ah-hooh," ending with a yell, piercing harsh and shrill, through the clenched teeth. He had but one means of escape—the lake. Into it he plunged, beneath a shower of poisoned arrows— plunged deeply—and swam under while he could endure the absence of air ; he rose, he was in the midst of his foes swimming and shouting around him ; down again, up to breathe, and on he swam with long and powerful sweeps. The pursuit was long, but at last our man entered the chasm he had explored, plunged along the cascade as near as he dared, clung to a shrub that grew from the crevice of the rock, and lay under water for the approach of his pursuers. On they came, they passed, they shrieked and plunged for ever into the abyss of mist.

Another individual of these veteran trappers was my guide, Kelly, a blacksmith by trade, from Kentucky. He left his native State about twelve years ago, and entered the service of the American Fur Company. Since that time, he has been in the States but once, and that for a few weeks only. In his opinion, every thing was so dull and tiresome that he was compelled to fly to the mountains again. The food, too, had well nigh killed him : " The villanous pies and cake, bacon and beef, and the nick-nacks that one is obliged to eat among cousins, would destroy the constitution of an ostrich." And if he could eat such stuff, he said he had been so long away from civilization that he could never again enjoy it. As long as he could get good buffalo cows to eat, the fine water of the snowy hills to drink, and good buckskins to wear, he was satisfied. The mountaineers were free ; he could go and come when he chose, with only his own will for law.

My intercourse with him, however, led me afterwards to assign another cause for his abandonment of home. There were times when we were encamped at night on the cold mountains about a blazing fire, that he re-lated anecdotes of his younger days with an intensity of feeling which discovered that a deep fountain of emotion was still open in his bosom, never to be sealed till he slum-ber under the sands of the desert.

We passed the night of the 11th of July at the Puebla. One of my companions who had, previously to the division of my company, used horses belonging to an individual who left us for Santa Fé, and the excellent Mr. Blair, were without riding animals. It became, therefore, an object for them to purchase here; and the more so, as there would be no other opportunity to do so for some hundreds of miles. But these individuals had no money nor goods that the owners of the horses would receive in exchange. They wanted clothing or cash, and as I had a surplus quantity of linen, I began to bargain for one of the animals. The first price charged was enormous. A little bantering, however, brought the owner to his proper senses; and the articles of payment were overhauled. In doing this, my whole wardrobe was exposed, and the vendor of horses became extremely enamoured of my dress-coat, the only one remaining, not out at the elbows. This he determined to have. I assured him it was impossible for me to part with it; the only one I possessed. But he, with quite as much coolness, assured me that it would then be impossible for him to part with his horse. These two impossibilities having met, all prospects of a trade were suspended, till one or the other of them should yield. After a little, the idea of walking cast such evident dissatisfaction over the countenances of my friends, that the coat was yielded, and then the pants and overcoat, and all my shirts save four, and various other articles to the value of three such animals in the States. The horse was then transferred to our keeping. And such a horse! The biography of her mischief, would fill a volume! and that of the vexations arising therefrom to us poor mortals? Would it not fill two volumes of "Pencillings by the Way," whose only deficiency would be the want of a love incident? Another horse was still necessary; but in this, as in the other case, a coat was a " sine quâ non ;" and there being no other article of the kind to dispose of among us, no bargain could be made. The night came on amidst these our little preparations. The owners of the horses and mules belonging to El Puebla, drove their animals into the court or quadrangle, around which their houses were built. We gathered our goods and chattels into a pile, in a corner of the most comfortable room we could obtain, and so

arranged our blankets and bodies, that it
would be difficult for any one to make
depredations upon them during the night,
without awaking us. After conversing
with my Dartmouth friend concerning the
mountainous country through which we
were to travel, and the incidents of feasting
and battle which had befallen him during
his trapping excursions, we retired to our
couches.

At eight o'clock on the 12th, we were
harnessed and on route again for the mountains. It was a fine mellow morning. The
snowy peaks of the Wolfano mountains,
one hundred and seventy miles to the south-
west, rose high and clear in view. The
atmosphere was bland like that of the
Indian summer in New England. Five
miles' travel brought us to the encampment
of Kelly's servant, who had been sent
abroad the night before to find grass for his
horses. Here another horse was purchased
of a Mexican, who had followed us from
Puebla. But on adjusting our baggage, it
appeared that three animals were required
for transporting it over the broken country
which lay before us. Messrs. Blair and
Wood would, therefore, still have but a
single saddle horse for their joint use.

This was felt to be a great misfortune, both on account of the hardships of such a journey on foot, as well as the delay it would necessarily cause in the prosecution of it. But these men felt no such obstacle to be insurmountable, and declared, that while the plain and the mountains were before them, and they could walk, they would conquer every difficulty that lay between them and Oregon. After we had eaten, Kelly's horses were rigged, and we moved on four or five miles up the river, where we halted for the night. Our provisions consisted of a small quantity of wheat meal, a little salt and pepper, and a few pounds of sugar and coffee. For meat we depended on our rifles. But as no game appeared during the day, we spent the evening in attempting to take cat-fish from the Arkansas. One weighing a pound, after much practical angling, was caught— a small consolation surely to the keen appetites of seven men! But this, and porridge made of wheat meal and water, constituted our supper that night and breakfast next morning.

July 13th, fifteen miles along the banks of the Arkansas ; the soil composed of sand slightly intermixed with clay, too loose to

retain moisture, and too little impregnated
with the nutritive salts to produce any thing
save a spare and stinted growth of bunch
grass and sun-flowers. Occasional bluffs
of sand and limestone bordered the valley
of the stream. In the afternoon, the range
of low mountains that lie at the eastern
base of the Great Cordilleras and Long's
ranges became visible; and even these,
though pigmies in the mountain race, were,
in midsummer, partially covered with snow.
Pike's peak in the south-west, and James'
peak in the north-west, at sunset showed
their hoary heads above the clouds which
hung around them.

On the 14th, made twenty miles. Kelly
relieved his servant by surrendering to him
his riding horse for short distances; and
others relieved Blair and Wood in a similar
manner. The face of the plain became more
broken as we approached the mountains.
The waters descending from the lower hills,
have cut what was once a plain into isolated
bluffs three or four hundred feet in height,
surmounted and surrounded with columnar
and pyramidal rocks. In the distance they
resemble immense fortresses, with towers
and bastions as skilfully arranged as they
could have been by the best suggestions of

art—embattlements raised by the commotions of warring elements—by the storms that have gathered and marshalled their armies on the heights in view, and poured their desolating power over these devoted plains!

The Arkansas, since we left Fort William, had preserved a medium width of a quarter of a mile, the waters still turbid; its general course east south-east; soil on either side as far as the eye could reach, light sand and clayey loam, almost destitute of vegetation.

On the 15th travelled about eighteen miles over a soil so light that our animals sunk over their fetlocks at every step. During the forenoon we kept along the bottom lands of the river. An occasional willow or cotton-wood tree, ragged and grey with age, or a willow bush trembling, it almost seemed, at the tale of desolation that the winds told in passing, were the only relieving features of the general dearth. The usual colour of the soil was a greyish blue. At twelve o'clock we stopped on a plat of low ground which the waters of the river moistened by filtration through the sand, and baited our horses. Here were forty or fifty decrepid old willows, so poor and shrivelled that one felt, after enjoying

their shade in the heat of that sultry day,
like bestowing alms upon them. At twelve
o'clock we mounted and struck out across
the plain to avoid a southward bend in the
river of twenty miles in length. Near the
centre of this bend is the mouth of the
river Fontequebouir, which the trappers
who have traversed it for beaver say, rises
in James' Peak eighty miles to the north-
west by north.

We came upon the banks of this stream
at sunset. Kelly had informed us that
we might expect to find deer in the groves
which border its banks. And, like a
true hunter, as soon as we halted at the
place of encampment, he sought them before they should hear or scent us. He
traversed the groves, however, in vain.
The beautiful innocents had, as it afterwards appeared, been lately hunted by a
party of Delaware trappers and in consideration of the ill usage received from these
gentlemen in red, had forsaken their old
retreat for a less desirable but safer one
among the distant hills in the north. So
that our expectations of game and meat
subsided in a supper of 'tole'—plain water
porridge. As our appetites were keen, we
all relished it well, except the Mexican

servant, who declared upon his veracity that 'tole was no bueno.' Our guide was, if possible, as happy at our evening fire as some one else was when he "shouldered his crutch and told how fields were won;" and very much for the same reasons. For, during the afternoon's tramp, much of his old hunting ground had loomed in sight. Pike's and James' peaks showed their bald, cold, shining heads as the sun set ; and the mountains on each side of the upper river began to show the irregularities of their surfaces. So that as we rode along gazing at these stupendous piles of rocks and earth and ice, he would often direct his attention to the outlines of chasms, faintly traced on the shadings of the cliffs, through which various streams on which he had trapped, tumbled into the plains. I was particularly interested by his account of Rio Wolfano, a branch of the Arkansas on the Mexican side, the mouth of which is twelve miles below that of the Fontequebouir. It has two principal branches. The one originates in Pike's peak, seventy or eighty miles in the south ; the other rises far in the west among the Eutaw mountains, and has a course of about two hundred miles, nearly parallel with the Arkansas.

We travelled twenty-eight miles on the 16th over broken barren hills sparsely covered with shrub cedars and pines. The foliage of these trees is a very dark green. They cover, more or less, all the low hills that lie along the roots of the mountains from the Arkansas north to the Missouri. Hence the name " Black Hills" is given to that portion of them which lie between the Sweetwater and the mouth of the Little Missouri. The soil of our track to-day was a grey barren loam, gravel knolls and bluffs of sand and limestone.

About four o'clock, P. M., we met an un-heard of annoyance. We were crossing a small plain of red sand, gazing at the mountains as they opened their outlines of rock and snow, when, in an instant, we were enveloped in a cloud of flying ants with greyish wings and dark bodies. They fixed upon our horses' heads, necks, and shoulders, in such numbers as to cover them as bees do the sides of a hive when about to swarm. They flew around our own heads too, and covered our hats and faces. Our eyes seemed special objects of their attention. We tried to wipe them off; but while the hand was passing from one side of the face to the other, the part that was left bare was instantly covered as thickly as before with these creeping, hovering, nauseous insects. Our animals were so much annoyed by their pertinacity, that they stopped in their tracks ; and finding it impossible to urge them along, guide them and keep our faces clear of the insects at the same time, we dismounted and led them. Having by this means the free use of our hands and feet, we were able in the course of half an hour to pass the infested sands, and once more see and breathe.

We dined at the mouth of Kelly's Creek, another stream that has its source in Jame's peak. Encamped at the mouth of Oakley's creek, another branch of the Arkansas. It rises in the hills which lie thirty-five miles to the north. It is a clear, cool little brook, with a pebbly bottom, and banks clothed with shrub cedars and pines. We had a pleasant evening here, a cloudless sky, a cold breeze from the snow-clad mountains, a blazing cedar-wood fire, a song from our merry Joe, a dish of ' tole' and a fine couch of sand. Who wants more comforts than we enjoyed ? My debilitated system had begun to thrive under the bracing influence of the mountain air ; my companions were well and happy ; our

horses and mules were grazing upon a plat
of rich grass ; we were almost within touch
of those stupendous ridges of rock and
snow which stay or send forth the tempest
in its course, and gather in their rugged
embrace the noblest rivers of the world.

July 17. We made twenty miles to-day
among the deep gullies and natural fortresses
of this great gateway to the mountains. All
around gave evidence that the agents of
nature have struggled here in their mightiest
wrath, not the volcano, but the floods of
ages. Ravines hundreds of feet in depth ;
vast insular mounds of earth towering in all
directions, sometimes surmounted by fragments of mountains, at others, with stratified rocks, the whole range of vision was a
flowerless, bladeless desolation ! Our encampment for the night was at the mouth
of Wood's creek, five miles from the debouchure of the Arkansas from the mountains. The ridges on the south of the river,
as viewed from this place, presented an embankment of congregated hills, piled one
above another to the region of snow, and
scored into deep and irregular chasms,
frowning precipices, tottering rocks, and
black glistening strata, whose recent frac-
tures indicated that they were continually

sending upon the humble hills below weighty testimony of their own superior height and might. Nothing could be more perfectly wild. The summits were capped with ice. The ravines which radiated from their apices were filled with snow far down their course ; and so utterly rough was the whole mass, that there did not appear to be a foot of plain surface upon it. Eternal, sublime confusion !

This range runs down the Arkansas, bearing a little south of a parallel with it, the distance of about fifty miles, and then turning southward, bears off to Taos and Santa Fé. At the back of this ridge to the westward, and connected with it, is said to be a very extensive tract of mountains which embrace the sources of the Rio Bravo del Norte, the Wolfano, and other branches of the Arkansas ; and a number of streams that fall into Rio Colorado of the West, and the Gulf of California. Among these heights live the East and West bands of the Eutaws. The valleys in which they reside are said to be overlooked by mountains of shining glaciers, and in every other respect to resemble the valleys of Switzerland. They are a brave, treacherous race, and said to number about eight thousand souls. They raise mules, horses, and sheep, and cultivate corn and beans, trap the beaver, manufacture woollen blankets with a darning-needle, and intermarry with the Mexican Spaniards.

Sixty miles east of these mountains, and fifty south of the Arkansas, stands (isolated on the plain), Pike's Peak, and the lesser ones that cluster around it. This Peak is covered with perpetual snow and ice down one-third its height. The subordinate peaks rise near to the line of perpetual congelation, and stand out upon the sky like giant watchmen, as if to protect the vestal snows above them from the polluting tread of man. On the north side of the river a range of mountains, or hills, as they have been called by those who are in the habit of looking on the Great Main Ridges, rise about two thousand feet above the plain. They resemble, in their general characteristics, those on the south. Like them, they are dark and broken; like them, sparsely covered on their sides with shrub pines and cedars. They diverge also from the river as they descend : and after descending it forty miles, turn to the north, and lose themselves in the heights which congregate around James' Peak.

On the morning of the 18th we rose early, made our simple repast of tole, and prepared to enter the mountains. A joyful occasion this. The storms, the mud, the swollen streams, the bleakness and barrenness of the Great Prairie Wilderness, in an hour's ride, would be behind us ; and the deep, rich vales, the cool streams and breezes, and transparent atmosphere of the more elevated regions, were to be entered.

Wood's Creek, on which we had passed the night, is a cold, heavy torrent, from the northern hills. At the ford, it was about three feet deep, and seven yards wide. But the current was so strong as to bear away two of our saddle-horses. One of these was my Puebla animal. She entered the stream with all the caution necessary for the result. Stepping alternately back, forward, and sidewise, and examining the effect of every rolling stone upon the laws of her own gravity, she finally gathered her ugly form upon one of sufficient size and mobility to plunge herself and rider into the stream. She floated down a few yards, and, contrary to my most fervent desire, came upon her feet again, and made the land. By dint of wading, and partially drowning, and other like agreeable ablutions, we found ourselves at last on the right side of the water : and having bestowed upon it sundry commendatory epithets of long and approved use under like circumstances, we remounted ; and shivering in the freezing winds from the neighbouring snows, trotted on at a pace so merry and fast, that three-quarters of an hour brought us to the buttress of the cliffs, where the Arkansas leaps foaming from them.

This river runs two hundred miles among the mountains. The first half of the distance is among a series of charming valleys, stocked with an endless number of deer and elk, which, in the summer, live upon the nutritious wild grass of the vales, and in the winter, upon the buds, twigs, and bark of trees. The hundred miles of its course next below, is among perpendicular cliffs rising on both sides hundreds, and sometimes thousands, of feet in height. Through this dismal channel, with a rapid current down lofty precipices, and through compressed passes, it plunges and roars to this point, where it escapes nobly and gleefully, as if glad at having fled some fearful edict of nature, consigning it to perpetual imprisonment in those dismal caverns.

Here we entered the Rocky Mountains

L 2

through a deep gorge at the right, formed
by the waters of a little brook which comes
down from the north.   It is a sweet stream.
It babbles so delightfully upon the ear, like
those that flowed by one's home, when youth
was dreaming of the hopes of coming years
in the shade of the hemlock by the family
spring.   On its banks grew the dandelion,
the angelica, the elder, the alder and birch,
and the mountain-flax.   The pebbles, too,
seemed old acquaintances, they were so like
those which I had often gathered, with a
lovely sister long since dead, who would
teach me to select the prettiest and best.
The very mountains were dark and mighty,
and overhanging, and striped with the departing snows, like those that I viewed in
the first years of remembrance, as I frolicked
with my brothers on the mossy rocks.

We soon lost sight of the Arkansas among
the small pines and cedars of the valley, and
this we were sorry to do.   The good old
stream had given us many a fine cat-fish,
and many a bumper of delicious water while
we travelled wearily along its parched banks.
It was like parting with an old companion
that had ministered to our wants, and stood
with us in anxious, dangerous times.   It was,
therefore, pleasant to hear its voice come

up from the caverns like a sacred farewell while we wound our way up the valley.

This gorge, or valley, runs about ten miles in a northwardly direction from the debouchure of the Arkansas, to the dividing ridge between the waters of that river and those of the southern head-waters of the south fork of the Great Platte.

About midway its length, the trail, or Indian track, divides: the one branch makes a circuit among the heights to the westward, terminates in the great valley of the south fork of the Platte, within the mountains, commonly called "Boyou Salade;" and the other and shorter leads northwardly up the gorge to the same point. Our guide carefully examined both trails at the diverging point, and finding the more western one most travelled, and believing, for this reason, the eastward one the least likely to be occupied by the Indians, he led us up to the foot of the mountain which separates it from the vales beyond. We arrived at a little open spot at the base of the height about twelve o'clock. The steepest part of the trail up the declivity was a loose, moving surface of sand and pebbles, constantly falling under its own weight. Other portions were precipitous, lying along overhanging cliffs and the brinks of deep ravines strewn with fallen rocks. To ascend it seemed impossible ; but our old Kentuckian was of a different opinion.

In his hunting expeditions he had often ascended and descended worse steeps with packs of beaver, traps, &c. So, after a description of others of a much more difficult nature, which he had made with worse animals and heavier packs, through storms of hail and heaps of snow ; and after the assurance that the Eutaw village of tents, and women, and children, had passed this not many moons ago, we felt nettled at our own ignorance of possibilities in these regions, and drove off to the task. Our worthy guide led the way with his saddle-horse following him ; the pack animals, each under the encouraging guardianship of a vigorous goad, and the men and myself leading our riding animals, brought up the rear. Now for a long pull, a strong pull, and a pull not all together, but each leg on its own account. Five or six rods of zigzag clambering, and slipping, and gathering, and tugging, advanced us one on the ascent ; and then a halt for breath and strength for a new effort. The puffing and blowing over, a general shout, " go on, go on," started the cavalcade again. The pack animals, with each one hundred and fifty pounds weight, struggled and floundered, as step after step gave way in the sliding sand; but they laboured madly, and advanced at intervals of a few yards, resting and then on again, till they arrived at the rocky surface, about midway the ascent. Here a short pause upon the declivity was interrupted by a call of " onward" from our guide; and again we climbed. The track wound around a beetling cliff, which crowded the animals upon the edge of a frightful precipice. In the most dangerous part of it, my Puebla mare ran her pack against a projecting rock, and for an instant reeled over an abyss three hundred feet in depth. But her fortune favoured her; she blundered away from her grave, and lived to make a deeper plunge farther along the journey.

The upper half, though less steep, proved to be the worst part of the ascent. It was a bed of rocks, at one place small and rolling, at another large and fixed, with deep openings between them; so that our animals were constantly falling, and tottering upon the brink of the cliffs, as they rose again and made their way among them. An hour and a half of this most dangerous and tiresome clambering deposited us in a grove of yellow pines, near the summit. Our animals were covered with sweat and dirt, and trembled as if at that instant from the race track. Nor were their masters free from every ill of weariness. Our knees smote each other with fatigue, as Belshazzar's did with fear.

Many of the pines on this ridge were two feet in diameter, and a hundred feet high, with small clusters of limbs around the tops. Others were low, and clothed with strong limbs quite near the ground. Under a number of these latter, we had seated ourselves, holding the reins of our riding horses, when a storm arose with the rapidity of a whirlwind, and poured upon us hail, rain, and snow with all imaginable liberality. It was a most remarkable tempest. Unlike those whose monotonous groans are heard among the Green Mountains for days before they assemble their fury around you, it came in its strength at once, and rocked the stately pines to their most distant roots. Unlike those long "blows," which, generated in the frozen zone of the Atlantic seas, bring down the frosty blasts of Greenland upon the warmer climes of the States, it was the meeting of different currents of the aërial seas, lashed and torn by the live thunder, among the sounding mountains. One portion of it had gathered its electricity and mist around James' Peak in the east; another among the white heights north-west; and a third among the snowy pyramids of the Eutaws in the south-west; and, marshalling their hosts, met over this connecting ridge between the eastern and central ranges, as if by general battle to settle a vexed question as to the better right to the Pass; and it was sublimely fought. The opposing storms met nearly at the zenith, and fiercely rolled together their angry masses. As if to carry out the simile I have here attempted, at the moment of their junction, the electricity of each leaped upon its antagonist transversely across the heavens, and in some instances fell in immense bolts upon the trembling cliffs; and then instantly came a volley of hail as large as grape-shot, sufficient to whiten all the towers of this horrid war. It lasted an hour. I never before, not even on the plains, saw such a movement of the elements. If anything had been wanting to establish the theory, this exhibition sufficed to convince those who saw its movements, and felt its power, that these mountains are the great laboratory of mist, wind, and electricity, which, formed into storms, are sent in such awful fury upon the great plains or prairies that stretch away from their bases to the States, and, that here alone may be witnessed the extreme power of the warring elements.

After the violence of the tempest had abated, we travelled up the remainder of the ascent, and halted a few minutes on the summit to view the scene around us. Behind was the valley up which we had travelled, covered with evergreen shrubs. On the east of this, rose a precipitous wall of stratified rock, two thousand or three thousand feet high, stretching off towards the Arkansas, and dotted here and there with the small shrub pine, struggling from the crevices of the rocks. In the south-west the mountains, less precipitous. rose one above another in a distance, till their blue tops faded into the semblance of the sky. To the east of our position, there was nothing in sight but piles of mountains, whose dark and ragged masses increased in height and magnitude, till they towered in naked grandeur around James' Peak. From that frozen height ran off to the north

that secondary range of mountains that lie
between the head-waters of the South Fork
of the Platte and the plains. This is a
range of brown, barren, and broken ridges,
destitute alike of earth and shrub, with an
average height of three thousand feet above
the plain. On the western side of it, and
north of the place where we were viewing
them, hills of a constantly decreasing height
fall off for fifty miles to the north-west, till
they sink in the beautiful valley of Boyou
Salade, and then rising again, tower higher
and higher in the west, until lost in the haze
about the base of the Anahuac range ; a vast
waste of undusted rocks, without a flower
or leaf to adorn it, save those that hide
their sweetness from its eternal winters in
the glens down which we were to travel.

The Anahuac ridge of the snowy range
was visible for at least one hundred miles of
latitude ; and the nearest point was so far
distant that the dip of the horizon concealed
all that portion of it below the line of perpetual congelation. The whole mass was
purely white. The principal irregularity
perceptible was a slight undulation on the
upper edge. There was, however, perceptible shading on the lower edge, produced, perhaps, by great lateral swells pro-

truding from the general outline. But the mass, at least ninety miles distant, as white as milk, the home of the frosts of all ages, stretching away to the north by west full a hundred miles, unscaled by any living thing, except perhaps by the bold bird of our national arms,

> " Broad, high, eternal and sublime,
>   The mock of ages, and the twin of time,"

is an object of amazing grandeur, unequalled probably on the face of the globe.

We left this interesting panorama, and travelled down five miles to the side of a little stream running north, and encamped. We were wet from head to foot, and shivering with cold. The day had indeed been one of much discomfort; yet we had been well repaid for all this by the absorbing freshness and sublimity that hung around us. The lightning bounding on the crags; the thunder breaking the slumber of the mountains; a cooler climate, and the noble pine again; a view of the Great Main snowy range of the " Rocky," " Stone," or " Shining" mountains, south of the Great Gap, from a height never before trodden by a civilized tourist, the sight of the endless assemblage of rocky peaks, among which

our weary feet were yet to tread along unexplored waters, were the delights which lay
upon the track of the day, and made us
happy at our evening fire. Our supper of
water porridge being eaten, we tried to
sleep. But the cold wind from the snow
soon drove us from our blankets to our fire,
where we turned ourselves like Christmas
turkeys, till morning. The mountain flax
grew around our encampment. Every stalk
was stiffened by the frosts of the night;
and the waters of the brooks were barred
with ice. This is the birth-place of the
Platte. From these gorges its floods receive existence, among the sturdy, solemn
pines and nursing tempests, twelve miles
north of the Arkansas's debouchement from
the mountains, and forty miles due west
from James' Peak.

On the 19th we travelled in a northward
course down the little streams bursting
from the hills, and babbling among the
bushes. We were upon an Indian trail, full
of sharp gravel, that annoyed our animals
exceedingly. The pines were often difficult
to pass, so thick were they. But the right
course was easily discovered among them,
even when the soil was so hard as to have
received no impression from previous

travelling, by small stones which the Eutaws had placed among the branches. About mid-day we saw scattering spears of the wild flax again, and a few small shrubs of the black birch near the water courses. The endless climbing and ascending of hills prevented our making much progress. At two o'clock we judged ourselves but ten miles from the last night's encampment. A cloud of hail then beginning to pelt and chill us, we took shelter in a small grove of pines. But as the hail had fallen two inches in depth, over the whole adjoining country, every movement of the atmosphere was like a blast of December. Too cold to sleep, we therefore built fires and dried our packs, &c., till the howl of the wolves gave notice of the approach of morning.

Tole for breakfast. It had been our only food for nine days. It seemed strange that we should have travelled one hundred and eighty miles, in a country like that we had passed through since leaving Fort William, without killing an animal. But it ceased to appear so, when our worthy guide informed us that no individual had ever come from the Arkansas, in the region of the Fort, to the mountains, with as little suffering as we had. " It is," said he, " a starv-

ing country; never any game found in it.
The buffalo come into these valleys from
the north through the Bull Pen, and go out
there when the storms of the autumn warn
them to fly to the south for warm winter
quarters. But that valley off there, (pointing to a low smooth spot in the horizon),
looks mighty like Boyou Salade, my old
stamping ground. If it should be, we will
have meat before the sun is behind the
snow."

We were well pleased with this prospect. Our Mexican servant cried, at
the top of his voice, " Esta muy bueno,
Señor Kelly, si, muy bueno, este Boyou
Salade ; mucho carne por nosotros." And
the poor fellow had some reasons for this
expression of joy, for the tole regimen had
been to him what the water gruel of the
Mudfog workhouse was to Oliver Twist,
except that its excellent flavour had never
induced the Mexican " to ask for more."
He had, on previous occasions, in company
with Kelly, gnawed the ribs of many a fat
cow in Boyou Salade ; and the instincts of
his stomach put him in such a frenzy at the
recollection, that although he could only
understand the words " Boyou Salade,"
these were sufficient to induce him to cross

himself from the forestep to the abdomen, and to swear by Santa Gaudaloupe that tole was not food for a Christian mouth.

On the 20th we were early on our way. The small prairie wolf which had howled us to sleep every evening, and howled us awake every morning since we left Independence, was continually greeting us with an ill-natured growl, as we rode along among his hiding places. The streams that were mere rivulets twenty miles back, having received a thousand tributaries, were now heavy and deep torrents. The peaks and mountain swells were clad with hail and snow. Every thing, even ourselves, shivering in our blankets, gave evidence that we were traversing the realms of winter. Still many of the grasses and flowers which usually flourish in high latitudes and elevated places were growing along the radices of the hills, and aided much in giving the whole scene an unusually singular aspect. We were in fine spirits, and in the enjoyment of a voracious appetite. Our expectations of having a shot soon at a buffalo, were perhaps an accessory cause of this last. But be that as it may, we dodged along among the pines and spruce and hemlock and firs

about ten miles, and rose over a swell of
land covered with small trees in full view of
a quiet littie band of buffalo.   Ye deities
who presided of old over the trencher and
goblet, did not our palates leap for a tender
loin ? A halt—our famous old Kentuckian
creeps away around a copse of wood —
we hear the crack of his deadly rifle—
witness the writhing of the buffalo ! He
lays himself gently down. All is now silent,
intense anxiety to observe whether he
will rise again and run, as buffalo often
do under the smart of a wound, beyond our
reach among the hills. No ! he curls his
tail as in the last agony ; he choaks ; he is
ours ! he is ours !

Our knives are quickly hauled from their
sheaths—he is rolled upon his brisket—his
hide is slit along the spine, and pealed down
midrib ; one side of it is cut off and spread
upon the sand to receive the meat ; the
flesh on each side of the spine is pared off ;
the mouth is opened, and the tongue
removed from his jaws ; the axe is laid to
his rib ; the heart—the fat—the tender
loins—the blood, are taken out—his legs
are rifled of their generous marrow bones ;
all wrapped in the green hide, and loaded
on animals, and off to camp in a charm-

ing grove of white pine by a cold stream of water under a woody hill!

Who that had seen us stirring our fires that night in the starlight of bright skies among the mountain forests; who that had seen the buffalo ribs propped up before the crackling blaze—the brisket boiling in our camp-kettles; who that had seen us with open countenances yield to these well cooked invitations to "drive dull care away," will not believe that we accepted them, and swallowed against time, and hunger, and tole? Indeed, we ate that night till there was a reasonable presumption that we had eaten enough; and when we had spent a half hour in this agreeable employment, that presumption was supported by a pile of bones, which if put together by Buffon in his best style, would have supported not only that but another presumption to the like effect. Our hearty old Kentuckian was at home, and we were his guests. He sat at the head of his own board, and claimed to dictate the number of courses with which we should be served. " No, no," said he, as we strode away from the bare ribs which lay round us, to our couches of pine leaves, "no, no, I have eaten with you, fared well, and now you

must take courage while you eat with me ;
no, no, not done yet ; mighty good eating
to come.   Take a rest upon it, if you like,
while I cook another turn ; but I'll insure
you to eat till day peeps.   Our meat here
in the mountains never pains one.   Nothing
harms here but pills and lead ; many's the
time that I have starvêd six and eight days,
and when I have found meat, ate all night ;
that's the custom of the country.   We
never borrow trouble from hunger or thirst,
and when we have a plenty, we eat the best
pieces first, for fear of being killed by some
brat of an Indian before we have enjoyed
them.   You may eat as much as you can ;
my word for it, this wild meat never hurts
one.   But your chickens and bacon, &c.,
in the settlements, it came right near shoving
me into the Kenyon when I was down there
last."

While the excellent man was giving
vent to these kind feelings, he was busy
making preparations for another course.
The marrow bones were undergoing a severe
flagellation ; the blows of the old hunter's
hatchet were cracking them in pieces, and
laying bare the rolls of " trapper's butter"
within them.   A pound of marrow was

thus extracted, and put into a gallon of
water heated nearly to the boiling point.
The blood which he had dipped from the
cavity of the buffalo was then stirred in till
the mass became of the consistency of rice
soup. A little salt and black pepper finished
the preparation. It was a fine dish; too
rich, perhaps, for some of my esteemed acquaintances, whose digestive organs partake
of the general laziness of their habits; but
to us who had so long desired a healthful
portion of bodily exercise in that quarter,
it was the very marrow and life-blood of
whatsoever is good and wholesome for
famished carniverous animals like ourselves. It was excellent, most excellent.
It was better than our father's foaming ale.
For while it loosed our tongues and warmed
our hearts towards one another, it had the
additional effect of Aaron's oil; it made our
faces to shine with grease and gladness.
But the remembrance of the palate pleasures of the next course, will not allow me
to dwell longer upon this. The crowning
gratification was yet in store for us.

While enjoying the soup, which I have
just described, we believed the bumper of
our pleasures to be sparkling to the brim;

and if our excellent old trapper had not
been there, we never should have desired
more. But how true is that philosophy
which teaches, that to be capable of happiness, we must be conscious of wants ! Our
friend Kelly was in this a practical as well
as theoretical Epicurean. "No giving up
the beaver so," said he ; "another bait
and we will sleep."

Saying this, he seized the intestines of
the buffalo, which had been properly
cleaned for the purpose, turned them
inside out, and as he proceeded stuffed
them with strips of well salted and peppered tender loin. Our "*boudies*" thus
made, were stuck upon sticks before the
fire, and roasted till they were thoroughly
cooked and brown. The sticks were then
taken from their roasting position and
stuck in position for eating ; that is to
say, each of us with as fine an appetite as
ever blessed a New England boy at his
grandsire's Thanksgiving dinner, seized a
stick pit, stuck it in the earth near our
couches, and sitting upon our haunches, ate
our last course—the desert of a mountain
host's entertainment. These wilderness sau-
sages would have gratified the appetite of

those who had been deprived of meat a
less time than we had been. The enve-
lopes preserve the juices with which while
cooking, the adhering fat, turned within,
mingles and forms a gravy of the finest
flavour. Such is a feast in the mountains.

Since leaving Fort William we had been
occasionally crossing the trails of the Eutaw
war parties, and had felt some solicitude for
the safety of our little band. An over-
whelming number of them might fall upon
us at night and annihilate us at a blow.
But we had thus far selected such encampments, and had such confidence in our
rifles and in our dog, who never failed to
give us notice of the least movement of a
wolf or panther at night, that we had not
stationed a guard since leaving that post.

Our guide too sanctioned this course;
always saying when the subject was introduced that the dawn of day was the time
for Indian attacks, and that they would
rise early to find his eyes shut after the
howl of the wolf on the hills had announced
the approach of light. We however took
the precaution to encamp at night in a deep
woody glen, which concealed the light of
our fire, and slept with our equipments

upon us, and our well primed rifles across
our breasts.

On the morning of the 21st we were
awakened at sunrise, by our servant who
had thus early been in search of our
animals. The sun rose over the eastern
mountains brilliantly, and gave promise of a
fine day. Our route lay among vast swelling hills, the sides of which were covered
with groves of the large yellow pine and
aspen. These latter trees exclude every
other from their society. They stand so
closely that not the half of their number
live until they are five inches in diameter.
Those also that grow on the borders of the
groves are generally destroyed, being deprived of their bark seven or eight feet up,
by the elk which resort to them yearly to
rub off the annual growth of their horns.
The snow on the tops of the hills was
melting, and along the lower edge of it,
where the grass was green and tender,
herds of buffalo were grazing. So far distant were they from the vales through which
we travelled, that they appeared a vast collection of dark specks on the line of the sky.

By the side of the pebbly brooks, grew
many beautiful plants. A species of con-
volvulus and honeysuckle, two species of

wild hops and the mountain flax, were among them. Fruits were also beginning to appear ; as wild plums, currants, yellow and black ; the latter like those of the same colour in the gardens, the former larger than either the red or black, but of an unpleasant astringent flavour.—We had not, since entering the mountains, seen any indication of volcanic action. The rocky strata and the soil appeared to be of primary formation. We made fifteen miles to-day in a general course of north by west.

On the 22nd we travelled eight miles through a country similar to that we had passed the day before. We were still on the waters of the Platte ; but seldom in sight of the main stream. Numerous noisy brooks ran among the hills over which we rode. During the early part of the morning buffalo bulls were often seen crossing our path : they were however so poor and undesirable, that we shot none of them. About ten o'clock we came upon a fresh trail, distinctly marked by hoofs and dragging lodge poles. Kelly judged these " signs" to be not more than twenty four hours old, and to have been made by a party of Eutaws which had passed into

Boyou Salade to hunt the buffalo. Hostile Indians in our immediate neighbourhood was by no means an agreeable circumstance to us. We could not contend with any hope of success against one hundred and fifty tomahawks and an equal number of muskets and bows and arrows. They would also frighten the buffalo back to the bull pen, and thus prevent us from laying in a stock of meat farther along to support us across the desert in advance. We therefore determined to kill the next bull that we should meet, cure the best pieces for packing, and thus prepare ourselves for a siege or a retreat, as circumstances might dictate ; or if the Indians should prevent our obtaining other and better meat, and yet not interrupt us by any hostile demonstration in pursuing our journey, we might, by an economical use of what we could pack from this point, be able to reach, before we should perish with hunger, the game which we hoped to find on tributaries of Grand River.

We, therefore, moved on with great caution ; and at about two o'clock killed a fine young bull. He fell in a glen through which a little brook murmured along to a copse just below. The bulls in consider-

able number were manifesting their surplus
wrath on the other side of the little wood
with as much apparent complacency as
certain animals with fewer legs and horns
often do, when there is not likely to be any
thing in particular to oppose them. But
fortunately for the reputation of their pretensions, as sometimes happens to their
biped brethren, a circumstance chanced to
occur, when their courage seemed waxing to
the bursting state, on which it could expend
its energies. The blood of their slaughtered companion scented the breeze, and on
they came, twenty or more, tail in air, to
take proper vengeance.

We dropped our butcher knives, mounted quickly, and were about to accommodate them with the contents of our rifles,
when, like many perpendicular bellowers,
as certain danger comes, they fled as
bravely as they had approached. Away
they racked, for buffalo never trot, over
the brown barren hills in the north-
east, looking neither to the right nor left,
for the long hair around the head does not
permit such aberrations of their optics ,
but onward gloriously did they roll their
massive bulks—now sinking in the vales
and now blowing up the ascents ; stop-

ping not an instant in their career until
they looked like creeping insects on the
brow of the distant mountain. Having
thus vanquished, by the most consum-
mate generalship and a stern patriotism
in the ranks never surpassed by Jew or
Gentile, these " abandoned rebels," we
butchered our meat, and as one of the works
of returning peace, loaded it upon our animals, and travelled in search of quaking-asp
wood wherewithal to dry it. The traders
and trappers always prefer this wood for
such purposes, because, when dry, it is
more inodorous than any other ; and consequently does not so sensibly change the
flavour of the meat dried over a fire made
of it. Half an hour's ride brought us to a
grove of this timber, where we encamped
for the night—dried our meat, and Eutaws
near or far, slept soundly. In this remark
I should except, perhaps, the largest piece
of human nature among us, who had, as his
custom was, curled down hard-by our brave
old guide and slept at intervals, only an eye
at a time, for fear of Indians.

23d. Eighteen miles to-day among rough
precipices, overhanging crags, and roaring
torrents. There were, however, between
the declivities and among the copses of

cotton-wood, quaking-asp and fir, and yellow pine, some open glades and beautiful
valleys of green verdure, watered by the
rivulets gushing from the stony hills, and
sparkling with beautiful flowers. Five or
six miles from our last encampment, we
came upon the brow of a woody hill that
overlooked the valley, where the waters on
which we were travelling unite with others
that come down from the mountains in the
north, and from what is properly called the
south fork of the Great Platte, within the
mountains. Here we found fresh Indian
tracks; and on that account deemed it
prudent to take to the timbered heights,
bordering the valley on the west, in order
to ascertain the position of the Indians,
their numbers, &c., before venturing within
their reach. We accordingly, for three
hours, wound our way in silence among
fallen timber and thick-set cotton-wood;
climbed every neighbouring height, and
examined the depressions in the plain,
which could not be seen from the lower
hills.

Having searched the valley thoroughly in this manner, and, perceiving from
the peaceable and careless bearing of
the small bands of buffalo around its bor-

ders, that if there were Indians within it
they were at some distance from our trail,
we descended from the heights, and struck
through a deep ravine across it, to the
junction of the northern and southern
waters of the stream.

We found the river at this place a hundred and fifty yards wide, and of an average
depth of about six feet, with a current of
five miles the hour. Its course hence is
E. N. E. about one hundred miles, where
it rushes through a magnificent kenyon or
chasm in the eastern range of the Rocky
Mountains to the plains of the Great
Prairie Wilderness. This valley is a con-
geries or collection of valleys. That is,
along the banks of the main and tributary
streams a vale extends a few rods or
miles, nearly or quite separated from a
similar one beyond, by a rocky ridge or
bute or a rounded hill covered with grass
or timber, which protrudes from the height
towards the stream. This is a bird's-eye
view of Boyou Salade, so named from the
circumstance that native rock salt is found
in some parts of it. We were in the central portion of it. To the north, and south,
and west, its isolated plains rise one above
the other, always beautiful, and covered

with verdure during the months of spring
and summer. But when the storms of
autumn and winter come, they are the re-
ceptacles of vast bodies of snow, which fall
or are drifted there from the Anahuac
Ridge, on its western horizon. A sweet
spot this, for the romance of the future as
well as the present and past. The buffalo
have for ages resorted here about the last
days of July, from the arid plains of the
Arkansas and the Platte; and thither the
Eutaws and Cheyennes from the mountains
around the Santa Fé, and the Shoshonies
or Snakes and Arrapahoes from the west,
and the Blackfeet, Crows and Sioux from
the north, have for ages met, and hunted,
and fought, and loved. And when their
battles and hunts were interrupted by the
chills and snows of November, they have
separated for their several winter resorts.
How wild and beautiful the past as it comes
up fledged with the plumage of the imagination!

These vales, studded with a thousand
villages of conical skin wigwams, with
their thousands of fires blazing on the
starry brow of night! I see the dusky
forms crouching around the glowing piles
of ignited logs, in family groups whispering

the dreams of their rude love ; or gathered
around the stalwart form of some noble
chief at the hour of midnight, listening to
the harangue of vengeance or the whoop of
war, that is to cast the deadly arrow with
the first gleam of morning light.   Or may
we not see them gathered, a circle of
braves around an aged tree, surrounded
each by the musty trophies of half a century's daring deeds.   The eldest and richest
in scalps, rises from the centre of the ring
and advances to the tree.   Hear him :

" Fifty winters ago, when the seventh
moon's first horn hung over the green
forests of the Eutaw hills, myself and five
others erected a lodge for the Great Spirit,
on the snows of the White Bute, and
carried there our wampum and skins and
the hide of a white buffalo. We hung
them in the Great Spirit's lodge, and seated
ourselves in silence till the moon had descended the western mountain, and thought
of the blood of our fathers that the Cumanches had killed when the moon was round
and lay on the eastern plain. My own
father was scalped, and the fathers of five
others were scalped, and their bloody heads
were gnawed by the wolf.   We could not
live while our fathers' lodges were empty,

and the scalps of their murderers were not
in the lodges of our mothers. Our hearts
told us to make these offerings to the Great
Spirit who had fostered them on the mountains ; and when the moon was down, and
the shadows of the White Bute were as
dark as the hair of a bear, we said to the
Great Spirit, ' No man can war with the
arrows from the quiver of thy storms ; no
man's word can be heard when thy voice is
among the clouds ; no man's hand is strong
when thy hand lets loose its winds. The
wolf gnawed the heads of our fathers, and
the scalps of their murderers hang not in
the lodges of our mothers. Great father
spirit, send not thine anger out ; hold in
thy hand the winds ; let not thy great voice
drown the death-yell while we hunt the
murderers of our fathers.' I and the five
others then built in the middle of the lodge
a fire, and in its bright light the Great
Spirit saw the wampum, and the skin, and
the white buffalo hide. Five days and
nights, I and the five others danced and
smoked the medicine, and beat the board
with sticks, and chaunted away the power
of the great Medicine, that they might not
be evil to us, and bring sickness into our
bones. Then when the stars were shining

in the clear sky, we swore (I must not tell
what, for it was in the ear of the Great
Spirit) and went out of the lodge with our
bosoms full of anger against the murderers
of our fathers, whose bones were in the
jaws of the wolf, and went for their scalps
to hang them in the lodges of our mothers.
See him strike the aged tree with his war
club again, again, nine times. So many
Cumanches did I slay, the murderers of
my father, before the moon was round
again, and lay upon the eastern plain."

This is not merely an imagined scene in
former times in Boyou Salade. All the
essential incidents related, happened yearly
in that and other hunting grounds, whenever the old braves assembled to celebrate
the valorous deeds of their younger days.
When these exciting relations were finished,
the young men of the tribe, who had not
yet distinguished themselves, were exhorted
to seek glory in a similar way. Woe
to him who passed his manhood without
ornamenting the door of his lodge with the
scalps of his enemies !

This valley is still frequented by some of
these tribes as a summer haunt, when the
heat of the plains renders them uncomfort-
able. The Eutaws were scouring it when we

passed. We therefore crossed the river to its northern bank, and followed up its northern branch eight miles, with every eye keenly searching for the appearance of foes ; and made our encampment for the night in a deep chasm, overhung by the long branches of a grove of white pines. We built our fire in the dry bed of a mountain torrent, shaded by bushes on the side towards the valley, and above, by a dense mass of boughs, so effectually, as not only to conceal the blaze from any one in the valley, but also to prevent the reflection from gilding too high the conspicuous foliage of the neighbouring trees. After our horses had fed themselves, we tied them close to our couches, that they might not, in case of an attack, be driven away before we had an opportunity of defending them; and when we retired, threw water upon our fire that it might not guide the Indians in a search for us ; put new caps upon our arms, and trusting to our dog and mule, the latter in such cases always the most skilful to scent their approach, tried to sleep. But we were too near the snows. Chilling winds sucked down the vale, and drove us from our blankets to a shivering watch during the remainder of the night. Not a cap, however, was burst. Alas ! for our brave intentions, they ended in an ague fit.

Our guide informed us, that the Eutaws reside on both sides of the Eutaw or Ana-huac mountains ; that they are continually migrating from one side to the other; that they speak the Spanish language ; that some few half breeds have embraced the Catholic faith ; that the remainder yet hold the simple and sublime faith of their fore-fathers, in the existence of one great creat-ing and sustaining cause, mingled with a belief in the ghostly visitations of their deceased Medicine men or diviners ; and that they number a thousand familiès. He also stated that the Cheyennes are a band of renegadoes from the Eutaws and Cuman-ches ; and that they are less brave and more thievish than any other tribe living in the plains south of Arkansas.

We started at seven o'clock in the morn-ing of the 24th, travelled eight miles in a north by west direction, killed another buffalo, and went into camp to jerk the meat. Again we were among the frosts and snows and storms of another dividing ridge. Our camp was on the height of land between the waters of the Platte and those of Grand River, the largest southern

branch of the Colorado of the west. From
this eminence we had a fine view of Boyou
Salade, and also of the Anahuac range,
which we had before seen from the ridge
between the Arkansas and the southern
waters of the Platte. To the south-east,
one hundred and sixty miles, towered the
bald head of James' Peak ; to the east, one
hundred miles distant, were the broken and
frowning cliffs through which the south
fork of the Platte, after having gathered all
its mountain tributaries, forces its roaring
cascade course to the plains. To the north,
the low, timbered and grassy hills, some
tipped with snow, and others crowned with
lofty pines, faded into a smooth, dim, and
regular horizon.

CHAPTER V.

An Ascent—A Misfortune—A Death—The Mountain of the Holy Cross—Leaping Pines—Killing a Buffalo —Asses and Tyrants—Panther, &c.—Geography— Something about Descending the Colorado of the West — Dividing Ridges — A Scene — Tumbleton's Park — A War Whoop — Meeting of Old Fellow Trappers—A Notable Tramp—My Mare—The etiquette of the Mountains—Kelly's Old Camp, &c.— A Great Heart—Little Bear River—Vegetables and Bitterness—Two White Men, a Squaw and Child— A Dead Shot—What is Tasteful—Trapping—Blackfoot and Sioux—A Bloody Incident—A Cave—Hot Spring—The Country—A Surprise—American and Canadian Trappers—The Grand River—Old Park— Death before us—The Mule—Despair.

THE ascent to this height was not so laborious as the one near the Arkansas. It lay up the face of a mountain which formed a larger angle with the plane of the horizon than did the other. But it was clothed with a dense forest of pines, a species of double-leaved hemlock, and spruce and fir trees, which prevented our animals from

falling over the precipices, and enabled us
to make long sweeps in a zigzag course,
that much relieved the fatigue of the ascent. We however met here a misfortune
of a more serious nature to us, than the
storm that pelted us on the other ridge.
One of the horses belonging to our guide
sickened just before arriving at the summit,
and refusing to bear farther the burthen
which he had heretofore borne with ease
and apparent pride, sunk under it. We
roused him ; he rose upon his legs, and
made a willing attempt to do his duty ; but
the poor animal failed in his generous
effort.

We, therefore, took off his pack, put
it upon my saddle horse, and drove him
before us to the summit, from whence we
enjoyed the beautiful prospect we have just
described. But we felt little interest in
the expanse of sublimity before us ; our
eyes and sympathies, too, were turned to
the noble animal which was now suffering
great pain. He had been reared in the
mountains ; and it seemed to be his highest
pleasure to tread along their giddy brinks.
Every morning at his post, with the other
horse belonging to his master, he would

stand without being fastened, and receive
his burthen ; and with every demonstration
of willingness, bear it over the mountains
and through torrents till his task was
ended in the night encampment. Such a
horse, in the desolate regions we were traversing, the bearer of our wearing apparel
and food, the leader of our band of animals, the property of our kind old Kentuckian, the one-third of all his worldly
estate, was no mean object of interest.
After noticing him awhile, we perceived
symptoms of his being poisoned, administered whatever medicine we possessed suited
to the case, and left him to his fate for the
night. Rain during the day, frost during
the night ; ice in our camp kettles an inch
in thickness.

We were out early on the morning of the
25th, and found our guide's horse living.
We accordingly saddled, packed and started down the valley of a small head stream
of Grand River. The sick horse was driven
slowly along for about five miles when he
refused to go farther. It now became evident that he had been eating the wild par-
snips at our last encampment on the other
side of the ridge. That he must die became, therefore, certain, and we unpacked

to see the breath from his body before he
should be left to the merciless wolves. He
died near daylight down, and as the path
before us was rough and bushy, we determined to remain on the spot for the night.
Our anxiety for the life of this excellent
animal had well nigh led us to pass unobserved one of the most singular curiosities in nature—a cross of crystallized
quartz in the eastern face of a conical
mountain !

On the western side of the stream which
we were following down, were a collection of butes or conical peaks clustered
around one, the top of which was somewhat
in the form of the gable end of an ancient
church. This cluster was flanked on each
side by vast rolls or swells of earth and
rock, which rose so high as to be capped
with snow. In the distance to the West,
were seen through the openings between
the butes, a number of spiral peaks that
imagination could have said formed the
western front of a vast holy edifice of the
eternal hills. On the eastern face of the
gable bute were two transverse seams
of what appeared to be crystallized quartz.
The upright was about sixty feet in length,
the cross seam about twenty feet, thrown

athwart the upright near its top and lying parallel to the plane of the horizon. I viewed it as the sun rose over the eastern mountains and fell upon the glittering crystals of this emblem of the Saviour's suffering, built with the foundations and treasured in the bosom of these granite solitudes. A cross in a church, however fallen we may suppose it to be from the original purity of worship, excites, as it should, in the minds of all reasonable men, a sacred awe arising from the remembrance of the scene in Judea which spread darkness like the night over the earth and the sun. But how much more impressive was this cross of living rock—on the temple of nature where priest never trod ; the symbol of redeeming love, engraven when Eden was unscathed with sin, by God's own hand on the brow of his everlasting mountains.

The trappers have reverently named this peak, the " Mountain of the Holy Cross." It is about eight hundred feet in height above the level of the little brook, which runs a few rods from its base. The upper end of the cross is about one hundred feet below the summit. There are many dark and stately groves of pine and balsam fir in the vicinity. About the brooks grow the black alder, the laurel, and honey-suckle, and a great variety of wild flowers adorn the crevices of the rocks. The virgin snows of ages whiten the lofty summits around; the voice of the low murmuring rivulets trembles in the sacred silence: " O solitude, thou art here," the lip moves to speak. " Pray, kneel, adore," one seems to hear softly breathed in every breeze. " It is holy ground."

26th. On march at six o'clock and tra-velled down the small stream which had accompanied us on the 24th and 25th. As we advanced, the valleys opened, and the trees, pine, fur, white oak, cotton wood, quaking-asp, &c., became larger and taller. The wild flowers and grass became more luxuriant. As we were on an Indian trail, our course was as nearly a right line as the eye of that race could trace among the lower hills. Hence we often left the stream and crossed the wood swells, not hills, not mountains; but vast swelling tracts of land that rise among these vales like half buried spheres, on which, frequently for miles about us, pine and fir trees of the largest size had been prostrated by the winds. To leap our animals over these, and among them, and into them, and out of them, and still among them, floundering, tearing packs and riders — running against knots and tumbling upon splintery stubs and rocks, were among the amusements of getting through them. The groves of small quaking-asp too, having been killed by the elk, in some places had fallen across our track so thickly that it became necessary to raise the foot over one at almost every step.

Here my Puebla mare performed many a feat of " high and lofty tumbling." She could leap the large pines, one at a time, with satisfaction to herself, that was worthy of her blood. But to step, merely step, over one small tree and then over another, seemed to be too much condescension. Accordingly she took a firm unalterable stand upon her reserved rights, from which neither pulling nor whipping seemed likely to move her. At length she yielded, as great men sometimes do, her own opinion of constitutional duty to the will of the people, and leaped among them with a desperation that ought to have annihilated a square mile of such obstacles. But instead

thereof, she turned a saumersault into about
the same quantity of them, and there lay
" alone in her glory," till she was tumbled
out and set up again.

The valley, during the day's journey, had
appeared five miles in width. On its
borders hung dark mountains of rock, some
of which lying westward, were tipped with
shining ice. Far beyond these appeared
the Anahuac ridge. Snow in the south
was yet in sight—none seen in the east
north. The valley itself was much broken,
with minor rocky declivities, bursting up
between the " swells," and with fields of
large loose stones laid bare by the torrents.
The buffalo were seen grazing in small
detached herds on the slopes of the mountains near the lower line of snow, those
green fields of the skies. Many " elk
signs," tracks, &c., were met; but none
of these animals were seen. Our guide informed me that their habit is to " follow
the snow." In other words, that as the
snow in summer melts away from the
lowlands, they follow its retiring banks
into the mountains; and when it begins
in autumn to descend again, they descend
with it, and pass the winter in the valley.

He also accounted for the absence of the male deer in a similar way; and added that the does, when they bring forth their young, forsake their male companions until the kids are four or five months old; and this for the reason that the unnatural male is disposed to destroy his offspring during the period of its helplessness. Some rain fell to-day.

27th. We commenced our march this morning at six o'clock, travelled, as our custom usually was, till the hour of eleven, and then halted to breakfast, on the bank of the stream. The face of the country along the morning's trail was much the same as that passed over the day before; often beautiful, but oftener sublime. Vast spherical swells covered with buffalo, and wild flowering glens echoing the voices of a thousand cascades, and countless numbers of lofty peaks crowding the sky, will give perhaps a faint idea of it. As the stream that we had been following bore to the westward of our course, we in the afternoon struck across a range of low hills to another branch of it that came down from the eastern mountains, and encamped upon its banks. These hills were composed of hard gravel, covered with two or three inches of

black loam.   In the deep vales the mountain torrents had swept away the soil, and
left the strata bare for miles along their
courses.   The mountain flax and the large
thistle flourished everywhere.   The timber
was the same in kind as we had passed the
three last days.   The groves were principally confined to the lower portions of the
ravines which swept down from the snowy
heights.   The Anahuac range in the west
appeared to dip deeper in the horizon, and
recede farther from us.   One half only of
its altitude as seen from the dividing ridges
was now visible.   We were doubtless less-
ening our own altitude materially, but the
difference in the apparent height of this
ridge was in part produced by its increased
distance.   It had evidently begun to tend
rapidly towards the Pacific.

An aged knight of the order of horns
strode across our path near four o'clock,
and by his princely bearing invited our
trapper to a tilt.   His Kentucky blood
could not be challenged with impunity.
He dropped upon one knee—drew a close
sight—clove the bull's heart in twain, and
sent him him groaning upon the sand.   He
was very poor, but as we had reason to
fear that we were leaving the buffalo

" beat," it was deemed prudent to increase
the weight of our packs with the better
portion of his flesh. Accordingly the tongue,
heart, leaf fat and the " fleece" were taken,
and were being lashed to our mule, when
an attack of bilious bravery seized our
giant in the extremities, and he began to
kick and beat his horse for presuming to
stand upon four legs, or some similar act,
without his permission, in such gallant
style, that our mule on which the meat was
placed, leaped affrighted from us and
dropped it on the sand. We were all
extremely vexed at this, and I believe made
some disparaging comparisons between the
intellects of asses and tyrants. Whether
our mule or Smith felt most aggrieved
thereby we were never informed. But the
matter was very pleasantly disposed of by
our benevolent old guide. He turned the
meat with his foot and kicked it good-
naturedly from him, saying in his blandest
manner, " No dirt in the mounting but
sand ; the teeth can't go that ;" and
mounted his horse for the march. We travelled twenty miles and encamped.

28th. Eighteen miles down the small
valleys between the sharp and rugged hills ;
crossed a number of small streams running

westward. The mountains along our way
differed in character from any we had heretofore passed. Some of them were composed entirely of earth, and semi-elliptical
in form ; others embraced thousands of
acres of what seemed to be mere elevations
of fine brown gravel, rising swell above
swell, and sweeping away to the height of
two thousand feet, destitute of timber save
a few slender strips which grew along the
rills that trickled at long intervals down
their sides. We encamped again on the
bank of the main stream. It was one
hundred yards in width ; water a foot and
a half deep, current six miles the hour.

29th. To-day we struck Grand River,
(the great southern branch of the Colorado
of the west), twenty miles from our last
night's encampment. It is here three
hundred yards wide ; current, six miles the
hour ; water, from six to ten feet in depth,
transparent, but, like the atmosphere, of
much higher temperature than we had met
with since leaving the Arkansas. The
valleys that lie upon this stream and some
of its tributaries, are called by the hunters
" The Old Park." If the qualifying term
were omitted, they would be well described
by their name. Extensive meadows run-

ning up the valleys of the streams, woodlands skirting the mountain bases and
dividing the plains, over which the antelope, black and white-tailed deer, the
English hare, the big horn or mountain
sheep, the grisly, grey, red and black
bears, and the buffalo and elk range—a
splendid park indeed; not old, but new
as in the first fresh morning of the creation.

Here also are found the prairie and the
large grey wolf, the American panther,
beaver, polecat, and land otter. The grisly
bear is the largest and most ferocious—
with hair of a dirty-brown colour, slightly
mixed with those of a yellowish white.
The males not unfrequently weigh five or
six hundred pounds. The grey bear is less
in size, hair nearly black, interspersed along
the shoulders and hips with white. The red
is still less, according to the trappers, and of
the colour indicated by the name. The black
bear is the same in all respects as those
inhabiting the States. The prairie dog is
also found here, a singular animal, partially
described in a previous page; but as they
may be better known from Lieutenant
Pike's description of them, I shall here
introduce it: " They live in towns and
villages, having an evident police esta-

blished in their communities. The sites of
these towns are generally on the brow of a
hill, near some creek or pond, in order to
be convenient to water and to be exempt
from inundation. Their residence is in
burrows, which descend in spiral form."
The Lieutenant caused one hundred and
forty kettles of water to be poured into one
of their holes in order to drive out the occupant, but failed. "They never travel
mcre than half a mile from their homes,
and readily associate with rattlesnakes.
They are of a dark brown colour, except
their bellies, which are red. They are
something larger than a grey squirrel, and
very fat ; supposed to be graminivorous.
Their villages sometimes extend over two
or three miles square, in which there must
be innumerable hosts of them, as there is
generally a burrow every ten steps. As
you approach the towns, you are saluted on
all sides by the cry of " *wishtonwish*," uttered in a shrill piercing manner."

The birds of these regions are the sparrow-
hawk, the jack-daw, a species of grouse of
the size of the English grouse ; colour brown,
a tufted head, and limbs feathered to the
feet ; the raven, very large, turkey, turkey-
buzzards, geese, all the varieties of ducks

known in such latitudes, the bald and grey
eagle, meadow lark and robin red breast.
Of reptiles, the small striped lizard, horned
frog and garter snake are the most common. Rattlesnakes are said to be found
among the cliffs, but I saw none.

We forded Grand River, and encamped
in the willows on the northern shore. The
mountains in the west, on which the snow
was lying, were still in sight. The view to
the east and south was shut in by the
neighbouring hills; to the north and north-
east it was open, and in the distance
appeared the Wind River and other mountains, in the vicinity of the 'Great Gap.'

During the evening, while the men were
angling for trout, Kelly gave me some
account of Grand River and the Colorado
of the west. Grand River, he said, is a
branch of the Colorado. It rises far in the
east among the precipitous heights of the
eastern range of the Rocky Mountains,
about midway from the Great Gap and the
Kenyon of the south Fork of the Platte.
It interlocks the distance of sixty miles
with the waters of the Great Platte; its
course to the point where we crossed, is
nearly due west. Thence it continues in
a west by north course one hundred and

sixty miles, where it breaks through the Anahuac Ridge. The cliffs of this Kenyon are said to be many hundred feet high, and overhanging; within them is a series of cascades, which, when the river is swollen by the freshets in June, roar like Niagara.

After passing this Kenyon, it is said to move with a dashing, foaming current in a westerly direction fifty miles, where it unites with Green River, or Sheetskadee, and forms the Colorado of the west. From the junction of these branches the Colorado has a general course from the north-east to the south-west, of seven hundred miles to the head of the Gulf of California. Four hundred of this seven hundred miles is an almost unbroken chasm of Kenyon, with perpendicular sides, hundreds of feet in height, at the bottom of which the waters rush over continuous cascades. This Kenyon terminates thirty miles above the Gulf. To this point the river is navigable. The country on each side of its whole course is a rolling desert of brown loose earth, on which the rains and dews never fall.

A few years since, two Catholic Missionaries and their servants, on their way from the mountains to California, attempted to descend the Colorado. They have never been seen since the morning they commenced their fatal undertaking. A party of trappers and others made a strong boat and manned it well, with the determination of floating down the river to take the beaver, which they supposed to live along its banks ; but they found themselves in such danger after entering the kenyon, that with might and main they thrust their trembling boat ashore, and succeeded in leaping upon the crags, and lightening it before it was swallowed in the dashing torrent. But the death which they had escaped in the stream, still threatened them on the crags. Perpendicular and overhanging rocks frowned above them ; these they could not ascend. They could not cross the river ; they could not ascend the river, and the foaming cascades below forbade the thought of committing themselves again to their boat.

Night came on, and the difficulty of keeping their boat from being broken to pieces on the rocks, increased the anxieties of their situation. They must have passed a horrible night ; so full of fearful expectations, of the certainty of starvation on the crags, or drowning in the stream. In the morning, however, they examined the rocks again, and found a small projecting crag, some twenty feet above them, over which, after many efforts, they threw their small boat-rope and drew the noose tight. One of their number then climbed to explore. He found a platform above the crag, of sufficient size to contain his six companions, and a narrow chasm in the overhanging wall through which it appeared possible to pass to the upper surface. Having all reached the platform, they unloosed their lasso, and, bracing themselves as well as they could, with their rifles in the moving, dry earth beneath their feet, they undertook the ascent. It was so steep that they were often in danger of being plunged together in the abyss below. But by digging steps in the rocks, (where they could be dug with their rifle-barrells), and by making use of their lasso where it could be used, they reached the upper surface near sunset, and made their way back to the place of departure.

This is a mountain legend, interesting, indeed, but—

> " I cannot tell how the truth may be,
> I tell the tale as 'twas told to me :"

At day-light, on the 30th, our cavalcade was moving across the woody ridges and verdant valleys between the crossings of

Grand River and its great north fork. We
struck that stream about ten o'clock. Its
water was beautifully clear, average depth
two feet, and current four miles the hour.
It is said to take its rise in the mountains,
near the south side of the ' Great Gap,' and
to flow, in a south-westerly course, through
a country of broken and barren plains, into
Grand River, twenty miles below the crossings. We ascended rapidly all the day.
There was no trail to guide us ; but our
worthy guide knew every mountain-top in
sight. Bee lines through immense fields of
wild sage and wormwood, and over gravelly
plains—a short halt for a short breakfast—
constant spurring, and trotting, and driving, deposited us at sunset, at the foot of a
lofty mountain, clothed with heavy timber.
This was the dividing ridge between the
waters of Grand and Green Rivers. It was necessary to cross it. We therefore, turned out
the animals to feed, ate a scanty morsel of
dried meat, and went to our couches, for
the strength requisite for the task. About
the middle of the night the panthers on the
mountain gave us a specimen of their
growling capacities. It was a hideous noise :
deep and broken by the most unearthly
screams ! They were gathering for prey ;

for our horses and ourselves. We drove up the animals, however, tied them near the camp, built a large and bright fire, and slept till daylight.

At sunrise, on the morning of the 31st, we stood on the summit of the mountain, at the base of which we had slept the previous night. It was the very place from which I wished to view the outline of the valley of Grand River, and the snowy ridge of the Anahuac ; and it was as favourable an hour for my purpose as I could have selected from the whole day. The sun had just risen over the eastern heights, sufficiently to give the valley of the Grand River to the south-east of me, those strong contrasts of light and shade which painters know so well how to use when sketching a mountain scene at early morning, or when the sun is half hidden at night. The peaks were bright, the deep shadows sprang off from the western sides, above faintly, and deepening as they descended to the bases, where the deep brown of the rocks and earth gave the vales the semblance of undisturbed night.

The depression of the valley, as I have termed it, was in truth a depression of a vast tract of mountains ; not unto a plane or vale ; but a great ravine of butes and ridges, decreasing in height from the limit of vision in the north-east, east and south — and falling one below another toward the stream, into the diminutive bluffs on its banks. The valley below the crossing was less distinctly seen. Its general course only could be distinguished among the bare hills upon its borders. But the great main chain, or Anahuac range, came sweeping up from the Arkansas more sublime, if possible, in its aspect than when viewed from the heights farther south. It was about one hundred miles distant, the length of the section in view about one hundred and sixty ; not a speck on all its vast outline. It did not show as glaciers do ; but like a drift of newly-fallen snow heaped on mountains, by some mighty efforts of the elements ; piled from age to age ; and from day to day widening and heightening its untold dimensions. Its width, its height, its cubic miles, its mass of rock, of earth, of snow, of ice, of waters ascending in clouds to shower the lowlands or renew its own robes of frosts, of waters sent rushing to the seas, are some of the vast items of this sublimity of existence. The light of the rising

N 3

sun falling upon it through the remarkable transparent atmosphere of these regions, made the view exceedingly distinct. The intervening space was thickly dotted with lesser peaks, which, in the lengthened distance, melted into an apparent plain. But the elevation of the great Anahuac ridge, presenting its broad, white side to the morning light in that dry, clear, upper air, seemed as distictly seen as the tree at my side. In the north-west it manifestly tended toward the north end of the Great Salt Lake. But I must leave this absorbing scene for the journey of the day. The ascent of the dividing ridge, from which I took this extensive survey of all this vast, unknown, unexplored portion of the mountains, was comparatively easy. We threaded, indeed, some half dozen precipices in going up, within an inch of graves five hundred feet deep. Yet, as none of us lost our brains on the rocks below, these narrow and slippery paths cannot be remembered in connexion with incidents either remarkable or sad.

With this notice of mountain turnpikes, I shall be obliged to my readers to step along with me over the bold summit and look at the descent, yes, the *descent*, my friends.

It is a bold one : one of the men said " four miles of perpendicular ;" and so it was. Or if it was not, it ought to have been, for many very good reasons of mathematical propriety that are as difficult to write as to comprehend. It was partially covered with bushes and trees, and a soft vegetable mould that yielded to our horses' feet, but we, by dint of holding, bracing, and sliding, arrived safely at the bottom, and jogged on merrily six or seven miles over barren ridges, rich plains, and woody hills to the head of Tumbleton park. We had turned out our animals to eat, hung our camp-kettle over the fire to boil some bits of grisly meat that we had found among the rubbish of our packs, and were resting our wearied frames in the shade of the willows, conversing about the tracts which we had seen five miles back ; one supposing that they were made by Indians, the Arrapahoes or the Shoshonies, while our old guide insisted that they were made by white men's horses ! and assigned as a reason for this opinion, that no Indians could be travelling in that direction, and that one of the horses had shoes on its fore feet ; when the Arrapahoe war-whoop and the clattering of hoofs upon the side hill above, brought us to our feet, rifle in hand,

for a conflict.   Kelly seemed for a moment
to be in doubt as to his own conclusions
relative to the tracks, and as to the colour of
those unceremonious visiters.   But as they
dashed up, he leaped the brook, and seized
the hands of three old fellow-trappers.   It
was a joyful meeting.   They had often
stood side by side in battle, and among the
solemn mountains dug the lonely grave of
some slaughtered companion, and together
sent the avenging lead into the hearts of the
Blackfeet.   They were more than brothers,
and so they met.   We shared with them
our last scraps of meat.

They informed us that they had fallen in
with our trail, and followed us under a belief
that we were certain friends whom they
were expecting from St. Louis with goods
for the post at Brown's Hole ; that the Arrapahoes were fattening on buffalo in the
Bull Pen, on the north fork of the Platte ;
that the Shoshonies or Snakes were starving
on roots on Great Bear River ; that the
Blackfeet and Sioux were in the neighbourhood ; that there was no game in the mountains except on the head waters of Snake
River ; and that they themselves were a
portion of a party of white men, Indians, and
squaws, on their way to Bent's Fort on the

Arkansas, to meet Mr. Thomson with the goods before named; that we might reasonably anticipate starvation and the arrows of the Sioux, and other kindred comforts along our journey to Brown's Hole. Mr. Craig, the chief of the party, and part owner with Mr. Thomson, assured us that the grass on the Columbia was already dry and scarce; and if there should prove to be enough to sustain our horses on the way down, that the snows on the Blue Mountains would prevent us from reaching Vancouver till the spring, and kindly invited us to pass the winter at his post. After two hours' tarry with us he and his party returned to their camp.

Tumbleton's Park is a beautiful savannah, stretching north-westerly from our camp in an irregular manner among groves of pine, spruce, fir, and oak. Three hundred yards from us rose Tumbleton's Rock, one of those singular spires found in the valley of the mountains, called Butes. It was about eighty feet in height, twenty feet in diameter at the base, and terminated at the top in a point. Soon after our new acquaintances had left us, we "caught up" and struck across the hills in a north-easterly course toward the north fork of Little Bear River. The travelling was very rough, now among fields of loose stones and bushes, and now among dense forests ; no trail to aid us in finding our way ; new ground even to our guide. But he was infallible.

Two hours' riding had brought us upon an Indian trail that he had heard of ten years before ; and on we rushed among the fallen pines, two feet, three feet in diameter, raised, as you see, one foot, two feet from the ground. The horses and mules are testing their leaping powers. Over they go, and tip off riders and packs, &c., &c. A merry time this. There goes my Puebla mare, head, heels, and neck, into an acre of crazy logs. Ho, halt! Puebla's down, mortally wounded with want of strength! She's unpacked, and out in a trice ; we move again. Ho! whistle that mule into the track! he'll be off that ledge there. Move them on! move! cut down that sapling by the low part of that fallen tree! drive over Puebla! There she goes! long legs a benefit in bestriding forests. Hold! hold! hold! that pack-horse yonder has anchored upon a pine! Dismount! back her out! she has hung one side of herself and pack upon that knot! away! ho! But silence! a deer springs up in yonder thicket! Kelly creeps forward – halt! hush!

hu! Ah! the varlet! he is gone; a mur-
rain on his fat loins! a poor supper we'll
have to-night! no meat left, not a particle; nor coffee, tea, nor salt! custom of
society here to starve! suppose you will
conform! Stay, here's trouble! but they
move! one goes down well! another, another,
and another! My Puebla mare, reader, that
six foot frame standing there, hesitating to
descend that narrow track around the precipice! she goes over it! bravely done! A
ten feet leap! and pack and all stuck in the
mud. That mule, also, is down in the quagmire! a lift at the pack there, man! the
active, tireless creature! he's up and off.
Guide, this forest is endless! shan't get out
to-night. But here we go merrily onward!
It is dark enough for the frogs of Egypt!
Halt! halt! ho! Puebla down again—laid
out among the logs! Pull away upon that
pack there, man! help the sinner to her feet
again for another attempt to kill herself.
Beautiful pines, firs, and hemlocks, these,
reader; but a sack of hurricanes has been
let loose among them not long since. The
prostrate shingle timber, eh? 'twould cover
a roof over the city of London; and make
a railroad to run the Thames into Holland.
Halt! halt! unpack! we camp here to-night.

A little prairie this, embosomed, nestled, &c., among the sweet evergreen woodlands. Wait a little now, reader, till we turn these animals loose to feed, and we'll strike up a fire wherewithal to dry our wet garments, and disperse a portion of this darkness. It is difficult kindling this wet bark. Joseph, sing a song; find a hollow tree; get some dry leaves. That horse is making into the forest! better tie him to a bough! That's it ; Joseph, that's a youthful blaze! give it strength! feed it oxygen! it grows. Now for our guest. Seat yourself, sir, on that log; rather damp comfort—the best we have—homespun fare—the ton of the country ! We're in the primeval state, sir. We regret our inability to furnish you food, sir. But as we have not, for the last few days indulged much in that merely animal gratification, we beg you to accommodate yourself with a dish of Transcendentalism ; and with us await patiently a broiled steak a few days along the track of time to come.

It was ten o'clock at night when we arrived at this encampment. It had been raining in torrents ever since night-fall. The rippling of a small stream had guided us after the darkness shut in. Drenched with rain, shivering with cold, destitute of food, and with the appetite of wolves, we availed ourselves of the only comforts within our reach —a cheering pine-knot fire, and such sleep as we could get under the open heavens in a pelting storm.

The general face of the country through which the afternoon's travel had carried us, was much broken; but the inequalities, or hills and valleys, to a very considerable extent, were covered with a rich vegetable loam, supporting a heavy growth of pine, spruce, quaking-asp, &c. The glades that intervened were more beautiful than I had seen. Many were covered with a heavy growth of timothy or herds grass, and red top in blossom. Large tracts in the skirts of the timber were thickly set with Sweet-sicily. The mountain flax was very abundant. I had previously seen it in small patches only; but here it covered acres as densely as it usually stands in fields, and presented the beautiful sheet of blue blossoms so graceful to the lords of the plough.

I had noticed some days previously, a few blades of the grasses just named, standing in a clump of bushes; but we were riding rapidly, and could not stop to ex-

amine them, and I was disposed to think
that my sight had deceived me. What!
the tame grasses of Europe, all that are
valuable for stock, the best and most sought
by every intelligent farmer in Christendom;
these indigenous to the vales of the Rocky
mountains?   It was even so.

August 1st. As our horses had found
little to eat during the past night, and
seemed much worn by the exceeding fatigues of the previous day, we at early dawn
drew them around our camp, loaded the
strongest of them with our packs, and led
and drove the poor animals through three
miles more of standing and fallen timber, to
the opening on Little Bear River, and turned
them loose to feed upon the first good grass
that we found.   It chanced to be in one of
Kelly's old encampments; where he had,
some years before, fortified himself with logs,
and remained seven days with a sick fellow
trapper.   At that time the valley was alive
with hostile Indians; but the good man
valued the holy principles of humanity more
than his life, and readily put it at hazard to
save that of his companion.   " A fearful
time that," said he; "the redskins saw every
turn of our heads during those seven days
and nights.   But I baited our horses within

reach of my rifle during the day, and put
them in that pen at night ; so that they
could not rush off with them, without losing
their brains.   The buffalo were plenty here
then.   The mountains were then rich.
The bulls were so bold that they would
come close to the fence there at night, and
bellow and roar till I eased them of their
blood by a pill of lead in the liver.   So you
see I did not go far for meat.   Now, the
mountains are so poor that one would stand
a right good chance of starving, if he were
obliged to hang up here for seven days. The
game is all driven out.   No place here for a
white man now. Too poor, too poor. What
little we get, you see, is bull beef. Formerly,
we ate nothing but cows, fat and young.
More danger then, to be sure ; but more
beaver too ; and plenty of grease about the
buffalo ribs.   Ah! those were good times ;
but a white man has now no more business
here."

Our general course since entering the
mountains at the Arkansas, had been north-
west by west. It now changed to north-west
by north.   Our horses and mules, having
eaten to their satisfaction the rich grass
about our guide's old encampment, we
moved on down Little Bear River.   The

country, as we descended, became more
and more barren.

The hills were destitute of timber and
grasses ; the plains bore nothing but prickly
pear and wild wormwood. The latter is a
shrub growing from two to six feet in height.
It branches in all directions from the root.
The main stem is from two to four inches
in diameter at the ground, the bark rough,
of a light greyish colour and very thin.
The wood is firm, fine grained, and difficult
to break. The leaves are larger, but
resemble in form and colour those of the
common wormwood of the gardens. The
flavour is that of a compound of garden
wormwood and sage : hence it has received
the names of " wild wormwood" and "wild
sage." Its stiff and knotty branches are
peculiarly unpleasant to the traveller among
them. It stands so thickly over thousands
of acres of the mountain valleys, that it is
well nigh impossible to urge a horse through
it ; and the individual who is rash enough
to attempt it, will himself be likely to be
deprived of his moccasins, and his horse of
his natural covering of his legs. There are
two species of the prickly pear (cactus)
here. The one is the plant of low growth,
thick elliptical leaves armed with thorns,

the same as is found in the gardens of
certain curious people in the States; the
other is of higher growth, often reaching
three feet; the colour is a deep green.
It is a columnar plant without a leaf; the
surface of the stalk is checked into dia-
monds of the most perfect proportions,
swelling regularly from the sides to the
centre. At the corners of these figures
grow strong thorns, from an inch to an inch
and a half in length. Six inches from the
ground, branches shoot from the parent
stalk in all directions, making an angle with
it of about forty-five degrees, and growing
shorter as the point of union with the
central stalk increases in height. The
consistency of the whole plant is alternately pulpy and fibrous. We were making
our tedious way among these thorny companions, musing upon our empty stomachs,
when we were overtaken by two men, a
squaw and child, from Craig's party. They
made their camp with us at night. Nothing
to eat, starving and weak; we followed the
example of the squaw, in eating the inner
portion of large thistle-stalks.

2nd. We rose at daybreak, somewhat
refreshed by sleep, but weak, weak, having
eaten but little for four days. The longings

of appetite—they are horrible !   Our guide
was used to long fasts, and was therefore
little incommoded.   He, however, had been
out with his rifle, since the peep of day,
and as we were lifting the packs upon our
mules, it cracked in the direction of the
trail we were about to travel.   We hastened
away to him with the eagerness of starving
men, and found him resting unconcernedly
upon his rifle, waiting for us to enjoy with
him the roasted loins of an elk, which had
tumbled from a neighbouring cliff, in obedience to his unerring aim.

Leaving his saddle-horse to pack the
meat on, passed along a mile, and encamped among the willows on the bank of
Little Bear River.   The first work, after
turning loose our animals, was to build a
fire to cook meat.   Our squaw companion
thought otherwise.   She selected a place
for her camp beneath the willows, cleared a
spot wide enough for her bed, formed an
arch of the boughs overhead, covered it
with a piece of buffalo tent leather, unloosed
her infant from its prison, and laid it upon
skins in the shade she had formed.   After
this, the horses of herself and husband were
unharnessed, and turned loose to feed.
She was a good, cleanly, affectionate body,

equally devoted to the happiness of her child, husband, and horses; and seemed disposed to initiate us into every little piece of knowledge that would enable us to discover the wild edible roots of the country, the best method of taking fish, hoppling horses, tying knots in ropes, repairing saddles, &c., which experience had taught her.

Our fire had just begun to burn brightly, when our guide arrived with the elk. It was very much bruised by its fall from the cliff when shot. Yet it was meat; it was broiled; it was eaten; it was sweet. No bread, or vegetables, or salt, to the contrary, it was delicious. Four days' fasting is confessed to be an excellent panacea for a bad appetite; and as all good and wholesome rules work both ways, it is without doubt a *tasteful* addition to bad food. I must, however, bear my humble testimony to the fact, that meat alone, unqualified with gravy, unsprinkled with salt or pepper, unaided by any vegetable or farinaceous accompaniment, is excellent food for men. It neither makes them tigers nor crocodiles. On the contrary, it prevents starvation, when nothing else can be had, and cultivates industry, the parent of virtue, in all the multiplied departments of the gastric system.

3rd. Remained in camp all day to refresh our animals, to eat, and hear yarns of mountain life. During these conversations, the great dangers of a residence among the mountains was often reverted to. One class of them was said to arise from the increasing scarcity of buffalo and beaver among them. This circumstance compelled the trappers to move over a wide range of country, and consequently, multiplied the chances of falling in with the Sioux and Blackfeet, their deadliest enemies—enemies on whom no dependence could be placed other than this, that they always fight well whenever and wherever met. Our new friends related, in this connexion, the death of one of their old companions, a brave old trapper of the name of Redman. This man, and another called Markhead, were trapping on the head-waters of Green River, when they were discovered by a war party of young Sioux, and robbed of their horses. This was a great annoyance to them. The loss of the value of their animals was inconvenient for the poor men ; but the loss of their services in transporting their traps and furs, and " possibles," (clothing, cooking utensils, &c.,) was severely felt. It was necessary to recover them, or *cache ;*" that is, bury in some secret place in the dry sand, their remaining property: forsake their hunt, and abandon all their prospects of gain for the season. Redman had lived with the Sioux, and relying on their former friendship for him in their village, determined to go with Markhead, and attempt to reason a Sioux war party into a surrender of their plunder. They approached them rifle in hand, and held a parley near the Pilot Bute. The result was, that the Indians demanded and obtained their rifles, discharged them at their owners, killed Redman instantly, and severely wounded his companion. This occurred in the spring of 1839.

4th. We were early on route this morning, down the banks of Little Bear River; course north-west. Our track lay so low, that the mountains were seldom seen. A portion of the Anahuac ridge in the south-west, was the only height constantly in view. The plains, as they are called, on either side of the river, were cut into vast ravines and bluffs. In their side sometimes appeared a thin stratum of slate. Few other rocky strata were seen during a march of fifteen miles. About twelve o'clock, we came upon a cave formed by the limestone and sulphur deposit of a small stream that burst from a hill hard by. The water had, by constant depositions, formed an elevated channel some five rods down the face of the hillside, at the termination of which it spread itself over a circular surface of one hundred and fifty or two hundred feet in circumference. In the centre of this, was an orifice, down which the water trickled into the cave below. As little of the cave could be seen from the ground above, myself and two others attempted to explore it. We found the roof hung with beautifully crystallized sulphur, and the bottom strewn with large quantities of the same material in a pulverized state. The odour was so offensive, however, that we were glad to retreat before we had formed a very perfect estimate of its extent and contents. It was about six rods long, eight feet wide, and four feet high. Near it were a number of warm springs. On the bluff, a few rods above it, was a small tract of fused rocks. In all the circle of vision, however, there were no elevations that indicate any powerful volcanic action in former times ; nor any from which these rocks could have tumbled or been thrown. The warm springs, however, in the vicinity may, perhaps, indicate their origin.

The face of the country passed to-day

was dry and barren.   A single quaking-asp tree here and there on the sterile bottom lands, and small strips of cotton wood, whose tops peered from the deep gorges just above the level of the wormwood plains, and a few withered patches of the wild grasses among the patched bluffs, present its whole aspect.

The sun had nearly set before we arrived at the desired place of encampment, the junction of the two principal forks of Little Bear River.   When within half a mile of it, one of the trappers who had joined us, suddenly started his horse into a quick gallop in advance of the rest of the party. We were surprised by this sudden movement, and hastened after him.   As we rose a sharp knoll, our surprise was changed to pleasure on seeing him in friendly converse with a white face, a fellow-trapper, one of the " white men" of the mountains.   He was a French Canadian, fourteen days from Brown's Hole.   We were soon across the river, and in his camp among the cotton-wood.   Here we found three others to welcome us, and give us information of the movements of the Indians.   They had been attacked by a Sioux war party, a few days before on Little Snake River, but had es-

o 2

caped with no other loss than that of a hat and a favourite dog. Their opinion was that we should have the pleasure of meeting them on their way to Brown's Hole. This prospect was extremely gratifying to our noble old Kentucky guide. " D—n them," said he ; " I'll try to pick up one of the rascals. Redman was as fine a fellow as ever came to the mountains, and they shot him with his own rifle. He was a fool to let them have it ; he ought to have shot one of them, d—n 'em, and then died, if he must."

Our elk meat was diminishing fast, under the kind administration of our own and our friends' appetites ; and the certain prospect that we should obtain no more for eight days was a source of no inconsiderable uneasiness to us. And yet we gave Ward, Burns, the squaw, and the four French trappers, being destitute of food, as freely as they would have given to us under similar circumstances, the best piece, and as much as they would eat for supper and breakfast. These solitary Frenchmen were apparently very happy. Neither hunger nor thirst annoy them, so long as they have strength to travel, and trap, and sing. Their camps are always merry, and they cheer themselves along the weary march in the wilderness with the wild border songs of " Old Canada." The American trappers present a different phase of character. Habitual watchfulness destroys every frivolity of mind and action. They seldom smile : the expression of their countenances is watchful, solemn, and determined. They ride and walk like men whose breasts have so long been exposed to the bullet and the arrow, that fear finds within them no resting-place. If a horse is descried in the distance, they put spurs to their animals, and are at his side at once, as the result may be, for death or life. No delay, no second thought, no cringing in their stirrups ; but erect, firm, and with a strong arm, they seize and overcome every danger, or " perish," as they say, " as white men should," fighting promptly and bravely.

5th. This morning we were to part with Burns and Ward, and the French trappers. The latter pursued their way to the " Old Park," as they called the valley of Grand River, in pursuit of beaver ; the former went into the heights in the south-west, for the same object, and the additional one of waiting there the departure of the Sioux and Blackfeet. These Americans had in-

terested us in themselves by their frankness
and kindness ; and before leaving them, it
was pleasant to know that we could testify
our regard for them by increasing their
scanty stock of ammunition. But for every
little kindness of this description, they
sought to remunerate us tenfold, by giving
us moccasins, dressed deer and elk skins,
&c. Every thing, even their hunting shirts
upon their backs, were at our service ;—
always kindly remarking when they made an
offer of such things, that " the country was
filled with skins, and they could get a
supply when they should need them."

About ten o'clock, we bade these fearless
and generous fellows a farewell as hearty
and honest as any that was ever uttered ;
wishing them a long and happy life in
their mountain home; and they bade us a
pleasant and prosperous journey. We took
up our march again down Little Bear River
for Brown's Hole. It was six or eight
" camps," or days' travel, a-head of us ;
the way infested with hostile Indians—destitute of game and grass ; a horrid journey !
We might escape the Sioux ; we might kill
one of our horses, and so escape death by
starvation ! But these few chances of saving our lives were enough. Dangers of

the kind were not so appalling to us then as they would have been when leaving the frontier. We had been sixty odd days among the fresh trails of hostile tribes, in hourly expectation of hearing the war-whoop raised around us; and certain that if attacked by a war party of the ordinary number, we should be destroyed. We had, however, crept upon every height which we had crossed with so much caution, and examined the plains below with so much care, and when danger appeared near, wound our way among the timber and heights till we had passed it with so much success, that our sense of danger was blunted to that degree, and our confidence in our ability to avoid it so great, that I verily believe we thought as little of Indians as we did of the lizards along our track.

We still clung to the stream. It was generally about fifty yards wide, a rapid current, six inches deep, rushing over a bed of loose rocks and gravel, and falling at the rate of about two hundred feet to the mile. During the day, a grisly bear and three cubs and an elk showed themselves. One of the men gave chase to the bears, with the intention of killing one of them for food; but they eluded his pursuit by run-ning into brush, through which a horse could not penetrate with sufficient speed to overtake them. The man in pursuit, however, found a charming prize among the brush; a mule—an excellent pack mule, which would doubtless be worth to him at Brown's Hole £20. It was feeding quietly, and so tame as to permit him to approach within ten yards, without even raising its head over the hazel bushes that partly concealed it. A double prize it was, and so accidental; obtained at so little expense; ten minutes time only — two pounds a minute! But alas for the £20! He was preparing to grasp it, and the mule most suddenly—most wonderfully—most cruelly metamorphosed itself into an elk! fat as marrow itself, and sufficient in weight to have fed our company for twelve days. It fled away, before our " maid and her milk pail companion " could shake his astonished locks, and send a little lead after it, by way of entreaty, to supply us starving wretches with a morsel of meat.

After this incident had imparted its comfort to our disappointed appetites, we passed on, over, around, in, and among deep ravines, and parched, sterile, and flinty plains for the remainder of our ten miles' march, and encamped on the bank of the river. The last of our meat was here cooked and eaten. A sad prospect! No game ahead, no provisions in possession. We caught three or four small trout from the river, for breakfast, and slept.

I had now become much debilitated by want of food and the fatigues of the journey. I had appropriated my saddle horse to bear the packs that had been borne by Kelly's before its death; and had, consequently, been on foot ever since that event, save when my guide could relieve me with the use of his saddle beast. But as our Spanish servant, the owner and myself, had only his horse's services to bear us along, the portion to each was far from satisfying to our exceeding weariness. Blair and Wood also, had had only one horse from El Peubla. We were, therefore, in an ill condition to endure a journey of seven days, over a thirsty country, under a burning sun, and without food.

END OF THE FIRST VOLUME.

LONDON:
PRINTED BY SCHULZE AND CO., 13, POLAND STREET.

TRAVELS

IN THE

GREAT WESTERN PRAIRIES.

—

VOL. II.

TRAVELS

IN THE

GREAT WESTERN PRAIRIES,

THE ANAHUAC AND ROCKY MOUNTAINS,

AND IN

THE OREGON TERRITORY.

BY THOMAS J. FARNHAM.

IN TWO VOLUMES.

VOL. II.

LONDON:

RICHARD BENTLEY, NEW BURLINGTON STREET.

Publisher in Ordinary to Her Majesty.

1843.

LONDON:

PRINTED BY SCHULZE AND CO., 13, POLAND STREET.

CONTENTS

TO

THE SECOND VOLUME.

CHAPTER I.

Bear Hunt—Sulphur Puddle—The River—Wolves and their Fare—Dog Eating—Little Snake River—Thirst — Deserts — Mountains — Mountain Hottentots — Brown's Hole—Fort David Crockett— Traders — Winter and its Hilarities—Lovs—The Way to get a Wife—A Recommendation to Civilized People—The Colorado of the West—Club Indians—The Shoshonies—An Indian Temperance Society—The Crows— The Blackfeet—Unburied Skeletons—The Arrapahoes, and Citizenship among them—War Parties— Lodge of the Great Spirit—Religious Ceremonies— The Vow and an Incident—The First Shoshonie who saw a White Man. .　　.　　.　　.　　.　　1—47

CHAPTER II.

An Arrival from Fort Hall—An Account from Oregon— Return of two of my companions to the States—A startling Condition—An Indian Guide—A Farewell—

How a Horse studies Geology—A Camp—Dog Mutton superseded — A Scene—Sheetskadee—Butes—Desolation—Midnight Scene in the Mountains—Indian Jim and the Buffalo—Hungry Stomachs—A fat Shot—Fine Eye-sight—An old Trapper picked up—Beautiful Desert—" Hos, Hos"—Meek the Bear Killer—A wild Vale—Steamboat Spring—Natural Soda Fountains—Neighbouring Landscape—A hard Drive —Valley of Chasm—Nature's Vase—A heavy March —Passing the Mountains—A charming Gorge—Entrance into Oregon—The South Branch of the Columbia—Fort Hall and its Hospitalities. . 48—90

CHAPTER III.

The Rocky Mountains and their Spurs—Geography of the Mountain Region — Wyeth — The Outset — The Beaver Catcher's Bride —Trois Butes—Addition from a Monastery — Orisons — A Merry Mountain Trapper — Root Diggers — Enormous Springs—Volcanic Hearths and Chasms—Carbo—An old Chief—A Bluff—Boisais River—Incident of Trade —The Bonaks—The Dead Wail—Fort Boisais, its Salmon, Butter, and Hearty Cheer—Mons. Payette—Curiosity—Departure—Passing the Blue Mountains —The Grandeur of them—Their Forests, Flowers, and Torrents—Descent of the Mountains—Plain, a Christian Crane—Arrival at Dr. Whitman's Mission —Wallawalla — People — Farm— Mill—Learning—Religion—Mr. Ermitinger — Blair — Nez Percés—Racing—Indian Horse Training—Sabbath and its joys in the Wilderness . . . . 90—140

CHAPTER IV.

Parting with Friends—Wallawalla Valley—Fort Walla-
walla—Mr. Pambrun—The Columbia—Country down
its banks—What was seen of Rock Earth—Wood,
Fire, and Water— Danger, &c. from the Heights—Fall-
ing Mountain—Mourning Hymn to God—Giant's
Causeway—A View of the Frozen Sublime—Tum Tum
Orter' and other appurtenances—Dalles—Methodists
Episcopal Mission—Mr. and Mrs. Perkins—Mr. Lee
—Mission Premises—Egyptian Pyramids—Indians—
How Fifty Indians can fight One—Boston—The Re-
sult of a War—Descent of the Columbia in a Canoe
—A Night on the River—The Poetry of the Wilder-
ness—The Cascades—Postage—Dr. McLaughlin—
Indian Tombs—Death—A Race—The River and its
Banks—Night again—Mounts Washington and Jef-
ferson—Arrival—Fort Vancouver—British Hospi-
tality . . . . . . 150—199

CHAPTER V.

Departure from Vancouver—Wappatoo Island—The
Willamette River—Its Mouth—The Moûntains—
Falls—River above the Falls—Arrival at the Lower
Settlement—A Kentuckian—Mr. Johnson and his
Cabin—Thomas M'Kay and his Mill—Dr. Bailey and
Wife and Home—The Neighbouring Farmers—The
Methodist Episcopal Mission and Missionaries—Their
Modes of Operations—The Wisdom of their Course
—Their Improvements, &c.—Return to Vancouver—
Mr. Young—Mr. Lee's Misfortune—Descent of the

Willamette—Indians—Arrival at Vancouver—Oregon—Its Mountains, Rivers and Soil, and Climate—Shipment for the Sandwich Islands—Life at Vancouver—Descent of the Columbia—Astoria—On the Pacific Sea—The Last view of Oregon—Account of Oregon, by Lieut. Wilkes, Commander of the late exploring expedition   .   .   .   200—315

TRAVELS

GREAT WESTERN PRAIRIES,

&c. &c.

CHAPTER I.

Bear Hunt—Sulphur Puddle—The River—Wolves and
their Fare—Dog Eating—Little Snake River—Thirst
— Deserts — Mountains — Mountain Hottentots —
Brown's Hole—Fort David Crockett—Traders—
Winter and its Hilarities—Love—The Way to get a
Wife—A Recommendation to Civilized People—The
Colorado of the West—Club Indians—The Shosho-
nies—An Indian Temperance Society—The Crows—
The Blackfeet—Unburied Skeletons—The Arrapa-
hoes, and Citizenship among them—War Parties—
Lodge of the Great Spirit—Religious Ceremonies—
The Vow and an Incident—The First Shoshonie
who saw a White Man.

6th August. Eighteen miles to-day over
the barren intervales of the river. The wild
wormwood and prickly pear were almost
the only evidences of vegetative powers
which the soil presented. A rugged deso-

lation of loam and sand bluffs, barren vales
of red earth, and an occasional solitary
boulder of granite; no mountains even, to
relieve the dreary monotony of the sick-
ening sight. About twelve o'clock it was
pleasant to see a small band of antelopes
show themselves on the brink of a bluff.

We halted, and attempted to approach
them; but they had been hunted a few
days before by the French trappers, whom
we had met, and by no means relished our
companionship. Away they ran like the
wind. Our hopes of finding game were at
an end; the French trappers had seen, on
all their way out, no other game than this
band of antelopes. Our faithful greyhound
could be eaten as a last resource, and we
travelled on. Our excellent guide insisted
upon walking nearly all the way that I
might ride. This was inestimably kind
in him. The act flowed from his own
goodness; for, during our long journey
together, he had never failed to take every
opportunity to make me comfortable. We
arranged our camp to-night with unusual
care. The Sioux were among the hills on
the right, and every preparation was therefore made to receive an attack from them.
But like many other expectations of the

kind, this vanished as the beautiful mountain morn dawned upon the silent desert.

7th. To-day we travelled across a great southward bend in the river. The face of the country a desert—neither tree nor shrub, nor grass, nor water in sight. During the afternoon we fell in with an old grisly bear and two cubs. It was a dangerous business, but starvation knows no fear.

Kelly and Smith, having horses that could run, determined to give chase and shoot one cub, while the greyhound should have the honour of a battle with the other. Under this arrangement the chase commenced. The old bear, unfaithful to her young, ran ahead of them in her fright, and showed no other affection for them than to stop occasionally, raise herself on her hind feet, and utter a most piteous scream. The horses soon ran down one cub, and the greyhound the other, so that in half an hour we were on the route again with the certain prospect of a supper when we should encamp. Had we found water and wood where we killed our meat, we should have believed it impossible to have proceeded further without food; but as necessity seldom deals in mercy, she compelled us in this case, to travel till dark, before we found wood enough to cook our food, and water enough to quench our parching thirst. At last, turning from our track and following down a deep ravine that ran toward the river, we came upon a filthy, oozing sulphurous puddle which our horses, though they had had no water the entire day, refused to drink. There was no alternative, however, between drinking this and thirsting still, and we submitted to the lesser of two evils. We drank it; and with the aid of dry wormwood for fuel, boiled our meat in it. These cubs were each of about twelve pounds weight. The livers, hearts, heads, and the fore quarters of one of them, made us a filthy supper. It, however, served the purpose of better food as it prevented starvation. We had travelled eighteen miles.

8th. The morning being clear and excessively warm, we thought it prudent to seek the river again, that we might obtain water for ourselves and animals. They had had no grass for the last twenty-four hours; and the prospect of finding some for the poor animals upon the intervales, was an additional inducement to adopt this course. We accordingly wound down the ravine two or three miles, struck the river at a point where its banks were productive, and unpacked to feed them, and treat ourselves to a breakfast of cub meat. Boiled or roasted, it was miserable food. To eat it, however, or not to eat at all, was the alternative. Furthermore, in a region where lizards grow poor, and wolves lean against sand banks to howl, cub soup, without salt, pepper, &c., must be acknowledged to be quite in style.

Having become somewhat comfortable by feasting thus, we travelled on down this river of deserts twenty miles, and encamped again on its banks. At this encampment we ate the last of our meat; and broke the bones with our hatchet for the oily marrow in them. The prospect of suffering from hunger before we could arrive at Brown's Hole, became every hour more and more certain. The country between us and that point was known to be so sterile, that not even a grisly bear was to be hoped for in it. It was a desert of black flint, sand and marl, rendered barren by perpetual drought.

9th. Travelled twenty-three miles along the river — nothing to eat, not even a thistle stalk. At night we tried to take

some fish ; the stream proved as ungene-
rous as the soil on its banks.

10th. Made fifteen miles to-day ; country covered with wild wormwood ; at intervals a little bunch grass—dry and dead ;
face of the country formerly a plain, now
washed into hills. Our dog was frantic
with hunger ; and although he had treated
us to a cub, and served us with all the fidelity of his race, we determined in full council
to-night, if our hooks took no fish, to breakfast on his faithful heart in the morning.
A horrid night we passed : forty-eight hours
without a morsel of food ! Our camp was
eight miles above the junction of Little Bear
and Little Snake Rivers.

11th. This morning we tried our utmost
skill at fishing. Patience often cried ' hold'
but the appearance of our poor dog would
admonish us to continue our efforts to obtain a breakfast from the stream. Thus we
fished and fasted till eight o'clock. A
small fish or two were caught—three or four
ounces of food for seven starving men !
Our guide declared the noble dog must die!
He was accordingly shot, his hair burnt
off, and his fore quarters boiled and eaten !
Some of the men declared that dogs made
excellent mutton ; but on this point, there

existed among us what politicians term an honest difference of opinion. To me, it tasted like the *flesh of a dog, a singed dog ;* and appetite keen though it was, and edged by a fast of fifty hours, could not but be sensibly alive to the fact that, whether cooked or barking, a dog is still a dog, every where. After our repast was finished, we saddled and rode over the plains in a northerly direction for Brown's Hole. We had been travelling the last five days, in a westerly course ; and as the river continued in that direction, we left it to see it no more, I would humbly hope, till the dews of Heaven shall cause its deserts to blos som and ripen into something more nutritive than wild wormwood and gravel.

We crossed Little Snake River about ten o'clock. This stream is similar in size to that we had just left. The water was clear and warm ; the channel rocky and bordered by barren bluffs. No trees grew upon its banks where we struck it ; though I was informed that higher up, it was skirted with pretty groves of cotton wood. But as the Sioux war party which had attacked the French trappers in this neighbourhood, was probably not far from our trail, perhaps on it, and near us, we spent little time in examining either groves or deserts ; for we were vain enough to suppose that the mere incident of being scalped here would not be so interesting, to ourselves at least, as would be our speedy arrival at Craig and Thomson's post—where we might eat Christian food and rest from the fatigues of our journey. For these, and several other palpable reasons, we drove on speedily and silently, with every eye watchful, every gun well primed, every animal close to his fellows, till ten o'clock at night. We then halted near a place where we had been told by the French trappers, we could find a spring of water. The day had been excessively warm, and our thirst was well nigh insufferable. Hence the long search for the cooling spring to slake its burnings. It was in vain. Near midnight therefore it was abandoned by all, and we wrapped ourselves in our blankets, hungry, thirsty, and weary, and sunk to rest upon the sand. Another dreadful night! Thirst, burning thirst! The glands cease to moisten the mouth, the throat becomes dry and feverish, the lungs cease to be satisfied with the air they inhale, the heart is sick and faint; and the nerves preternaturally active, do violence to every vital organ. It is an incipient throe of death.

21st. We arose at break of day, and

pursued our journey over the grey, barren wastes. This region is doomed to perpetual sterility. In many portions of it there appears to be a fine soil. But the trappers say that very little rain or snow falls upon it; hence its unproductiveness. And thus it is said to be with the whole country lying to the distance of hundreds of miles on each side of the whole course of the Colorado of the West. Vast plateaux of desolation, yielding only the wild wormwood and prickly pear! So barren, so hot, so destitute is it of water that can be obtained and drunk, that the mountain sheep, and hare even, animals which drink less than any others that inhabit these regions, do not venture there. Travellers along that stream are said to be compelled to carry it long distances upon animals, and draw it where it is possible so to do, with a rope and skin bucket from the chasm of the stream. And yet their animals frequently die of thirst and hunger; and men often save their lives by eating the carcasses of the dead, and by drinking the blood which they from time to time draw from the veins of the living.

Between this river and the Great Salt Lake, there is a stream called Severe River, which rises in the high plateaux to the S.E.

of the lake, and running some considerable distance in a westerly course, terminates in its own lakes.   On the banks of this river there is said to be some vegetation, as grasses, trees, and edible roots.   Here live the "Piutes" and "Land Pitches," the most degraded and least intellectual Indians known to the trappers.   They wear no clothing of any description—build no shelters.   They eat roots, lizards, and snails. Their persons are more disgusting than those of the Hottentots.

They provide nothing for future wants. And when the lizard and snail and wild roots are buried in the snows of winter, they are said to retire to the vicinity of timber, dig holes in the form of ovens in the steep sides of the sand hills, and, having heated them to a certain degree, deposit themselves in them, and sleep and fast till the weather permits them to go abroad again for food.   Persons who have visited their haunts after a severe winter, have found the ground around these family ovens strewn with the unburied bodies of the dead, and others crawling among them, who had various degrees of strength, from a bare sufficiency to gasp in death, to those that crawled upon their hands and feet, eating grass like cattle. It is said that they have no weapons of defence except the club, and that in the use of that they are very unskilful. These poor creatures are hunted in the spring of the year, when weak and helpless, by a certain class of men, and when taken, are fattened, carried to Santa Fé and sold as slaves during their minority. "A likely girl" in her teens brings oftentimes £60 or £80. The males are valued less.

At about eleven o'clock we came to a stream of good water and halted to slake our thirst and cook the remainder of our dog mutton. Our animals' sufferings had nearly equalled our own. And while we ate and rested under the shade of a tree, it added much to our enjoyment to see the famished beasts regale themselves upon a plat of short wiry grass beside the stream. Some marks of dragging lodge poles along the now well defined trail, indicated to us that a portion of the Shoshonie or Snake tribe had lately left Brown's Hole. From this circumstance we began to fear what afterwards proved true, that our hopes of finding the Snakes at that post and of getting meat from them would prove fallacious. Our filthy meal being finished, we gathered

up our little caravan and moved forward at
a round pace for three hours, when the
bluffs opened before us the beautiful plain
of Brown's Hole. As we entered it we
crossed two cool streams that tumbled down
from the stratified cliffs near at hand on the
right ; and a few rods beyond, the whole
area became visible. The Fort, as it is
called, peered up in the centre, upon the
winding bank of the Sheetskadee. The
dark mountains rose around it sublimely,
and the green fields swept away into the
deep precipitous gorges more beautifully
than I can describe.

How glad is man to see his home again
after a weary absence! Every step becomes
quicker as he approaches its sacred portals ;
and kind smiles greet him ; and leaping
hearts beat upon his ; and warm lips press
his own. It is the holy sacrament of friendship. Yet there is another class of these
emotions that appears to be not less holy.
They arise when, after having been long
cut off from every habit and sympathy of
civilized life, long wandering among the
deep and silent temples of the eternal
mountains, long and hourly exposed to the
scalping knife of savages and the agonies of

starvation, one beholds the dwellings of
civilized men—kindred of the old Patriot
blood, rearing their hospitable roofs among
those heights, inviting the houseless, way-
worn wanderer to rest ; to relax the tension
of his energies, close his long watching
eyes, and repose the heart awhile among
generous spirits of his own race. Is not
the hand that grasps yours then, an honest
hand ? Does it not distil, by its sacred
warmth and hearty embrace, some of the
dearest emotions of which the soul is capable ; friendship unalloyed, warm, holy, and
heavenly ?

Thus it seemed to me, at all events,
as we rode into the hollow square and
received from St. Clair, the person in
charge, the hearty welcome of an old hunter to "Fort David Crockett." A room was
appropriated immediately for our reception,
our horses were given to the care of his
horse guard, and every other arrangement
within his means, was made, to make us
feel that within that little nest of fertility,
amid the barrenness of the great Stony
Range—far from the institutions of law
and religion—far from the sweet ties of
family relations, and all those nameless
endearing influences that shed their rich

fragrance over human nature in its cultivated abiding places—that there even could
be given us the fruits of the sincerest friendship.   Such kindness can be appreciated
fully by those only who have enjoyed it in
such places ; who have seen it manifested
in its own way ; by those only, who have
starved and thirsted in these deserts and
been welcomed, and made thrice welcome,
after months of weary wandering, to " Fort
David Crockett."

After partaking of the hospitality of Mr.
St. Clair, I strolled out to examine more
minutely this wonderful little valley.   It is
situated in or about latitude 42° north ;
one hundred miles south of Wind River
mountains, on the Sheetskadee (Prairie
Cock) River.   Its elevation is something
more than eight thousand feet above the
level of the sea. It appeared to be about six
miles in diameter ; shut in, in all direction,
by dark frowning mountains, rising one
thousand five hundred feet above the plain.
The Sheetskadee, or Green River, runs
through it, sweeping in a beautiful curve
from the north-west to the south-west part
of it, where it breaks its way through the encircling mountains, between cliffs, one thousand feet in height, broken and hanging as

if poised on the air. The area of the plain is thickly set with the rich mountain grasses, and dotted with little copses of cotton wood and willow trees. The soil is alluvial, and capable of producing abundantly all kinds of small grains, vegetables, &c., that are raised in the northern States. Its climate is very remarkable. Although in all the country, within a hundred miles of it, the winter months bring snows, and the severe cold that we should expect in such a latitude, and at such an elevation above the level of the sea, yet in this little nook, the grass grows all the winter; so that, while the storm rages on the mountains in sight, and the drifting snows mingle in the blasts of December, the old hunters here heed it not. Their horses are cropping the green grass on the banks of the Sheetskadee, while they themselves are roasting the fat loins of the mountain sheep, and laughing at the merry tale and song.

The Fort is a hollow square of one story log cabins, with roofs and floors of mud, constructed in the same manner as those of Fort William. Around these we found the conical skin lodges of the squaws of the white trappers, who were away on their " fall hunt," and also the lodges of a few

Snake Indians, who had preceded their tribe to this, their winter haunt. Here also were the lodges of Mr. Robinson, a trader, who usually stations himself here to traffic with the Indians and white trappers. His skin lodge was his warehouse ; and buffalo robes were spread upon the ground and counter, on which he displayed his butcher knives, hatchets, powder, lead, fish-hooks, and whisky. In exchange for these articles he receives beaver skins from trappers, money from travellers, and horses from the Indians. Thus, as one would believe, Mr. Robinson drives a very snug little business. And. indeed, when all the " independent trappers" are driven by approaching winter into this delightful retreat, and the whole Snake village, two or three thousand strong, impelled by the same necessity, pitch their lodges around the Fort, and the dances and merry makings of a long winter are thoroughly commenced, there is no want of customers.

These winters in Brown's hole are somewhat like winters among the mountains of New England, in the effects they produce on the rise and progress of the art of all arts—the art of love. For, as among the good old hills of my native clime, quiltings,

and singing-schools, and evening dances,
when the stars are shining brightly on the
snow crust, do soften the heart of the mountain lad and lassie, and cause the sigh and
blush to triumph over all the counsels of
maiden aunts and fortune-tellers ; so here
in this beautiful valley, and in the skin
lodge village of the Snakes, there are bright
evenings, beaming stars, and mellow moons,
and social circles for singing the wild dit-
ties of their tribe, and for sewing with the
sinews of the deer, their leggings, moccasins and buffalo robes, and for being be-
witched with the tender passion.

The dance, too, enlivens the village.
The musician chants the wild song, and
marks the time by regular beatings with
a stick upon a sounding board ; and
light heels, and sturdy frames, and buxom
forms respond to his call. To these, and
other gatherings, the young go, to see
who are the fairest, and best, and most
loved of the throng. Our friend Cupid
goes there too. Yes, Cupid at an Indian dance ! And there measuring bow
and arrow with those who invented them,
he often lays at his feet, I am told, the
proudest hawk's feather that adorns the
brow of Chief or Chiefess. For, on the

morning after the dance, it not unfrequently happens that he of the beard is compelled, by force of certain uneasy sensations about the heart, to apply to some beardless one for the balm of sweet smiles for his relief.

He does not wait for the calm hour of a Sunday night. Nor does he delay putting the question by poetical allusions to the violet and firmament. No! Calm hours and the poetry of nature have no charms for him. He wants none of these. Our friend Cupid has cast an arrow into his heart, bearded with the stings of irresistible emotion; and he seeks that mischievous fair one, her alone who selected the arrow and the victim; her alone who was a " particips criminis" in the loss of that great central organ of his life, called in the annals of Christian countries, " the heart." No! his course is vastly more philosophical and single-minded, (I mean no offence to my countrymen—none to you, ye Britons over the waters,) than the ginger-bread, sugar-candy courtships of Christian people. He first pays his addresses to his band of horses ; selects the most beautiful and valuable of them all, and then goes with his chosen horse to the lodge of his chosen

girl's father or mother, or if both these be
dead, to the lodge of her eldest sister, ties
the animal to the tent pole, and goes away.
After his departure, the inmates of the
lodge issue from it, and in due form examine
the horse, and if it appears to be worth as
much as the girl whom the owner seeks, an
interview is had, the horse taken by the
parents, or sister, as the case may be, and
the lover takes the girl. A fair business
transaction, you perceive, my readers—" a
quid pro quo"—a compensation in kind.

The girl, received in exchange for the
horse, becomes the absolute personal property of the enamoured jockey, subject to
be re-sold whenever the state of the market
and his own affection will allow. But if
those, whose right it is to judge in the
matter, are of opinion that the girl is worth
more than the horse, another is brought;
and if these are not enough, he of the beard
may bring another, or get Cupid to shoot
his heart in another direction.

There are many benefits in this mode of
obtaining that description of legal chattels
called a wife, over the mode usually
adopted among us. As for example : by
this mode there is a price given for a valuable article. Now to my apprehension, this
is an improvement upon our plan ; for it

removes entirely from certain old daddies, the necessity of disposing of their daughters by gift, to certain worthless, portionless young men, who are merely virtuous, talented, honest and industrious ; an evil of no small magnitude, as may be learned by inquiry in the proper quarter. But the Indian system of matrimony extirpates it. Wealth measures off affection and property by the peck, yard or dollar's worth, as circumstances require ; and no young lady of real genuine property, respectability and standing, and family, will think of placing her affections upon a talented, virtuous and industrious, promising and prosperous coxcomb of poverty ; nor, vice versâ, will a young man of these vulgar qualities have the unfathomable barefacedness to propose himself to a young lady of real genuine property respectability, property form, property face, property virtue, property modesty, and property intelligence.

No, bless the day ! such impudence will cease to interfere with the legitimate pretensions of those who are able—while they declare their passion mighty, unalterable and pure—to place in the hands from which they receive the dear object of their property love, the last quoted prices of the family stock.

But I pass to the consideration of another view of this matter which I deem, if possible, of still greater importance. As, if in disposing of young ladies in marriage, a valuation in money should be made of their property beauty, property modesty, property intelligence, &c., and required to be paid before marriage, the false opinion that honesty, probity, intelligence, integrity, virtue and respectability can exist without a property basis, would gradually fade away before the influence of our rich daddies' daughters. Oh the age that would then bless our earth! The piety of the church would fan itself in the property pew. The forum of jurisprudence would then echo to the lofty strains of property eloquence. The groves of Academus would breathe the wisdom of property philosophy. The easel of the artist would cast upon the canvas the inspirations of property genius. And music, and sculpture, and poetry, born in garrets, would give place to another race of these arts—a property race, that could be kept in one's apartments without compelling one to blush for their origin. We should then have a property fitness of things, that would place our property selves in a state of exalted property beatitude.

It is hoped that the Legislators of the world
will bestow upon this matter their most
serious attention, and from time to time
pass such laws as will aid mankind in
attaining this splendid and brilliant ex-
altation of our nature, when the precious metals shall be a universal measure
of value.

This is diverging. But after my reader
is informed that the only distinct aim I
proposed to myself in writing my journal,
was to keep the day of the month correctly,
and in other respects " keep a blotter,"
the transition from this strain of true philosophy, to a notice of the white men and
their squaws, will be thought easy and
natural.

If, then, a white man is disposed to take
unto himself a squaw among the Snakes, he
must conform to the laws and customs of
the tribe, which have been ordained and established for the regulation of all such
matters.   And, whether the colour in any
individual case be of black or white, does
not seem to be a question ever raised to
take it out of the rules.   The only difference is, that the property, beauty, &c. of
the whites frequently give them the preference on 'change, and enable them to

obtain the best squaws of the nation.
These connexions between the white trappers and squaws I am told, are the cause
of so many of the former remaining during
life in these valleys of blood.—They seem
to love them as ardently as they would
females of their own colour.

A trader is living there with a young
Eutaw squaw, through whose charms he has
forsaken friends, wealth and ease, and civilization, for an Indian lodge among all the
dangers and wants of a wilderness. This
gentleman is said to have a standing offer
of £140 for his dear one, whenever, in the
course of a limited time, he will sell her
graces. But it is believed that his heart
has so much to do with his estimation of
her value, that no consideration could induce him voluntarily to deprive himself of
her society.

The above anecdotes were related to
me during the first evening I spent at Fort
David Crockett. It was a bright ethereal
night. The Fort stood in the shade of the
wild and dark cliffs, while the light of the
moon shone on the western peaks, and cast
a deeper darkness into the inaccessible
gorges on the face of the mountains. The
Sheetskadee flowed silently among the al-

ders—the fires in the Indian lodges were
smouldering ; sleep had gathered every ani-
mate thing in its embrace. It was a night
of deep solitude. I enjoyed the lovely
scene till near midnight in company with
Mr. St. Clair; and when at last its excite-
ments and the thrilling pleasure of being
relieved from the prospect of death by
hunger allowed me to slumber, that gentleman conducted me to his own room and
bed, and bade me occupy both while I
should remain with him. He expressed
regret that he had so little provisions in the
Fort ;—a small quantity of old jerked meat ;
a little tea and sugar.

" But," said he, " share it with me as
long as it lasts. I have hunters out; they
will be here in ten or twelve days; you
have been starving; eat while there is any
thing left, and when all is gone we'll have
a mountain sheep, or a dog to keep off
starvation till the hunters come in."

My companions and guide were less
fortunate. We purchased all the meat
which either money or goods could induce
the Indians to sell. It amounted to one
day's supply for the company. And as
there was supposed to be no game within a
circuit of one hundred miles, it became

matter of serious inquiry whether we should seek it in the direction of Fort Hall, or on the head waters of Little Snake River, one hundred miles off our proper route to Oregon.

In the latter place there were plenty of fine, fat buffalo; but on the way to the other point there was nothing but antelope, difficult to kill, and poor. A collateral circumstance turned the scale of our deliberations. That circumstance was dog meat. We could get a supply of these delectable animals from the Indians; they would keep life in us till we could reach Fort Hall; and by aid thereof we could immediately proceed on our journey, cross the Blue Mountains before the snow should render them impassable, and reach Vancouver, on the lower Columbia, during the autumn. On the contrary, if we sought meat on the waters of Little Snake River, it would be so late before we should be prepared to resume our journey, that we could not pass those mountains until May or June of the following spring.

The dogs, therefore, were purchased; and preparations were made for our departure to Fort Hall, as soon as ourselves and our animals were sufficiently

recruited for the undertaking.   Meanwhile
my companions ate upon our stock of barking mutton.   And thus we spent seven
days—delightful days ; for although our
fare was humble and scanty, yet the flesh
began to creep upon our skeletons, our
minds to resume their usual vivacity, and
our hearts to warm again with the ordinary
emotions of human existence.

The trials of a journey in the western
wilderness can never be detailed in words.
To be understood, they must be endured.
Their effects upon the physical and mental
system are equally prostrating.   The desolation of one kind and another which meets
the eye every where ; the sense of vastness
associated with dearth and barrenness, and
of sublimity connected with eternal, killing frost ;—of loneliness coupled with a
thousand natural causes of one's destruction ; perpetual journeyings over endless
declivities, among tempests, through freezing torrents ; one half the time on foot,
with nothing but moccasins to protect the
feet from the flinty gravel and the thorns of
the prickly pear along the unbeaten way ;
and the starvings and thirstings wilt the
muscles, send preternatural activity into
the nervous system, and through the whole

animal and mental economy a feebleness, an irritability altogether indescribable.

At Fort David Crockett there were rest, and food, and safety ; and old Father Time, as he mowed away the passing moments and gathered them into the great garner of the Past, cast upon the Future a few blossoms of hope, and sweetened the hours, now and then, with a bit of information about this portion of his ancient dominion. I heard from various persons, more or less acquainted with the Colorado of the West, a confirmation of the account of that river given in the journals of previous days ; and also that there resides at the lower end of its great kenyon, a band of the Club Indians —very many of whom are seven feet high, and well proportioned ; that these Indians raise large quantities of black beans upon the sandy intervales on the stream ; that the oval-leaf prickly-pear grows there from fifteen to twenty feet in height ; that these Indians make molasses from its fruit ; that their principal weapon of warfare is the club, which they wield with amazing dexterity and force ; that they inhabit a wide extent of country north-west, and south-east of this lower part of the river ; that they have never been subdued by the

Spaniards, and are inimical to all white people. Subsequent inquiry in California satisfied me that this river is navigable only thirty or forty miles from its mouth, and that the Indians who live upon its barren banks near the Gulf, are such as I have described.

The Snakes, or Shoshonies, are a wandering tribe of Indians who inhabit that part of the Rocky Mountains which lies on the Grand and Green River branches of the Colorado of the West, the valley of Great Bear River, the habitable shores of the Great Salt Lake, a considerable portion of country on Snake River above and below Fort Hall, and a tract extending two or three hundred miles to the west of that post. Those who reside in the place last named, are said to subsist principally on roots ; they, however, kill a few deer, and clothe themselves with their skins. The band living on Snake River subsist on the fish of the stream, buffalo, deer, and other game. Those residing on the branches of the Colorado, live on roots, buffalo, elk, deer, the mountain-sheep, and antelope. The Snakes own many horses. These, with their thousands of dogs, constitute all the domestic animals among them. They have conical skin-lodges, a few camp-kettles, butcher-knives and guns. Many of them, however, still use the bow and arrow. In dress, they follow the universal Indian costume — moccasins, leggings, and the hunting-shirt. Nothing but the hair covers the head ; and this, indeed, would seem sufficient, if certain statements made in relation to it be true ; as that it frequently grows four and five feet in length, and in one case eleven feet. In these instances, it is braided and wound round the head in the form of a Turkish turban. If only two or three feet in length, it is braided on the female head in two queues, which hang down the back : on the male, it is only combed behind the ears, and lies dishevelled around the shoulders. The female dress differs from that of the male in no other respect than this : the shirt or chemise of the former extends down to the feet. Beaver, otter, bear and buffalo skins, and horses are exchanged by them with the Arrapahoes, and the Americans, and British traders, for some few articles of wearing apparel ; such as woollen blankets and hats. But as their stock of skins is always very limited, they find it necessary to husband it with much care, to obtain therewith a supply of tobacco, arms and ammunition.

From the first acquaintance of the whites
with them, these people have been remarkable for their aversion to war, and those
cruelties generally practised by their race.
If permitted to live in peace among their
mountains, and allowed to hunt the buffalo
—that wandering patrimony of all the
tribes—when necessity requires, they make
war upon none, and turn none hungry away
from their humble abodes. But these
peaceable dispositions in the wilderness,
where men are left to the protection of
their impulses and physical energies, have
yielded them little protection. The Blackfeet, Crows, Sioux and Eutaws have alternately fought them for the better right to
the Old Park, and portions of their Territory, with varied success ; and, at the present time, do those tribes yearly send predatory parties into their borders to rob them
of their horses. But as the passes through
which they enter the Snake country are becoming more and more destitute of game on
which to subsist, their visits are less frequent, and their number less formidable.
For several years, they have been in a
great measure relieved from these annoy-
ances.

From the time they met Lewis and Clark
on the head-waters of the Missouri to the

present day, the Snakes have opened their lodges to whites, with the most friendly feelings. And many are the citizens of the States, and the subjects of Britain, who have sought their villages, and by their hospitality have been saved from death among those awful solitudes. A guest among them is a sacred deposit of the Great Spirit. His property, when once arrived within their camp, is under the protection of their honour and religious principle ; and should want, cupidity, or any other motive, tempt any individual to disregard these laws of hospitality, the property which may have been stolen, or its equivalent, is returned, and the offender punished. The Snakes are a very intelligent race. This appears in the comforts of their homes, their well-constructed lodges, the elegance and useful form of their wardrobes, their horse-gear, &c.

But more especially does it exhibit itself in their views of sensual excesses and other immoralities. These are inhibited by immemorial usages of the tribe. Nor does their code of customs operate upon those wrong doings only which originate among a savage people. Whatever indecency is offered them by their intercourse with the

whites, they avoid. Civilized vice is quite as
offensive as that which grows up in their own
untrained natures. The non-use of intoxi-
cating liquor is an example of this kind.
They abjured it from the commencement of
its introduction among them. And they
give the best of reasons for this custom :—
" It unmans us for the hunt, and for defending ourselves against our enemies ; it
causes unnatural dissensions among ourselves ; it makes the Chief less than his
Indian ; and by its use, imbecility and ruin
would come upon the Shoshonie tribe."

Whatever difference of opinion may exist
among civilized men on this matter, these
Indians certainly reason well for themselves,
and, I am inclined to think, for all others.
A voice from the depth of the mountains—
from the lips of a savage—sends to our ears
the startling rebuke—" Make not, vend not,
give not to us the *strong water*. It pros-
trates your superior knowledge, your en-
larged capacities for happiness, your cultivated understandings.   It breaks your
strong laws ; it rots down your strong
houses ; it buries you in the filthiest ditch
of sin.   Send it not to us ; we would rather
die by the arrows of the Blackfeet."

The Crows are a wandering tribe, and

usually found in the upper plains around
the head-waters of the north fork of Great
Platte, Snake, and Yellowstone rivers.
Their number is estimated to be about five
thousand. They are represented as the
most arrant rascals among the mountains.
The traders say of them that "they have
never been known to keep a promise or do
an honourable act." No white man or
Indian trusts them. Murder and robbery
are their principal employments. Much of
their country is well watered, timbered, and
capable of yielding an abundant reward to
the husbandman.

The Blackfeet Indians reside on the Marias
and other branches of the Missouri above
the Great Falls. In 1828 they numbered
about two thousand five hundred lodges or
families. During that year they stole a
blanket from the American Fur Company's
steamboat on the Yellowstone, which had
belonged to a man who had died of the
small-pox on the passage up the Missouri.
The infected article being carried to their
encampment upon the "left hand fork of
the Missouri," spread the dreadful infection
among the whole tribe. They were amazed
at the appearance of the disease. The red
blotch, the bile, congestion of the lungs,

liver, and brain, were all new to their medicine-men; and the rotten corpse falling in
pieces while they buried it, struck horror
into every heart.   In their phrenzy and
ignorance they increased the number of
their sweat ovens upon the banks of the
stream, and whether the burning fever or
the want of nervous action prevailed; whether frantic with pain, or tottering in death,
they were placed in them, sweated profusely
and plunged into the snowy waters of the
river. The mortality which followed this
treatment was a parallel of the Plague in
London. They endeavoured for a time to
bury the dead, but these were soon more
numerous than the living. The evil-minded
medicine-men of all ages had come in a
body from the world of spirits, had entered
into them, and were working the annihilation of the Blackfeet race.

The Great Spirit had also placed the
floods of his displeasure between himself
and them. He had cast a mist over the
eyes of their conjurors, that they might not
know the remedial incantation. Their hunts
were ended; their bows were broken; the
fire in the Great Pipe was extinguished for
ever; their graves called for them; and the
call was now answered by a thousand dying

groans. Mad with superstition and fear,
brother forsook sister ; father his son ; and
mother her sucking child ; and fled to the
elevated vales among the western heights,
where the influences of the climate, operat-
ing upon the already well-spent energies of
the disease, restored the remainder of the
tribe again to health. Of the two thousand
five hundred families existing at the time
the pestilence commenced, one or more
members of eight hundred only survived its
ravages ; and even to this hour do the
bones of seven or eight thousand Blackfeet
lie unburied among the decaying lodges of
their deserted village, on the banks of the
Yellowstone. But this infliction has in no
wise humanized their blood-thirsty nature.
As ever before, they wage exterminating
war upon the traders and trappers, and the
Oregon Indians.

The Arrapahoes reside south of the
Snakes. They wander in the winter season
over the country about the head of the
Great Kenyon of the Colorado of the West,
and to a considerable distance down that
river ; and in summer hunt the buffalo in
the New Park, or " Bull Pen," in the " Old
Park" on Grand River, and in " Boyou Salade," on the south fork of the Platte. Their

number is not well ascertained. Some estimate it at three thousand, others more, and
others still less. They are said to be a
brave, fearless, thrifty, ingenious, and hospitable people. They own large numbers
of horses, mules, dogs, and sheep. The
dogs they fatten and eat. Hence the name
Arrapahoes—dog eaters. They manufacture the wool of their sheep into blankets of
a very superior quality. I saw many of
them; possessed one; and believe them to
be made with something in the form of a
darning-needle. They appeared to be
wrought, in the first time, like a fishing-
net; and on this, as a foundation, darned
so densely that the rain will not penetrate
them. They are usually striped or checked
with yellow and red.

There is in this tribe a very curious law
of naturalization; it is based upon property.
Any one, whether red or white, may avail
himself of it. One horse, which can run
with sufficient speed to overtake a buffalo
cow, and another horse or mule, capable of
bearing a pack of two hundred pounds,
must be possessed by the applicant.

These being delivered to the principal
chief of the tribe, and his intentions being
made known, he is declared a citizen of the

Arrapahoe tribe, and entitled to a wife and
other high privileges thereunto appertain-
ing. Thus recognized, he enters upon a life
of savage independence. His wife takes
care of his horses, manufactures his saddles
and bridles, and leash ropes and whips, his
moccasins, leggings, and hunting-shirts,
from leather and other materials prepared
by her own hands ; beats with a wooden
adze his buffalo robes, till they are soft and
pleasant for his couch ; tans hides for his
tent covering, and drags from the distant
hills the clean white-pine poles to support
it ; cooks his daily food and places it before
him. And should sickness overtake him,
and death rap at the door of his lodge, his
squaw watches kindly the last yearnings of
the departing spirit. His sole duty, as her
lord in life, and as a citizen of the Arrapahoe tribe, is to ride the horse which she
saddles and brings to his tent, kill the game
which she dresses and cures ; sit and
slumber on the couch which she spreads ;
and fight the enemies of the tribe. Their
language is said to be essentially the same
as that spoken by the Snakes and Cumanches.

This, and other tribes in the mountains,
and in the upper plains, have a custom, the

same in its objects as was the ceremony of
the " toga virilis " among the Romans.

When ripened into manhood, every young
man of the tribe is expected to do some act
of bravery that will give promise of his disposition and ability to defend the rights of
his tribe and family. Nor can this expectation be disregarded. So, in the spring of
the year, those of the age alluded to, associate themselves forty or fifty in a band, and
devote themselves to the duties of man's
estate in the following manner :—They take
leave of their friends, and depart to some
secret place near the woodlands ; collect
poles twenty or thirty feet in length, and
raise them in the form of a cone ; and cover
the structure so thickly with leaves and
boughs as to secure the interior from the
gaze of persons outside. They then hang a
fresh buffalo's head inside, near the top of
the lodge where the poles meet ; and below
this, around the sides, suspend camp-kettles,
scalps, and blankets, and the skin of a
white buffalo, as offerings to the Great Spirit.
After the lodge is thus arranged, they enter
it with much solemnity, and commence the
ceremonies which are to consecrate themselves to war, and the destruction of their
own enemies, and those of the tribe. The

first act, is to seat themselves in a circle round a fire built in the centre of the lodge, and "make medicine;" that is,—invoke the presence and aid of protecting spirits, by smoking the great mystic pipe.

One of their number fills it with tobacco and herbs, places upon the bowl a bright coal from the fire within the lodge, draws the smoke into his lungs, and blows it thence through his nostrils. He then seizes the stem with both hands, and leaning forward, touches the ground between his feet with the lower part of the bowl, and smokes again as before. The feet, and arms, and breast, are successively touched in a similar way; and after each touching, the sacred smoke is inhaled as before. The pipe is then passed to the one on his right, who smokes as his fellow has done. And thus the Great Pipe goes round, and the smoke rises and mingles with the votive offerings to the Great Spirit which are suspended above their heads. Immediately after this smoking is believed to be a favoured time for offering prayer to the Great Spirit. They pray for courage, and victory over their foes in the campaign they are about to undertake; and that they may be protected from the spirits of evil-minded medicine men. They then make a solemn and irrevocable vow, that if these medicine men do not make them sick —do not enter into their bosoms and destroy their strength and courage, they will never again see their relatives and tribe, unless they do so in garments stained with the blood of their enemies.

Having passed through these ceremonies, they rise and dance to the music of a war chant, till they are exhausted and swoon. In this state of insensibility, they imagine that the spirits of the brave dead visit them and teach them their duty, and inform them of the events that will transpire during the campaign. Three days and nights are passed in performing these ceremonies; during which time, they neither eat nor drink, nor leave the lodge. At early dawn of the fourth day they select a leader from their number, appoint a distant place of meeting; and emerging from the lodge, each walks away from it alone to the place of rendezvous. Having arrived there, they determine whose horses are to be stolen, whose scalps taken, and commence their march. They always go out on foot, wholly dependent upon their own energies for food and every other necessary. Among other things, it is considered a great disgrace to be long without meat and the means of riding.

It sometimes happens that these parties

are unable to satisfy the conditions of their
consecration during the first season ; and
therefore are compelled to resort to some
ingenious and satisfactory evasion of the obligations of their vow, or to go into winter
quarters till another opening spring allows
them to prosecute their designs.   The
trappers relate a case of this kind, which
led to a curious incident.   A war party of
Blackfeet had spent the season in seeking
for their enemies without success.   The
storms of approaching winter had begun to
howl around, and a wish to return to the
log fires and buffalo meat, and hilarities and
friendships of the camp of the tribe in the
high vales of the Upper Missouri, had become ardent, when a forlorn, solitary trapper
who had long resided among them, entered
their camp.   Affectionate and sincere greetings passed at the moment of meeting.

The trapper, as is the custom, was invited
to eat ; and all appeared friendly and glad.
But soon the Indians became reserved, and
whispered ominously among themselves. At
length came to the ear of the trapper high
words of debate in regard to his life.   They
all agreed that his white skin indubitably
indicated that he belonged to the " Great
Tribe of their natural enemies, and that

with the blood of a white upon their garments, they would have fulfilled the terms
of their vow, and could return to their
friends and tribe.   A part of them seriously questioned whether the sacred names
of friend and brother, which they had for
years applied to him, had not so changed
his natural relationship to them, that the
Great Spirit, to whom they had made their
vow, had sent him among them in the character which they themselves had given him
—as a friend and brother.   If so, they reasoned that the sacrifice of his life would only
anger Him, and by no means relieve them
from the obligations of their vow.

Another party reasoned that the Great
Spirit had sent this victim among them to
test their fidelity to Him.   He had indeed
been their friend ; they had called him brother, but he was also their natural enemy ;
and that the Great One to whom they had
made their vow, would not release them at
all from its obligations, if they allowed this
factitious relation of friendship to interfere
with obedience to Himself.   The other party
rejoined, that although the trapper was
their natural enemy, he was not one within
the meaning of their vow ; that the taking
of his life would be an evasion of its sacred

obligations, a blot upon their courage, and an outrage upon the laws of friendship ; that they could find other victims, but that their friend could not find another life. The other party rebutted, that the trapper was confessedly their natural enemy ; that the conditions of their vow required the blood of their natural enemy ; and that the Great Spirit had sufficiently shown His views of the relative obligations of friendship and obedience to Himself in sending the trapper to their camp.

The trapper's friends perceiving that the obstinacy of their opponents was unlikely to yield to reason, proposed as a compromise, that, since, if they should adjudge the trapper their enemy within the requirements of their vow, his blood only would be needed to stain their garments, they would agree to take from him so much as might be necessary for that purpose ; and that in consideration of being a brother, he should retain enough to keep his heart alive. As their return to their tribe would be secured by this measure, little objection was raised to it. The flint lancet was applied to the veins of the white man ; their garments were dyed with his blood ; they departed for their nation's village, and the poor trapper for the beaver among the hills.

My worthy old guide, Kelly, had often seen these medicine lodges. He informed me that many of the votive offerings, before mentioned, are permitted to decay with the lodge in which they are hung; that the penalty to any mortal who should dare appropriate them to his use was death. A certain white man, however, who had been robbed of his blanket at the setting in of winter, came upon one of these sacred lodges, erected by the young Arrapahoes which contained, among other things, a blanket that seemed well calculated to shield him from the cold. He spread it over his shivering frame, and very unadvisedly went into the Arrapahoe village. The Indians knew the sacred deposit, held a council, called the culprit before them, and demanded why he had stolen from the Great Spirit? In exculpation, he stated that he had been robbed; that the Great Spirit saw him naked in the wintry wind; pitied him; showed him the sacred lodge, and bade him take the blanket. "That seems to be well," said the principal chief to his fellow-counsellors. "The Great Spirit has an undoubted right to give away his own property;" and the trader was released.

Among the several personages whom I

chanced to meet at Brown's Hole, was an old Snake Indian, who saw Messrs. Lewis and Clark on the head waters of the Missouri in 1805.   He is the individual of his tribe, who first saw the explorers' cavalcade.   He appears to have been galloping from place to place in the office of sentinel to the Shoshonie camp, when he suddenly found himself in the very presence of the whites.   Astonishment fixed him to the spot.   Men with faces pale as ashes, had never been seen by himself or nation. "The head rose high and round, the top flat; it jutted over the eyes in a thin rim ; their skin was loose and flowing, and of various colours."   His fears at length overcoming his curiosity, he fled in the direction of the Indian encampment ; but being seen by the whites, they pursued and brought him to their camp ; exhibited to him the effects of their fire-arms, loaded him with presents, and let him go.   Having arrived among his own people, he told them he had seen men with faces pale as ashes, who were makers of thunder, lightning, etc. This information astounded the whole tribe.   They had lived many years, and their ancestors had lived many more, and there were many legends which spoke of many wonderful

things ; but a tale like this they never had
heard.

A council was, therefore, assembled to
consider the matter. The man of strange
words was summoned before it, and he re-
hearsed, in substance, what he had before
told to others, but was not believed. " All
men were red, and therefore he could not
have seen men as pale as ashes." " The
Great Spirit made the thunder and the lightning ; he therefore could not have seen
men of any colour that could produce these.
He had seen nothing ; he had lied to his
chief, and should die."

At this stage of the proceedings, the
culprit produced some of the presents
which he had received from the pale
men. These being quite as new to them
as pale faces were, it was determined
" that he should have the privilege of
leading his judges to the place where he
declared he had seen these strange people ;
and if such were found there, he should be
exculpated ; if not, these presents were to
be considered as conclusive evidence against
him, that he dealt with evil spirits, and that
he was worthy of death by the arrows of his
kinsfolks." The pale men, the thunder-
makers, were found, and were witnesses of

the poor fellow's story.   He was released ;
and has ever since been much honoured and
loved by his tribe, and every white man in
the mountains.   He is now about eighty
years old, and poor.   But as he is always
about Fort David Crockett, he is never
permitted to want.

CHAPTER II.

An Arrival from Fort Hall—An Account from Oregon—
Return of two of my companions to the States—A
startling Condition—An Indian Guide—A Farewell—
How a Horse studies Geology—A Camp—Dog Mut-
ton superseded—A Scene—Sheetskadee—Butes—
Desolation—Midnight Scene in the Mountains—In-
dian Jim and the Buffalo—Hungry Stomachs—A fat
Shot—Fine Eye-sight—An old Trapper picked up—
Beautiful Desert—" Hos, Hos"—Meek the Bear Kil-
ler—A wild Vale—Steamboat Spring—Natural Soda
Fountains—Neighbouring Landscape—A hard Drive
—Valley of Chasm—Nature's Vase—A heavy March
—Passing the Mountains—A charming Gorge — En-
trance into Oregon—The South Branch of the Co-
lumbia—Fort Hall and its Hospitalities.

17th. An event of great interest occurred
this day. It was the arrival of Paul Richardson and three of his companions from
Fort Hall. This old Yankee woodsman
had been upon one of his favourite summer
trips from St. Louis to the borders of Oregon. He had acted as guide and hunter to
a party of missionaries to the Oregon In-

dians. Several other persons from the western states had accompanied them : one with the lofty intention of conquering California ; and others with the intention of trading, farming, &c., on the lower Columbia ; and others to explore the Rocky Mountains, and the wonders of nature along the shores of the Pacific. The events of their tour were freely discussed. They had storms of hail and human wrath. The conqueror of California had been disposed to act the general before he had received his epaulettes ; had proved to be so troublesome that he was expelled from camp a short distance from the frontier, and obliged to ride, sleep, and eat, at a comfortable distance from his companions, during the remainder of the journey.

The missionaries, too, Messrs. Monger and Griffith, and their ladies, had had causes of irritability ; so that between all the conflicting feelings and opinions of the party, their little camp, it was said, was frequently full of trouble. Oregon also came under discussion. Mr. Richardson had travelled over the territory ; knew it well ; it was not so productive as New England ; fifteen bushels of wheat to the acre was an extraordinary crop ; corn and potatoes did not yield the seed planted ; rain fell incessantly five months of the year ; the remainder was unblessed even with dew ; the Indians and whites residing there had the fever and ague, or bilious fever, the year through ; that what little of human life was left by these causes of destruction, was consumed by musquitoes and fleas ; that the Columbia river was unfit for navigation— fit only for an Indian fish-pond. Such a description of Oregon (the part of the American domain represented by traders, trappers, and travellers, as most delightful, beautiful, and productive) was astonishing, unlooked-for, and discouraging. And did I not recollect that Mr. Richardson had reasons for desiring to increase the strength of his party through the dangerous plains towards the States, I should, after having seen Oregon, be at a loss to divine the purpose of such a representation of it.

18th. Mr. Richardson's description of Oregon had the effect of drawing off two of my companions. They had no evidence to oppose to his account ; he had resided two years in the Territory, and on the knowledge acquired by that means, had represented it to be in no sense a desirable place of abode. They therefore forsook the chase after a desert, and joined him for the green glades of the valley States. On the morning of the 18th, they left me. It was the most disheartening event which had befallen me on the journey. Oakley and Wood had stood by me in the trials and storms of the plains; had evinced a firmness of purpose equal to every emergency that had occurred, were men on whom reliance could be placed; humane men, always ready to do their duty promptly and cheerfully. It was painful therefore to part with them at a time when their services were most needed. Alone in the heart of the Rocky Mountains, a traveller through the range of the Blackfeet war parties, in bad health, no men save poor old Blair, and the worse than useless vagabond Smith, alias Carroll, to aid me in resisting these savages: I felt alone.

I was indeed kindly offered quarters for the winter at Brown's Hole ; but if I accepted them, I should find it impossible to return to the States the next year. I determined therefore to reach the Columbia river that season, be the risk and manner what it might. Accordingly I engaged a Snake Indian, whom the whites called " Jim," to pilot me to Fort Hall, the march to commence on the morning of the 19th—distance two hundred miles, compensation fifty loads of ammunition, and three bunches of beads.

There is in this valley, and in some other parts of the mountains, a fruit called bulberry. It is the most delightful acid in the vegetable kingdom; of the size of the common red currant, with larger seeds than are found in that fruit; colour deep red. It grows upon bushes eight or ten feet high, which in general appearance resemble a young beech tree. Of these berries I obtained a small quantity, had a dog butchered, took a pound or two of dried buffalo meat which Mr. St. Clair kindly gave me, purchased a horse of Mr. Robinson for the use of Blair, and on the morning of the 19th of August left the hospitalities of Fort David Crockett for the dreary waste and starving plains between it and Fort Hall. Blair, Smith, and my guide Jim, constituted my whole force. Numerous war-parties of Blackfeet and Sioux were hovering over my trail. If discovered by them, death was certain; if not, and starvation did not assail us, we might reach the waters of Snake river. At all events the trial was to be made; and at ten o'clock, A.M., we were winding our way up the Sheetskadee.

Of the regrets at leaving this beautiful

little valley, there was no one that I remember more vividly than that of parting with my old guide. Kelly was a man of many excellent qualities. He was brave without ostentation, kind without making you feel an obligation ; and preferred on all occasions the happiness of others to his own ease or safety. The river during the twelve miles' travel of the day, appeared to be about one hundred yards wide, a rapid current two feet deep, water limpid. The mountains on either side rose half a mile from the river in dark stratified masses, one thousand feet above the level of the stream. On their sides were a few shrub cedars. The lower hills were covered with the hated wild wormwood and prickly pear. The banks were of white clay, alternated with the loose light coloured sandy soil of the mountain districts. The rocks were quartz, red sand-stone, and lime-stone. Our camp was pitched at night on the high bank of the stream among the bushes ; and a supper of stewed dog-meat prepared us for sleep.

20th. At seven o'clock in the morning we had breakfasted and were on our way. We travelled three miles up the east bank of the river, and came to a mountain, through which it broke its way with a noise which indicated the fall to be great, and the

channel to be a deep rugged chasm.   Near
the place where it leaves the chasm, we
turned to the right, and followed up a
rough, deep gorge, the distance of five
miles, and emerged into a plain.   This
gorge had been formed by the action of a
tributary of Green River, upon the soft
red sand stone that formed the precipices
around.   It winds in the distance of five
miles to every point of the compass.   Along
much of its course also the cliffs hang over
the stream in such a manner as to render
it impossible to travel the water-side.
Hence the necessity, in ascending the
gorge, of clambering over immense precipices, along brinks of yawning caverns, on
paths twelve or fourteen inches in width,
with not a bush to cling to in the event of
a false step.   And yet our Indian horses
were so well used to passes of the kind,
that they travelled them without fear or
accident till the worst were behind us.

How delusive the past as a test of the
future !   I was felicitating myself upon our
good fortune, as the caravan wound its
way slowly over a sharp cliff before me,
when the shout from the men in advance,
" Well done, Puebla," made me hasten to
the top of the ridge.   My Puebla mare had
left the track.   Instead of following a wide,

well-beaten way down the mountain, she
in her wisdom had chosen to tread the
shelf of a cliff, which, wide at the place
where it sprang from the pathway, gradually became narrower, till it was lost in
the perpendicular face of the mountain.
She was under a high bulky back at the
time, and before she had quite explored the
nethermost inch of the interesting stratum
which she was disposed to trace to its lowest
dip, the centre of gravity was suddenly
thrown without the base, and over she
reeled, and fell ten or twelve feet among
broken rocks, then rolled and tumbled six
hundred feet more of short perpendicular
descents and inclined plains, into the
stream below. On descending and examining her, I found her horribly mangled,
the blood running from the nostrils, ears,
and other parts of the body. As it was
apparent she would soon die, I stripped her
of her packs and gear, drove her to a
plat of grass where she could find food,
should she need it, and left her to her
fate.

This accident being disposed of, we
emerged from this gorge, travelled over
barren gravelly plains, dotted with pyramidal hills of the same material, whose

sides were belted with strata of coarse
grey sand-stone. About four o'clock, P.M.,
Jim halted beside a little brook, and pointing ahead, said, "Wat, ugh, u—gh;" by
which I understood that the next water on
our way was too far distant to be reached that night ; and we encamped. The
scenery to the west was very beautiful. A
hundred rods from our camp, in that direction, rose an apparently perfect pyramid of
regular stratified black rocks, about six
hundred feet in height, with a basilar diameter of about eight hundred feet, and
partially covered with bushes. Beyond it,
some five hundred yards, crept away a
circling ridge of the same kind of rocks,
leaving a beautiful lawn between. And
still beyond, sixty miles to the south-west,
through a break in the hills that lay in clusters over the intervening country, a portion
of the Anahuac range was seen, sweeping
away in the direction of the Great Salt
Lake.

Jim had turned his horse loose as soon as
he saw we were disposed to encamp according to his wishes, and was away with his
rifle to the hills. In an instant he was on
their heights, creeping stealthily among
the bushes and rocks ; and the crack of

his rifle, and the tumbling of some kind of
game over the cliffs, immediately succeeded.
More nimble and sure of step than the
mountain goat, he sprang down again from
cliff to cliff, reached the plain, and the next
moment was in camp, crying "hos, ugh,
yes." I sent my horse and brought in his
game ; a noble buck antelope, of about
forty pounds weight. In consequence of
this windfall, our dog meat was thrown
among the willows for the behoof of the
wolves. My guide, poor fellow, had eaten
nothing since we left the Fort. His tribe
have a superstition of some kind which
forbids them the use of such meat. A
dog-eater is a term of reproach among
them. If one of their number incurs the
displeasure of another, he is called "Arrapahoe," the name of the tribe previously
described, who fatten these animals for
some great annual feast. Jim's creed,
however, raised no objections to the flesh
of the antelope. He ate enormously, washed
himself neatly, combed his long dark hair,
pulled out his beard with his right thumb
and left fore-finger nails, and "turned in."

21st. Twenty miles to-day. The ride of
the forenoon was over plains and hills of
coarse gravel, destitute of grass, timber,

or brush, the everywhere present wild
wormwood excepted ; that of the afternoon was among broken hills, alternately
of gravel and brown sand, here and there
dotted with a tuft of bunch grass. From
some few of the hills protruded strata of
beautiful slate. The bottom lands of the
river, even, were as barren as Sahara. The
only living things seen, were the small
prairie wolf, and flocks of magpie. This
bird inhabits the most dreary portions of
the mountains, and seems to delight in
making the parched and silent deserts more
lonely by its ominous croak of welcome to
its desolate habitation.

The raven indeed was about us, throwing his funeral wing upon the light of
the setting sun. In fine, to-day, as often
before, I found nothing in nature from
which to derive a single pulse of pleasure, save the vastness of desolate wastes,
the tombs of the washing of the flood!
Towards night, however, we were gratified
by finding a few decrepid old cotton-wood
trees, on the bank of the Sheetskadee,
among which to encamp. Our horses
having had little food for the last forty-
eight hours, devoured with eager appetite
the dry grass along the banks. Since

leaving Brown's Hole, our course had been
nearly due north.

22nd. Travelled up Green River about
three miles, crossed it three times, and
took to the hills on its western side. The
course of the river, as far as seen in this
valley, is nearly south ; the bottom and
banks generally of gravel ; the face of the
country a dry, barren, undulating plain.
Our course, after leaving the river, was
north-west by north. About two o'clock,
we struck Ham's Fork, a tributary of
Green River, and encamped near the water-
side. This stream probably pours down
immense bodies of water when the snow
melts upon the neighbouring highlands ;
for its channel, at the place where we
struck it, was half a mile in width, and two
hundred feet deep. Very little water is
said to run in it during July, August and
September. The current was three or four
inches in depth, a rod wide, and sluggish.
Three butes appeared in the north-east,
about twelve o'clock, fifteen miles distant.
One of them resembled a vast church, surmounted by a perpendicular shaft of rock,
probably three hundred feet in height.
The swelling base resembled in colour the
sands of this region. The rock shaft was
dark, probably basalt.

By the side of this, springing immediately from the plain, rose another shaft of rock, about one hundred and fifty feet high, of regular outline, and about fifteen feet in diameter. Seven or eight miles to the north, rose another bute, a perpendicular shaft, fifty or sixty feet in height, resting upon a base of hills which rise about three hundred feet above the plain. Beyond these butes, to the east, the country seemed to be an open plain. To the south of them extends a range of dark mountains, reaching far into the dimly-discerned neighbourhood of Long's Peak. The whole circle of vision presented no other means of life for man or beast than a few small patches of dry grass, and the water of the stream. Many of the sandy bluffs were covered with the prickly pear and wild wormwood. Generally, however, nothing green, nothing but the burnt, unproductive waste appeared, which no art of man can reclaim. Yet far in the north, the snowy peaks of Wind River Mountains, and to the south-west, a portion of the Anahuac ridge indicated that it might be possible to find along the borders of this great grave of vegetation, green vales and purling brooks to alleviate the desolation of the scene.

We travelled fifteen miles to-day, and

encamped upon the bank of the stream ;
cooked supper, and wrapping ourselves in
our blankets, with saddles for pillows, and
curtained by the starry firmament, slept
sweetly among the overhanging willows.
Near midnight, the light of the moon
aroused me. It was a lovely night. The
stars seemed smaller than they do in less
elevated situations, but not less beautiful.
For, although they are not so brilliant, they
burn steadily, brightly on the hours of night
in these magnificent wastes. It was midnight. The wolves are correct time-keepers.

I had scarcely viewed the delightful scene
around me, when these sleepless sentinels
of the deserts raised their midnight howl.
It rung along the chambers of the mountains, was, at intervals, taken up by kennel
after kennel, till, in the deep and distant
vales, it yielded again to the all-pervading
silence of night. This is one of the habits
that instinct has taught their race. As soon
as the first light of morning appears in the
east, they raise a *reveille* howl in the prairies
of the Western States which, keeping company with the hours, swells along the vast
plains from Texas to the sources of the
Mississippi, and from Missouri to the
depths of the Rocky Mountains. All day

they lurk in silence. At midnight, another howl awakens the sleeping wilderness— more horrible and prolonged; and it is remarkable with what exactness they hit the hour.

23d. We were up this morning before the light; and while the sun rose in the Great Gap, mounted our jaded horses for the day's ride. As we moved onward upon the elevated bluffs which border the river, the light of the morning showed the butes clearly on the eastern horizon. Jim paid little regard to the course of the stream to-day; but struck a bee line for some object, unseen by us, across the hills—at times among wild wormwood, at others among sharp, flinty stones, so thickly laid over the ground that none but an Indian horse would travel over them. We occasionally approached the stream, and were gratified with the appearance of a few solitary old cotton-wood trees on its banks. A poor, stinted shrub willow, too, made great effort here and there to prolong existence, but with little success. Even in one little nook, the wild rose, currant, and bulberry bushes had the effrontery to bear leaves.

About four o'clock, P.M., small patches of dry grass were seen in the ravines. On one

of these were five buffalo ; but they proved
to us more delightful to the sight than to
any other sense, since I was unable to induce my guide to halt and hunt them.
This apparently unpardonable stubbornness
was afterward explained. He had the only
animal which could run fast enough to approach them—he alone could ride him—
and having lost his right thumb, protested
that he could not discharge his piece from
a running horse. But having no interpreter with us to render his furious protesta-
tions intelligible, I attributed his unwillingness to lay in a supply of good meat here to
mere malicious indifference. At five o'clock,
we came upon a plat of excellent grass,
around a clump of yellow pines. Near this,
weary and hungry, we made our camp for
the night ; ate the half of the meat in our
possession —a mere mite—and gorged ourselves with wild currants, which grew plentifully among the pines, until the darkness
bade us cease. Course as yesterday : the
butes out of sight during the afternoon.
We supposed we had travelled twenty miles;
weather exceedingly warm.

24th. Rode on a fast trot till about three
o'clock, P.M. Made about twenty-five
miles. Our route lay over sandy and grav-

elly swells, and the bottom lands of Ham's Fork ; the latter, like the former, were well nigh destitute of vegetation.   When about to encamp, we had the excellent fortune to espy an antelope on a bluff hard by.   He fell before the well levelled rifle of our one-thumbed guide.   A fat one he was too ; just such an one as the imaginations of our hungry stomachs had all the day been figuring to themselves would afford a pleasant variety in the matter of starvation.   The circle of vision, the last day or two, had been very much circumscribed by the increasing size of the undulating bluffs, among which our way usually ran.   And from their tops, whenever we chanced to go over them, neither the Wind River Mountains nor the Anahuac range were visible.   In all directions, to the limit of sight, rolled away the dead, leafless, thirsty swells.   Wolves and ravens live among them ; but whence they derive subsistence is a difficult problem even for themselves to solve.   Their howlings and croakings evidently came from famished mouths.

25th. Fifteen miles to-day along the river; course as on the 24th, N.W. by W., among the bluffs that border the stream ; or if that were tortuous, we travelled from bend to bend, over the table lands on either side. In the valley of the stream, small groves of young and thrifty cotton-wood trees, currant bushes, and the black alder, gave us hopes of soon seeing the grasses and flowers, and the cool springs of the highlands, between us and the Great Beaver River. The day, however, was sultry; scarcely a breath of wind moved; the dust that rose from our track lay on the air as the smoke of a village does on a still May morning. So that these occasional appearances of vegetable life imparted less pleasure than they would have done if we had been able to see them through another medium than the dripping mud, manufactured from dust and perspiration.

Near mid-day, we crossed the river from its northern to its southern side, and were emerging from the bushes which entangled our egress, when Jim, uttering a shrill whoop, pointing to a solitary horseman urging his horse up the bluff a half mile below us. Beckoning him to us, we dismounted to allow our jaded animals to feed until he should arrive. In the style of a true mountaineer, he dashed up to us on a rapid gallop, greeting us with as hearty a shake of the hand as he could have bestowed

upon a brother, and asked our names and
destination ; said his name was " Midison
Gordon, an independent trapper, that he
was bound to Brown's Hole for his squaw
and ' possibles,' and was glad to see us," in
less time than is usually employed in saying
half as much ; and accepting an invitation
to encamp with us, he continued to express
his pleasure at seeing us, till our attention
was diverted from him by a halt for the
night.

These remnants of the great trapping
parties of the American Fur Company,
commonly make Brown's Hole their winter
quarters. Indeed, I believe the owners of
that post to be old trappers of the Company,
who, having lost all their relish for former
habits of life, by a long residence in the
mountains, have established themselves
there in order to bring around them, not
only the means of subsistence according to
their tastes, but their merry old companions
with their tales, jests, and songs, and honest
and brave hearts. Gordon, like all other
trappers whom I saw in the mountains, was
convinced that there were so few beaver, so
little meat, and so many dangers among
them, that " a white man had no business
there." He, therefore, was going for his

squaw and "possibles," preparatory to descending the Columbia to open a farm in the valley of the Willamette. He said that was also the intention of nearly all his fellow-trappers. They proposed to take with them their Indian wives and children, settle in one neighbourhood, and cultivate the earth, or hunt, as inclination or necessity might suggest, and thus pass the evening of their days among the wild pleasures of that delightful wilderness.

26th. Course north-west; distance twenty miles; sometimes on the banks of the river, and again over the swells, to avoid its windings. The country through which we passed to-day, was in some respects more interesting than any we had seen since leaving Brown's Hole. Instead of plateaux, baked and flinty, or hills of loose unproductive loam and sand, shorn by perpetual drought of flower, shrub, and tree, a journey of twenty miles over which would hardly cross grass enough to feed a dozen horses a single day, the slopes of a thousand spherical hills, as green as the fields of the States in May, sent forth the sweet fragrance of teeming vegetation; little streams ran away among the black, white, and orange pebbles; and the dandelion, anemone, and other flowers rejoiced in the spring-day breezes which crept over them. It was May indeed here. The snow had lately disappeared, and the rains had still later been falling, as they do in April in other places. The insects were piping the note of an opening year.

It was the dividing ridge between the tributaries of the Sheetskadee and Great Bear River; and yet not a ridge. When viewed from its highest points, it appeared an elevated plateau of slightly conical swells, so raised above the vast deserts on the east of it, as to attract the moisture of the clouds. The soil of this region is, however, poor,— not sufficient to bear timber. The grasses grow rankly over most of its surface; and those parts which are barren are covered with red or white sand, that contrasts beautifully with the matted green of other portions. In a word, it was one of those places among the mountains where all is pure. There the air is dense—the water cold—the vegetation fresh; there the snow lies nine months of the year, and when it eventually melts before the warm suns of June and July, the earth is clothed with vegetation almost in a day. About sunset, we descended a sharp declivity of broken rocks, and encamped on a small stream running north. My indefatigable Jim Shoshonie killed an antelope for our suppers. An unexpected favour this; for, from the representations given me of this part of my route, I expected to commence here a long-consuming fast, which would not be broken till I reached Fort Hall, or my grave.

27th. Our last night's encampment proved to have been on a branch of the Great Bear River—the principal, if not the only feeder of the Great Salt Lake. We started down along its verdant little valley about seven o'clock in the morning, and reached the main river about twelve at noon. It was twenty yards wide—water two feet deep, and transparent, current four miles per hour, bottom of brown sand and gravel. After feeding our animals, we descended the river till four o'clock, and halted on its banks for the night. We had travelled thirty miles. The mountains which hemmed in the valley were generally of a conical form, primitive, and often verdant. Their height varied from five hundred to two thousand five hundred feet above the level of the stream. The bottom lands were from one to three miles wide, of a loose, dry, gravelly soil, covered with withered bunch grass. By the water side grew various kinds of trees, as quaking-asp, black birch, and willows; also shrubs of various kinds, as the black alder, small willow, wild wormwood, black currant, and service berry. In the ravines of the mountains, groves of trees sometimes appeared peering up luxuriantly among the black projecting cliffs.

28th. An early rising, a hurried meal, and a rapid saddling and packing of horses, started us from camp at six o'clock. While girding our saddle animals, the last act done in breaking up camp in mountain life, Jim's eagle eye discerned in the distance down the river, " hos, hos." Indian like, for we had become such in our habits, we put new caps on our rifles, mounted quickly, and circled out behind a barricade of brushwood, in order to ascertain the number, colour, and purpose of such unceremonious intruders upon the territories of our solitude. Jim peered through the leaves with the utmost intensity of an Indian's vision. It was the place for war-parties of the Crows, Sioux, and Blackfeet; and this early appearance of individuals approaching our camp was a circumstance that scented strongly of bows and arrows. But suspense became certainty, a pleasant certainty, as Jim reined his horse from concealment, and galloped away to the stranger, now within rifle-shot of us.

A strong and warm shake of the hand, and various contortions of the face, and uncouth gestures of recognition between them, completed their interview, and the swarthy old trapper approached myself and men. He was no less a personage than the bear-killer, Meek, who figures in the St. Louis Museum, with the paws of an immense grisly bear upon his shoulders in front, the fingers and thumb of his left hand bitten off, while with his right hand he holds the hunter's knife, plunged deeply in the animal's jugular vein. He accosted me with, " Good morning, how are ye ?—stranger in the mountains, eh ?" And before I could make a monosyllabic reply, he continued, " Have you any meat ? Come, I've got the shoulder of a goat, (antelope) ; let us go back to your camp, and cook, and eat, and talk awhile." We were harnessed for the day's ride, and felt unwilling to lose the cool hours of the morning, and much more so to consume the generous man's last pound of meat. Thanking him,

therefore, for his honest kindness, we satisfied him with our refusal, by the assurance
that we had meat, and had already breakfasted.   On hearing that we were travelling
to the Columbia river, he informed us that
we   might   probably   go   down   with   the
Nez Percés Indians, who, he stated, were
encamped at the time on Salmon river, one
day's journey from Fort Hall.   He was on
his way to Brown's Hole for his squaw
and " possibles," with the design of joining
their camp.   These Indians would leave
their hunting grounds for their homes about
ten days from that date.

This was another remnant of the American Fur Company's trapping parties.   He
came to the mountains many years ago, and
has so long associated with Indians that
his manners much resemble theirs.   The
same wild, unsettled, watchful expression of
the eye, the same unnatural gesticulation
in conversation, the same unwillingness to
use words when a sign, a contortion of the
face or body, or movement of the hand will
manifest thought ;   in standing, walking,
riding, in all but complexion, he was an
Indian.   Bidding us good morning, and
wheeling away to the day's ride, he said,
" Keep your eye shining for the Blackfeet.

They are about the 'Beer Springs'; and stay, my white horse tired, one camp down the river; was obliged to ' *cache*' my pack and leave him ; use him if you can, and take him on to the Fort; and look here, I have told you I am Meek, the bear-killer, and so I am. But I think the boys at the museum in St. Louis might have done me up as it really was. The beast only jumped on my back, and stripped off my blanket ; scratched some, but didn't pull my shoulder blade off. Well, after he had robbed me of my blanket, I shoved my rifle against him, and blew out his heart. That's all—no fingers bitten off, no knifing; I merely drove a little lead into his palpitato ."

So saying, he spurred his weary animal to a trot, and was soon hidden among the underbrush of the intervales. Meek was evidently very poor. He had scarcely clothing enough to cover his body ; and while talking with us, the frosty winds which sucked up the valley, made him shiver like an aspen leaf. He reverted to his destitute situation, and complained of the injustice of his former employers, the little remuneration he had received for the toils and dangers he had endured on their account, &c., a complaint which I had heard from every trapper whom I had met on my journey. The valley opened wider as we pursued our way along its northern side ; the soil, the water, and vegetation much the same in quantity and quality as those which we had passed on the 27th. The mountains on either hand spread into rocky precipitous ridges, piled confusedly one above another in dark threatening masses. Among them hung, in beautiful wildness from the crevices of the cliffs, numerous shrub cedars.

The mountain flax was very abundant and ripe. The root resembled that of perennial plants, the fibres that of the annual bluebowl of the States, the flower the same, the seed vessel the same ; but the seeds themselves were much smaller, and of a very dark brown colour. This valley is the grain-field and root-garden of the Shoshonie Indians ; for there grow in it a number of kinds of edible roots, which they dig in August, and dry for winter use. There is also here a kind of grass, bearing a seed of half the size of the common rye, and similar in form. This they also gather, and parch and store away in leather sacks, for the season of want. These Indians had been gathering in their roots, &c., a few days previous to our arrival. I was informed, however, that the crop was barely sufficient to subsist them while harvesting it. But, in order to prevent their enemies from finding whatever might have escaped their own search, they had burned over large sections of the most productive part. This day's ride was estimated at thirty miles. Our camp at night was in a dense copse of black alders by the water-side. Ate our last meat for supper—no prospect of getting more until we should arrive at Fort Hall, four days' ride.

29th. Up with the sun and on march. After an hour's ride, we came upon Meek's white horse. He came to us on as fast a gallop, and with as noisy a neighing as if Zimmerman had never dipt his quill in solitude, and wrote the laws for destroying nature, for nature's good. Jim now put spur to his noble animal, with the regularity of the march of the tread-mill. And, by way of apology for his haste, pointed to the ground, and laying his head on one shoulder, and snoring, said, " u—gh, ugh," which being interpreted, meant that our next snoring place was a very, very long day's journey away. And one acquainted with Indian firmness, would have read in

E 2

his countenance, while making this communication, a determination to reach it before
night-fall, whatever might be the consequences. And so we did. At sunset our
camp kettle was bubbling over the bones of
a pelican at the " Steamboat spring." The
part of the valley seen to-day was generally
covered with a stout coat of bunch grass.
This, and other indications, led me to suppose it fertile. Yet it appeared question-
able if it would yield the ordinary fruits of
agriculture without being irrigated.

I noticed, however, during the day's ride, a
number of points at which the waters of the
river might be conducted over very large
tracts of excellent soil. The scarcity of
fencing timber appeared an obstacle, certainly ; but other than this, there seemed to
me no considerable cause of doubt that the
valley of the Great Bear River will, in the
course of time, become one of the most
prosperous abodes of cultivated life. Its
situation, so remote from either ocean,
only increases our expectation of such an
event, when it is recollected that the most
practicable waggon route between the States
and Oregon Territory and the Californias,
runs through it.

The north end of the Great Salt Lake is

thirty miles from our present encampment, and the mountains on the borders of the valley are more abrupt and craggy, the water of the stream more abundant, and the soil more productive, than in the part already described. A number of creeks also entering the main stream from the East, open up among the black heights a number of lesser and charming vales; and around the union of the river with the Lake are excellent water, soil and timber, under skies of perpetual spring. Of the Lake itself I heard much from different individuals who had visited different portions of its coast.

The substance of their statements, in which they all agree, is that it is about two hundred miles long, eighty or one hundred wide; the water exceedingly heavy; and so salt, say they in their simple way, that pieces of wood dipped in it and dried in the sun are thickly frosted with pure white salt; that its coasts are generally composed of swells of sand and barren brown loam, on which sufficient moisture does not fall to sustain any other vegetation than the wild wormwood and prickly pear; that all attempts to go round it in canoes have, after a day or two of trial, been aban-

doned for want of fresh water; that the
Great Bear River is the only considerable
stream putting into it; that high land is
seen near the centre of it;—but whether
this be an island or a long peninsula there
was a difference of opinion among my infor-
mants.   The valleys of the Great Bear
River and its tributaries, as well as the
northern portion of the Lake, are supposed
to be within the territory of the States.

The immediate neighbourhood of our encampment is one of the most remarkable in
the Rocky Mountains.   The facts that the
trail to Oregon and California will for ever
of necessity, pass within three hundred
yards of the place where our camp fire is
burning; that near this spot must be erected
a resting-place for the long lines of caravans
between the harbours of the Pacific and the
waters of the Missouri, would of themselves
interest all who are witnessing the irresistible movements of civilization upon the
American continent.   But this spot has
other objects of interest: its Geology and
its Mineralogy, and I might well say the
Chemistry of it, (for there are laboratories
and gases here in the greatest profusion), will
hereafter occupy the attention of the lovers
of these sciences.   The Soda Springs, called

by the fur traders Beer Springs, are the
most remarkable objects of the kind
within my knowledge. They are situated on
the north-west side of the river, a few rods
below a grove of shrub cedars, and about two
hundred yards from the shore. There are
six groups of them; or in other words,
there are six small hollows sunken about
two feet below the ground around, of circular form, seven or eight feet in diameter, in
which are a number of fountains sending
up large quantities of gas and water, and
emitting a noise resembling the boiling of
immense cauldrons. These pools are
usually clear, with a gravelly bottom. In
some of them, however, grow bogs or has-
socks of coarse grass, among which are
many little wells, where the water bubbled
so merrily that I was tempted to drink at
one of them. But as I proceeded to do so,
the suffocating properties of the gas instantly drove me from my purpose. After
this rebuff, however, I made another attempt
at a more open fountain, and drank with
little difficulty.

The waters appeared to be more highly
impregnated with soda and acid than
those of Sarotoga; were extremely pleasant to the taste, and fumed from the

stomach like the soda water of the shops. Some of them threw off at least four gallons of gas a second. And although they cast up large masses of water continually, for which there appeared no outlet, yet at different times of observation I could perceive no increase or diminution of the quantity visible. There are five or six other springs in the bank of the river just below, the waters of which resemble those I have described. One of them discharges about forty gallons a minute.

One fourth of a mile down stream from the Soda Spring, is what is called " The Steamboat Spring." The orifice from which it casts its water is in the face of a perpendicular rock on the brink of the stream, which seems to have been formed by the depositions of the fountain. It is eight inches in diameter. Six feet from this, and on the horizontal plane of the rock, is another orifice in the cavern below. On approaching the spring, a deep gurgling, hissing sound is heard underground. It appears to be produced by the generating of gas in a cavernous receiver. This, when the chamber is filled, bursts through another cavern filled with water, which it thrusts frothing and foaming into the stream. In passing the smaller orifice, the pent gas escapes with very much the same sound as steam makes in the escape-pipe of a steam-boat. Hence the name. The periods of discharge are very irregular. At times, they occur once in two, at others, once in three, four or five minutes. The force of its action also is subject to great variation. Those who have been there, often say that its noise has been heard to echo far among the hills. When I visited it I could not hear it at the distance of two hundred yards. There is also said to be a difference at different times in the temperature of the water. When I examined it, it was a little above blood heat. Others have seen it much higher.

The most remarkable phenomenon connected with these springs, remains yet to be noticed. The whole river, from the Steamboat spring to the Soda Springs, (a distance of more than a fourth of a mile), is a sheet of springs, thousands in number, which bursting through two feet of superincumbent running water, throw their foaming jets, some six inches, and some less, above the surface. The water is much the same in its constituent qualities, as that of the Soda springs.

E 3

There are in the immediate vicinity of the Steamboat Spring, and on the opposite side of the river numerous rocks with orifices in their centres, and other evidences of having been formed by intermittent springs that have long ago ceased to act.

The scenery around these wonderful fountains, is very wild. To the east northeast, opens up the upper valley of Great Bear River, walled in on either side by dark primitive mountains, beetling over the vale, and towering on the sky. To the south south-west sweeps away the lower valley.— On either side of it rise lofty mountains of naked rocks, the wild sublimity of which contrasts strikingly with the sweet beauty of the stream and vale below.

Although statements in regard to what shall transpire in the future, are always a work more befitting a seer than a journalist, yet I cannot forbear expressing the belief that the healthiness and beauty of their locality—the magnificence of the scenery on the best routes to them from the States and from the Pacific, the manifest superiority of these waters over any others, will cause "The Soda Springs" to be thronged with the gay and fashionable of both sides of the continent.

30th. Our sleep had been interrupted at midnight by the blazing fires of an Indian encampment on a neighbouring hill. And once awakened by such a cause, the tracks of a war party, probably of Blackfeet, which we had crossed during the day, were sufficient to put us on duty the remainder of the night. At early dawn, we saddled and moved in silence a few hundred yards down the river, turned to the right around the Bute in the rear of the Steamboat spring, entered the " Valley of chasms," and soon brought the mountains on its northern border, between us and our suspicious neighbours.

This valley derives its name from the numerous cracks or chasms in the volcanic rocks on which it rests. They are so wide and deep that the natives, for many miles at the lower part of it, have been obliged to run their trail over the lower swells of the hills on its north-western side. Up this trail Jim rode on a brisk trot, beckoning us, in an ominous manner to follow, and keep in a body near him. The " cut rock" and scoriæ lay every where, and crippled the poor animals at almost every step. Onward he led us, with all the speed which the severest inflictions of spur and whip could

produce, till the shutting in of night deposited us among the willows on the stream of
the valley, forty miles from our last night's
encampment. The rapidity of our travelling to-day, allowed me little time to examine this singular valley. I noticed merely
that it was, like the intervales of Bear River,
covered with bunch-grass, which the thirsty
suns of summer had dried to hay. A curious gas spring also attracted my attention
about nine o'clock in the morning. Its
bubbling and its beautiful reservoir appeared to arouse the admiration even of my
dogged guide Jim : he halted to look at it.
Jim, for the first time since I had had
the honour of his acquaintance, absolutely
stopped to look at, and admire a portion
of the earth. It was a fine specimen of
Nature's masonry. The basin was about
six feet in diameter ; the bottom a circular
horizontal plane ; around the edge rose a
rim or flanche, eight inches in height ; all
one solid rock. In the centre of the bottom
arose the gas and water : the latter was six
inches deep, limpid, and slightly acid. This
fountain was situated a few rods to the right
of the trail.

31st. We took to our saddles, and in
three hours reached the foot of the moun-

tains which divide the " Valley of chasms"
from Snake River.   There is a wide depression through the heights here of so gentle a
declination, that loaded waggons can pass
from one valley to the other without difficulty.   Up this we turned.   It was covered
with green grass and shrubs and trees,
among which a little brook was whispering
to the solitude.

The small birds, too, were chirping
among the bright flowers and bending
boughs ; and on either hand, as if to
guard so much loveliness from the winds of
surrounding desolation, the black crags rose
and frowned one thousand five hundred feet
in air.   But hunger!!   Every bud was fed;
every bird had its nourishment ; the lizards
even were not starving.   We were.   When
about half way up the gorge, one of Smith's
horses tired and refused to go farther.   The
fellow's wound, received in the plains, had
healed ; and with strength from time to
time, his petty tyranny towards his animals
increased till being entirely recovered, he
seemed to have resumed a degree of malignity towards them whenever they did not
chance to comprehend his wishes, or were
unable to comply with them, that would be
incredible if described.   In this case, he

cut a strong goad ; and following the slow steps of the worn-out animal, struck her lengthwise over the almost denuded ribs as frequently and as long as he had strength to do it ; and then would rest and strike again with renewed vengeance, until his beast dropped her head and received his blows without a movement. Remonstrance, and the astonished gazing of my savage guide, only increased his severity. And thus he continued to beat the poor animal, till, being convinced against his will, that he even could not make a dying horse heed his command, he bestowed upon her a farewell kick and curse and left her.

About four o'clock we stood on the high ground which divides the waters of the little brook which we had followed up, from a small head stream of Portneuf. The valley of the great southern branch of the Columbia, was spread out before us. Slaking our thirst at a cool spring, we travelled five miles down the mountain, and encamped in sight of the Trois Butes. When we halted, I was two much exhausted with hunger and fatigue to unsaddle my horse. We had been on short allowance most of the time since leaving Fort David Crockett. The day on which we arrived at the Soda Springs, I ate

the eighth part of a pelican; the two last
past days, nothing. But I suffered less
from the gnawings of hunger than I had on
the previous night. A deadly stupor per-
vaded the gastric and nervous systems; a
sluggish action of the heart, a dimness of
vision and painful prostration of every
energy of life were creeping upon me. After
a little rest, however, I crept to the bushes,
and after a long search, found two red rose-
buds! These I gladly ate, and went to my
couch to dream of feasts.

The 1st of September was a fine day.
The sun was bright and unclouded, as he
came in his strength over the eastern mountains, and awakened us from our slumbers
among the alders on the bank of Portneuf.
Hunger, indeed, was still gnawing at our
vitals. But sleep had banished weariness,
and added something to the small stock of
our remaining strength; and the recollection of past perils—perils of floods, of tempests, of Indian foes—death threatened at
every step during a journey of three months
in the plains and mountains—the inspiring
view of the vale of the great southern branch
of the Columbia, so long promised us in
hope along our weary way—the fact that we
were in Oregon, unmoored the mind from

its anxieties, and shed over us a gladness
which can only be comprehended by those
who, having suffered as we had, have viewed
as we did, from some bright height, their
sufferings ended, in the rich, ripe possession
of the objects so ardently sought. We were
in Oregon. Fort Hall lay in the plain before us. Its hospitalities would be enjoyed
ere sunset. Our wardrobes were overhauled,
our razors put on duty, our sun-burnt frames
bathed in the Portneuf; and equipped in
our best, our hearts beat joyfully back the
rapid clattering of our horses' hoofs on the
pavements of the mountains, as we rushed
to the plains. An hour among the sands
and wild wormwood, an hour among the
oozing springs, and green grass around
them, an hour along the banks of Saptin
River, and we passed a line of timber
springing at right angles into the plain;
and before us rose the white battlements of
Fort Hall!

As we emerged from this wood, Jim
intimated that we should discharge our
rifles; and as we did so, a single armed
horseman issued from the gate of the Fort,
approached us warily, and skulking among
the copses, scanned us in the most inquisi-
tive manner. Having satisfied himself at

last that our skins were originally intended to be white, he came alongside ; and learning that we were from the States ; that we had no hostile intentions ; that we knew Mr. Walker to be in the Fort, and would be glad to have our compliments conveyed to him, he returned ; and Mr. Walker immediately appeared. A friendly salutation was followed by an invitation to enter the Fort ; and a " welcome to Fort Hall," was given in a manner so kind and obliging, that nothing seemed wanting to make us feel that we were at home. A generous flagon of Old Jamaica, wheaten bread, and butter newly churned, and buffalo tongues fresh from the neighbouring mountains, made their appearance as soon as we had rid ourselves of the equipage and dust of journeying, and allayed the dreadful sense of starvation.

CHAPTER III.

The Rocky Mountains and their Spurs—Geography of
the Mountain Region — Wyeth — The Outset —
The Beaver Catcher's Bride — Trois Butes — Ad-
dition from a Monastery — Orisons — A Merry
Mountain Trapper — Root Diggers — Enormous
Springs—Volcanic Hearths and Chasms—Carbo—An
old Chief—A Bluff—Boisais River—Incident of Trade
—The Bonaks—The Dead Wail—Fort Boisais, its
Salmon, Butter and Hearty Cheer—Mons. Payette—
Curiosity—Departure—Passing the Blue Mountains
—The Grandeur of them—Their Forests, Flowers,
and Torrents—Descent of the Mountains—Plain, a
Christian Crane—Arrival at Dr. Whitman's Mission
—Wallawalla—People — Farm— Mill —Learning—
Religion—Mr. Ermitinger —Blair—Nez Percés —
Racing— Indian Horse Training — Sabbath and its
joys in the Wilderness.

It will not be uninteresting while pausing
here, and making preparations to descend
Snake, Lewis, or Saptin river, to lead my
readers back over that portion of my journey which lay among the mountains. I do
not design to retrace my steps here, however, in order again to attempt a description
of sufferings which can never be described.
They are past; and let their remembrance

die. But a succinct account of the region lying west of the Anahuac ridge, and between latitudes 39° and 42° north — its mountains, its plains, its rivers, &c , will, I persuade myself, be new, and not without interest to the reader.

James' Peak, Pike's Peak, and Long's Peak, may be called the outposts of a lofty range of rocky mountains, which, for convenience in description, I have called Long's Range, extending nearly due north from the Arkansas, in latitude 39°, to the Great Gap in latitude 42° north.

The range is unconnected with any other. It is separated from the Wind River Mountains by the Great Gap or Great Southern Pass, and from the Great Anahuac Range by the upper valleys of the Arkansas, those of the South Fork of the Platte, and those of the Green and Grand rivers. Two spurs spring off from it to the west: the one from James' Peak, the other from Long's Peak. These spurs, as they proceed westward, dip lower and lower till they terminate—the first in the rough cliffs around the upper waters of the Arkansas, and the latter in spherical sand-hills around the lower waters of Grand river. The Anahuac Mountains were seen from about latitude 39° to

42° north. This range lies about two hundred miles west of Long's Range, and between latitude 39 and 40°, has a general course of north north-west. It appeared an unbroken ridge of ice and snow, rising in some points, I think, more than fifteen thousand feet above the level of the sea. From latitude 41° it tends to the north-west by west, past the north-eastern shore of the Great Salt Lake to the northern end of it; and thence west-wardly to a point south of Portneuf, where it unites with the range of the Snowy Mountains.

The Snowy Mountains are a transverse range or spur of the Rocky Mountains, which run from the Wind River Mountains, latitude 42° north, in nearly a right line to Cape Mendocino, latitude 40°, in Upper California. Many portions of this range, east as well as west of Fort Hall, are very lofty, and covered with perpetual snow. About one hundred miles from the coast of the Pacific it intersects that range of snowy peaks called the President's Range, which comes down from Puget's sound, and terminates in the arid plains about the mouth of the Colorado of the West.

The Wind River Mountains are a spur which shoots from the great northern chain, commonly called the Rocky Mountains, in latitude 42° and odd minutes north; and running in a south-easterly direction into the Great Prairie Wilderness, forms the northern wall of the Great Gap or Great Southern Pass.

On the northern side of the Wind River Peaks, are the sources of Jefferson, Madison, and Gallatin rivers; on the south-eastern side rises the Sweetwater, the north-westernmost branch of the North Fork of the Great Platte; on the southern side the Sheetskadee or Green river, the northern branch of the Colorado of the West; on the north-western side and north of the Snowy Mountains, spring down the Saptin, Snake, or Lewis river, the great southern branch of the Columbia.

On the western side of Long's Range, rises the Grand river, the principal branch of the Colorado of the West. It furnishes four times the quantity of water that Green river does. Further south, in the vicinity of James' Peak, and on the west side of this range, rises the South Fork of the Great Platte.

Close under the eastern base of the Anahuac or Great Main Ridge, and nearly in latitude $39\frac{1}{2}°$ north, are the sources of the Arkansas.

The immense parallelogram lying within these ranges of mountains, may be described by saying that it is a desert of arid plains and minor mountains. And if this general appellation be qualified by the accounts given on previous pages of Boyou Salade, Old Park, &c. very small portions of the whole area, the description will be complete.

Fort Hall was built by Captain Wyeth, of Boston in 1832, for the purposes of trade with the Indians in its vicinity. He had taken goods into the lower part of the Territory, to exchange for salmon. But competition soon drove him from his fisheries to this remote spot, where he hoped to be permitted to purchase furs of the Indians without being molested by the Hudson's Bay Company, whose nearest post was seven hundred miles away.

In this he was disappointed. In pursuance of the avowed doctrine of that company, that no others have a right to trade in furs west of the Rocky Mountains, whilst the use of capital and their incomparable skill and perseverance can prevent it, they established a fort near him, preceded him,

followed him, surrounded him every where,
and cut the throat of his prosperity with
such kindness, and politeness, that Wyeth
was induced to sell his whole interest, exist-
ent and prospective, in Oregon, to his generous but too indefatigable, skilful, and
powerful antagonists.

From what I saw and heard of Wyeth's
management in Oregon, I was impressed
with the belief that he was, beyond comparison, the most talented business-man from
the States that ever established himself in
the Territory.

The business of this post consists in exchanging blankets, ammunition, guns, tobacco, &c., with the neighbouring Indians,
for the skins of the beaver and land otter;
and in furnishing white men with traps,
horses, saddles, bridles, provisions, &c., to
enable them to hunt these animals for the
benefit and sole use of the owners, the
Hudson's Bay Company. In such cases the
horses are borrowed without price; the other
articles of the " outfit" sold on credit till
the termination of the hunt; and the only
security which the Company requires for the
return of their animals, is the pledge of
honour to that effect, and that the furs taken
shall be appropriated at a stipulated price
to the payment of arrears.

Goods are sold at this establishment fifty per cent lower than at the American posts. White trappers are paid a higher price for their furs than is paid the Indians; are charged less for the goods which they receive in exchange; and are treated in every respect by this shrewd Company with such uniform justice, that the American trappers even are fast leaving the service of their countrymen, for the larger profits and better treatment of British employment. There is also a company of men connected with this Fort, under the command of an American mountaineer, who, following various tribes in their migratory expeditions in the adjacent American and Mexican domain, collect whatever furs may chance to be among them.

By these means, and various others subsidiary to them, the gentlemen in charge of this trading establishment, collected, in the summer of 1839, more than thirty packs of the best beaver of the mountains.

We spent the 2d and 3d most agreeably with Mr. Walker, in his hospitable adobie castle; exchanged with him our wearied horses for fresh ones; and obtained dried buffalo meat, sugar, cocoa, tea, and corn meal, a guide, and every other necessary within that gen-

tleman's power to furnish for our journey to
Wallawalla. And at ten o'clock, A. M., of the
4th of September, we bade adieu to our
very obliging countryman, and took to our
saddles on the trail down the desert banks
of the Saptin. As we left the Fort, we
passed over the ground of an affray, which
originated in love and terminated in death.
Yes, love on the western declivity of the
Rocky Mountains! and love of a white man
for an Indian dame!

It appeared that a certain white trapper
had taken to himself a certain bronze dam-
sel of the wilderness to be his slave-wife,
with all the solemn ceremonies of purchase and payment for the same in sundry horses, dogs, and loads of ammunition, as required by the custom in such
affairs governing; and that by his business
of trapping for beaver, &c., he was, soon
after the banns were proclaimed, separated
from his beloved one, for the term of three
months and upwards, much against his tender inclination and interest, as the following
showeth: for during the terms of his said
absence, another white man, with intent to
injure, &c., spoke certain tender words unto
the said trapper's slave-wife, which had the

effect to alienate from him the purchased and rightfully possessed affections of his slave-spouse, in favour of her seducer. In this said condition did the beaver-catcher find his bride when he came in from the hunt. He loaded his rifle, and killed the robber of his heart. The grave of the victim is there—a warning to all who would trifle with the vested rights of an American trapper in the love of an Indian beauty.

We made about ten miles, and halted for the night. Our guide displayed himself a five feet nine inch stout Wallawalla. He had been in the service of the Hudson Bay Company many years, and was consequently assiduous and dutiful. Yes, consequently so; for neither Indian nor white man is long in their service without learning his place, and becoming active and faithful in doing his duty. As soon as we entered camp, our pack-horses were stripped of their burdens, and turned loose to feed; wood was gathered, and a fire blazing under the kettles, and " all out door" immediately rendered as comfortable to us, as skies spangled with stars, and earth strewn with snowy sand could be made. Wallawalla was a jolly oddity of a mortal. The frontal region of his head had been pressed in infancy most aristocratically into the form of the German idiots; his eyes were forced out upon the corners of the head; his nose hugged the face closely like a bunch of affectionate leeches; hair black as a raven, and flowing over a pair of herculean shoulders; and feet——but who can describe that which has not its like under the skies. Such was Carbo, our Palinurus over the burnt plains of Snake River.

The short ride of the day had shown us the western limit of the partial fertility about Fort Hall. The earth had begun to be red, burnt, and barren; grass, sparse and dry; the shrubs and cotton-woods stinted and shrivelled.

The plain of the Trois Butes is situated between the Snowy mountain range on the south, and another ridge which, diverging from it above the sources of the Saptin River, follows that stream down to the Blue Mountains near Wallawalla. This plain by experiment is found to be eight thousand feet above the level of the sea. In the vicinity of the post, there is an abundance of grass for the subsistence of many thousands of animals. The soil, in various parts of it, also appears well adapted to the cultivation of the small grains and esculent roots. But

the fact that frosts occur almost every month
of the year, shows the extent to which the
arable sections can be rendered available
for such purposes.

The Trois Butes rise on the plain fifteen
or twenty miles east of the Fort. They
are pyramidal peaks, probably of volcanic
origin, of two thousand feet in height above
the plain, and twelve thousand feet above the
level of the sea. Around their dark bases
grow evergreen trees ; from their sides burst
small brooks, rendering verdant strips of the
plain which radiate beautifully in all directions from them ; and over all, during most
of the year, hang their crests of glittering
snows ! East of the Butes, vegetation continually decreases till it ceases in the black
crags which embosom the head streams of
the river.

On the 5th, travelled thirty miles down
the western bank of the river ; soil sandy
and volcanic, bearing wild wormwood—in
fact a desert ; crossed a number of small
streams putting into the Saptin ; on these a
little bunch of grass, and a few alders and
willows, tried to grow. Whilst baiting at
noon, we were agreeably surprised with an
addition to our company, of a young Swiss
trapper, eight years in the mountains ; he

learned the silversmith business when in
youth ; afterwards entered a monastery and
studied Latin, &c., for the order of Priests ;
ran away from the monastery, entered the
French army, deserted, and came to America ; sickened, was visited by a Roman priest
who had been a classmate with him at the
monastery ; and having had a more numerous family than was required by the canons
of his order, had fled to America, where his
orisons would not be disturbed by the cries
of infants.   On entering our trapper's
chamber they mutually recognized each
other ; and horror immediately seized the
pious priest at the recollection of the trapper's sinfulness ; and particularly the sin of
forsaking the holy places of the mother
church ; of taking carnal weapons in hands
that had been employed in making crosses
in the sacred precincts of the cloister. The
trapper had contracted the dangerous habit
of thinking for himself, and replied to the
godly man in a sharp and retaliatory manner ; and among other things drew a very
ungracious comparison between escaping
from prayers and chants, and flying from
an unlawful family.

This reference to former delinquencies in

a country to which he had fled to escape the remembrance of them, aroused the holy indignation of the priest to such an extent, that he immediately consigned the witness of his fault to worms, and his soul to an apprenticeship at fire eating in purgatory. Our trapper had become a heretic.   In the blindness of his heart he had forgotten that the power to save and destroy the soul of man, had been committed to an order of men chosen, and set apart as the repositories of that portion of Omnipotence; and that whatever errors of conduct may occur in the life of these men, the efficiency of the anathematizing and saving commission is not thereby annulled; and he rose from his bed and hurled at the priest sundry counter anathemas in the form of chairs, and shovel and tongs. I could perceive in him no returning belief in the Omnipotent key of the "Roman Catholic apostolical mother Church." Instead of saying his prayers, and counting the beads of his rosary, he talked of the stirring scenes of a trapper's life, and recounted the wild adventures of the mountains; instead of the sublime Te Deum, he sang the thrilling martial airs of his native land; instead of the crosier, he bore the faithful rifle ; instead of the robes of sacred office, he wore the fringed deer skin frock of the children of the wilderness. He was a trapper—a merry mountain trapper.

6th. Twenty-five miles to-day; face of the country, black, hard and barren swells; encamped on a small tributary of the Saptin ; very little grass for the animals ; found here a family of the Root Digger Indians ; the man half clad, children naked, all filthy. She was clad in a wrapper of mountain sheep skin.

7th. Twenty miles. About mid-day heard a loud roaring of waters ; descended the chasm of the river and discovered two enormous springs bursting from the basaltic cliffs of the opposite shore. Their roaring was heard three miles. The lower one discharged water enough to turn the machinery of twenty ordinary manufactories. The water foamed and rushed down inclined planes of rocks the distance of two hundred feet. The country, an undulating, barren, volcanic plain; near the river cut into bluffs; lava every where ; wild wormwood and another shrub two feet in height, bearing a yellow blosom, the only wood seen ; encamped on a small stream about three miles from the river.　Found here the only grass which I had observed during the day.

8th. Still on the western bank of the Saptin ; river one-fourth of a mile wide ; water extremely clear ; current five miles the hour ; depth of water about four feet. On the eastern side, the soil appeared a dark mass of imbedded fused rock, stretching in broken undulations to the distant highlands. In that direction twenty miles lay a range of mountains like an irregular line of darkness on the horizon.　Every thing touched by our horses' feet claimed a volcano for its birth-place.　Thirty miles to-day.

9th. Face of the country the same as that passed over on the 8th — scarcely grass enough to feed our animals, and that dried to hay.　The mountains on the west side of the river gradually nearing it.　No timber since we left the immediate vicinity of Fort Hall.　We cooked our food with the willow bushes which the Indians had killed and rendered dry for such purposes.　All the rocks more or less fused ; many large tracts of lava ; a number of clear little brooks bubbling over the cinders of this great hearth of Nature's fire.　Made forty miles.

10th. Fifteen miles over " cut rock" and wormwood deserts ; and at mid-day descended about six hundred feet in the chasm of the Saptin, and travelled along the brink of the river a short distance; crossed at a place called " The Islands," to the eastern shore.

The river has been dipping deeper in the plain the last three days. A bird's eye view of it for sixty miles above the Islands would present a tortuous chasm, walled by basalt, trap, &c., and sunk along the centre of the valley, from one hundred to eight hundred feet deep, a black chasm, destitute of timber and other evidences of fertility, from a quarter to half a mile in width. In the centre of the bottom rushes the Saptin; over rocks and gravel a clear, pure, strong stream, with a current of five miles to the hour; water three and four feet in depth. Travelled seven or eight miles from the ford and fell in with eight or ten springs of limpid water, bubbling through the flinty crust of the plain. The sun was pouring upon us his fiercest rays, and our thirst was excessive. A halting, dismounting and rushing to the water, the application of our giant's lips to the liquid—a paralysis of his thirst produced by the boiling hot sensation which it imparted to his swearing apparatus, prepared us to resume our ride. Hot springs,

boiling hot—no apparent mineral properties.

11th. Travelled to-day thirty-five miles
over an irregular, rough, unseemly desert;
volcanic stones strewn every where on a
black, impenetrable, baked surface; soil
too poor to bear the wormwood—trail too
far east to see the river. At ten o'clock,
met a petty chief of the Snake Root Diggers
and his son on horseback, from Boisais
river. He was dressed in a blanket coat,
deer skin pants, and moccasins garnished
with cut glass beads and strips of red flannel;
the boy entirely naked. Carbo learned
from him the situation of his tribe, and a
few bits of Indian scandal ascertained that
we could reach Boisais river the next day,
and that we could probably obtain fresh
horses there. His copper-coloured high-
ness then left us to pursue his way to Fort
Hall, to get his guns repaired, and we continued ours to the lower Columbia, to get
out of this grave of desolation. I had not
seen an acre of land since leaving Fort Hall,
capable of producing the grains or vegetables. Encamped on a small brook running
westwardly towards the Saptin.

12th. On route at six o'clock in the morning; horses weary, and getting crippled

pitifully on the " cut rock ;" face of the
country absolute sterility ; our trail near
the mountains, about two hundred miles
east of the Saptin. At nine o'clock, came
to the bluff overlooking Boisais river.
Here the valley is sunken six or seven
hundred feet ; the whole of it below, to the
limit of sight, appears to have subsided
nearly to a level with the waters of the
Saptin. Lines of timber ran along the
Boisais, and plats of green grass and shrubs
dotted its banks. The mountains, whence
the river came, rose in dark stratified
ridges. Where the stream escaped from
them, there was an immense chasm, with
perpendicular sides, which seemed to open
into their most distant bases. Horrid crags
beetled over its dismal depths. Lofty,
rocky ridges extended far into the north.
In the west and northwest towered the Blue
Mountains.

We descended the bluff, followed down
the Boisais three or four miles, and crossed
the river into an encampment of Snake
fishermen. They were employed in laying
in their winter store of salmon. Many
horses were feeding on the plain. We
turned ours loose also for a bite of the fresh

grass, while we bought fish, &c., and made
other arrangements to improve digestion
and our speed in travelling.   Our business was transacted as follows :—For one
large fish-hook we bought one salmon ; for
one paper of vermillion, six bunches of
spawn ; for one butcher-knife, one leathern
fish rope.   Carbo exchanged horses ; disposed of one worth five shillings for one
worth three, and gave a blanket and ten
loads of ammunition to boot. He was vastly
pleased with his bargain, and endeavoured
to show himself so, by trying to grin like a
white man ; but he was not skilled in the
science of manufacturing laughter, and
made a deplorable failure of it.   One of my
own horses, whose feet were worn and tender, was exchanged with like profit to the
shrewd jockeys.

These Indians are more filthy than the
Hottentots.   Both sexes were nearly naked.
Their shelters were made with rush mats
wrapped around cones of poles.

Having finished our trading, we travelled
about ten miles down the stream, and encamped upon its bank.   The plains were
well covered with grass ; many portions
seemed susceptible of cultivation. The bed of

the river presented the usual characteristics of a mountain torrent; broad, shallow, with extensive bars of coarse gravel crossing the channel in all directions. The water limpid, and its quantity might be expressed by saying that the average depth was six inches, width ten yards, rate of current three miles an hour. In the month of June, however, it is said to bring from its maternal mountains immense floods.

13th. A breakfast of boiled spawn, and on trail at sunrise; travelled rapidly down the grassy intervales of Boisais; passed many small groves of timber. Many Indians employed in drying salmon, nearly naked, and dirty and miserable, ran after us for tobacco, and to drive a bargain for horses. All Indians have a mania for barter. They will trade for good or evil to themselves, at every opportunity. Here they beset us on every side. And if at any moment we began to felicitate ourselves on having at last escaped from their annoying petitions for "shmoke" and "hos," the next moment the air would resound with whips and hoofs, and "shmoke, shmoke," "hos," from half a dozen new applicants, more troublesome than their predecessors. No Jew, with old clothes and a pinch-beck watch to sell, ever

pressed customers with more assiduity than
did these savages.   But when we had
travelled about thirty miles from our night
camp, they all suddenly disappeared ; and
neither hut nor Shoshonie was seen more.
They dare not pass the boundary between
themselves and the Bonaks.

Soon after being relieved from these
pests, our guide, Carbo, intimated that it
would be according to the rules of etiquette
in that country for him to leave us, unac-
quainted though we were with the right
trail among the ten thousand that crossed
the country in every direction, and proceed
to Fort Boisais, to make the important an-
nouncement that four white faces were approaching the post.   I remonstrated ; but
remonstrance was mere air in comparison
with the importance of doing his duty
in the most approved style ; and away
he shot, like an arrow from the bows
of his tribe, over hillock and through the
streams and copses, till lost from view.   It
was about four o'clock.   The trails were
so numerous, that we found it useless to
continue on any of them.   For if we
selected any single one, that one branched
into many every half mile.   Thus we
deemed it best to ' take our course,' as the

mariner would say, and disregard them altogether. In following this determination,
we crossed the Boisais again and again ;
floundered in quagmires, and dodged along
among whipping boughs and underbrush ;
and, when unimpeded by such obstacles,
pelted the dusty plain with as sturdy a trot
as ever echoed there, till the sun went
down, and his twilight had left the sky.
No Fort yet ! nor had we yet seen the
Saptin. We halted, held a council, and determined to " hold our course" westward ;
listened—heard nothing but the muttering
Boisais, and travelled on. In half an hour,
came to us a frightful, mournful yell, which
brought us to an instantaneous halt. We
were within fifty yards of the Bonak Indians, and were discovered !

This tribe is fierce, warlike, and ath-
letic, inhabiting the banks of that part of
Saptin, or Snake River, which lies between
the mouth of Boisais, or Reed's River, and
the Blue Mountains. They make war upon
the Blackfeet and Crows ; and for that purpose often cross the mountains, through a
gap between the track of Lewis and Clarke
and the ' Great Gap.' By these wars, their
number has been much reduced. They are
said to speak a language peculiar to them-

selves ; and are regarded by the whites as
a treacherous and dangerous race. We had
approached so near their camp, that whatever might be their disposition toward us,
it was impossible to retreat. Darkness
concealed the surrounding country, and hid
the river and the trails. We could not escape without their permission and aid.

Our young Swiss trapper was the very
man to grapple the dilemma. He bribed their
good will and their safe conduct to the Fort.
Five or six of them quickly seized horses,
and, mounting without saddle or bridle, led
the way. While these things were being
done, horrid wails came from their huts
among the bushes ; and those who were
with us responded to them. The only word
uttered was one, which sounded like ' yap.'
This they spoke at first in a low, plaintive
key, and slowly ; and then, on a higher
note and rapidly, as if under stronger emotions of grief ; and then fell away again to
the low plaint of desponding sorrow. I
noticed, as we rode along, that the tails of
many of their horses were shorn of the hair
in the most uncouth manner. The manes
also were miserably haggled. The men who
rode them wept, and at intervals wailed.

I was afterwards informed that their tribe

was mourning the death of some of their number who had lately died ; and that it is a custom with them and other western tribes, on the death of friends, in war or by disease, for all the surviving relatives to shear the manes and tails of their horses to the skin—kill all the animals of the deceased —pile all his personal property around his burial-place, and mourn, in the manner I have described, for several days. Their camp was eight miles south of Fort Boisais.

We rode the distance in three quarters of an hour. Other Bonak horsemen joined us along the way. Each one, as he overtook us, uttered the wail ; and then one and another took it up and bore it along the scattered line of the cavalcade. It was not very dark—but it was night, and all its air was filled with these expressions of savage grief. Tears flowed, and sobs arrested oftentimes the wail half spoken. The sympathy of the poor creatures for each other appeared very sincere, and afforded strong inducement to doubt the correctness of the usually received opinion that the American Indians possess little of the social affections. They certainly manifested enough on this occasion to render the hour I passed with them more oppressively painful than I hope ever again to experience.

Mr. Payette, the person in charge at Boisais, received us with every mark of kindness ; gave our horses to the care of his
servants, and introduced us immediately to
the chairs, table and edibles of his apartments. He is a French Canadian ; has been
in the service of the Hudson's Bay Company more than twenty years, and holds the
rank of clerk ; is a merry, fat old gentleman
of fifty, who, although in the wilderness all
the best years of his life, has retained that
manner of benevolence in trifles, in his mode
of address, of seating you and serving you at
table, of directing your attention continually to some little matter of interest, of
making you speak the French language
'*parfaitement*' whether you are able to do so
or not, so strikingly agreeable in that mer-
curial people. The 14th and 15th were
spent very pleasantly with this gentleman.
During that time he feasted us with excellent bread, and butter made from an American cow, obtained from some of the missionaries ; with baked, boiled, fried and
broiled salmon—and, at my request, with
some of his adventures in the wilderness.

Fort Boisais was established in 1832, as
the post whence to oppose Wyeth's operations at Fort Hall. From it, the Hudson's
Bay Company sent their trading parties over

the country south, in advance and rear and around every movement of Wyeth. And by using liberally the fund laid by annually for that purpose, they undersold the American till he was forced from the country.

On the part of the Hudson's Bay Company, I see nothing strange or unmanly in this conduct, if looked at as a business transaction. People having equal rights in trade, assume necessarily the relative positions which their skill and capital can command. This is the position of Americans and Britons in Oregon. By a pusillanimous policy on the part of the American Government, we have given British subjects an equal right with our own citizens to trade in all that part of the Public Domain lying west of the Rocky Mountains. In the exercise of the rights thus granted, the Hudson's Bay Company employ their incomparable ingenuity and immense wealth in driving every American trader from the coasts of the North Pacific. And who is to be blamed for this? The Government of the United States, that has, through want of wisdom or firmness or justice, permitted these important rights of its citizens to be monopolized by foreign capitalists for the last thirty years.

This fort stands on the eastern bank of

the Saptin, eight miles north of the mouth of Boisais or Reed's river. It consists of a parallelogram about one hundred feet square, surrounded by a stockade of poles about fifteen feet in height. It was entered on the west side. Across the area north and south runs the principal building. It is constructed of logs, and contains a large dining room, a sleeping apartment and kitchen. On the north side of the area, in front of this, is the store ; on the south side the dwellings of the servants ; back of the main building, an out-door oven ; and in the north-east corner of the stockade is the bastion. This was Fort Boisais in 1839. Mons. Payette was erecting a neat adobie wall around it. He expected soon to be able to tear away the old stockade, and before this has doubtless done so.

Among the curiosities of this establishment were the fore wheels, axletree and thills of a one-horse waggon, said to have been run by the American missionaries from the State of Connecticut through the mountains thus far toward the mouth of the Columbia. It was left here under the belief that it could not be taken through the Blue Mountains. But fortunately for the next that shall attempt to cross the continent, a safe and easy passage has lately been discovered by which vehicles of the kind may be drawn through to Wallawalla.

At ten o'clock on the 16th we found ourselves sufficiently rested to recommence our journey. Our packs and ourselves were sent across the Saptin in a canoe; and our horses having swam it, and having been packed and saddled firmly for a rapid march, and a '*bon jour*' having been returned by Mons. Payette, with the additional kind wish of a '*bon voyage*' to us, over the mountains, we left the old gentleman to his solitary dominion.

He usually collects, during the twelvemonth, twelve or fifteen packs of beaver, and employs himself in the salmon season in curing large quantities of that fish for the supply of other posts. Our course was down the west bank of the river. The soil was sand and clay mixed in nearly equal proportions. Its composition is such as to render it fruitful; but the absence of dews and rains forbids the expectation that it will ever be so. Vegetation, bunch-grass and wild wormwood. Travelled fifteen miles and encamped near a small bute, at the foot of which ran a little tributary of the Saptin. From the south bank of this stream near our camp burst a great number of hot springs. Water impregnated with sulphur : temperature at the boiling point.

17th. Soil as on the track of the 16th, save that the hills became higher and more gravelly.   In the afternoon, crossed a brook putting into the Saptin.   At mid-day, touched the Saptin, and left it again for the hills.   Mid-afternoon, struck another small stream, and followed up its valley till night. Estimated our day's journey at thirty miles.

18th. The hills higher and more rocky ; those in the distance to the west and north-west partially covered with pines and cedars. Immediately around our track, the hills were clothed with dry bunch grass. Some of them had been burnt by the Indians. Many beautiful little valleys were seen among the highlands.   Black birch, rose, and willow shrubs, and quaking-asp trees on the banks of the little brooks.   En-camped under the cliffs of a bute.   The moon was in the first quarter.   Its cold beams harmonized well with the chilling winds of the mountains.   The atmosphere all the day smoky, as in Indian summer-time in the highlands of New England. Estimated distance travelled, twenty-five miles.

19th. Forenoon, over gently rising conical hills, clothed with bunch grass ; soil in the valleys sand and clay. Cooked dinner at L'Arbor Seul, a lonely pine in an extensive plain. Encamped at night on a stream coming from the Blue Mountains, in the north-west. Distance to-day, thirty miles.

20th. Track up the valley in which we encamped the preceding night, over gently undulating hills ; high broken mountains on either side. About twelve o'clock, came to a very steep descent, a mile in length. The upper part of it was so precipitous that the animals with packs were obliged to make a zigzag track of a mile, to descend the half that distance ; the lower part was less precipitous, but covered with loose volcanic rocks. Among these the horses plunged and bruised themselves badly ; but fortunately none were seriously injured. Some rich soil in the valleys ; heavy groves of yellow pine, spruce, and hemlock ; quaking-asp on the streams, and in the ravines. From high swells, over which ran the trail, we saw an extensive valley, deeply sunken among the lofty mountains in the north-east. It appeared to be thickly coated with grass, some portions dry, others green. The meadow lark made its appearance to-day. Toward night, we came again into the valley which we had entered at mid-day, and encamped under a majestic yellow pine. Freezing breezes swept down from the woody mountain around us, and made our fire, blazing high under the dark groaning boughs, extremely agreeable. Travelled twenty-five miles.

21st. A day of severe travelling. In the forenoon, the trail ran over a series of mountains swelling one above another in long and gentle ascents, covered with noble forests of yellow pine, fir, and hemlock. Among these were frequent glades of rich pasture land ; grass green, and numerous brooks of pure water leaping from the cliffs, or murmuring among the shrubbery. The snow-ball, the wax plant, the yellow and black currant—a species of whortleberry— the service berry—choke cherry—the elder —the shrub maple—and all the beautiful flowers that gem a mountain landscape during its short summer, clothed the ground. At twelve o'clock, we entered a deep ravine, at the bottom of which ran a brook of sweet clear water ; we dined on its bank. A dish of rich cocoa, mush, and sugar, and dried buffalo tongue, on the

fresh grass, by a cool rivulet on the wild
mountains of Oregon! Nature stretched
her bare and mighty arms around us! The
mountains hid the lower sky, and walled
out the lower world! We looked upon the
beautiful heights of the Blue Mountains,
and ate among its spring blossoms, its singing pines, and holy battlements, ten thousand feet above the seas.

In the afternoon, we continued to ascend ; vast rolls lifted themselves over one
another, in a northerly direction, higher
and higher, till in the distance their tops
mingled with the blue of the sky. We
followed this grassy ridge till near four
o'clock, when we commenced descending.
A mile over slowly declining hills, and
then the descent became frightful. It appeared to stand 45° to the plane of the
horizon. The horses, when they turned at
the angles of the zigzag trail, often found the
greatest difficulty to keep on their feet. Two
miles of such descent, of bracing with
might and main, deposited us in a ravine
of great depth, hung far and near with
cliffs and abrupt earthy borders, partially
covered with pines. At the bottom a brook
running in a northerly direction, struggled
and roared among the fallen rocks. We

made our way with much difficulty down
its banks a short distance, crossed it, and
proceeding in a north-westerly direction to
another stream flowing eastward, encamped
among the pines. These valleys were filled
with cold winds, which rushed through them
in irregular gusts, chilling every thing they
touched. We set fire to large piles of dry
pine logs in camp, spread our couches,
and wayworn as men ever were, ensconced
ourselves in them for repose. Carbo did not
retire ; but went whistling about among the
horses ; untied his wallet of provisions, and
ate a second time, punched the fire, and
looked at the eastern sky with evident
interest. The vales below had been set on
fire by Indians ; and I more than half supposed that he expected to see some of his
tribe at our quarters. But my supposition
was groundless.

As soon as the moon peeped over the
eastern heights, he roused me to hear in
broken French that our horses had nothing
to eat in the place where they were ; and
that we, being rested, must climb the
mountain to find food for them. No proposition, and the facts brought to urge its
adoption, could have been more unfortunately reasonable and true—at that parti-

cular time. My first impulse was to order him to his couch ; but a hungry whinney from my roan pony, browsing near me, awakened me fully to the propriety of the measure proposed. I, therefore, summoned my weary limbs and bruised and ulcered feet, to their best efforts, and at twelve o'clock at night we were on march.

For some time we led our animals through the tangled wood, and then along a steep gravelly side of the chasm, where the foot-hold slipped at every step ; awhile among rolling stones so thickly strewn upon the ground, that the horses touched it only when their weight drove their feet down between them ; and then, awhile we seemed to hang on the cliffs, and pause between advancing and following the laws of gravitation to the bed of the torrent that battled its way in the caverns far below ; and in the desperation of a last effort, climbed the bank to a place of safety. At length we arrived at a large indentation in the face of the mountain, up the encircling rim of which, the trail for half a mile was of comparatively easy ascent. At the end of this distance, another difficulty was superadded to all we had yet experienced.

The steeps were covered to the depth of

several feet with " cut rock"—dark shining cubes from one to three inches in diameter, with sharp corners and edges. It was well nigh impossible to force our horses on them. The most obedient one, however, was at length led and scourged upon them; and by repeating the same inflictions, the remainder were finally induced to follow. All walked except Smith. His horse was "a d—d brute, and was made to carry him or die."

The poor animals would slip, and gather, and cripple; and when unable longer to endure the cutting stone under their feet, would suddenly drop on their knee; but the pain caused by that position would soon force them to rise again, and struggle up the ascent. An half hour of such travelling conducted us over this stony surface to the smooth grassy swells, the surface of which was pleasant to the lacerated feet of our horses. The green grass grew thickly all around. The moon poured her bright beams through the frosty air on the slumbering heights; in the deep pine-clad vales dimly burned the Indian fires; from mountain to mountain sounded the deep bass of a thousand cascades.

We encamped in a grove of pines which

crowned the mountain, at three o'clock in the morning.

2nd. We saddled early, and ascending for two hours a line of gentle grassy elevations, came to the beginning of the north-western declivities of the Blue Mountains. The trail ran down the ravines of small brooks flowing northwest, and occasionally over high swells which stretched down the plain that lies about the south-western branches of the Wallawalla River : we halted to dine. In the afternoon we struck off north-westerly over the rolling plain. The soil in the depressions was a light and loose compound of sand and clay, and thinly covered with bunch grass. The swells were of gravel, and generally barren ; trees on the brooks only, and these few, small and of little value.

About three o'clock we came into the camp of a middle-aged Skyuse Indian, who was on his onward march from the buffalo hunt in the mountain valleys east and north-east of Fort Hall. He was a spare man of five feet eight inches, dressed in a green camlet frock-coat, a black vest, striped cotton shirt, leather pants, moccasins, and a white felt hat. There were two children, boys, neatly clad in deerskin. His camp equipage was very comfortable—four or five camp-kettles with tin covers, a number of pails with covers, a leathern tent, and an assortment of fine buffalo robes. He had had a very successful hunt. Of the seventeen horses in his caravan, six were loaded with the best flesh of the buffalo cow, cured in the best manner; two others bore his tent, utensils, clothing, robes, &c.; four others were ridden by himself and family; the five remaining were used to relieve those that, from time to time, might tire. These were splendid animals, as large as the best horses of the States, well knit, deep and wide at the shoulders; a broad loin, and very small lower limbs and feet; of extreme activity and capacity for endurance.

Learning that this Indian was proceeding to Dr. Whitman's mission establishment, where a considerable number of his tribe had pitched their tents for the approaching winter, I determined to leave the cavalcade and accompany him there. My guide Carbo, therefore, having explained my intentions to my new acquaintance, departed with the remainder of his charge for Fort Wallawalla. Crickie, (in English " poor crane,") was a very kind man.

Immediately after the departure of Carbo and company, he turned my worn-out animals loose, and loaded my packs upon his own, gave me a splendid saddle-horse to ride, and intimated by significant gestures that we would go a short distance that afternoon, in order to arrive at the mission early the next day. I gave my assent, and we were soon on the way. Our course was north-easterly over sharp swells, among which ran many clear and beautiful brooks ; soil gravel, loam, sand and clay, and well covered with dry bunch grass, incapable of producing the grains without irrigation. The swells and streams run northwesterly from the Blue Mountains. Our course was diagonally across them.

Having made about ten miles at sunset, we encamped for the night. I noticed, during the drive, a degree of forbearance towards each other, in this family of savages which I had never before observed in that race. When we halted for the night the two boys were behind. They had been frolicking with their horses, and as the darkness came on, lost the trail. It was a half-hour before they made their appearance, and during this time, the worthy parents exhibited the most affectionate solicitude for them. One of them was but three years old, and was lashed to the horse he rode; the other only seven years of age. Young pilots in the wilderness at night! But the elder, true to the sagacity of his race, had taken his course, and struck the brook on which we had encamped, within three hundred yards of us. The pride of the parents at this feat, and their ardent attachment to their children, were perceptible in the pleasure with which they received them at their evening fire, and heard the relation of their childish adventure.

The weather was so pleasant that no tent was pitched. The willows were beat, and buffalo robes spread over them. Underneath were laid other robes, on which my Indian host seated himself with his wife and children on one side, and myself on the other. A fire burned brightly in front. Water was brought, and the evening ablutions having been performed, the wife presented a dish of meat to her husband, and one to myself. There was a pause. The woman seated herself between her children. The Indian then bowed his head and prayed to God! A wandering savage in Oregon calling upon Jehovah in the name of Jesus

Christ! After the prayer, he gave meat to his children, and passed the dish to his wife.

While eating, the frequent repetition of the words Jehovah and Jesus Christ, in the most reverential manner, led me to suppose they were conversing on religious topics; and thus they passed an hour. Meanwhile, the exceeding weariness of a long day's travel admonished me to seek rest.

I had slumbered, I know not how long, when a strain of music awoke me. I was about rising to ascertain whether the sweet notes of Tallis's Chant came to these solitudes from earth or sky, when a full recollection of my situation, and of the religious habits of my host, easily solved the rising inquiry, and induced me to observe instead of disturbing. The Indian family was engaged in its evening devotions. They were singing a hymn in the Nez Percés language. Having finished it, they all knelt and bowed their faces upon the buffalo robes, and Crickie prayed long and fervently. Afterwards they sang another hymn and retired. This was the first breathing of religious feelings that I had seen since leaving the States. A pleasant evidence that the Oregon wilderness was beginning to bear the rose of Sha-

G 3

ron on its thousand hills, and that on the barren soil of the Skyuse heart was beginning to bud and blossom and ripen the golden fruits of faith in Jehovah, and hope in an after-state.

23rd. We were on our way before the sun rose. The dawn on an Oregon sky, the rich blue embankment of mountains over which the great day-star raised his glowing rim, the blandness of the air, the lively ambling of the caravan towards the neighbouring abode of my countrymen, imparted to my mind and body a most agreeable exhilaration. Crickie, and his wife and children also, appeared to enjoy the atmosphere and scenery of their native valley; and we went on together merrily over the swelling plains and murmuring streams till about eight o'clock, when Crickie spurred his horse in advance of the cavalcade, and mctioned me to follow him.

We rode very rapidly for about three hours over a country gently undulating, well set with bunch grass, and intersected with small streams flowing north-west. The dust had risen in dark clouds during our ride, and rendered it necessary to bathe before presenting ourselves at the mission. We therefore halted on the bank of a little brook overhung with willows, and proceeded to make our toilet. Crickie's paraphernalia was ample for the purpose, and showed that among his other excellencies, cleanliness held a prominent place. A small mirror, pocket-comb, soap and a towel, were immediately produced; and the dust was taken from his person and wardrobe with a nicety that would have satisfied a town exquisite.

A ride of five miles afterward brought us in sight of the groves around the mission. The plains far and near were dry and brown. Every form of vegetation was dead save the forest trees, whose roots drank deeply of the waters of the stream. We crossed the river, passed the Indian encampment hard by, and were at the gate of the mission fields in presence of Dr. Whitman. He was speaking Skyuse at the top of his voice to some lazy Indians who were driving their cattle from his garden, and giving orders to others to yoke their oxen, get the axes, and go into the forest for the lower sleepers of the new mission house. Mr. Hall, printer at the Sandwich Islands, soon appeared in working dress, with an axe on his shoulder; next came Mr. Monger, pulling the pine shavings from his foreplane. All seemed desirous to ask me how long a balloon line had been running between the States and the Pacific, by which single individuals crossed the continent. The oxen, however, were yoked, and axes glistening in the sun, and there was no time to spend, if they would return from their labour before nightfall. So that the whence and wherefore of my sudden appearance among them, were left for an after explanation. The doctor introduced me to his excellent lady, and departed to his labour.

The afternoon was spent in listless rest from the toils of my journey. At sunset, however, I strolled out and took a bird's-eye view of the plantation and plain of the Wallawalla. The old mission-house stands on the north-east bank of the river, about four rods from the water-side, at the northeast corner of an enclosure containing about two hundred and fifty acres; two hundred of which are under good cultivation. The soil is a thin stratum of clay, mixed with sand and a small proportion of vegetable mould, resting on a base of coarse gravel. Through this gravel, water from the Wallawalla filtrates, and by capillary attraction is raised to the roots of vegetation in the incumbent earth. The products are wheat,

Indian corn, onions, turnips, ruta baga, water, musk and nutmeg melons, squashes, asparagus, tomatoes, cucumbers, peas, &c., in the garden—all of good quality, and abundant crops.

The Wallawalla is a pretty stream. Its channel is paved with gravel and sand, and about three rods in width ; water two feet deep, running five or six miles the hour, and limpid and cool through the year. A hundred yards below the house, it makes a beautiful bend to the south west for a short distance, and then resumes its general direction of north-west by north, along the border of the plantation. On the opposite bank is a line of timber and underwood, interlaced with flowering brambles. Other small groves occur above and below along the banks.

The plain about the waters of this river is about thirty miles square. A great part of this surface is more or less covered with bunch grass. The branches of the river are distributed over it in such manner that most of it can be grazed. But, from what came under my own observation, and the information received from respectable American citizens, who had examined it more minutely than I had time to do, I suppose there to be scarcely two thousand acres of this vast extent of surface, which can ever be made available for the purposes of cultivation.   The absence of rains and dews in the season of crops, and the impossibility of irrigating much of it on account of the height of the general surface above the streams, will afford sufficient reasons for entertaining this opinion.

The doctor returned near night with his timber, one elm and a number of quaking-asp sticks ; and appeared gratified that he had been able to find the requisite number of sufficient size to support his floor.   Tea came on, and passed away in earnest conversation about native land and friends left there—of the pleasure they derived from their present occupation—and the trials that befel them while commencing the mission and afterwards.

Among the latter, was mentioned the drowning of their child in the Wallawalla the year before, a little girl two years old. She fell into the river at the place where they took water for family use.   The mother was in the house, the father a short distance away on the premises.   The alarm was conveyed to them almost instantly, and they and others rushed to the stream, and sought for their child with frantic eagerness. But the strong heavy current had carried it down and lodged it in a clump of bushes under the bank on which they stood. They passed the spot where it lay, but found it too late. Thus these devoted people were bereft, in the most afflicting manner, of their only child—left alone in the wilderness.

The morning of the 24th opened in the loveliest hues of the sky. Still none of the beauty of the harvest field—none of the fragrance of the ripened fruits of autumn were there. The wild horses were frolicking on the plains; but the plains smoked with dust and dearth. The green woods and the streams sent up their harmonies with the breeze; but it was like a dirge over the remains of the departed glories of the year. And yet when the smoking vegetables, the hissing steak, bread white as snow, and the newly-churned golden butter graced the breakfast table, and the happy countenances of countrymen and countrywomen shone around, I could with difficulty believe myself in a country so far distant from, and so unlike my native land, in all its features. But during breakfast, this pleasant illusion was dispelled by one of the causes which induced it.

Our steak was of horse-flesh! On such meat this poor family subsist most of the time. They do not complain. It enables them to exist to do the Indian good, and thus satisfies them. But can it satisfy those who give money for the support of missionaries, that the allowance made by their agents for the support of those who abandon parents and freedom and home, and surrender not only themselves to the mercy of the savages, but their offspring also, should be so meagre, as to compel them to eat horse-flesh! This necessity existed in 1839, at the mission on the Wallawalla, and I doubt not exists in 1843.

The breakfast being over, the doctor invited me to a stroll over his premises. The garden was first examined; its location, on the curving bank of the Wallawalla; the apple trees, growing thriftily on its western border; the beautiful tomato and other vegetables, burdening the grounds. Next to the fields. The doctor's views of the soil, and its mode of receiving moisture from the river, were such as I have previously expressed. " For," said he, " in those places where you perceive the stratum of gravel to be raised so as to interrupt the capillary attraction of the superincumbent earth, the crop failed." Then to the new house. The adobie walls had been erected a year. These were about forty feet by twenty, and one and a half stories high. The interior area consisted of two parlours of the ordinary size, separated by an adobie portion. The outer door opened into one of them; and from this a door in the partition led to the other. Above were to be sleeping apartments. To the main building was attached another of equal height designed for a kitchen, with chambers above for servants. Mr. Monger and a Sandwich Islander were laying the floors, making the doors, &c.

The lumber used was a very superior quality of yellow pine plank, which Dr. Whitman had cut with a whip saw among the blue mountains, fifteen miles distant. Next to the " caral." A fine yoke of oxen, two cows, an American bull, and the beginning of a stock of hogs were thereabout. And last to the grist-mill on the other side of the river. It consisted of a spherical wrought iron burr four or five inches in diameter, surrounded by a counterburred surface of the same material. The spherical burr was permanently attached to the shaft of a horizontal water-wheel. The surrounding burred surface was firmly fastened to

timbers, in such a position that when the
water-wheel was put in motion, the operation of the mill was similar to that of a
coffee-mill.   It was a crazy thing, but for it
the doctor was grateful.

It would, with the help of himself and an
Indian, grind enough in a day to feed his
family a week, and that was better than to
beat it with a pestle and mortar.   It appeared to me quite remarkable that the
doctor could have made so many improvements since the year 1834.   But the industry
which crowded every hour of the day, his untiring energy of character, and the very efficient aid of his wife in relieving him in a
great degree from the labours of the school,
are, perhaps, circumstances which will
render possibility probable, that in five
years one man without funds for such purposes, without other aid in that business
than that of a fellow missionary at short intervals, should fence, plough, build, plant an
orchard, and do all the other laborious acts
of opening a plantation on the face of that
distant wilderness; learn an Indian language
and do the duties, meanwhile, of a physician
to the associate stations on the Clear Water
and Spokan.

In the afternoon, Dr. Whitman and his

lady assembled the Indians for instruction in
reading. Forty or fifty children between the
ages of seven and eighteen, and several other
people gathered on the shady side of the
new mission-house at the ringing of a hand-
bell, and seated themselves in an orderly
manner on wooden benches. The doctor
then wrote monosyllables, words, and in-
structive sentences in the Nez Percés language, on a large black-board suspended on
the wall, and proceeded first to teach the
nature and power of the letters in representing the simple sounds of the language, and
then the construction of words and their
uses in forming sentences expressive of
thought. The sentences written during these
operations were at last read, syllable by
syllable, and word after word, and explained
until the sentiments contained in them were
comprehended ; and it was delightful to
notice the undisguised avidity with which
these people would devour a new idea. It
seemed to produce a thrill of delight
that kindled up the countenance and ani-
mated the whole frame. A hymn in the
Nez Percés language, learned by rote from
their teachers, was then sung, and the exercises closed with prayer by Dr. Whitman
in the same tongue.

25th. I was awakened at early dawn by the merry sounds of clapping boards, the hammer, the axe and the plane ; the sweet melodies of the parent of virtue, at this cradle of civilization. When I rose every thing was in motion. Dr. Whitman's little herd was lowing in the river ; the wild horses were neighing at the morning breeze ; the birds were caroling in the groves. I said, every thing was alive. Nay, not so. The Skyuse village was in the deepest slumber, save a few solitary individuals who were stalking with slow and stately tread up a neighbouring bute, to descry the retreat of their animals. Their conical skin lodges dotted the valley above the mission, and imparted to the morning landscape a peculiar wildness. As the sun rose, the inmates began to emerge from them.

It was a chilly hour ; and their buffalo robes were drawn over their shoulders, with the hair next the body. The snow-white flesh side was fringed with the dark fur that crept in sight around the edges, and their own long black glistening tresses fell over it far down the back. The children were out in all the buoyancy of young life, shouting to the prancing steed, or betting gravel stones that the arrows upon their little bows would be the first to clip the sturdy thistle head upon which they were waging mimic war. The women were busy at their fires, weaving mats from the flag; or sewing moccasins, leggings, or hunting shirts. Crickie was giving meat to his friends, who the past winter had fed him, and taken care of him, while lying sick.

This is the imperial tribe of Oregon. They formerly claimed a prescriptive right to exercise jurisdiction over the country down the Columbia to its mouth; and up the North and South Forks to their sources. In the reign of the late high Chief, the brother of him who now holds that station, this claim was acceded to by all the tribes within those districts. But that talented and brave man left at his death but one son, who, after receiving a thorough education at the Selkirk settlement on Red River of Lake Winnepeg, also died — and with him the imperial dignity of the Skyuse tribe.

The person in charge at Fort Wallawalla, indeed dressed the present incumbent in better style than his fellows; proclaimed him high chief, and by treating him with the formality usually tendered to his deceased brother, has obtained for him the name, but not the respect and influence belonging to the office. He is a man of considerable mental power, but has none of the fire and energy attributed to his predecessor. The Wallawallas and Upper Chinooks are the only tribes that continue to recognise the Skyuse supremacy.

The Skyuse are also a tribe of merchants. Before the establishment of Forts Hall and Boisais, they were in the habit of rendezvousing at " La Grande Rounde," an extensive valley in the Blue Mountains, with the Shoshonies and other Indians from the Saptin, and exchanging with them their horses for furs, buffalo robes, skin tents, &c. But since the building of these posts, that portion of their trade is nearly destroyed. In the winter season, a band of them usually descends to the Dalles, barters with the Chinooks for salmon, and holds councils over that mean and miserable band to ascertain their misdemeanors, and punish them therefore by whipping. The Wallawallas, however, are their most numerous and profitable customers. They may well be termed the fishermen of the Skyuse camp. They live on both banks of the Columbia, from the Blue Mountains to the Dalles, and employ themselves principally

in taking salmon.   For these, their betters,
who consider fishing a menial business,
give them horses.   They own large numbers of these animals.   A Skyuse is thought
to be poor who has but fifteen or twenty of
them.   They generally have many more.
One fat, hearty old fellow, owns something
more than two thousand ; all wild, except
many as he needs for use or sale.

To these reports of the Indians, Dr.
Whitman gave little credence ; so at va-
riance were some of the facts related, with
what he presumed the Hudson's Bay Company would permit to be done by any one
in their employment, or under their patron-
age—the abuse of American citizens, and
the ungentlemanly interference with their
characters and calling.

On the morning of the 27th, the arrival
of Mr. Ermetinger, the senior clerk at Fort
Hall from Fort Wallawalla, created quite a
sensation.   His uniform kindness to the
Missionaries has endeared him to them.
My companion, Blair, accompanied him.
The poor old man had become lonely and
discouraged, and as I had encouraged him to
expect any assistance from me which his
circumstances might demand, it afforded
me the greatest pleasure to make his merits

known to the Missionaries, who needed an artisan to construct a mill at the station on the Clear Water. Dr. Whitman contracted with him for his services and Blair was happy. I sincerely hope he may for ever be so.

I attended the Indian school to-day. Mrs. Whitman is an indefatigable instructress. The children read in monosyllables from a primer lately published at the Clear Water station. After reading, they repeated a number of hymns in the Nez Percés, composed by Mr. Smith, of the Spokan station. These were afterwards sung. They learn music readily. At nightfall, I visited the Indian lodges in company with Dr. Whitman In one of them we saw a young woman who imagined that the spirit of a Medicine man, or conjuror, had entered into her system, and was wasting her life. She was resorting to the native remedy for such evils—singing wild incantations, and weeping loudly. This tribe, like all others west of the mountains, believe in witchcraft under various forms — practice sleight-of-hand, fire-eating, &c. They insert rough sticks into their throats, and draw them up and down till the blood flows freely, to make them long-winded on march. They flatten the head, and perforate the septum, or partition of the nose. In this orifice they wear various ornaments. The more common one that I noticed was a wolf's tooth.

The Skyuse have two distinct languages : the one used in ordinary intercourse, the other on extraordinary occasions ; as in war-councils, &c. Both are said to be copious and expressive. They also speak the Nez Percés and Wallawalla.

On the 28th, Mr. Ermetinger started for Fort Hall, and Blair for the Clear Water. Early in the day, the Indians brought in large numbers of their horses to try their speed. These are a fine race of animals ; as large, and of better form, and more activity than most of the horses in the States. Every variety of colour is found among them, from the shining coal-black to the milk-white. Some of them are pied very singularly ; for instance, a roan body with bay ears, and white mane and tail. Some are spotted with white on a roan, or bay, or sorrel ground, with tail and ears tipped with black. They are better trained to the saddle than those of civilized countries.

When an Indian wishes an increase of his serving animals, he mounts a fleet horse, and, lasso in hand, rushes into his band of wild animals, throws it upon the neck of the chosen one, and chokes him down; and while in a state of insensibility, ties the hind and fore feet firmly together. When consciousness returns, the animal struggles violently, but in vain, to get loose. His fear is then attacked by throwing bear-skins, wolf-skins, and blankets at his head till he becomes quiet. He is then loosened from the cord, and rears and plunges furiously at the end of a long rope, and receives another introduction to bear-skins, &c. After this, he is approached and handled; or, if still too timid, he is again beset with blankets and bear-skins, as before, until he is docile. Then come the saddling and riding. During this training, they uniformly treat him tenderly when near, and rudely when he pulls at the end of the halter. Thus they make their wild steed the most fearless and pleasant riding animals I ever mounted.

The course pursued by Mr. Whitman, and other Presbyterian Missionaries, to improve the Indians, is to teach them the Nez Percés language, according to fixed grammatical rules, for the purpose of opening to them the arts and religion of civilized

nations through the medium of books.
They also teach them practical agriculture
and the useful arts, for the purpose of civilizing their physical condition. By these
means, they hope to make them a better
and a happier people. Perhaps it would be
an easier way to the same result, if they
would teach them the English language,
and thus open to them at once the treasures which centuries of toil, by a superior
race, have dug from the mines of intelligence and truth.

This was the evening before the sabbath,
and Dr. Whitman, as his custom was, invited one of the most intelligent Indians to
his study, translated to him the text of
scripture from which he intended to teach
the tribe on the morrow, explained to him
its doctrines, and required of him to explain
in turn. This was repeated again and
again, until the Indian obtained a clear understanding of its doctrines.

The 29th was the sabbath, and I had an
opportunity of noticing its observance by
the Skyuse. I rose before the sun. The
stars were waxing dim on the morning sky,
the most charming dawn I ever witnessed.
Every possible circumstance of sublimity
conspired to make it so. There was the

pure atmosphere ; not a wisp of cloud on all its transparent depths. The light poured over the Blue Mountains like a cataract of gold ; first on the upper sky, then deepening its course through the lower air, it gilded the plain with a flood of brightness, mellow, beautiful brightness ; the charms of morning light, on the brown, boundless solitudes of Oregon. The breeze scarcely rustled the leaves of the dying flowers ; the drumming of the woodpecker on the distant tree, sounded a painful discord ; so grand, so awful, and yet so sweet, were the unuttered symphonies of the sublime quiet of the wilderness.

At ten o'clock the Skyuse assembled for worship in the open air. The exercises were according to the Presbyterian form ; the invocation, the hymn, the prayer, the hymn, the sermon, a prayer, a hymn, and the blessing ; all in the Nez Percés tongue. The principal peculiarity about the services was the mode of delivering the discourse. When Dr. Whitman arose and announced the text, the Indian who had been instructed on the previous night, rose and repeated it ; and as the address proceeded, repeated it also by sentence or paragraph, till it was finished. This is the custom of the Skyuse in all their public speaking. The benefit resulting from it in this case, apparently, was the giving the doctrines which the Doctor desired to inculcate, a clearer expression in the proper idiom of the language.

During the recess, the children were assembled in sabbath school. In the afternoon, the service was similar to that of the morning. Every thing was conducted with much solemnity. After worship, the Indians gathered in their lodges, and conversed together concerning what they had heard. If doubt arose as to any point, it was solved by the instructed Indian. Thus passed the sabbath among the Skyuse.

On the 29th, I hired Crickie to take me to the Dalles; and, Mrs. Whitman having filled my sacks with bread, corn-meal, and other edibles, I lashed my packs once more for the lower Columbia.

CHAPTER IV.

Parting with Friends—Wallawalla Valley—Fort Walla-
walla—Mr. Pambrun—The Columbia—Country down
its banks—What was seen of Rock Earth—Wood,
Fire and Water—Danger, &c. from the Heights—Fall-
ing Mountain—Morning Hymn to God—Giant's
Causeway—A View of the Frozen Sublime—Tum Tum
Orter' and other appurtenances—Dalles—Methodist
Episcopal Mission—Mr. and Mrs. Perkins—Mr. Lee
—Mission Premises—Egyptian Pyramids—Indians—
How Fifty Indians can fight One Boston—The Re-
sult of a War—Descent of the Columbia in a Canoe
—A Night on the River—The Poetry of the Wilder-
ness—The Cascades—Postage—Dr. McLaughlin—
Indian Tombs—Death—A Race—The River and its
Banks—Night again—Mounts Washington and Jef-
ferson—Arrival—Fort Vancouver—British Hospital-
ity.

30th.   Left the kind people of the mission at ten o'clock for Fort Wallawalla.
Travelled fifteen miles ; face of the country
dry, barren, swelling plains ; not an acre
capable of cultivation ; some bunch grass,
and a generous supply of wild wormwood.
Encamped on the northern branch of the
Wallawalla River.

October 1. At ten o'clock to-day, I was kindly received by Mr. Pambrun at Fort Wallawalla. This gentleman is a half-pay officer in the British army. His rank in the Hudson Bay Company, is that of " clerk in charge" of this post. He is of French extraction, a native of Canada. I breakfasted with him and his family. His wife, a half breed of the country, has a numerous and beautiful family. The breakfast being over, Mr. Pambrun invited me to view the premises. The fort is a plank stockade, with a number of buildings within, appropriated to the several uses of a store, blacksmith-shop, dwellings, &c. It has a bastion in the north-east corner, mounted with cannon. The country around has sometimes been represented as fruitful and beautiful. I am obliged to deny so foul an imputation upon the fair fame of dame Nature. It is an ugly desert ; designed to be such, made such, and is such.

About seven miles up the Wallawalla River, are two or three acres of ground fenced with brush, capable of bearing an inferior species of Yankee pumpkin ; and another spot somewhere, of the fourth of an acre, capable of producing anything that grows in the richest kind of unmoistened sand. But aside from these distinguished exceptions, the vicinity of Fort Wallawalla is a desert. There is, indeed, some beauty and sublimity in sight, but no fertility. The wild Columbia sweeps along under its northern wall.   In the east, roll up to heaven dark lofty ridges of mountains ; in the north-west, are the ruins of extinct and terrible volcanic action ; in the west, a half mile, is the entrance of the river into the vast chasm of its lower course, abutted on either side by splendidly castellated rocks, a magnificent gateway for its floods.

But this is all. Desert describes it as well as it does the wastes of Arabia. I tarried only two hours with the hospitable Mr. Pambrun.   But as if determined that I should remember that I would have been a welcome guest a much longer time, he put some tea and sugar and bread into my packs, and kindly expressed regrets that our mutual admiration of Napoleon should be thus crowded into the chit-chat of hours instead of weeks.   A fine companionable fellow ; I hope he will command Fort Wallawalla as long as Britons occupy it, and live a hundred years afterwards.

Travelled down the south bank of the Columbia along the water-side ; the river half a mile in width, with a deep strong current; water very clear. A short distance from this brink, on both sides, rose the embankments of the chasm it has worn for itself, in the lapse of ages—a noble gorge, worthy of its mighty waters. The northern one might properly be termed a mountain running continuously along the water's edge, seven hundred or eight hundred feet in height, black, shining, and shrubless. The southern one consisted of earthy bluffs, alternating with cliffs from one hundred to four hundred feet above the stream, turreted with basaltic shafts, some twenty, others one hundred feet above the subjacent hills.

Passed a few horses travelling industriously formed from one wisp of dry bunch grass to another. Every thing unnatural, dry, brown, and desolate. Climbed the heights near sunset, and had an extensive view of the country south of the river. It was a treeless, brown expanse of dearth, vast rolling swells of sand and clay, too dry to bear wormwood. No mountains seen in that direction. On the north they rose precipitously from the river, and hid from view the country beyond. The Wallawalla Indians brought us drift-wood and fresh salmon, for which they desired " shmoke," tobacco.

H 3

2nd. Continued to descend the river. Early in the day, basalt disappeared from the bluffs; and the country north and south opened to view five or six miles from the stream. I was partially covered with dry bunch grass; groups of Indian horses occasionally appeared. But I was impressed with the belief that the journeyings from one quid of grass to another, and from these to water, were sufficient to enfeeble the constitution of the best horse in Christendom. The wild wormwood, of " blessed memory," greeted my eyes and nose, wherever its scrags could find sand to nourish them.

During the day I was gratified with the sight of five or six trees, and these a large species of willow, themselves small and bowed with age; stones and rocks more or less fused. A strong westerly wind buffeted me; and much of the time filled the air with drifting sand. We encamped at the water side about three o'clock. I had thus a fine opportunity of ascending the heights to view the southern plain. The slopes were well covered with grass, and seemed easy of ascent; but on trial proved extremely laborious. I however climbed slowly and patiently the long sweeps for two hours, and gained nothing. Nay, I could see the noble

river, like a long line of liquid fire blazing
with the light of the western sun ; and the
rush wigwams of the Wallawallas, dotting
the sands of the opposite shore ; and the
barren bluffs and rocks beyond them piled
away into space. But to the south my vision was hemmed in by the constantly rising
swells. No extensive view could be obtained
from any of the heights.

The sun was fast sinking, and the hills
rose as I advanced. I was so weary that I
could go little further. But taking a careful
view of the peaks which would guide me
back to my camp, I determined to travel on
till it should become too dark to see what
might open before me. I climbed slowly
and tediously the seemingly endless swells,
lifting themselves over and beyond each
other in beautiful, but to my wearied limbs,
and longing eyes in most vexatious con-
tinuity, till the sun dipped his lower rim beneath the horizon.

A volcano burst the hills, thought I ; and
on I trudged with the little strength that a
large quantity of vexation gave me. Fires
blister your beautiful brows, I half uttered,
as I dragged myself up the crowning eminence, and saw the plateau declining in irregular undulations far into the southwest—

a sterile waste, clothed in the glories of the
last rays of a splendid sunset. The crests of
the distant swells were fringed with bunch
grass ; not a shrub or a tree on all the field
of vision ; and evidently no water nearer
than the Columbia. Those cattle which are,
in the opinions of certain travellers, to de-
pasture these plains in future time, must be
of sound wind and limb to gather food and
water the same day. I found myself so
wearied on attaining this goal of my wishes,
that, notwithstanding the lateness of the
hour, I was literally compelled to seek some
rest before attempting to descend.

I therefore seated myself, and in the
luxury of repose permitted darkness to commence creeping over the landscape, before
I could rouse myself to the effort of moving.
When I did start, my style of locomo-
tion was extremely varied, and withal sometimes not the most pleasant to every portion
of the mortal coil. My feet were not unfrequently twice or thrice the length of that
measure in advance of my body. But the
reader must not suppose that this circumstance diminished my speed. I continued to slide down the hills, using as vehicles the small sharp stones beneath me,
until an opportunity offered to put my

nether extremities under me again. Once I
had nearly plunged headlong from a precipice some fifty feet high, and saved myself
by catching a wormwood bush standing
within three feet of the brink. Finally,
without any serious mishap, I arrived in
camp, so completely exhausted, that, without tasting food, I threw myself on my couch
for the night.

3rd. The earthy bluffs continued to bind
the chasm of the river till mid-day, when
buttresses of basalt took their place. A
little bunch grass grew among the wild
wormwood. Turkeys, grouse, and a species
of large hare frequently appeared ; many
ducks in the stream. For three hours before sunset the trail was rugged and precipitous, often overhanging the river, and so
narrow that a mis-step of four inches would
have plunged horse and rider hundreds of
feet into the boiling flood. But as Skyuse
horses never make such disagreeable mis-
takes, we rode the steeps in safety. Encamped in a small grove of willows. The
river along the day's march was hemmed in
by lofty and rugged mountains. The rocks
showed indubitable evidences of a volcanic origin. As the sun went down, the
Wallawalla village on the opposite shore

sang a hymn in their own language, to a
tune which I have often heard sung in Catholic Churches, before the image of the
Virgin. The country in the south, as seen
from the heights, was broken and barren;
view limited in all directions by the un-
evenness of the surface.

4th. Awakened this morning by the fall
of a hundred tons of rock from the face of
the mountain near us. The earth trembled
as if the slumbering volcanoes were wrest-
ling in its bowels. We were brought to our
feet, and opened and rubbed our eyes with
every mark of despatch. My " poor crane"
and his hopeful son condescended to appear shocked; an event in an Indian's life
that occurs as seldom as his birth. I had
stationed myself near the fallen rocks as the
sun's first rays awoke the morning hymn of
the Indian village.

It was a sweet wild tune that they sung
to God among the dark mountains of the
Columbia. And sweeter, perhaps, in such
a place, where every motion of the heart
is a monition that one is alone, and every
thought brings with it the remembrance that
the social affections are separated from the
objects of their fondness, and where every
moral sensibility is chilled by a sense of

desolation and danger, calling into exercise the resisting and exterminating propensities, and where the holy memories of home find no response but in some loved star in the unchanging heavens. In such a place how far sweeter than anything beside is the evidence of the religious principle—the first teaching of a mother's love, rising over the wastes of nature from the altar of a pure heart—the incense of love going up to the heavenly presence.

At eight o'clock we were on route; at nine o'clock approached the bend in the river, where it changes from a south-west to a north-west course. At this place the cliffs which overhang the southern bank presented a fine collection of basaltic columns. Along the margin of the river lay hillocks of scoriæ, piled together in every imaginable form of confusion. Among them grew considerable quantities of bunch grass, on which a band of Wallawalla horses were feeding. Sand-hills on the opposite shore rose one thousand feet in the air. Basalt occurred at intervals, in a more or less perfect state of formation, till the hour of noon, when the trail led to the base of a series of columns extending three-fourths of a mile down the bank. These were more perfectly formed than any previously seen.

They swelled from a large curve of the
mountain side, like the bastions of ancient
castles ; and one series of lofty columns towered above another, till the last was surmounted by a crowning tower, a little above
the level of the plain beyond. And their
pentagonal form, longitudinal sections, dark
shining fracture, and immense masses
strewn along my way, betokened me if not
in the very presence of the Giant's Causeway, yet on a spot where the same mighty
energies had exerted themselves which
built that rare, beautiful wonder of the Emerald Isle. The river was very tortuous, and
shut in by high dykes of basalt and sand
hills the remainder of the day ; saw three
small rapids in the Columbia ; encamped at
sunset ; too weary to climb the heights.

5th. Arose at break of day, and ordering
my guide to make arrangements for starting
as soon as I should return, I ascended the
neighbouring heights.   Grassy undulating
plains in all directions south of the river.
Far in the north-east towered the frozen
peak of Mount Washington, a perfect pyramid, clothed with eternal snows. The view
in the north was hemmed in by mountains
which rose higher than the place of observation. On descending, my guide Crickie
complained of ill-health ; and assigned that

circumstance as a reason why he should not proceed with me to the Dalles. I was much vexed with him at the time, for this unseasonable desertion, and believed that the real inducement to his course was the danger to be apprehended from the Indians at the Shutes. But I was sorry to learn from Dr. Whitman afterwards that the poor fellow was actually sick, and that he suffered much at the sand bank encampment, where I left him. After paying Crickie for his faithful services thus far along, and giving him four days' provision for himself and boy, a Wallawalla Indian who had encamped with us the previous night, took charge of Crickie's horses, bearing himself and packs, and led the way down the river.

The " poor crane" was an honest, honourable man ; and I can never think of all his kind acts to me, from the time I met him in the plains beyond the Wallawalla mission, till I left him sick on the bank of the Columbia, without wishing an opportunity to testify my sense of his moral worth and goodness of heart in some way which shall yield him a substantial reward for all he suffered in my service. Two hours' ride brought to my ears the music of the " tum tum ort-

er ;" the Indian-English for the "thunder-
ing waters" of the Shutes. These are the
only perpendicular falls of the Columbia, in
its course from the junction of its great
northern and southern branches, to the
ocean. And they do indeed thunder. A
stratum of black rock forming the bed of
the river above, by preserving its horizontal
position, rises at this place above the natural
surface of the stream, and forms an abrupt
precipice, hanging sixty feet in height over
the bed below.

The river, when I passed was unfortunately at its lower stage—still the Shutes
were terribly grand. The main body of the
water swept around near its southern bank,
and being there compressed into a narrow
rough channel, chafed its angry way to the
brink, where, bending a massive curve, as
if hesitating to risk the leap, it plunged into
a narrow cavern sixty feet deep, with a force
and volume which made the earth tremble.
The noise was prodigious, deafening, and
echoed in awful tumult among the barren
mountains. Further towards the other
shore, smaller jets were rushing from
the imprisoned rocks which clustered near
the brow of the cliff, into other caverns ;

and close under the north bank, and farther
down the stream, thundered another, nearly
equal in grandeur to the one first described.

On the portions of the rocky stratum left
by the chafing waters, in wearing out numerous channels below the present situation
of the Shutes, were the flag huts of one hundred Wallawalla fishermen.   They were
taking salmon with scoop nets and bone
pointed spears. These people are filthy and
naked. Some sat by fires swallowing roasted
salmon ; others greasing themselves with
the oil of that fish ; others were dressing and
drying them ; others stood down on the pro-
jections in the chasms, sweeping their nets
in the foaming waters; untaught, unelevated,
least intelligent, least improvable human
nature !   It was not deemed safe to remain
long among these savages, who had begun
to examine my packs with more interest
than strictly honest intentions towards them
seemed to require, and I took to the trail
again on a fast trot.

Some of them endeavoured to follow on
foot, demanding a tribute of " smoke" for
the privilege of passing their dominions.
But having none at hand I pushed on, without regarding their suit, over sand hills,

beds of volcanic stones, and hanging declivities, till rounding a basaltic buttress, I
came in view of the little plain on the south
western shore of the Dalles. The " Dalles,"
a French term for " flat stones," is applied
to a portion of the river here, where, by a
process similar to that going on at Niagara,
the waters have cut channels through an
immense stratum of black rock, over which
they used to fall as at the Shutes.

At low stages these are of sufficient capacity to pass all the waters. But the annual
floods overflow the " flat stones," and produce a lashing and leaping, and whirling of
waters, too grand for the imagination to
conceive. These " Dalles" are covered
with the huts of the Chinooks, a small
band of a tribe of the same name, which inhabits the banks of Columbia from this
place to its mouth. They flatten their
heads and perforate the septum of the nose,
as do the Wallawallas, Skyuse and Nez
Percés.

The depression of the southern embankment of the chasm of the river at the
Dalles, extends eight miles along the stream,
and from a half mile to a mile in width. It
is broken by ledges bursting through the

surface, and in parts loaded with immense boulders of detached rocks. Along the north-western border are groves of small white oaks; and on the highlands in that direction are forests of pine, spruce and other evergreens, clothing the whole country westward to the snowy peaks of the President's Range.

In the south-west, specked with clusters of bunch grass, is an open rolling plain, which stretches beyond the reach of vision. In the north rise sharp mountains, thinly clad with evergreen trees; through an opening among the peaks of which, appeared the shining apex of Mount Adams. In the north-east sweep away in brown barrenness, naked cliffs and sandy wastes. I had taken a bird's-eye view of the Dalles and the region round about, when my Indian cried out "Lee house." And there it was, a mission house of the American P. E. Methodist Church, in charge of Messrs. Lee and Perkins.

I spent a week at the Dalles' mission, eating salmon and growing fat; an event that had not lately occurred in the republic of the members of my mortal confederacy.

The buildings of the mission, are a dwelling-house, a house for worship and for school purposes, and a workshop, &c. The first is a log structure thirty by twenty feet, one and a half floor high, shingle roofs, and floors made of plank cut with a whip-saw from the pines of the hills. The lower story is divided into two rooms—the one a dining-room, the other the family apartment of Mr. Perkins and lady. These are lined overhead and at the sides with beautiful rush mats manufactured by the Indians. The upper story is partitioned into six dormitories, and a school-room for Indian children ; all neatly lined with mats. Underneath is an excellent cellar. The building designed for a house of worship, was being built when I arrived. Its architecture is a curiosity.

The frame is made in the usual form, save that instead of four main posts at the corners, and others at considerable distances, for the support of lateral girders, there were eleven on each side, and six on each end, beside the corner posts—all equal in size and length. Between these billets of wood were driven transversely, on which as lathing, mortar made of clay, sand and straw, were laid to a level with their exterior and interior faces. There is so little falling weather here, that this mode of building was considered sufficiently substantial.

Messrs. Lee and Perkins were formerly connected with the mission on the Willamette. Eighteen months before I had the happiness of enjoying their hospitality, they came to this spot with axes on their shoulders, felled trees, ploughed, fenced, and planted twenty acres of land with their own hands, and erected these habitations of civilization and Christianity on the bosom of the howling wilderness. Their premises are situated on elevated ground, about a mile south-west from the river. Immediately back is a grove of small white oaks and yellow pines ; a little north, is a sweet spring bursting from a ledge of rocks which supplies water for house use, and moistens about an acre of rich soil. About a mile to the south, are two or three hundred acres of fine land, with groves of oaks around, and an abundant supply of excellent water. Here it was the intention of the mission to open a farm under the care of a layman from the States.

A mile and a half to the north, is a tract of about two hundred acres, susceptible of being plentifully irrigated by a number of large streams that pour down upon it from the western mountains. Here, too, they intended to locate laymen to open farms, and extract from the idle earth the means of feeding themselves, the Indians, and the way-worn white man from the burnt solitudes of the mountains. No location, not even the sacred precincts of St. Bernard, on the snows of the Alps, could be better chosen for the operations of a holy benevolence.

The Indians from many quarters flock to the Dalles and the Shutes in the spring, and autumn, and winter to purchase salmon; the commercial movements between the States and the Pacific will pass their door; and there in after-days, the sturdy emigrants from the States will stop, (as did the pilgrims on Plymouth rock,) to give grateful praise to Him who stood forth in their aid, not indeed while struggling on the foamy billow, but on the burning plain and the icy cliff, and in the deadly turmoil of Indian battles on the way, and will seek food and rest for their emaciated frames, before entering the woody glen and flowing everglades of Lower Oregon.

A saw-mill, a grist-mill, and other machinery necessary to carry out a liberal plan of operations, are in contemplation. The

fruit of the oak, it is supposed, will support
1,000 hogs from the middle of August to
the middle of April; the products of the
arable soil will suffice to make that number
into marketable pork; and as the grass
and other vegetation grow there during the
winter months, twenty-five or thirty square
miles of pasturage round about, will enable
them to raise, at a trifling expense, immense
numbers of sheep, horses and cattle. Five
acres of ground cultivated in 1839, produced twenty-five bushels of the small
grains, seventy-five bushels of potatoes, and
considerable quantities of other vegetables.
This was an experiment only on soil not
irrigated. Gentlemen suppose it capable
of producing double that amount, if irrigated. The season, too, was unusually
dry.

Around about the mission are clusters of
friable sandstone rocks of remarkable form.
Their height varies from ten to thirty feet;
their basilar diameters from three to ten
feet: their shape generally resembles that
of the obelisk. These (fifteen or twenty in
number) standing among the oaks and pines,
often in clusters, and sometimes solitary,
give a strange interest of antiquity to the
spot. And this illusion is increased by a

rock of another form, an immense boulder resting upon a short, slender pedestal, and strikingly resembling the Egyptian sphynx. The Indian tradition in regard to them is, that they were formerly men, who, for some sin against the Great Spirit, were changed to stone.

At the Dalles is the upper village of the Chinooks. At the Shutes, five miles above, is the lower village of the Wallawallas. One of the missionaries, Mr. Lee, learns the Chinook language, and the other, Mr. Perkins, the Wallawalla ; and their custom is to repair on Sabbath days each to his own people, and teach them the Christian religion. The Chinooks flatten their heads more, and are more stupid than any other tribe on the Columbia. There was one among the Dalles' band, who, it was said, resisted so obstinately the kind efforts of his parents to crush his skull into the aristocratic shape, that they abandoned him to the care of nature in this regard ; and much to the scandal of his family, his head grew in the natural form. I saw him every day while I staid there. He was evidently the most intelligent one of the band. His name is Boston ; so called, because the form of his head resembles that of Americans, whom the Indians call "Boston," in order to distinguish them from "King George's men,"—the Hudson Bay Company gentlemen. Boston, although of mean origin, has, on account of his superior energy and intelligence, become the war chief of the Dalles.

On the morning of the 14th, I overhauled my baggage, preparatory to descending the river. In doing so, I was much vexed to find that the Indians had, in some manner, drawn my saddle to the window of the workshop in which it was deposited, and stripped it of stirrups, stirrup-straps, surcingle, girths, and crupper. They had also stolen my bridle.

The loss of these articles, in a region where they could not be purchased — articles so necessary to me in carrying out my designs of travelling over the lower country, roused in me the bitterest determination to regain them at all hazards. Without reflecting for a moment upon the disparity of numbers between my single self and forty or fifty able-bodied Indians, I armed myself completely, and marched my solitary battalion to the camp of the principal chief, and entered it. He was away. I explained to some persons there by signs and a few words, the object of my search, and marched my army to an elevated position and halted.

I had been stationed but a short time, when the Indians began to collect in their chief's lodge, and whisper earnestly. Ten minutes passed thus, and Indians were constantly arriving and entering. I was supported in the rear by a lusty oak, and so far as I remember, was ready to exclaim with the renowned antagonist of Roderick Dhu,

" Come one, come all;" &c.

but never having been a hero before or since, I am not quite certain that I thought any such thing. My wrath, however, was extreme. To be robbed for the first time by Indians, and that by such cowardly wretches as these Chinooks were; and robbed too of my means of exploring Oregon, when on the very threshold of the most charming part of it, was an inconvenience and an ignominy worth a battle to remove.

Just at the moment of this lofty conclusion, thirty-eight or forty Indians rushed around me; eight or ten loaded muskets were levelled at my chest, within ten feet of me, and the old chief stood within five feet, with a duelling pistol loaded, cocked, and pointed at my heart. While this movement was being made, I brought my rifle to bear upon the old chief's vital organs. Thus both armies stood for the space of five minutes, without the movement of tongue or muscle. Then one of the braves intimated that it was " not good" for me to be out with arms; and that I must immediately accommodate myself within doors. But to this proposition the bravery of my army would not submit. I accordingly informed him to that effect; whereupon the opposing army went into a furious rage.

At this juncture of affairs, Mr. Lee came up, and acted as interpreter. He inquired into the difficulty, and was told that the " whole Chinook tribe was threatened with invasion, and all the horrors of a general war, on what account they knew not." The commander of my army reported that they had robbed him, and deserved such treatment; and that he had taken arms to annihilate the tribe, unless they had restored to him what they had stolen.

I was then told that "it was not good for me to appear in arms—that it was good for me to go into the house " To this, my army with one voice replied, " Nay, never,

never leave the ground, or the Chinooks
alive, tribe or chief, if the stolen property
be not restored;" and wheeling my battalion, drove first one flank and then the
other of the opposing hosts, fifty yards into
the depths of the forests.

During this movement, worthy of the best
days of Spartan valour, the old chief stood
amazed to see his followers, with guns loaded
and cocked, fly before such inferior numbers. After effecting the complete rout of
the opposing infantry, the army under my
command took up the old position without
the loss of a single man. But the old chief
was still there, as dogged and sullen as
Indian ever was. On approaching him, he
presented his pistol again near my chest,
whereupon my rifle was instantly in a position to reach his; and thus the renowned
leaders of these mighty hosts stood for the
space of an hour without bloodshed.

Perhaps such another chief was never
seen; such unblenching coolness—excepting always the heat which was thrown off
in a healthful and profuse perspiration—
and such perfect undauntedness, except an
unpleasant knocking of the knees together,
produced probably by the anticipated blasts
of December. But while these exhibitions

of valour were being enacted, one stirrup
was thrown at my feet, and then the other,
and then the straps, the crupper, &c.,
until all the most valuable articles lost, were
piled before me. The conquest was complete, and will doubtless shed immortal
lustre upon the gallant band, who, in the
heart of the wilderness, dared to assert and
maintain, against the encroachments of a
numerous and well-disciplined foe, the
" élite" of the Chinook army, the rights
and high prerogative of brave freemen and
soldiers. The number of killed and wounded
of the enemy had not been ascertained,
when the troops under my command departed for the lower country.

In the evening which succeeded this day
of carnage, the old chief assembled his surviving followers, and made war speeches
until midnight. His wrath was immeasur-
able. On the following morning, the Indians in the employ of the mission left their
work.

About ten o'clock, one of the tribe appeared with a pack-horse, to convey Mr.
Lee's and my own packs to the water-side.
The old chief also appeared, and bade him
desist. He stood armed before the house
an hour, making many threats against the

Bostons, individually and collectively ; but finally retired. As soon as he had entered his lodge, the horse of his disobedient subject was loaded, and rushed to the river. An effort was made to get oarsmen for our canoe, but the old hero of a legion of devils told them, " the high Bostons would kill them all, and that they must not go with him." Mr. Lee, however, did not despair.

We followed the baggage towards the river. When within a quarter of a mile of it, two Americans, members of Richardson's party, Mr. Lee and an Indian or two, whom the old chief had not succeeded in frightening, took the canoe from the bushes, and bore it to the river on their shoulders.

The natives were stationed beyond rifle-shot upon the rocks on either side of the way, bows and arrows, and guns in hand. Indian Boston was in command. He stood on the loftiest rock, grinding his teeth, and growling like a bloodhound, "Bostons ugh;" and springing upon his bow, drove his arrows into the ground with demoniac madness. I stopped, and drew my rifle to my face, whereupon there was a grand retreat behind the rocks. My army marched slowly and majestically on, as became the dignity of veteran victors. The women and children fled from the wigwams by the way; and the fear of the annihilation of the whole tribe only abated when my wrath was, to their understanding, appeased by the interference of Mr. Lee. Thus the tribe was saved from my vengeance—the whole number, fifty or sixty stout savages, were saved! an instance of clemency, a parallel to which will scarcely be found in the history of past ages.

Being convinced, at last, that my intentions towards them had become more pacific, six oarsmen, a bowsman, and steersman, were readily engaged by Mr. Lee, and he shoved off from that memorable battle-ground on a voyage to the Willamette. These Indians have been notorious thieves ever since they have been known to the whites. Their meanness has been equally well known. Destitute of every manly and moral virtue, they and their fathers have hung around the Dalles, eaten salmon, and rotted in idleness and vice; active only in mischief, and honest only in their crouching cowardice towards those they suppose able to punish their villany.

There is some very curious philosophy among them: as for example, they believe human existence to be indestructible by the laws of nature ; and never diseased, unless made so by the Medicine men or conjurers, who are believed to enter into the system in an unseen manner, and pull at the vitals. They also hold that one Medicine man can cast out another. Accordingly, when one of them is called to a patient and does not succeed in restoring him to health, he is believed to be accessory to his death, and is punished as such by the relatives of the deceased.

Their mode of treating patients is to thrust them into a sweat oven, and thence, reeking with perspiration, into the cold streams. After this, they are stretched out at length on the ground, wrapped very warmly, and kneaded, and rolled, and rubbed, with great severity. The abdomen is violently pressed down to the spine, and the forehead pressed with the might of the operator ; the arms and limbs, pinched and rubbed, rolled and bruised. Meanwhile, the conjuror is uttering most beastly noises. As might be supposed, patients labouring under the febrile diseases, are soon destroyed.

In order, however, to keep up their influence among the people, the conjurors of

a tribe, male and female, have cabalistic
dances. After the darkness of night sets
in, they gather together in a wigwam, build
a large fire in the centre, spread the floor
with elk skins, set up on end a wide cedar
board, and suspend near it a stick of wood
in a horizontal position. An individual
seizes the end of the stick, swings the other
end against the cedar board, and thus beats
noisy time to a still more noisy chant. The
dance is commenced sometimes by a man
alone, and often by a man and woman.
And various and strange are the bodily contortions of the performers. They jump up
and down, and swing their arms with more
and more violence, as the noise of the singing and thumping accompaniment increases,
and yelp, and froth at the mouth, till the
musician winds up with the word "*ugh*"—
a long, strong, gutteral grunt; or until
some one of the dancers falls apparently
dead.

When the latter is the case, one of the
number walks around the prostrate individual, and calls his or her name loudly at
each ear, at the nose, fingers, and toes.
After this ceremony, the supposed dead
shudders greatly, and comes to life. And
thus they continue to sing, and thump, and

dance, and die, and come to life through
the night. They are said to be very expert
at sleight of hand.

The Chinooks, like all other Indians, believe in existence after death ; but their
views of the conditions of that existence,
I could not learn. The conjurors teach
them, that they themselves shall be able to
visit their tribe after the body shall have
decayed ; and when approaching the end
of their days, inform the people in what
shape they will manifest themselves. Some
choose a horse, others a deer, others an
elk, &c., and when they die, the image of
their transmigrated state is erected over
their remains.

The reader is desired to consider Mr. Lee
and myself gliding, arrow-like, down the
deep clear Columbia, at two o'clock in the
afternoon of the 15th, and to interest himself in the bold mountain embankments
clothed with the deep, living green of lofty
pine and fir forests, while I revert to the
kind hospitalities of the Dalles' mission.
Yet how entirely impossible is it to relate
all that one enjoys in every muscle of the
body, every nerve and sense, and every affection of the spirit when he flies from the
hardships and loneliness of deserts to the

comforts of a bed, a chair, and a table,
and the holy sympathy of hearts moulded
and controlled by the higher sentiments. I
had taken leave of Mr. and Mrs. Perkins
with the feelings that one experiences in
civilized lands, when leaving long-tried and
congenial friends.

The good man urged me to return and
explore with him, during the rainy season
in the lower country, some extensive and
beautiful prairies, which the Indians say lie
sixty or seventy miles in the north, on the
east side of the President's range ; and Mrs.
Perkins kindly proposed to welcome my
return for that object with a splendid suit
of buckskin, to be used in my journeyings.

But I must leave my friends to introduce
the reader to the " Island of the Tombs."
Mr. Lee pointed to it, as the tops of the
cedar board houses of the dead peered over
the hillocks of sand and rock among which
they stood. We moored our canoe
on the western side, and climbed up a
precipice of black shining rocks two hundred feet ; and winding among drifts of
sand the distance of one hundred yards
came to the tombs. They consisted of
boxes ten or twelve feet square on the
ground, eight or ten high, made of cedar

boards fastened to a rough frame, in an
upright position at the sides, and horizontally over the top.   On them, and about
them, were the cooking utensils, and other
personal property of the deceased.   Within
were the dead bodies, wrapped in many
thicknesses of deer and elk skins, tightly
lashed with leather thongs, and laid in a
pile with their heads to the east.   Underneath the undecayed bodies were many
bones from which the flesh and wrappings
had fallen : in some instances a number
of waggon loads.   Three or four of the
tombs had gone to ruins, and the skulls
and other bones lay strewn on the ground.
The skulls were all flattened.   I picked up
one with the intention of bringing it to the
States.   But as Mr. Lee assured me that
the high veneration of the living for the
dead would make the attempt very dangerous, I reluctantly returned it to its resting place.

We glided merrily down the river till
sunset, and landed on the northern shore to
sup.   The river had varied from one to one
and a half miles in width, with rather a
sluggish current ; water clear, cool, and
very deep.   Various kinds of duck, divers,
&c., were upon its beautiful surface.   The

hair seal was abundant. The mountains rose abruptly on either side from five hundred to two thousand feet, in sweeping heights, clad with evergreen trees. Some few small oaks grew in the nooks by the water side. Among these were Indian wigwams, constructed of boards split from the red cedar on the mountains. I entered some of them. They were filthy in the extreme. In one of them was a sick man. A withered old female was kneeding and pinching the devil out of him. He was labouring under a bilious fever. But as a " Medicine man" was pulling at his gall, it was necessary to expel him ; and the old hag pressed his head, bruised his abdomen, &c., with the fury and groaning of a bedlamite.

Not an acre of arable land appeared along the shores. The Indians subsist on fish and acorns of the white oak. The former they eat fresh during the summer ; but their winter stores they dry and preserve in the following manner :—The spine of the fish being taken out, and the flesh being slashed into checks with a knife, so as to expose as much surface as possible, is laid on the rocks to dry. After becoming thoroughly

hard, it is bruised to powder, mixed with
the oil of the leaf fat of the fish, and packed
away in flag sacks. Although no salt is
used in this preparation, it remains good
till May of the following year. The acorns,
as soon as they fall from the trees, are buried
in sand constantly satured with water, where
they remain till spring. By this soaking
their bitter flavour is said to be destroyed.

After supper, Mr. Lee ordered a launch,
and the Indian paddles were again dipping
in the bright waters. The stars were out
on the clear night, twinkling as of old,
when the lofty peaks around were heaved
from the depths of the volcano. They now
looked down on a less grand, indeed, but
more lovely scene. The fires of the natives
blazed among the woody glens, the light
canoe skimmed the water near the shore,
the winds groaned over the mountain tops,
the cascades sang from cliff to cliff, the loon
shouted and dove beneath the shining
wave; it was a wild, almost unearthly
scene, in the deep gorge of the Columbia.
The rising of the moon changed its features.
The profoundest silence reigned, save the
dash of paddles that echoed faintly from
the shores; our canoe sprang lightly over

the rippling waters, the Indian fires smouldered among the waving pines; the stars
became dim, and the depths of the blue sky
glowed one vast nebula of mellow light.
But the eastern mountains hid awhile the
orb from sight.

The south-western heights shone with its
pale beams, and cast into the deeply sunken
river a bewitching dancing of light and
shade, unequalled by the pencil of the wildest imagination. The grandeur, too, of
grove, and cliff, and mountain, and the
mighty Columbia wrapped in the drapery
of a golden midnight! It was the new and
rapidly opening panorama of the sublime
wilderness. The scene changed again when
the moon was high in heaven.

The cocks crew in the Indian villages;
the birds twittered on the boughs; the wild
fowl screamed, as her light gilded the
chasm of the river, and revealed the high
rock Islands with their rugged crags and
mouldering tombs. The winds from Mount
Adams were loaded with frosts, and the
poetry of the night was fast waning into an
ague, when Mr. Lee ordered the steersman
to moor. A crackling pine fire was soon
blazing, and having warmed our shivering

frames, we spread our blankets, and slept
sweetly till the dawn.

Early on the morning of the 16th, our
Indians were pulling at the paddles. The
sky was overcast, and a dash of rain occasionally fell, the first I had witnessed since
leaving Boyou Salade. And although the
air was chilly, and the heavens gloomy, yet
when the large clear drops pattered on my
hat, and fell in glad confusion around our
little bark, a thrill of pleasure shot through
my heart. Dangers, wastes, thirst, starvation, eternal dearth on the earth, and dew-
less heavens, were matters only of painful
recollection. The present was the reality
of the past engrafted on the hopes of the
future; the showery skies, the lofty green
mountains, the tumbling cataracts, the
mighty forests, the sweet savour of teeming
groves, among the like of which I had
breathed in infancy, hung over the
threshold of the lower Columbia, the goal
of my wayfaring.

Hearken to that roar of waters! see
the hastening of the flood! hear the sharp
rippling by yonder rock; the whole river
sinks from view in advance of us. The
bowsman dips his paddle deeply and
quickly; the frail canoe shoots to the

northern shore between a string of islands and the main land; glides quickly down a narrow channel; passes a village of cedar board wigwams on a beautiful little plain to the right; it rounds the lower island; behold the Cascades!—an immense trough of boulders of rocks, down which rushes the "Great River of the West." The baggage is ashore; the Indians are conveying the canoe over the portage, and while this is being done, the reader will have time to explore the lower falls of the Columbia, and their vicinage.

The trail of the Portage runs near the torrent, along the rocky slope on its northern bank, and terminates among large loose rocks, blanched by the floods of ages, at the foot of the trough of the main rapid. It is about a mile and a half long. At its lower end voyagers re-embark when the river is at a low stage, and run the lower rapids. But when it is swollen by the annual freshets, they bear their boats a mile and a half farther down, where the water is deep and less tumultuous. In walking down this path, I had a near view of the whole length of the main rapids. As I have intimated, the bed of the river here is a vast inclined trough of white rocks, sixty

or eighty feet deep, about four hundred
yards wide at the top, and diminishing to
about half that width at the bottom. The
length of this trough is about a mile. In
that distance the water falls about one
hundred and thirty feet ; in the rapids,
above and below it, about twenty feet,
making the whole descent about one
hundred and fifty feet. The quantity of
water which passes here is incalculable.
But an approximate idea of it may be obtained from the fact that while the velocity
is so great, that the eye with difficulty follows objects floating on the surface, yet
such is its volume at the lowest stage of
the river, that it rises and bends like a sea
of molten glass over a channel of immense
rocks, without breaking its surface, except
near the shores, so deep and vast is the
mighty flood !

In the June freshets, when the melted
snows from the western declivities of seven
hundred miles of the Rocky Mountains,
and those on the eastern sides of the President's Range, come down, the Cascades
must present a spectacle of sublimity
equalled only by Niagara. This is the
passage of the river through the President's
Range, and the mountains near it on either

side are worthy of their distinguished name.
At a short distance from the southern shore
they rise in long ridgy slopes, covered with
pines, and other terebinthine trees of extraordinary size, over the tops of which rise
bold black crags, which, elevating themselves in great grandeur one beyond another, twenty or thirty miles to the southward, cluster around the icy base of Mount
Washington. On the other side of the
Cascades is a similar scene. Immense and
gloomy forests, tangled with fallen timber
and impenetrable underbrush, cover mountains, which in the States, would excite the
profoundest admiration for their majesty
and beauty, but which dwindle into insig-
nificance as they are viewed in presence of
the shining glaciers, and massive grandeur
of Mount Adams, hanging over them.

The river above the Cascades runs north-
westwardly ; but approaching the descent,
it turns westward, and, after entering the
trough, south westwardly, and having
passed this, it resumes its course to the
north west. By this bend, it leaves between its shore and the northern mountains, a somewhat broken plain, a mile in
width, and about four miles in length. At
the upper end of the rapids, this plain is

nearly on a level with the river, so that an inconsiderable freshet sets the water up a natural channel half way across the bend. This circumstance, and the absence of any serious obstructions in the form of hills, &c., led me to suppose that a canal might be cut around the Cascades at a trifling expence, which would not only open steamboat navigation to the Dalles, but furnish at this interesting spot, an incalculable amount of water power.

The canoe had been deposited among the rocks at the lower end of the trough, our cocoa and boiled salmon, bread, butter, potatoes, &c., had been located in their proper depositories, and we were taking a parting gaze at the rushing flood, when the sound of footsteps, and an order given in French to deposit a bale of goods at the water side, drew our attention to a hearty old gentleman of fifty or fifty-five, whom Mr. Lee immediately recognized as Dr. McLaughlin. He was about five feet eleven inches in height, and stoutly built, weighing about two hundred pounds, with large green blueish eyes, a ruddy complexion, and hair of snowy whiteness. He was on his return from London with despatches from the Hudson's Bay Company's Board in

England, and with letters from friends at home to the hundreds of Britons in its employ in the north-western wilderness. He was in high spirits. Every crag in sight was familiar to him, had witnessed the energy and zeal of thirty years' successful enterprise; had seen him in the strength of ripened manhood, and now beheld his undiminished energies crowned with the frosted locks of age. We spent ten minutes with the doctor, and received a kind invitation to the hospitalities of his post; gave our canoe, freighted with our baggage, in charge of the Indians, to take down the lower rapids, and ascended the bluff to the trail which leads to the tide-water below them. We climbed two hundred feet among small spruce, pine, fir, and hemlock trees, to the table land.

The track was strewn with fragments of petrified trees, from three inches to two feet in diameter, and rocks, (quartz and granite, *ex loco*), mingled with others more or less fused. Soon after striking the path on the plain, we came to a beautiful little lake, lying near the brink of the hill. It was clear and deep; and around its western, northern, and eastern shores, drooped the boughs of a thick hedge of small evergreen

trees, which dipped and rose charmingly
in its waters. All around stood the lofty
pines, sighing and groaning in the wind.
Nothing could be seen, but the little lake
and the girding forest; a gem of perfect
beauty, reflecting the deep shades of the
unbroken wilderness. A little stream
creeping away from it down the bluff,
babbled back the roar of the Cascades.

The trail led us among deep ravines,
clad with heavy frosts, the soil of which
was a coarse gravel, thinly covered with a
vegetable mould. A mile from the lake,
we came upon a plain level again. In this
place was a collection of Indian tombs,
similar to those upon the "Island of
tombs." These were six or eight in number, and contained a great quantity of
bones. On the boards around the sides
were painted the figures of death, horses,
dogs, &c. The great destroyer bears the
same grim aspect to the savage mind
that he does to ours.—A skull and the
fleshless bones of a skeleton piled around,
were his symbol upon these rude resting
places of the departed. One of them,
which our Indian said, contained the remains of a celebrated " Medecine man,"
bore the figure of a horse rudely carved

from the red cedar tree. This was the form in which his *posthumous* visits were to be made to his tribe. Small brass kettles, wooden pails, and baskets of curious workmanship, were piled on the roof.

Thence onward half a mile over a stony soil, sometimes open, and again covered with forests, we reached our canoe by the rocky shore at the foot of the rapids. Mr. Lee here pointed out to me a strong eddying current on the southern shore, in which Mr. Cyrus Shepard and Mrs. Doctor White and child, of the Methodist Mission on the Willamette, were capsized the year before, in an attempt to run the lower rapids. Mr. Shepard could not swim—had sunk the second time, and rose by the side of the upturned canoe, when he seized the hand of Mrs. White, who was on the opposite side, and thus sustained himself and her, until some Indians came to their relief. On reaching the shore, and turning up the canoe, the child was found entangled among the cross-bars, dead!

The current was strong where we re-entered our canoe, and bore us along at a brisk rate.—The weather, too, was very agreeable ; the sky transparent, and glowing with a mild October sun. The scenery

about us was truly grand. A few detached
wisps of mist clung to the dark crags of
the mountains on the southern shore, and
numerous cascades shot out from the peaks,
and tumbling from one shelf to another,
at length plunged hundreds of feet among
confused heaps of rocks in the vale. The
crags themselves were extremely picturesque ; they beetled out so boldly, a thousand feet above the forests on the sides of
the mountain, and appeared to hang so easily
and gracefully on the air. Some of them
were basaltic. One appeared very remarkable. The mountain on which it stood
was about one thousand two hundred feet
high. On its side there was a deep rocky
ravine. In this, about three hundred feet
from the plain, arose a column of thirty or
forty feet in diameter, and, I judged more
than two hundred feet high, surmounted
by a cap resembling the pediment of an
ancient church.

Far up its sides grew a number of shrub
cedars, which had taken root in the crevices,
and, as they grew, sunk down horizontally, forming an irregular fringe of green
around it. A short distance further down
was seen a beautiful cascade. The stream
appeared to rise near the very apex of the

mountain, and having run a number of rods in a dark gorge between two peaks, it suddenly shot from the brink of a cliff into the copse of evergreen trees at the base of the mountain. The height of the perpendicular fall appeared to be about six hundred feet. Some of the water was dispersed in spray before reaching the ground; but a large quantity of it fell on the plain, and sent among the heights a noisy and thrilling echo. On the north side of the river, the mountains were less precipitous, and covered with a dense forest of pines, cedars, firs, &c.

The bottom lands of the river were alternately prairies and woodlands; the former clad with a heavy growth of the wild grasses, dry and brown—the latter, with pine, fir, cotton-wood, black ash, and various kinds of shrubs. The river varied in width from one to two miles, generally deep and still, but occasionally crossed by sand-bars. Ten or twelve miles below the cascades we came upon one, that, stretching two or three miles down the river, turned the current to the southern shore. The wind blew freshly, and the waves ran high in that quarter; so it was deemed expedient to lighten the canoe. To this

K 2

end Mr. Lee, the two Americans and myself, landed on the northern shore for a
walk, while the Indians should paddle
around to the lower point of the bar. We
travelled along the beach. It was generally
hard and gravelly.

Among the pebbles, I noticed several
splendid specimens of the agate. The soil
of the flats was a vegetable mould, eighteen
inches or two feet in depth, resting on a stratum of sand and gravel, and evidently overflown by the annual floods of June. The flats
varied from a few rods to a mile in width.
While enjoying this walk, the two Americans started up a deer, followed it into the
woods, and, loth to return unsuccessful,
pursued it till long after our canoe was
moored below the bar. So that Mr. Lee
and myself had abundant time to amuse
ourselves with all manner of homely wishes
towards our persevering companions till
near sunset, when the three barges of Dr.
McLaughlin, under their Indian blanket
sails and sapling masts, swept gallantly by
us, and added the last dreg to our vexation.
Mr. Lee was calm, I was furious. What,
for a paltry deer, lose a view of the Columbia hence to the Fort! But I remember
with satisfaction that no one was materially

injured by my wrath, and that my truant countrymen were sufficiently gratified with their success to enable them to bear with much resignation, three emphatic scowls, as they made their appearance at the canoe.

The dusk of night was now creeping into the valleys, and we had twenty miles to make. The tide from the Pacific was setting up, and the wind had left us; but our Indians suggested that the force of their paddles, stimulated by a small present of " shmoke" (tobacco,) would still carry us in by eleven o'clock. We therefore gave our promises to pay the required quantum of the herb, ensconced ourselves in blankets, and dozed to the wild music of the paddles, till a shower of hail aroused us. It was about ten o'clock. An angry cloud hung over us, and the rain and hail fell fast; the wind from Mounts Washington and Jefferson chilled every fibre of our systems; the wooded hills, on both sides of the river were wrapped in cold brown clouds; the owl and wolf were answering each other on the heights; enough of light lay on the stream to show dimly the islands that divided its waters, and the fires of the wigwams disclosed the naked groups of savages around them.

It was a scene that the imagination loves. The canoe, thirty feet in length, (such another had cut those waters centuries before); the Indians, kneeling two and two, and rising on their paddles; their devoted missionary surveying them and the villages on the shores, and rejoicing in the anticipation, that soon the songs of the redeemed savage would break from the dark vales of Oregon; that those wastes of mind would soon teem with a harvest of happiness and truth, cast a breathing unutterable charm over the deep hues of that green wilderness, dimly seen on that stormy night, which will give me pleasure to dwell upon while I live. "On the bar!" cried Mr. Lee; and while our Indians leaped into the water, and dragged the canoe to the channel, he pointed to the dim light of the Hudson Bay Company's saw and grist mill two miles above on the northern shore.

We were three miles from Vancouver. The Indians knew the bar, and were delighted to find themselves so near the termination of their toil. They soon found the channel, and leaping aboard plied their paddles with renewed energy. And if any one faltered, the steersman rebuked him with his own hopes of "shmoke" and "schejotecut," (the Fort) which never failed to bring the delinquent to duty. Twenty minutes of vigorous rowing moored us at the landing. A few hundred yards below, floated a ship and a sloop, scarcely seen through the fog. On the shore rose a levee or breastwork, along which the dusky savages were gliding with stealthy and silent tread; in the distance were heard voices in English speaking of home. We landed, ascended the levee, entered a lane between cultivated fields, walked a quarter of a mile, where, under a long line of pickets, we entered Fort Vancouver—the goal of my wanderings, the destination of my weary footsteps!

Mr. James Douglass, the gentleman who had been in charge of the post during the absence of Dr. McLaughlin, conducted us to a room warmed by a well-fed stove; insisted that I should exchange my wet garments for dry ones, and proffered every other act that the kindest hospitality could suggest to relieve me of the discomforts resulting from four months' journeying in the wilderness.

CHAPTER V.

Departure from Vancouver—Wappertoo Island—The Willamette River—Its Mouth—The Mountains—Falls—River above the Falls—Arrival at the Lower Settlement—A Kentuckian—Mr. Johnson and his Cabin—Thomas M'Kay and his Mill—Dr. Bailey and Wife and Home—The Neighbouring Farmers—The Methodist Episcopal Mission and Missionaries—Their Modes of Operations—The Wisdom of their Course —Their Improvements, &c.—Return to Vancouver— Mr. Young—Mr. Lee's Misfortune—Descent of the Willamette—Indians—Arrival at Vancouver—Oregon—Its Mountains, Rivers and Soil, and Climate— Shipment for the Sandwich Islands—Life at Vancouver—Descent of the Columbia—Astoria—On the Pacific Sea—The Last View of Oregon—Account of Oregon, by Lieut. Wilkes, Commander of the late exploring Expedition.

ON the morning of the 21st, I left the Fort and dropped down the Columbia, five miles, to Wappatoo Island. This large tract of low land is bounded on the south-west, south and south-east, by the mouths of the Willamette, and on the north by the Columbia. The side contiguous to the latter river is about fifteen miles in length; the side bounded by the eastern mouth of

the Willamette about seven miles, and that
bounded by the western mouth of the same
river about twelve miles.   It derives its
name from an edible root called *Wappatoo*,
which it produces in abundance.   It is generally low, and, in the central parts broken
with small ponds and marshes, in which
the water rises and falls with the river.
Nearly the whole surface is overflown by
the June freshets.   It is covered with a
heavy growth of cotton-wood, elm, white-
oak, black-ash, alder, and a large species
of laurel, and other shrubs.   The Hudson
Bay Company, some years ago, placed a
few hogs upon it, which have subsisted
entirely upon roots, acorns, &c. and increased to many hundreds.

I found the Willamette deep enough for
ordinary steam-boats, for the distance of
twenty miles from its western mouth.   One
mile below the falls are rapids on which the
water was too shallow to float our canoe.
The tide rises at this place about fourteen
inches.   The western shore of the river,
from the point where its mouths diverge to
this place, consists of lofty mountains rising
immediately from the water-side, and
covered with pines.   On the eastern side,
beautiful swells and plains extend from the

Columbia to within five or six miles of the
rapids. They are generally covered with
pine, white oak, black-ash, and other kinds
of timber. From the point last named to the
rapids, wooded mountains crowd down to the
verge of the stream. Just below the rapids
a very considerable stream comes in from
the east. It is said to rise in a champaign
country, which commences two or three
miles from the Willamette, and extends
eastward twenty or thirty miles to the
lower hills of the President's range. This
stream breaks through the mountain tumultuously, and enters the Willamette with
so strong a current, as to endanger boats
attempting to pass it. Here were a number of Indian huts, the inmates of which
were busied in taking and curing salmon.
Between the rapids and the falls, the country adjacent to the river is similar to that
just described; mountains clothed with
impenetrable forests.

The river, thus far, appeared to have an
average width of four hundred yards, water
limpid. As we approached the falls, the
eastern shore presented a solid wall of basalt,
thirty feet in perpendicular height. On
the top of this wall was nearly an acre of
level area, on which the Hudson Bay Com-

pany have built a log-house. This plain
is three or four feet below the level of the
water above the falls, and protected from
the floods by the intervention of a deep
chasm, which separates it from the rocks
over which the water pours. This is the
best site in the country for extensive flour
and lumber-mills. The valley of the
Willamette is the only portion of Oregon
from which grain can ever, to any extent,
become an article of export ; and this splendid waterfall can be approached at all seasons, from above and below, by sloops,
schooners, &c. The Hudson Bay Company
aware of its importance, have commenced a
race-way, and drawn timber on the ground,
with the apparent intention of erecting such
works. On the opposite side is an acre or
two of broken ground, which might be simi-
larly occupied.

The falls are formed by a line of dark
rock, which stretches diagonally across the
stream. The river was low when I passed
it, and all the water was discharged at three
jets. Two of these were near the eastern
shore ; the other was near the western
shore, and fell into the chasm which divides
the rocky plain before named, from the cliffs
of the falls. At the mouth of this chasm

my Indians unloaded their canoe, dragged it up the crags, and having borne it on their shoulders eight or ten rods, launched it upon a narrow neck of water by the shore ; reloaded, and rowed to the deep water above.

The scene, however, was too interesting to be left so soon, and I tarried awhile to view it. The cataract roared loudly among the caverns, and sent a thousand foaming eddies into the stream below. Countless numbers of salmon were leaping and falling upon the fretted waters ; savages almost naked were around me, untrained by the soothing influences of true knowledge, and the hopes of a purer world ; as rude as the rocks on which they trod ; as bestial as the bear that growled in the thicket. On either hand was the primeval wilderness, with its decaying and perpetually-renewing energies; nothing could be more intensely interesting. I had passed but a moment in these pleasant yet painful reflections, when my Indians, becoming impatient, called me to pursue my voyage.

A mile above the falls a large creek comes in from the west. It is said to rise among the mountains near the Columbia, and to run south and south-east and eastwardly through a series of fine prairies, interspersed

with timber. Above the falls, the mountains rise immediately from the water's edge,
clothed with noble forests of pine, &c.; but
at the distance of fifteen miles above, their
green ridges give place to grassy and wooded
swells on the west, and timbered and prairie
plains on the eastern side. This section of
the river appeared navigable for any craft
that could float in the stream below the
falls.

It was dark when I arrived at the level
country ; and emerging suddenly in sight of
a fire on the western bank, my Indians cried
" Boston!" Boston!" and turned the canoe
ashore to give me an opportunity of speaking with a fellow countryman. He was sitting in the drizzling rain, by a large log-fire
—a stalwart six foot Kentucky trapper.
After long service in the American Fur
Companies, among the rocky mountains, he
had come down to the Willamette, accompanied by an Indian woman and his child,
selected a place to build his home, made
an " improvement," sold it, and was now
commencing another. He entered my canoe
and steered across the river to a Mr. Johnson's. " I am sorry I can't keep you," said
he, " but I reckon you'll sleep better under
shingles, than this stormy sky. Johnson

will be glad to see you. He's got a good shantee, and something for you to eat."

We soon crossed the stream, and entered the cabin of Mr. Johnson. It was a hewn log structure, about twenty feet square, with a mud chimney, hearth and fire-place. The furniture consisted of one chair, a number of wooden benches, a rude bedstead covered with flag mats, and several sheet-iron kettles, earthen plates, knives and forks, tin pint cups, an Indian wife, and a brace of brown boys. I passed the night pleasantly with Mr. Johnson ; and in the morning rose early to go to the Methodist Episcopal Mission, twelve miles above. But the old hunter detained me to breakfast ; and afterwards insisted that I should view his premises, while his boy should gather the horses to convey me on my way. And a sight of fenced fields, many acres of wheat and oat-stubble, potato-fields, and garden-vegetables of all description, and a barn well stored with the gathered harvest compensated me for the delay. Adjoining Mr. Johnson's farm were four others, on all of which there were from fifty to a hundred acres under cul-vation, and substantial log-houses and barns.

One of these belonged to Thomas M'Kay,

son of M'Kay, who figured with Mr. Astor in the doings of the Pacific Fur Company.

After surveying these marks of civilization, I found a Dr. Bailey waiting with his horses to convey me to his home. We accordingly mounted, bade adieu to the old trapper of Hudson Bay and other parts of the frozen north, and went to view M'Kay's mill. A grist-mill in Oregon! We found him working at his dam. Near by lay French burr stones, and some portions of substantial and well-fashioned iron work. The frame of the mill-house was raised and shingled ; and an excellent structure it was. The whole expense of the establishment, when completed, is expected to be £1,400 or £1,600. M'Kay's mother is a Cree or Chippeway Indian; and M'Kay himself is a compound of the two races. The contour of his frame and features, is Scotch ; his manners and intellects strongly tinctured with the Indian. He has been in the service of the Fur Companies all his life, save some six or seven years past; and by his daring enterprise, and courage in battle has rendered himself the terror of the Oregon Indians.

Leaving M'Kay's mill, we travelled along a circuitous track through a heavy forest of fir and pine, and emerged into a beautiful

little prairie, at the side of which stood the
doctor's neat hewn log cabin, sending its
cheerful smoke among the lofty pine tops in
its rear. We soon sat by a blazing fire, and
the storm that had pelted us all the way,
lost its unpleasantness in the delightful society of my worthy host and his amiable
wife. I passed the night with them. The
doctor is a Scotchman, his wife a Yankee.
The former had seen many adventures in
California and Oregon and had his face very
much slashed in a contest with the Shasty
Indians near the southern border of Oregon.
The latter had come from the States, a
member of the Methodist Episcopal Mission,
and had consented to share the bliss and ills
of life with the adventurous Gael ; and a
happy little family they were.

The next day Mrs. Bailey kindly undertook to make me a blanket coat by the time
I should return, and the worthy doctor and
myself started for the Mission. About a
mile on our way, we called at a farm occupied by an American, who acted as blacksmith and gunsmith for the settlement. He
appeared to have a good set of tools for his
mechanical business, and plenty of custom.
He had also a considerable tract of land
under fence, and a comfortable house and

out-buildings. A mile or two farther on, we came upon the cabin of a Yankee tinker : an odd fellow, this ; glad to see a countryman, ready to serve him in any way, and to discuss the matter of a canal across the isthmus of Darien, the northern lights, English monopolies, Symmes's Hole, Tom Paine, and wooden nutmegs. Farther on, we came to the Catholic Chapel, a low wooden building, thirty-five or forty feet in length ; and the parsonage, a comfortable log cabin.

Beyond these, scattered over five miles of country, were fifteen or twenty farms, occupied by Americans and retired servants of the Hudson Bay Company. Twelve or thirteen miles from the doctor's we came in sight of the Mission premises. They consisted of three log cabins, a blacksmith's shop, and outbuildings, on the east bank of the Willamette, with large and well cultivated farms round about ; and a farm, on which were a large frame house, hospital, barn, &c., half a mile to the eastward. We alighted at the last-named establishment, and were kindly received by Dr. White and his lady. This gentleman is the physician of the Mission, and is thoroughly devoted to the amelioration of the physical condition of the natives.

For this object, a large hospital was being erected near his dwelling, for the reception of patients. I passed the night with the doctor and his family, and the following day visited the other Mission families. Every one appeared happy in his benevolent work.—Mr. Daniel Leslie, in preaching and superintending general matters ; Mr. Cyrus Shepard, in teaching letters to about thirty half-breed and Indian children ; Mr. J. C. Whitecomb, in teaching them to cultivate the earth ; and Mr. Alanson Beers, in blacksmithing for the mission and the Indians, and instructing a few young men in his art. I spent four or five days with these people, and had a fine opportunity to learn their characters, the objects they had in view, and the means they took to accomplish them. They belong to that zealous class of Protestants called Methodist Episcopalians. Their religious feelings are warm, and accompanied with a strong faith and great activity. In energy and fervent zeal, they reminded me of the Plymouth pilgrims, so true in heart, and so deeply interested were they with the principles and emotions which they are endeavouring to inculcate upon those around them. Their hospitality and friendship were of the purest and most disinterested character. I shall have reason to remember long and gratefully the kind and generous manner in which they supplied my wants.

Their object in settling in Oregon I understood to be twofold ; the one and principal, to civilize and christianize the Indians ; the other, and not less important, the establishment of religious and literary institutions for the benefit of white emigrants. Their plan of operation on the Indians, is to learn their various languages, for the purposes of itinerant preaching, and of teaching the young the English language. The scholars are also instructed in agriculture, the regulations of a well-managed household, reading, writing, arithmetic and geography.

The principles and duties of the Christian religion form a very considerable part of the system. They have succeeded very satisfactorily in the several parts of their undertaking. The preachers of the Mission have traversed the wilderness, and by their untiring devotion to their work, wrought many changes in the moral condition of these proverbially debased savages; while with their schools they have afforded them ample means for intellectual improvement.

They have many hundred acres of land under the plough, and cultivated chiefly by the native pupils. They have more than a hundred head of horned cattle, thirty or forty horses, and many swine. They have granaries filled with wheat, oats, barley, and peas, and cellars well stored with vegetables.

A site had already been selected on the opposite side of the river for an academical building; a court of justice had been organised by the popular voice; a military corps was about to be formed for the protection of settlers, and other measures were in progress, at once showing that the American, with his characteristic energy and enterprize, and the philanthropist, with his holy aspirations for the improvement of the human condition, had crossed the snowy barrier of the mountain, to mingle with the dashing waves of the Pacific seas the sweet music of a busy and virtuous civilization.

During my stay here, several American citizens, unconnected with the Mission, called on me to talk of their fatherland, and inquire as to the probability that its

laws would be extended over them. The
constantly repeated inquiries were —

" Why are we left without protection in
this part of our country's domain ? Why
are foreigners permitted to domineer over
American citizens, drive their traders from
the country, and make us as dependent on
them for the clothes we wear, as are their
own apprenticed slaves?"

I could return no answer to these questions, exculpatory of this national delin-
quency, and therefore advised them to
embody their grievances in a petition, and
forward it to Congress. They had a meeting for that purpose, and afterwards put
into my hand a petition, signed by sixty-
seven citizens of the United States, and
persons desirous of becoming such, the
substance of which was, a description of
the country, their unprotected situation,
and, in conclusion, a prayer that the Federal Government would extend over them
the protection and institutions of the Republic. Five or six of the Willamette settlers, for some reason, had not an opportunity to sign this paper. The Catholic priest
refused to do it.

These people have put fifty or sixty fine

farms under cultivation in the Willamette valley, amidst the most discouraging circumstances. They have erected for themselves comfortable dwellings and outbuildings, and have herds of excellent cattle, which they have from time to time driven up from California, at great expense of property and even life. The reader will find it difficult to learn any sufficient rea- sons for their being left by the Government without the institutions of civilised society. Their condition is truly deplorable. They are liable to be arrested for debt or crime, and conveyed to the jails of Canada!

For, in that case, the business of British subjects is interfered with, who, by way of retaliation, will withhold the supplies of clothing, household goods, &c., which the settlers have no other means of obtaining. Nor is this all. The civil condition of the territory being such as virtually to prohibit the emigration to any extent of useful and desirable citizens, they have nothing to anticipate from any considerable increase of their numbers, nor any amelioration of their state to look for, from the accession of female society.

In the desperation incident to their lonely lot, they take wives from the Indian tribes around them. What will be the ultimate consequence of this unpardonable negligence on the part of the Government upon the future destinies of Oregon cannot be clearly predicted; but it is manifest that it must be disastrous in the highest degree, both as to its claims to the sovereignty of that territory, and the moral condition of its inhabitants.

Mr. W. H. Wilson, superintendent of a branch mission on Puget's Sound, chanced to be at the Willamette station, whose polite attentions it affords me pleasure to acknowledge. He accompanied me on many excursions in the valley, and to the heights, for the purpose of showing me the country. I was also indebted to him for much information relative to the Cowelitz and its valley, and the region about the sound, which will be found on a succeeding page.

My original intention had been to pass the winter in exploring Oregon, and to have returned to the States the following summer, with the American Fur traders. But having learned from various credible sources, that

little dependence could be placed upon
meeting them at their usual place of rendezvous on Green river, and that the prospect of getting back to the States by that
route would, consequently, be exceedingly
doubtful, I felt constrained to abandon the
attempt.   My next wish was to have gone
by land to California, and thence home
through the northern States of Mexico.   In
order, however, to accomplish this with
safety, a force of twenty-five men was in-
dispensable ; and as that number could not
be raised, I was compelled to give up all
hopes of returning by that route.

The last and only practicable means then
of seeking home during the next twelve
months, was to go to the Sandwich Islands,
and ship thence for New York or California,
as opportunity might offer.   One of the
company's vessels was then lying at Vancouver, receiving a cargo of lumber for the
Island market, and I determined to take
passage in her.   Under these circumstances, it behoved me to hasten my return
to the Columbia.   Accordingly, on the 20th
I left the mission, visited Dr. Bailey and
lady, and went to Mr. Johnson's to take a
canoe down the river.   On reaching this

place, I found Mr. Lee, who had been to the Mission establishment on the William-ette for the fall supplies of wheat, pork, lard, butter, &c., for his station of the "Dalles."

He had left the Mission two days before my departure, and giving his canoe, laden with these valuables, in charge of his Indians, proceeded to the highlands by land. He had arrived at Mr. Johnson's, when a message reached him to the effect that his canoe had been upset, and its entire contents discharged into the stream. He immediately repaired to the scene of this disaster, where I found him busied in at-tempting to save some part of his cargo. All the wheat, and a part of the other sup-plies, together with his gun and other para-phernalia, were lost. I made arrangements to go down with him when he should be ready, and left him to call upon a Captain Young, an American ex-trader, who was settled near. This gentleman had formerly explored California and Oregon in quest of beaver—had been plundered by the Mexican authorities of £4,000 worth of fur; and, wearied at last with his ill-luck, settled nine or ten years ago on a small tributary of the Willamette coming in from the west.

Here he has erected a saw and grist mill, and opened a farm. He has been many times to California for cattle, and now owns about one hundred head, a fine band of horses, swine, &c. He related to me many incidents of his hardships, among which the most surprising was, that for a number of years, the Hudson Bay Company refused to sell him a shred of clothing; and as there were no other traders in the country, he was compelled during their pleasure to wear skins.* A false report that he had been guilty of some dishonourable act in California was the alleged cause for this treatment; but perhaps, a better reason would be, that Mr. Young occasionally purchased beaver skins in the American territory.

I spent the night of the 12th with the excellent old captain, and in the afternoon of the 13th, in company with my friend Mr. Lee, descended the Willamette as far as the Falls. Here we passed the night, more to the apparent satisfaction of vermin than of ourselves. These creature comforts abound in Oregon. But it was not these alone that made our lodging at the

---

* The reader will take notice that this is an ex-parte statement.—ED.

Falls a rosy circumstance for memory's wastes. The mellifluent odour of salmon offal regaling our nasal sensibilities, and the squalling of a copper-coloured baby, uttered in all the sweetest intonations of such an instrument, falling with the liveliest notes upon the ear, made me dream of war to the knife, till the sun called us to our day's travel.

Five miles below the Falls, Mr. Lee and myself left the canoe, and struck across about fourteen miles to an Indian village on the bank of the Columbia opposite Vancouver. It was a collection of mud and straw huts, surrounded and filled with filth which might be smelt two hundred yards. We hired one of these cits to take us across the river, and at sunset of the 15th, were comfortably seated by the stove in " Bachelor's Hall" of Fort Vancouver.

The rainy season had now thoroughly set in. Travelling any considerable distance in open boats, or among the tangled underbrush on foot, or on horseback, was quite impracticable. I therefore determined to avail myself of whatever other means of information were in my reach; and as the gentleman in charge of the various trading-

posts in the territory, had arrived at Vancouver to meet the express from London, I
could not have had for this object a more
favourable opportunity.   The information obtained from these gentlemen, and
from other residents in the country, I have
relied on as correct, and combined it with
my own observations in the following general account of Oregon.

Oregon Territory is bounded on the north
by the parallel of 54 deg. 40 min. north
latitude ; on the east by the Rocky Mountains ; on the south by the parallel of 42
deg. north latitude ; and on the west by the
Pacific Ocean.

Mountains of Oregon. Different sections
of the great chain of highlands which
stretch from the straits of Magellan to the
Arctic sea, have received different names—
as the Andes, the Cordilleras, the Anahuac,
the Rocky and the Chippewayan Mountains.
The last mentioned appellation has been
applied to that portion of it which lies
between 58° of north latitude and the
Arctic sea. The Hudson Bay Company, in
completing the survey of the Arctic coast,
have ascertained that these mountains preserve a strongly defined outline entirely to
the sea, and hang in towering cliffs over it,

and by other surveys have discovered that they gradually increase in height from the sea southward.

The section to which the term Rocky Mountains has been applied, extends from latitude 58° to the Great Gap, or southern pass, in latitude 42° north. Their altitude is greater than that of any other range on the northern part of the continent. Mr. Thompson, the astronomer of the Hudson Bay Company, reports that he found peaks between latitudes 53 and 56 north, more than twenty-six thousand feet above the level of the sea. That portion lying east of Oregon, and dividing it from the Great Prairie Wilderness, will be particularly noticed. Its southern point is in the Wind River cluster, latitude 42° north, and about seven hundred miles from the Pacific Ocean. Its northern point is in latitude 54° 40′, about seventy miles north of Mount Browne, and about four hundred miles from the same sea. Its general direction between these points is from N. N. W. to S. S. E.

This range is generally covered with perpetual snows; and for this and other causes is generally impassable for man or beast. There are, however, several gaps through which the Indians and others cross to the great Prairie Wilderness. The northernmost is between the peaks Browne and Hooker. This is used by the fur traders in their journeys from the Columbia to Canada. Another lies between the head waters of the Flathead and the Marias rivers. Another runs from Lewis and Clarke's river to the southern head waters of the Missouri. Another lies up Henry's fork for the Saptin, in a north-easterly course to the Big-horn branch of the Yellow-stone. And still another, and most important of all, is situated between Wind river cluster and Long's mountains.

There are several spurs or lateral branches protruding from the main chain, which are worthy of notice. The northernmost of these parts off north of Fraser's river, and embraces the sources of that stream. It is a broad collection of heights, thinly covered with pines. Some of the tops are covered with snow nine months of the year. A spur from these passes far down between Fraser's and Columbia rivers. This is a line of rather low elevations, thickly clothed with pines, cedar, &c. The highest portions of them lie near the Columbia. Another spur puts out on the south of Mount Hooker, and lies in the bend of the Columbia, above the two lakes.

These are lofty and bare of vegetation. Another lies between the Flatbow and Flathead rivers; another between the Flathead and Spokan rivers ; another between the Kooskooskie and Wapicakoos rivers. These spurs, which lie between the head waters of the Columbia and the last mentioned river have usually been considered in connexion with a range running off S. W. from the lower part of the Saptin, and called the Blue Mountains. But there are two sufficient reasons why this is an error. The first is, that these spurs are separate and distinct from each other, and are all manifestly merely spurs of the Rocky Mountains, and closely connected with them.

And the second is, that no one of them is united in any one point with the Blue Mountains. They cannot therefore be considered a part of the Blue Mountain chain, and should not be known by the same name. The mountains which lie between the Wapicakoos river and the upper waters of the Saptin, will be described by saying that they are a vast cluster of dark naked heights, descending from the average elevation of fifteen thousand feet—the altitude of the great western ridge—to about eight thousand feet—the elevation of the eastern wall of the valley of the Saptin. The only qualifying fact that should be attached to this description is, that there are a few small hollows among these mountains, called "holes;" which in general appearance resemble Brown's hole, mentioned in a previous chapter; but unlike the latter, they are too cold to allow of cultivation.

The last spur that deserves notice in this place is that which is called the "Snowy Mountains." It has already been described in this work; and it can only be necessary here to repeat that it branches off from the Wind river peak in latitude 41° north, and runs in an irregular broken line to Cape Mendocino, in Upper California.

The Blue Mountains are a range of heights which commence at the Saptin, about twenty miles above its junction with the Columbia, near the 46° of north latitude, and run south-westerly about two hundred miles, and terminate in a barren, rolling plain. They are separated from the Rocky Mountains by the valley of the Saptin, and are unconnected with any other range. Some of their loftiest peaks are more than ten thousand feet above the level of the sea. Many beautiful valleys, many hills covered with bunch grass, and very many extensive swells covered with heavy yellow pine forests, are found among them.

The President's range is in every respect the most interesting in Oregon. It is a part of a chain of highlands, which commences at Mount St. Elias, and gently diverging from the coast, terminates in the arid hills about the head of the Gulf of California. It is a line of extinct volcanoes, where the fires, the evidences of whose intense power are seen over the whole surface of Oregon, found their principal vents. It has twelve lofty peaks; two of which, Mount St. Elias and Mount Fairweather, lie near latitude 55° north; and ten of which lie south of latitude 49° north. Five of these latter have received names from British navigators and traders.

The other five have received from American travellers, and Mr. Kelly, the names of deceased Presidents of the Republic. Mr. Kelly, I believe, was the first individual who suggested a name for the whole range. For convenience in description I have adopted it. And although it is a matter in which no one can find reasons for being very much interested, yet if there is any propriety in adopting Mr. Kelly's name for the whole chain, there might seem to be as much in following his suggestion, that all the principal peaks should bear the names of those distinguished men, whom the suffrages of the people that own Oregon* have from time to time called to administer their national government. I have adopted this course.

Mount Tyler is situated near latitude forty-nine degrees north, and about twenty miles from the eastern shore of those waters between Vancouver's Island, and the continent. It is clad with perpetual snow. Mount Harrison is situated a little more than a degree south of Mount Tyler, and about thirty miles east by north of Puget's Sound. It is covered with perpetual snow. Mount Van Buren stands on the isthmus between Puget's Sound and the Pacific. It is a lofty, wintry peak, seen in clear weather eighty miles at sea. Mount Adams lies under the parallel of forty-five degrees, about twenty-five miles north of the cascades of the Columbia. This is one of the finest peaks of the chain, clad with eternal snows, five thousand feet down its sides. Mount Washington lies a little north of the forty-fourth degree north, and about twenty miles

* The reader will remember that our Author is an American.—ED.

south of the Cascades.   It is a perfect cone, and is said to rise seventeen thousand or eighteen thousand feet above the level of the sea. More than half its height is covered with perpetual snows.   Mount Jefferson is an immense peak under latitude forty-one and a half degrees north.   It received its name from Lewis and Clark.   Mount Madison is the Mount McLaughlin of the British fur-traders.   Mount Monroe is in latitude forty-three degrees twenty minutes north, and Mount John Quincy Adams is in forty-two degrees ten minutes ; both covered with perpetual snow.

Mount Jackson is in latitude forty-one degrees ten minutes.   It is the largest and highest pinnacle of the President's range. This chain of mountains runs parallel with the Rocky Mountains, between three hundred and four hundred miles from them. Its average distance from the coast of the Pacific, south of latitude forty-nine degrees, is about one hundred miles.   The spaces between the peaks are occupied by elevated heights, covered with an enormous growth of the several species of pines, and firs, and the red cedar, many of which rise two hundred feet without a limb ; and are five, six, seven, eight, and even nine fathoms in circumference at the ground.

On the south side of the Columbia, at
the Cascades, a range of low mountains
puts off from the President's range, and
running down parallel to the river, terminates in a point of land on which Astoria
was built. Its average height is about one
thousand five hundred feet above the river.
Near the Cascades the tops are higher;
and in some instances are beautifully castellated. They are generally covered with
dense pine and fir forests. From the north
side of the Cascades, a similar range runs
down to the sea, and terminates in Cape
Disappointment. This range also is covered
with forests. Another range runs on the
brink of the coast, from Cape Mendocino in
Upper California to the Straits de Fuca.
This is generally bare of trees ; mere
masses of dark stratified rocks, piled many
hundred feet in height. It rises immediately from the borders of the sea, and
preserves nearly a right line course, during
their entire length. The lower portion
of the eastern sides is clothed with heavy
pine and spruce, fir and cedar forests.

I have described in previous pages the
great southern branch of the Columbia,
called Saptin by the natives who live on its
banks, and the valley of volcanic deserts,
through which it runs, as well as the Co-

lumbia and its cavernous vale, from its junction with the Saptin to Fort Vancouver, ninety miles from the sea. I shall therefore in the following notice of the rivers of Oregon, speak only of those parts of this and other streams, and their valleys about them, which remain undescribed.

That portion of the Columbia, which lies above its junction with the Saptin, latitude forty-six degrees eight minutes north, is navigable for bateaux to the boat encampment at the base of the Rocky Mountains, about the fifty-third degree of north latitude, a distance, by the course of the stream, of about five hundred miles. The current is strong, and interrupted by five considerable and several lesser rapids, at which there are short portages. The country on both sides of the river, from its junction with the Saptin to the mouth of the Spokan, is a dreary waste. The soil is a light yellowish composition of sand and clay, generally destitute of vegetation. In a few nooks, irrigated by mountain streams, are found small patches of the short grass of the plains interspersed with another species which grows in tufts or bunches four or five feet in height. A few shrubs (as the small willow, the sumac, and furze), appear in distant and solitary

groups.   There are no trees; generally
nothing green; a mere brown drifting
desert; as far as the Oakanagan River,
two hundred and eight miles, a plain, the
monotonous desolation of which is relieved
only by the noble river running through it,
and an occasional cliff of volcanic rocks
bursting through its arid surface.

The river Oakanagan is a large, fine
stream, originating in a large lake of the
same name situate in the mountains, about
one hundred miles north of its mouth. The
soil in the neighbourhood of this stream is
generally worthless.   Near its union, however, with the Columbia, there are a number
of small plains tolerably well clothed with
the wild grasses; and near its lake are
found hills covered with small timber.   On
the point of land between this stream and
the Columbia, the Pacific Fur Company in
1811 established a trading post.   This in
1814 passed by purchase into the hands of
the North-West Fur Company of Canada,
and in 1819 by the union of that body
with the Hudson Bay Company, passed into
the possession of the united company under
the name of Hudson Bay Company.   It is
still occupied by them under its old name
of Fort Oakanagan.

From this post, latitude forty-eight degrees six minutes, and longitude one hundred and seventeen degrees west, along the
Columbia to the Spokan, the country is as
devoid of wood as that below. The banks
of the river are bold and rocky, the stream
is contracted with narrow limits, and the
current strong and vexed with dangerous
eddies.

The Spokan river rises among the spurs
of the Rocky Mountains east south-east of
the mouth of the Oakanagan, and, after
a course of about fifty miles, forms the
Pointed Heart Lake, twenty-five miles in
length, and ten or twelve in width ; and
running thence in a north-westerly direction
about one hundred and twenty miles,
empties itself into the Columbia. About sixty
miles from its mouth, the Pacific Fur Company erected a trading-post, which they
called the " Spokan House." Their successors are understood to have abandoned it.
Above the Pointed Heart Lake, the banks
of this river are usually high and bold
mountains, sparsely covered with pines
and cedars of a fine size. Around the lake
are some grass lands, many edible roots,
and wild fruits. On all the remaining
course of the stream, are found at inter-

vals productive spots capable of yielding moderate crops of the grains and vegetables. There is considerable pine and cedar timber on the neighbouring hills ; and near the Columbia are large forests growing on sandy plains. In a word, the Spokan valley can be extensively used as a grazing district ; but its agricultural capabilities are limited.

Mr. Spaulding, an American missionary, made a journey across this valley to Fort Colville, in March 1837, in relation to which, he thus writes to Mr. Levi, Chamberlain of the Sandwich Islands : " The third day from home we came to snow, and on the fourth, came to what I call quicksands, plains mixed with pine trees and rocks. The body of snow upon the plains was interspersed with bare spots under the standing pines. For these, our poor animals would plunge whenever they came near, after wallowing in the snow and mud until the last nerve seemed almost exhausted, naturally expecting a resting-place for their struggling limbs ; but they were no less disappointed and discouraged, doubtless, than I was astonished, to see the noble animals go down by the side of a rock or pine tree, till their bodies struck the surface."

The same gentleman, in speaking of this valley, and the country generally, lying north of the Columbia, and claimed by the United States and Great Britain, says, " It is probably not worth half the money and time that will be spent in talking about it."

The country, from the Spokan to Kettle Falls, is broken into hills and mountains thinly covered with wood, and picturesque in appearance, among which there is supposed to be no arable land. A little below Kettle Falls, in latitude 48°, 37' is a trading post of the Hudson's Bay Company, called Fort Colville. Mr. Spaulding thus describes it :—" Fort Colville is two hundred miles west of north from this, (his station on the Clear Water), three days below Flatland River, one day above Spokan, one hundred miles above Oakanagan, and three hundred miles above Fort Wallawalla. It stands on a small plain of two thousand or three thousand acres, said to be the only arable land on the Columbia, above Vancouver. There are one or two barns, a blacksmith shop, a good flour mill, several houses for labourers, and good buildings for the gentlemen in charge."

" Mr. McDonald raises this year (1837)

about three thousand five hundred bushels
of different grains, such as wheat, peas,
barley, oats, corn, buckwheat, &c., and as
many potatoes; has eighty head of cattle,
and one hundred hogs. This post furnishes supplies of provisions for a great
many forts north, south, and west. The
country on both sides of the stream, from
Kettle Falls to within four miles of the
lower Lake, is covered with dense forests
of pine, spruce, and small birch. The
northwestern shore is rather low, but the
southern high and rocky. In this distance
are several tracts of rich bottom land,
covered with a kind of creeping red
clover, and the white species common to the
States. The lower lake of the Columbia
is about thirty-five miles in length, and
four or five in breadth. Its shores are bold,
and clad with a heavy growth of pine,
spruce, &c. From these waters the voya-
ger obtains the first view of the snowy
heights in the main chain of the Rocky
Mountains.

The Flathead River enters into the
Columbia a short distance above Fort Colville. It is as long, and discharges nearly
as much water as that part of Columbia
above their junction. It rises near the

sources of the Missouri and Sascatchawine. The ridges which separate them are said to be easy to pass. It falls into the Columbia over a confused heap of immense rocks, just above the place where the latter stream forms the Kettle Falls, in its passage through a spur of the Rocky Mountains. About one hundred miles from its mouth, the Flathead River forms a lake thirty-six miles long and seven or eight wide. It is called Lake Kullerspelm. A rich and beautiful country spreads off from it in all directions, to the bases of lofty mountains covered with perpetual snows. Forty or fifty miles above this lake, is the " Flathead House," a trading post of the Hudson Bay Company.

McGillivray's, or Flat Bow River, rises in the Rocky Mountains, and running a tortuous westerly course about three hundred miles, among the snowy heights, and some extensive and somewhat productive valleys, enters the Columbia four miles below the Lower Lake. Its banks are generally mountainous, and in some places covered with pine forests. On this stream, also, the indefatigable British fur traders have a post, " Fort Kootania," situated about one hundred and thirty miles from its mouth. Between the lower and upper lakes of the Columbia, are '' the Straits,'' a narrow, compressed passage of the river among jutting rocks. It is four or five miles in length, and has a current, swift, whirling, and difficult to stem. The upper lake is of less dimensions than the lower ; but, if possible, surrounded by more broken and romantic scenery, forests overhung by lofty tiers of wintry mountains, from which rush a thousand torrents, fed by the melting snows.

Two miles above this lake, the Columbia runs through a narrow, rocky channel. This place is called the Lower Dalles. The shores are strewn with immense quantities of fallen timber, among which still stand heavy and impenetrable forests. Thirty-five miles above is the Upper Dalles ; the waters are crowded into a compressed channel, among hanging and slippery rocks, foaming and whirling fearfully. A few miles above this place, is the head of navigation, '' The Boat encampment,'' where the traders leave their bateaux, in their overland journeys to Canada. The country from the upper lake to this place, is a collection of mountains, thickly covered with pine, and spruce, and fir trees of very large size.

Here commences the "Rocky Mountain portage," to the navigable waters on the other side. Its track runs up a wide and cheerless valley, on the north of which, tiers of mountains rise to a great height, thickly studded with immense pines and cedars, while on the south are seen towering cliffs, partially covered with mosses and stinted pines, over which tumble, from the ices above, numerous and noisy cascades. Two days' travel up the desolate valley, brings the traveller to "La Grande Cote," the principal ridge. This you climb in two hours. Around the base of this ridge, the trees, pines, &c., are of enormous size; but in ascending, they decrease in size, till on the summit they become little else than shrubs.

On a table land of this height, are found two lakes a few hundred yards apart; the waters of one of which flow down the valley just described, to the Columbia, and thence to the North Pacific; while those of the other, forming the Rocky Mountain River, run thence into the Athabasca, and thence through Peace River, the Great Slave Lake, and McKenzie's River, into the Northern Arctic Ocean. The scenery around these lakes is highly interesting. In the north, rises Mount Browne, sixteen thousand feet, and in the south, Mount Hooker, fifteen thousand seven hundred feet above the level of the sea. In the west, descends a vast tract of secondary mountains, bare and rocky, and noisy with tumbling avalanches. In the vales are groves of the winter-loving pine. In the east roll away undulations of barren heights beyond the range of sight. It seems to be the very citadel of desolation ; where the god of the north wind elaborates his icy streams, and frosts, and blasts, in every season of the year.

Frazer's River rises between latitudes 55° and 56° north, and after a course of about one hundred and fifty miles, nearly due south, falls into the Straits de Fuca, under latitude 49° north. It is so much obstructed by rapids and falls, as to be of little value for purposes of navigation. The face of the country about its mouth, and for fifty miles above, is mountainous and covered with dense forests of white pine, cedar, and other evergreen trees. The soil is an indifferent vegetable deposit six or seven inches in depth, resting on a stratum of sand or coarse gravel. The whole remaining portion of the valley is said to be cut with low mountains running north-westwardly and south-eastwardly ; among which are immense tracts of marshes and lakes, formed by cold torrents from the heights that encircle them. The soil not thus occupied, is too poor for successful cultivation. Mr. Macgillivray, the person in charge at Fort Alexandria, in 1827, says : " All the vegetables we planted, notwithstanding the utmost care and precaution, nearly failed ; and the last crop of potatoes did not yield one-fourth of the seed planted." The timber of this region consists of all the varieties of the fir, the spruce, pine, poplar, willow, cedar, cyprus, birch and alder.

The climate is very peculiar. The spring opens about the middle of April. From this time the weather is delightful till the end of May. In June the south wind blows, and brings incessant rains. In July and August the heat is almost insupportable. In September the whole valley is enveloped in fogs so dense, that objects one hundred yards distant cannot be seen till ten o'clock in the day. In October the leaves change their colour and begin to fall. In November, the lakes, and portions of the rivers are frozen. The winter months bring snow. It is seldom severely cold. The mercury in Fahrenheit's scale sinks a few days only, as low as ten or twelve degrees below zero.

That part of Oregon bounded on the north by Shmillamen River, and on the east by Oakanagan and Columbia Rivers, south by the Columbia, and west by the President's Range, is a broken plain, partially covered with the short and bunch grasses ; but so destitute of water, that a small portion only of it, can ever be depastured. The eastern and middle portions of it are destitute of timber — a mere sunburnt waste. The northern part has a few wooded hills and streams, and prairie valleys. Among the lower hills of the President's Range, too, there are considerable pine and fir forests ; and rather extensive prairies, watered by small mountain streams ; but nearly all of the whole surface of this part of Oregon, is a worthless desert.

The tract bounded north by the Columbia, east by the Blue Mountains, south by the forty-second parallel of north latitude, and west by the President's Range, is a plain of vast rolls or swells, of a light, yellowish, sandy clay, partially covered with the short and bunch grasses, mixed with the prickly pear and wild wormwood. But water is so very scarce, that it can never be generally fed; unless, indeed, as some travellers, in their praises of this region, seem to suppose, the animals that usually live by eating and drinking, should be able to dispense with the latter, in a climate where nine months in the year, not a particle of rain or dew falls, to moisten a soil as dry and loose as a heap of ashes. On the banks of the Luhon, John Days, Umatalla, and Wallawalla Rivers — which have an average length of thirty miles — without doubt, extensive tracts of grass may be found in the neighbourhood of water; but it is also true that not more than a fifth part of the surface within twenty-five miles of these streams, bears grass or any other vegetation.

The portion also which borders the Columbia, produces some grass. But of a strip six miles in width, and extending from the Dalles to the mouth of the Saptin, not an hundredth part bears the grasses; and the sides of the chasm of the river are so precipitous, that not a fiftieth part of this can be fed by animals which drink at that stream. In proceeding southward on the head waters of the small streams, John Days and Umatalla, the face of the plain rises gradually into vast irregular swells, destitute of timber and water. On the Blue Mountains are a few pine and spruce trees of an inferior growth. On the right tower the white peaks and thickly wooded hills of the President's Range.

The space south-east of the Blue Mountains is a barren, thirsty waste, of light, sandy, and clayey soil—strongly impregnated with nitre. A few small streams run among the sand hills; but they are so strongly impregnated with various kinds of salts, as to be unfit for use. These brooks empty themselves into the lakes, the waters of which are salter than the ocean. Near latitude 43° north, the Klamet River rises and runs westerly, through the President's Range. On these waters are a few productive valleys; westwardly from them to the Saptin the country is dry and worthless.

The part of Oregon lying between the Straits de Fuca on the north, the President's Range on the east, the Columbia on the south, and the ocean on the west, is thickly covered with pines, cedars, and firs of extraordinary size; and beneath these, a growth of brush and brambles which defies the most vigorous foot to penetrate. Along the banks of the Columbia, indeed, strips of prairie may be met with, varying from a few rods to three miles in width, and often several miles in length ; and even amidst the forests are found a few open spaces.

The banks of the Cowelitz, too, are denuded of timber for forty miles ; and around the Straits de Fuca and Puget's Sound, are large tracts of open country. But the whole tract lying within the boundaries just defined, is of little value except for its timber. The forests are so heavy and so matted with brambles, as to require the arm of a Hercules to clear a farm of one hundred acres in an ordinary life-time ; and the mass of timber is so great that an attempt to subdue it by girdling would result in the production of another forest before the ground could be disencumbered of what was thus killed. The small prairies among the woods are covered with wild grasses, and are useful as pastures.

The soil of these, like that of the timbered portions, is a vegetable mould, eight or ten inches in thickness, resting on a stratum of hard blue clay and gravel. The valley of the Cowelitz is poor—the soil, thin, loose, and much washed, can be used as pasture grounds for thirty miles up the stream. At about that distance some tracts of fine land occur. The prairies on the banks of the Columbia would be valuable land for agricultural purposes, if they were not generally overflown by the freshets in June—the month of all the year when crops are most injured by such an occurrence. It is impossible to dyke out the water; for the soil rests upon an immense bed of gravel and quicksand, through which it will leach in spite of such obstructions.

The tract of the territory lying between the Columbia on the north, the President's range on the east, the parallel of forty-two degrees of north latitude on the south, and the ocean on the west, is the most beautiful and valuable portion of the Oregon Territory. A good idea of the form of its surface may be derived from a view of its mountains and rivers as laid down on the map. On the south tower the heights of the snowy mountains ; on the west the naked peaks of the coast range ; on the north the green peaks of the river range ; and on the east the lofty shining cones of the President's range— around whose frozen bases cluster a vast collection of minor mountains, clad with the mightiest pine and cedar forests on the face of the earth! The principal rivers are the Klamet and the Umpqua in the south-west, and the Willamette in the north.

The Umpqua enters these in a latitude forty-three degrees, thirty minutes north. It is three-fourths of a mile in width at its mouth ; water two-and-a-half fathoms on its bar ; the tide sets up thirty miles from the sea ; its banks are steep and covered with pines and cedars, &c. Above tide water the stream is broken by rapids and falls. It has a westwardly course of about one hundred miles. The face of the country about it is somewhat broken ; in some parts covered with heavy pine and cedar timber, in others with grass only ; said to be a fine valley for cultivation and pasturage. The pines on this river grow to an enormous size : two hundred and fifty feet in height— and from fifteen to more than fifty feet in circumference ;* the cones or seed vessels are in the form of an egg, and oftentimes more than a foot in length ; the seeds are as large as the castor bean. Farther south is another stream, which joins the ocean twenty-three miles from the outlet of the Umpqua. At its mouth are many bays ; and the surrounding country is less broken than the valley of the Umpqua.

---

* This appears extravagant, but the fact cannot be disputed. It may be observed, however, that the wood, from its rapid growth, has but little weight—half that of the common pine or deal —ED.

Farther south still, is another stream called the Klamet. It rises, as is said, in the plain east of Mount Madison, and running a westerly course of one hundred and fifty miles, enters the ocean forty or fifty miles south of the Umpqua. The pine and cedar disappear upon this stream; and instead of them are found a myrtaceous tree of small size, which, when shaken by the least breeze, diffuses a delicious fragrance through the groves. The face of the valley is gently undulating, and in every respect desirable for cultivation and grazing.

The Willamette rises in the President's range, near the sources of the Klamet. Its general course is north north-west. Its length is something more than two hundred miles. It falls into the Columbia by two mouths; the one eighty-five, and the other seventy miles from the sea. The arable portion of the valley of this river is about one hundred and fifty miles long, by sixty in width. It is bounded on the west by low wooded hills of the coast range; on the south by the highlands around the upper waters of the Umpqua; on the east by the President's range; and on the north by the mountains that run along the southern bank of the Columbia. Its general appearnce as seen from the heights, is that of a

rolling, open plain, intersected in every direction by ridges of low mountains, and long
lines of evergreen timber; and dotted here
and there with a grove of white oaks. The
soil is a rich vegetable mould, two or three
feet deep, resting on a stratum of coarse
gravel or clay. The prairie portions of it
are capable of producing, with good cultivation, from twenty to thirty bushels of wheat
to the acre, and other small grains in proportion. Corn cannot be raised without irrigation. The vegetables common to such
latitudes yield abundantly, and of the best
quality. The uplands have an inferior soil,
and are covered with such an enormous
growth of pines, cedars and firs, that the
expense of clearing would be greatly beyond
their value. Those tracts of the second
bottom lands, which are covered with timber
might be worth subduing, but for a species
of fern growing on them, which is so difficult to kill, as to render them nearly worthless for agricultural purposes.

The climate of the country between the
President's range and the sea, is very tem-
perate. From the middle of April to the
middle of October, the westerly winds prevail, and the weather is warm and dry.
Scarcely a drop of rain falls. During the
remainder of the year, the southerly winds

blow continually, and bring rains; sometimes in showers, and at others in terrible
storms, which continue to pour down incessantly for many weeks.

There is scarcely any freezing weather
in this section of Oregon.. Twice within the
last forty years the Columbia has been frozen
over; but this was chiefly caused by the ac-
cumulation of ice from the upper country.
The grasses grow during the winter months,
and wither to hay in the summer time.

The mineral resources of Oregon have
not been investigated. Great quantities of
bituminous coal have however been disco
vered on Puget's Sound, and on the Willamette. Salt springs also abound; and other
fountains highly impregnated with sulphur,
soda, iron, &c., are numerous.

Many wild fruits are to be met with in the
territory, that would be very desirable for cultivation in the gardens of the States. Among
these are a very large and delicious straw-
berry, the service berry, a kind of whortleberry, and a cranberry growing on bushes
four or five feet in height. The crab apple,
choke cherry, and thornberry are common.
Of the wild animals, there are the white
tailed, black tailed, jumping and moose
deer; the elk; red and black and grey
wolf; the black, brown, and grisly bear;

the mountain sheep ; black, white, red and mixed foxes ; beaver, lynxes, martin, otters, minks, musk-rats, wolverines, marmot, ermines, wood-rats, and the small curled tailed short eared dog, common among the Chippeways.

Of the feathered tribe, there are the goose, the brant, several kinds of cranes, the swan, many varieties of the duck, hawks of several kinds, plovers, white eagles, ravens, crows, vultures, thrush, gulls, woodpeckers, pheasants, pelicans, partridges, grouse, snowbirds, &c.

In the rivers and lakes are a very superior quality of salmon, brook and salmon trout, sardines, sturgeon, rock cod, the hair seal, &c. ; and in the bays and inlets along the coast, are the sea otter and an inferior kind of oyster.

The trade of Oregon is limited entirely to the operations of the British Hudson Bay Company. A concise account of this association is therefore deemed apposite in this place.

A charter was granted by Charles II, in 1670, to certain British subjects associated under the name of " The Hudson's Bay Company," in virtue of which they were allowed the exclusive privilege of establish-

ing trading factories on the Hudson's Bay
and its tributary rivers. Soon after the
grant, the Company took possession of the
territory, and enjoyed its trade without
opposition till 1787; when was organized
a powerful rival under the title of the
" North American Fur Company of Canada." This company was chiefly composed
of Canadian-born subjects — men whose
native energy and thorough acquaintance
with the Indian character, peculiarly qualified them for the dangers and hardships
of a fur trader's life in the frozen regions
of British America. Accordingly we soon
find the North-westers outreaching in enterprise and commercial importance their
less active neighbours of Hudson's Bay ;
and the jealousies naturally arising between parties so situated, led to the most
barbarous battles, and the sacking and
burning each others posts. This state of
things in 1821, arrested the attention of
Parliament, and an act was passed conso-
lidating the two companies into one, under
the title of " The Hudson's Bay Company."

This association is now, under the operation of their charter, in sole possession of
all that tract of country bounded north by

the northern Arctic Ocean; east by the Davis' Straits and the Atlantic Ocean; south and south-westwardly by the northern boundary of the Canadas, and a line drawn through the centre of Lake Superior; thence north-westwardly to the Lake of the Wood; thence west on the 49th parallel of north latitude to the Rocky Mountains, and along those mountains to the 54th parallel; thence westwardly on that line to a point nine marine leagues from the Pacific Ocean; and on the west by a line commencing at the last mentioned point, and running northwardly parallel to the Pacific coast till it intersects the 141st parallel of longitude west from Greenwich, England, and thence due north to the Arctic Sea.

They have also leased for twenty years, commencing in March, 1840, all of Russian America, except the post of Sitka; the lease renewable at the pleasure of the Hudson's Bay Company. They are also in possession of Oregon under treaty stipulation between Britain and the United States. Thus this powerful Company occupy and control more than one-ninth of the soil of the globe. Its stockholders are British capitalists, resident in Great Britain. From these are elected a board of managers, who hold their meetings and transact their business at "The Hudson's Bay House" in London. This board buy goods and ship them to their territory, sell the furs for which they are exchanged, and do all other business connected with the Company's transactions, except the execution of their own orders, the actual business of collecting furs in their territory. This duty is entrusted to a class of men who are called partners, but who in fact receive certain portions of the annual net profits of the Company's business, as a compensation for their services.

These gentlemen are divided by their employers into different grades. The first of these is the Governor-General of all the Company's posts in North America. He resides at York Factory, on the west shore of Hudson's Bay. The second class are chief factors; the third, chief traders; the fourth, traders. Below these is another class, called clerks. These are usually younger members of respectable Scottish families. They are not directly interested in the Company's profits, but receive an annual salary of £100, food, suitable clothing, and a body servant, during an apprenticeship of seven years. At the expiration

of this term they are eligible to the trader-
ships, factorships, &c. that may be vacated
by death or retirement from the service.
While waiting for advancement they are
allowed from £80 to £120 per annum.
The servants employed about their posts
and in their journeyings are half-breed Iroquois and Canadian Frenchmen. These
they enlist for five years, at wages varying
from £68 to £80 per annum.

An annual Council composed of the
Governor-General, chief factors and chief
traders, is held at York Factory. Before
this body are brought the reports of the
trade of each district ; propositions for new
enterprises, and modifications of old ones;
and all these and other matters deemed
important, being acted upon, the proceedings had thereon and the reports from
the several districts are forwarded to the
Board of Directors in London, and subjected
to its final order.

This shrewd Company never allow their
territory to be overtrapped. If the annual
return from any well trapped district be less
in any year than formerly, they order a less
number still to be taken, until the beaver
and other fur-bearing animals have time to
increase. The income of the company

is thus rendered uniform, and their business perpetual.

The nature and annual value of the Hudson Bay Company's business in the territory which they occupy, may be learned from the following table, extracted from Bliss' work on the trade and industry of British America, in 1831 :

Skins.	No.	each £.	s.	d.	£.	s.	d.
Beaver	126,944	,, 1	5	0	158,680	0	0
Muskrat	375,731	,, 0	0	6	9,393	5	6
Lynx	58,010	,, 0	8	0	23,204	0	0
Wolf	5,947	,, 0	8	0	2,378	16	0
Bear	3,850	,, 1	0	0	3,850	0	0
Fox. . . . , . .	8,765	,, 0	10	0	4,382	10	0
Mink.	9,298	,, 0	2	3	929	16	0
Raccoon	325	,, 0	1	6	24	7	6
Tails	2,290	,, 0	1	0	114	10	0
Wolverine . . .	1,744	,, 0	3	0	261	12	0
Deer	645	,, 0	3	0	96	15	0
Weasel	34	,, 0	0	6	00	16	0
					£203,316	9	0

Some idea may be formed of the net profit of this business, from the facts that the shares of the company's stock, which originally cost £100, are at 100 per cent premium, and that the dividends range from ten per cent upward, and this too while they are creating out of the net proceeds an immense reserve fund, to be expended in keeping other persons out of the trade.

In 1805 the Missouri Fur Company established a trading-post on the head-waters of the Saptin. In 1806 the North-West Fur Company of Canada established one on Frazer's Lake, near the northern line of Oregon. In March, 1811, the American Pacific Fur Company built Fort Astoria, near the mouth of the Columbia. In July of the same year, a partner of the North-West Fur Company of Canada de-scended the great northern branch of the Columbia to Astoria. This was the first appearance of the British fur traders in the valleys drained by this river.

On the 16th of October, 1813, (while war was raging between England and the States) the Pacific Fur Company sold all its establishments in Oregon to the North-West Fur Company of Canada. On the 1st of December following, the British sloop of war Raccoon, Captain Black com-manding, entered the Columbia, took for-mal possession of Astoria, and changed its name to Fort George. On the 1st of October, 1818, Fort George was surren-dered by the British Government to the Government of the States, according to a stipulation in the Treaty of Ghent.

By the same treaty, British subjects were granted the same rights of trade and settlement in Oregon as belonged to the citizens of the Republic, for the term of ten years; under the condition, that as both nations claimed Oregon, the occupancy thus authorized should in no form affect the question as to the title to the country. This stipulation was by treaty of London, August 6, 1827, indefinitely extended; under the condition that it should cease to be in force twelve months from the date of a notice of either of the contracting powers to the other, to annul and abrogate it; provided such notice should not be given till after the 20th of October, 1828. And this is the manner in which the British Hudson's Bay Company, after its union with the North-West Fur Company of Canada, came into Oregon.

They have now in the territory the following trading posts: Fort Vancouver, on the north bank of the Columbia, ninety miles from the Ocean, in latitude $45\frac{1}{2}°$, longitude 122° 30′; Fort George, (formerly Astoria), near the mouth of the same river; Fort Nasqually, on Puget's Sound, latitude 47°; Fort Langly, at the outlet of Fraser's River, latitude 49° 25′; Fort McLaughlin, on the Millbank Sound, latitude 52°; Fort

Simpson, on Dundas Island, latitude 54½°. Frazer's Fort, Fort James, McLeod's Fort, Fort Chilcotin, and Fort Alexandria, on Frazer's river and its branches between the 51st and 54½ parallels of latitude ; Thompson's Fort, on Thompson's River, a tributary of Frazer's River, putting into it in latitude 50° and odd minu·es ; Kootania Fort, on Flatbow River ; Flathead Fort, on Flathead River ; Forts Hall and Boisais, on the Saptin ; Forts Colville and Oakanagan, on the Columbia, above its junction with the Saptin; Fort Nez Percés or Wallawalla, a few miles below the junction ; Fort McKay, at the mouth of the Umpqua river, latitude 43° 30′, and longitude 124° west.

They also have two migratory trading and trapping establishments of fifty or sixty men each. The one traps and trades in Upper California ; the other in the country lying west, south, and east of Fort Hall. They also have a steam-vessel, heavily armed, which runs along the coast, and among its bays and inlets, for the twofold purpose of trading with the natives in places where they have no post, and of outbidding and outselling any American vessel that attempts to trade in those seas. They likewise have five sailing vessels, measuring from one hundred to five hundred tons burthen, and armed with cannon, muskets, cutlasses, &c. These are employed a part of the year in various kinds of trade about the coast and the islands of the North Pacific, and the remainder of the time in bringing goods from London, and bearing back the furs for which they are exchanged.

One of these ships arrives at Fort Vancouver in the spring of each year, laden with coarse woollens, cloths, baizes, and blankets; hardware and cutlery; cotton cloths, calicoes, and cotton handkerchiefs; tea, sugar, coffee and cocoa : rice, tobacco, soap, beads, guns, powder, lead, rum, wine, brandy, gin, and playing cards; boots, shoes, and ready-made clothing, &c. ; also, every description of sea stores, canvas, cordage, paints, oils, chains and chain cables, anchors, &c. Having discharged these "supplies," it takes a cargo of lumber to the Sandwich Islands, or of flour and goods to the Russians at Sitka or Kamskatka; returns in August; receives the furs collected at Fort Vancouver, and sails again for England.

The value of peltries annually collected in Oregon, by the Hudson Bay Comp., is about £140,000 in the London or New York market. The prime cost of the goods ex-

changed for them is about £20,000. To
this must be added the per centage of the
officers as governors, factors, &c. the wages
and food of about four hundred men, the
expense of shipping to bring supplies of
goods and take back the returns of furs,
and two years' interest on the investments.
The Company made arrangements in 1839
with the Russians at Sitka and at other
ports, about the sea of Kamskatka, to supply them with flour and goods at fixed
prices.   As they are now opening large
farms on the Cowelitz, the Umpqua, and in
other parts of the Territory, for the production of wheat for that market ; and as they
can afford to sell goods purchased in England under a contract of fifty years' standing,
20 or 30 per cent cheaper than American
merchants can, there seems a certainty that
the Hudson's Bay Company will engross
the entire trade of the North Pacific, as it
has that of Oregon.

Soon after the union of the North-West
and Hudson's Bay Companies, the British
Parliament passed an act extending the jurisdiction of the Canadian courts over the
territories occupied by these fur traders,
whether it were " owned" or " claimed by
Great Britain." Under this act, certain

gentlemen of the fur company were appointed justices of the peace, and empowered to entertain prosecutions for minor offences, arrest and send to Canada criminals of a higher order, and try, render judgment, and grant execution in civil suits where the amount in issue should not exceed £200 ; and in case of non-payment, to imprison the debtor at their own forts, or in the jails of Canada.

It is thus shown that the trade, and the civil and criminal jurisdiction in Oregon are held by British subjects ; that American citizens are deprived of their own commercial rights ; that they are liable to be arrested on their own territory by officers of British courts, tried in the American domain by British judges, and imprisoned or hung according to the laws of the British empire, for acts done within the territorial limits of the Republic.

It has frequently been asked if Oregon will hereafter assume great importance as a thoroughfare between the States and China? The answer is as follows :

The Straits de Fuca, and arms of the sea to the eastward of it, furnish the only good harbours on the Oregon coast ? Those in Puget's Sound offer every requisite facility for the most extensive commerce. Ships beat out and into the straits with any winds of the coast, and find in summer and winter fine anchorage at short intervals on both shores; and among the islands of the Sound, a safe harbour from the prevailing storms. From Puget's Sound eastward, there is a possible route for a railroad to the navigable waters of the Missouri; flanked with an abundance of fuel and other necessary materials. Its length would be about six hundred miles. Whether it would answer the desired end, would depend very much upon the navigation of the Missouri.

As, however, the principal weight and bulk of cargoes in the Chinese trade would belong to the homeward voyage, and as the lumber used in constructing proper boats on the upper Missouri would sell in Saint Louis for something like the cost of construction, it may perhaps be presumed that the trade between China and the States could be conducted through such an overland communication.

The first day of the winter months came with bright skies over the beautiful valleys of Oregon. Mounts Washington and Jefferson reared their vast pyramids of ice and

snow among the fresh green forests of the
lower hills, and overlooked the Willamette,
the lower Columbia, and the distant sea.
The herds of California cattle were lowing
on the meadows, and the flocks of sheep
from the downs of England were scamper-
ing and bleating around their shepherds on
the plain ; and the plane of the carpenter,
the adze of the cooper, the hammer of the
tinman, and the anvil of the blacksmith
within the pickets, were all awake when I
arose to breakfast for the last time at Fort
Vancouver.

The beauty of the day, and the busy hum
of life around me, accorded well with the
feelings of joy with which I made preparations to return to my family and home.
And yet when I met at the table Dr. Mc
Laughlin, Mr. Douglas, and others with
whom I had passed many pleasant hours,
and from whom I had received many
kindnesses, a sense of sorrow mingled
strongly with the delight which the occasion
naturally inspired. I was to leave Vancouver for the Sandwich Islands, and see them
no more. I confess that it has seldom
been my lot to feel so deeply pained at
parting with those whom I had known so
little time. But it became me to hasten

my departure; for the ship had dropped down to the mouth of the river, and awaited the arrival of Mr. Simpson, one of the company's clerks, Mr. Johnson, an American from St. Louis, and myself. While we are making the lower mouth of the Willamette, the reader will perhaps be amused with the sketch of life at Fort Vancouver.

Fort Vancouver is, as has been already intimated, the depot at which are brought the furs collected west of the Rocky Mountains, and from which they are shipped to England; the place also at which all the goods for the trade are landed; and from which they are distributed to the various posts of that territory by vessels, bateaux, or pack animals, as the various routes permit. It was established by Governor Simpson, in 1824, as the great centre of all commercial operations in Oregon; is situated in a beautiful plain on the north bank of the Columbia, ninety miles from the sea, in latitude $45\frac{1}{2}°$ north, and in longitude $122°$ west; and stands four hundred yards from the water side. The noble river before it is sixteen hundred and seventy yards wide, and from five to seven fathoms in depth; the whole surrounding country is covered with forests of pine, cedar, and fir, &c., interspersed here and there with small open spots ; all overlooked by the vast snowy pyramids of the President's Range, thirty-five miles in the east.

The fort itself is an oblong square two hundred and fifty yards in length, by one hundred and fifty in breadth, enclosed by pickets twenty feet in height. The area within is divided into two courts, around which are arranged thirty-five wooden buildings, used as officers' dwellings, lodging apartment for clerks, storehouses for furs, goods, and grains ; and as workshops for carpenters, blacksmiths, coopers, tinners, wheelwrights, &c. One building near the rear gate is occupied as a school-house ; and a brick structure as a powder-magazine. The wooden buildings are constructed in the following manner. Posts are raised at convenient intervals, with grooves in the facing sides ; in these grooves planks are inserted horizontally ; and the walls are complete. Rafters raised upon plates in the usual way, and covered with boards, form the roofs.

Six hundred yards below the fort, and on the bank of the river, is a village of fifty-three wooden houses, generally constructed

like those within the pickets.   In these live
the Company's servants.   Among them is a
hospital, in which those who become diseased are humanly treated.   At the back,
and a little east of the fort, is a barn containing a mammoth threshing machine ; and
near this are a number of long sheds, used
for storing grain in the sheaf.   And behold
the Vancouver farm, stretching up and
down the river (3,000 acres, fenced into
beautiful fields) sprinkled with dairy houses,
and herdsmen and shepherds' cottages !   A
busy place.

The farmer on horseback at break of day,
summons one hundred half-breeds and Iroquois Indians from their cabins to the
fields.   Twenty or thirty ploughs tear open
the generous soil ; the sowers follow
with their seed, and pressing on them
come a dozen harrows to cover it ; and
thus thirty or forty acres are planted in
a day, till the immense farm is under crop.
The season passes on, teeming with daily
industry, until the harvest waves on all
these fields.   Then sickle and hoe glisten
in tireless activity to gather in the rich
reward of this toil ; the food of seven
hundred at this post, and of thousands more
at the posts on the deserts in the east and

north. The saw mill, too, is a scene of constant toil. Thirty or forty Sandwich Islanders are felling the pines and dragging them to the mill; sets of hands are plying two gangs of saws by night and day. Three thousand feet of lumber per day; nine hundred thousand feet per annum; are constantly being shipped to foreign ports.

The grist mill is not idle. It must furnish bread stuff for the posts, and the Russian market in the north-west. And its deep music is heard daily and nightly half the year.

We will now enter the fort. The blacksmith is repairing ploughshares, harrow teeth, chains and mill irons; the tinman is making cups for the Indians, and camp-kettles, &c.; the wheelright is making waggons, and the wood parts of ploughs and harrows; the carpenter is repairing houses and building new ones; the cooper is making barrels for pickling salmon and packing furs; the clerks are posting books, and preparing the annual returns to the board in London; the salesmen are receiving beaver and dealing out goods. Listen to the voices of those children from the school house. They are the half-breed offspring of the gentlemen and servants of the Company, educated at the Company's expense, preparatory to their being apprenticed to trades in Canada. They learn the English language, writing, arithmetic and geography. The gardener, too, is singing out his honest satisfaction, as he surveys from the northern gate ten acres of apple trees laden with fruit, his bowers of grapevines, his beds of vegetables and flowers. The bell rings for dinner; we will now pay a visit to the "Hall" and its convivialities.

The dining-hall is a spacious room on the second floor, ceiled with pine above and at the sides. In the south-west corner of it is a large close stove, giving out sufficient caloric to make it comfortable.

At the end of a table twenty feet in length stands Governor McLaughlin, directing guests and gentlemen from neighbouring posts to their places; and chief-traders, traders, the physician, clerks, and the farmer, slide respectfully to their places, at distances from the Governor corresponding to the dignity of their rank in the service. Thanks are given to God, and all are seated. Roast beef and pork, boiled mutton, baked salmon, boiled ham; beets, carrots, turnips, cabbage and potatoes, and wheaten bread, are tastefully distributed over the table among a dinner-set of elegant queen's ware, burnished with glittering glasses and decanters of various-coloured Italian wines. Course after course goes round, and the Governor fills to his guests and friends ; and each gentleman in turn vies with him in diffusing around the board a most generous allowance of viands, wines, and warm fellow-feeling. The cloth and wines are removed together, cigars are lighted, and a strolling smoke about the premises, enlivened by a courteous discussion of some mooted point of natural history or politics, closes the ceremonies of the dinner hour at Fort Vancouver. These are some of the incidents of life at Vancouver.

But we moor on the lower point of Wappatoo Island, to regale ourselves with food and fire. This is the highest point of it, and is said to be never overflown. A bold rocky shore, and the water is deep enough to float the largest vessels, indicate it to be a site for the commercial mart of the island. But the southern shore of the river, half a mile below, is past a doubt the most important point for a town site on the Columbia. It lies at the lower mouth of the Willamette, the natural outlet of the best agricultural district of

Oregon. It is a hillside of gentle acclivity, covered with pine forests. There is a gorge in the mountains through which a road from it to the prairies on the south can easily be constructed. At this place the Hudson's Bay Company have erected a house, and occupy it with one of their servants.

Having eaten our cold lunch, we left Wappatoo Island to the dominion of its wild hogs, and took again to our boat. It was a drizzly, cheerless day. The clouds ran fast from the south-west, and obscured the sun. The wind fell in irregular gusts upon the water, and made it difficult to keep our boat afloat. But we had a sturdy old Sandwich Islander at one oar, and some four or five able-bodied Indians at others, and despite winds and waves, slept that night a dozen miles below the Cowelitz. Thus far below Vancouver, the Columbia was generally more than one thousand yards wide, girded on either side by mountains rising very generally, from the water side, two or three thousand feet in height, and covered with dense forests of pine and fir. These mountains are used by the Chinooks as burial-places. During the epidemic fever of 1832, which almost swept this

portion of the Columbia valley of its inhabitants, vast numbers of the dead were
placed among them. They were usually
wrapped in skins, placed in the canoes,
and hung from the boughs of trees six or
eight feet from the ground. Thousands of
these were seen.

They hung in groups near the water side.
One of them had a canoe inverted over the
one containing the dead, and lashed tightly
to it. We were often driven close to the
shore by the heavy wind, and always noticed that these sepulchral canoes were perforated at the bottom. I was informed that
this is always done for the twofold purpose
of letting out the water which the rains
may deposit in them, and of preventing
their ever being used again by the living.

The 3rd was a boisterous day. The
southerly winds drove in a heavy tide from
the Pacific, and lashed the Columbia into
foam ; but by keeping under the windward
shore, we made steady progress till sunset,
when the increased expanse of the river
indicated that we were about fifteen miles
from the sea. The wind died away, and
we pushed on rapidly ; but the darkness
was so great that we lost our course, and
grounded upon a sand-bar three miles to the

north of Tongue Point. After considerable trouble, we succeeded in getting off, steered to the northern shore, and in half an hour were again in deep water. But "the ship, the ship," was on every tongue. Was it above or below Tongue Point? If the latter, we could not reach it that night, for the wind freshened again every instant, and the waves grew angry and fearful, and dashed into the boat at every sweep of the paddles.

We were beginning to calculate our prospects of another hour's breathing when the shadowy outline of the ship was brought between us and the open horizon of the mouth of the river, a half mile below us. The oars struck fast and powerfully now, and the frail boat shot over the whitened waves for a few minutes, and lay dancing and surging under the lee of the noble "Vancouver." A rope was hastily thrown us, and we stood upon her beautiful deck, manifestly barely saved from a watery grave. For now the sounding waves broke awfully all around us. Captain Duncan received us very kindly, and introduced us immediately to the cordial hospitalities of his cabin. The next morning we dropped down to Astoria, and anchored one hundred yards from the shore. The captain and passengers landed about ten o'clock; and as I felt peculiar interest in the spot, immortalized no less by the genius of Irving than the enterprize of John Jacob Astor, I spent my time very industriously in exploring it.

The site of this place is three quarters of a mile above the point of land between the Columbia and Clatsop Bay. It is a hillside, formerly covered with a very heavy forest. The space which has been cleared may amount to four acres. It is rendered too wet for cultivation by numberless springs bursting from the surface. The back ground is still a forest rising over lofty hills; in the foreground is the Columbia, and the broken pine hills of the opposite shore. The Pacific opens in the west.

Astoria has passed away; nothing is left of its buildings but an old batten cedar door; nothing remaining of its bastions and pickets, but half a dozen of the latter, tottering among the underbrush. While scrambling over the grounds, we came upon the trunk of an immense tree, long since prostrated, which measured between six and seven fathoms in circumference. No information could be obtained as to the length of time it had been decaying.

The Hudson's Bay Company are in possession, and call the post Fort George. They have erected three log buildings, and occupy them with a clerk, who acts as a telegraph keeper of events at the mouth of the river. If a vessel arrives, or is seen laying off and on, information of the fact is sent to Vancouver, with all the rapidity which can be extracted from arms and paddles.

This individual also carries on a limited trade with the Chinook and Clatsop Indians ; such is his influence over them, that he bears among the Company's gentlemen the very distinguished title of " King of the Chinooks." He is a fine, lusty, companionable fellow, and I am disposed to believe, wears the crown with quite as little injury to his subjects as to himself.

In the afternoon we bade adieu to Astoria, and dropped down toward Cape Disappointment.—The channel of the river runs from the fort in a north-western direction to the point of the Cape, and thence close under it in a south-westerly course the distance of four miles, where it crosses the bar. The wind was quite baffling while we

were crossing to the northern side ; and we
consequently began to anticipate a long residence in Baker's Bay.   But as we neared
the Cape, a delightful breeze sprang up in
the east, filled every sail, and drove the
stately ship through the heavy seas and
swells most merrily.

The lead is dipping, and the sailors are
chanting each measure as they take it ; we
approach the bar ; the soundings decrease ;
every shout grows more and more awful !
the keel of the Vancouver is within fifteen
inches of the bar !   Every breath is suspended, and every eye fixed on the leads, as
they are quickly thrown again !   They sink ;
and the chant for five fathoms enables us to
breathe freely.   We have passed the bar ;
Captain Duncan grasps his passengers
by the hand warmly, and congratulates
them at having escaped being lost in those
wild waters, where many a noble ship
and brave heart have sunk together and
for ever.

Off the mouth of the Columbia—on the
deep, long swells of the Pacific seas.   The
rolling surges boom along the mountainous
shores.   Up the vale one hundred miles
the white pyramid of Mount Washington
towers above the clouds, and the green

forest of Lower Oregon. That scene I shall never forget. It was too wild, too unearthly to be described. It was seen at sunset ; and a night of horrid tempest shut in upon this, the author's last view of Oregon.

The following abstract of Commander Wilkes' Report on Oregon came to hand while this work was in the press, and the author takes great pleasure in appending it to his work. Mr. Wilkes' statistics of the Territory, it will be seen, agree in all essential particulars with those given in previous pages. There is one point only of any importance that needs to be named, in regard to which truth requires a protest ; and that is contained in the commander's concluding remarks. It will be seen on reference to them, that the agricultural capabilities of Oregon are placed above those of any part of the world beyond the tropics. This is a most surprising conclusion ; at war with his own account of the several sections which he visited, and denied by every intelligent man living in the territory. What! Oregon, in this respect, equal to California, or the Valley of the Mississippi ! This can never be, until Oregon be blessed with a vast increase of productive soil, and Cali-

fornia and our own unequalled Valley be
greatly changed.

---

*Extracts from the Report of Lieutenant Wilkes
to the Secretary of the Navy, of the examination, by the Exploring Expedition, of the
Oregon Territory.*

The Territory embraced under the name
of Oregon, extends from latitude 42° north
to that of 53° 40′ north, and west of the
Rocky Mountains. Its natural boundaries,
were they attended to, would confine it
within the above geographical boundaries.

On the east it has the range of Rocky
Mountains along its whole extent ; on the
south those of the Klamet range, running on
the parallel of 42° and dividing it from
California ; on the west the Pacific Ocean ;
and on the north the western trend of the
Rocky Mountains, and the chain of lakes
near and along the parallels of 54° and 55°
north, dividing it from the British territory.
It is remarkable that, within these limits,
all the rivers which flow through the Territory take their rise.

The Territory is divided into three natural
felts or sections, viz :

1st. That between the Pacific Ocean and Cascade Mountains, (President's range) or western section ;

2nd. That between the Cascade mountains and blue mountain range, or middle section ;

3rd. That between the Blue and Rocky Mountain chains, or eastern section.

And this division will equally apply to the soil, climate, and productions.

The mountain ranges run, for the most part, in parallel lines with the coast, and, rising in many places above the snow line, (here found to be 6,500 feet), would naturally produce a difference of temperature between them, and also affect their productions.

Our surveys and explorations were confined, for the most part, to the two first, claiming more interest from being less known, and more in accordance with my instructions.

MOUNTAINS.—The Cascade range, or that nearest the coast, runs from the southern boundary, on a parallel with the sea coast, the whole length of the territory, north and south, rising, in many places, in high peaks, from twelve to fourteen thousand feet above the level of the sea, in regular cones. Their distance from the coast line is from one hundred to a hundred and fifty miles, and they almost interrupt the communication between the section, except where the two great rivers, the Columbia and Frazer's, force a passage through them.

There are a few mountain passes, but they are difficult, and only to be attempted late in the spring and summer.

A small range (the Claset) lies to the northward of the Columbia, between the coast and the waters of Puget's Sound, and along the strait of Juan de Fuca. This has several high peaks, which rise above the snow line, but, from their proximity to the sea, they are not at all times covered.

Their general direction is north and south, but there are many spurs or offsets that cause this portion to be very rugged.

The Blue mountains are irregular in their course, and occasionally interrupted, but generally tend from north by east to northeast, and from south to south-west.

In some parts they may be traced as spurs or offsets of the Rocky Mountains. Near the southern boundary they unite with the Klamet range, which runs east and west from the rocky mountains.

The Rocky Mountains are too well known to need description. The different passes will, however, claim attention hereafter. North of 48° the ranges are nearly parallel and have the rivers flowing between them.

ISLANDS.—Attached to the territory are groups of islands, bordering its northern coast. Among these are the large islands of Vancouver and Washington or Queen Charlotte; the former being two hundred and sixty miles in length, and fifty in width, containing about fifteen thousand square miles, and the latter a hundred and fifty miles in length and thirty in breadth, containing four thousand square miles.

Though somewhat broken in surface, their soil is said to be well adapted to agriculture.

They have many good harbours, and have long been the resort of those engaged in the fur trade; they enjoy a mild and salubrious climate, and have an abundance of fine fish frequenting their waters, which are taken in large quantities by the natives. Coal of good quality is found, specimens of which I obtained. The Hudson's Bay Company have made a trial of it, but, owing to its having been taken from near the surface, it was not very highly spoken of. Veins of minerals are also said to exist by those acquainted with these islands.

They both appear to be more densely inhabited than other portions of the territory. The natives are considered a treacherous race, particularly those in the vicinity of Johnson's Straits, and are to be closely watched when dealing with them.

At the south-east end of Vancouver's, there is a small archipelago of islands, through which the canal de Arro runs. They are for the most part uninhabited, well wooded, and composed of granite and pudding stone, which appear to be the prevailing rock to the northward of a line east from the strait of Juan de Fuca. They are generally destitute of fresh water, have but few anchorages, and strong currents render navigation among them difficult.

The islands nearer the main land, called on the maps Pitt's Banks, or the Prince Royal islands, are of the same character, and are only occasionally resorted to by the Indians, for the purpose of fishing.

The coast of the mainland, north of the parallel of 49°, is broken up by numerous inlets called canals, having perpendicular sides, and very deep water in them, affording no harbours, and but few commercial inducements to frequent them.

The land is equally cut up by spurs from the Cascade range, which here intersects the country in all directions, and prevents its adaptation for agriculture.

Its value is principally in its timber, and it is believed that few if any countries can compare with it in this respect.

There is no part on this coast where a settlement could be formed between Frazer's river, or 49° north, and the northern boundary of 54° 40′ north, that would be able to supply its own wants.

The Hudson's Bay Company have posts within this section of the country: Fort McLaughlin, in Millbank sound, in latitude 52° 10′ north, and Fort Simpson, in latitude 54° 30′ north, within Dundas island, and at the entrance of Chatham sound; but they are only posts for the fur trade of the coast, and are supplied twice a year with provisions, &c.

It is believed that the Company have yet no establishment on any of the islands; but I understood it was in contemplation to make one on Vancouver's island, in the vicinity of Nootka sound, or that of Clyoquot.

Owing to the dense fogs, the coast is extremely dangerous; and they render it at all times difficult to approach and navigate it. The interior of this portion of the territory is traversed by the three ranges of mountains, with the several rivers which take their rise in them, and is probably unequalled for its ruggedness, and from all accounts incapable of anything like cultivation.

The Columbia in its trend to the westward, along the parallel of 48°, cuts off the central or Blue mountain range, which is not again met with until on the parallel of 45°. From 45° they trend away to the southward and westward, until they fall into the Klamet range. This latter portion is but partially wooded.

Rivers.—The Columbia claims the first notice. Its northern branch takes its rise in the Rocky mountains, in latitude 50° north, longitude 116° west; from thence it pursues a northern route to near McGillivray's Pass, in the Rocky mountains. At the boat encampment, the river is three thousand six hundred feet above the level of the sea (here it receives two small tributaries, the Canoe river and that from the Committee's Punch Bowl), from thence it turns south, having some obstructions to its safe navigation, and receiving many tributaries in its course to Colville, among which are the Kootanie, or Fat Bow, and the Flat Head or Clarke river from the east, and that of Colville from the west.

This great river is bounded thus far on its course by a range of high mountains, well-wooded, and in places expands into a line of lakes before it reaches Colville, where it is two thousand and forty-nine feet above the level of the sea, having a fall of five hundred and fifty feet in two hundred and twenty miles. To the south of this it trends to the westward, receiving the Spokan river from the east, which is not navigable, and takes its rise in the Lake of Cœur d'Alène. Thence it pursues a westerly course for about sixty miles, receiving several smaller streams, and at its bend to the south it is joined by the Okanagan, a river that has its source in a line of lakes, affording canoe and boat navigation for a considerable extent to the northward.

The Columbia thence passes to the southward until it reaches Wallawalla, in the lattitude of 45° a distance of one hundred and sixty miles, receiving the Piscous, Y'Akama, and Point de Boise, or Entyatecoom, from the west, which take their rise in the Cascade range, and also its great south-eastern branch, the Saptin or Lewis, which has its source in the Rocky mountains, near our southern boundary, and being a large quantity of water to increase the volume of the main stream. The Lewis is not navigable, even for canoes, except in reaches. The rapids are extensive and of frequent occurrence. It generally passes between the Rocky mountain spurs and the Blue mountains. It receives the Koos-koos-ke, Salmon, and several other rivers, from the east and west (the former from the Rocky mountains, the latter from the Blue mountains) and, were it navigable, would much facilitate the intercourse with this part of the country. Its length to its junction with the Columbia is five hundred and twenty miles.

The Columbia at Wallawalla is one thousand two hundred and eighty-six feet above the level of the sea, and about three thousand five hundred wide; it now takes its last turn to the westward, receiving the Umatilla, Quisnel's, John Day's, and de Chute rivers from the south, and Cathlatate's from the north, pursuing its rapid course of eighty miles, previous to passing through the range of Cascade moutains, in a series of falls and rapids that obstruct its flow, and form insurmountable barriers to the passage of boats by water during the floods. These difficulties, however, are overcome by portages.

From thence there is a still water navigation for forty miles, when its course is again obstructed by rapids.

Thence to the ocean, one hundred and twenty miles, it is navigable for vessels of twelve feet draught of water at the lowest state of the river, though obstructed by many sand-bars.

In this part it receives the Willamette from the south, and the Cowelitz from the north. The former is navigable for small vessels twenty miles, to the mouth of the Klackamus, three miles below its falls; the latter cannot be called navigable except for a small part of the year, during the floods, and then only for canoes and barges.

The width of the Columbia, within twenty miles of its mouth, is much increased, and it joins the ocean between Cape Disappointment and Point Adams, forming a sand-pit from each by deposit, and causing a dangerous bar, which greatly impedes its navigation and entrance.

Frazer's river next claims attention. It

takes its rise in the Rocky mountain, near the source of Canoe river, taking a north-western course of eighty miles ; it then turns to the southward, receiving the waters of Stuart's river, which rises in a chain of lakes near the northern boundary of the Territory.

It then pursues a southerly course, receiving the waters of the Chilcotin, Pinkslitsa, and several smaller streams, from the west, and those of Thompson's river, Quisnell's, and other streams, from the east, (these take their rise in lakes, and are navigable in canoes, by making portages ;) and under the parallel of 49° it breaks through the Cascade range in a succession of falls and rapids, and, after a westerly course of seventy miles it empties itself into the gulf of Georgia, in the latitude of 49° 07′ north. This latter portion is navigable for vessels that can pass its bar drawing twelve feet water ; its whole length being three hundred and fifty miles.

The Chikeelis is next in importance. It has three sources among the range of hills that intersect the country north of the Columbia river. After a very tortuous course, and receiving some small streams issuing from the lakes in the high ground near the head-quarters of Hood's canal and Puget's Sound, it disembogues in Grey's harbour ; it is not navigable except for canoes ; its current is rapid, and the stream much obstructed.

To the south of the Columbia there are many small streams, three of which only deserve the name of rivers : the Umpqha, Too-too-tut-na, or Rogues' river, and the Klamet, which latter empties itself into the ocean south of the parallel of 42°. None of these form harbours capable of receiving a vessel of more than eight feet draught of water, and the bars for most part of the year are impassable from the surf that sets in on the coast. The character of the great rivers is peculiar—rapid and sunken much below the level of the country, with perpendicular banks ; indeed they are, as it were, in trenches, it being extremely difficult to get at the water in many places, owing to the steep basaltic walls ; and during the rise they are in many places confined by dalles, which back the water some distance, submerging islands and *tracts of low prairie*, giving the appearance of extensive lakes.

Lakes.—There are in the various sections of the country many lakes. The Okanagan, Stuart's, Quisnell's, and Kamloop's are the largest in the northern section.

The Flat Bow, Cœur d'Alène, and Kulluspelm, in the middle section, and those forming the head-waters of the large rivers in the eastern section. The country is well watered, and there are but few places where an abundance of water, either from rivers, springs, or rivulets, cannot be obtained.

The smaller lakes add much to the picturesque beauty of the country. They are generally at the head-waters of the smaller streams. The map will point out more particularly their extent and locality.

HARBOURS.—All the harbours formed by the rivers on the sea-coast are obstructed by extensive sand-bars, which make them difficult to enter. The rivers bring down large quantities of sand, which is deposited on meeting with the ocean, causing a gradual increase of the impediments already existing at their mouths. None of them can be deemed safe ports to enter. The entrance to the Columbia is impracticable two-thirds of the year, and the difficulty of leaving is equally great.

The north sands are rapidly increasing, and extending further to the southward. In the memory of several of those who have been longest in the country, Cape Disappointment has been encroached upon some hundred feet by the sea, and, during my short experience, nearly half an acre of the middle sands was washed away in a few days. These sands are known to change every season.

The exploration made of the Clatsop, or South channel, it is believed, will give more safety to vessels capable of entering the river. The depth of water on the bar seems not to have changed, though the passage has become somewhat narrow.

Grey's harbour will admit of vessels of light draught of water, (ten feet), but there is but little room in it, on account of the extensive mud and sand flats. A survey was made of it, to which I refer for particulars.

This, however, is not the case with the harbours formed within the straits of Juan de Fuca, of which there are many ; and no part of the world affords finer inland sounds or a greater number of harbours than can be found here, capable of receiving the largest class of vessels, and without a danger in them which is not visible. From the rise and fall of the tides, (eighteen feet), every facility is afforded for the erection of works for a great maritime nation. For further information, our extensive surveys of these waters are referred to.

CLIMATE.—That of the western section is mild throughout the year, neither experiencing the cold of winter nor the heat of summer. By my experiments, the mean temperature was found to be 54° of Fahrenheit.

The prevailing winds in the summer are from the northward and westward, and in the winter, from the southward and westward, and south-east, which are tempestuous. The winter is supposed to last from December to February; rains usually begin to fall in November, and last till March, but they are not heavy though frequent.

Snow sometimes falls, but it seldom lies more than three days. The frosts are early, occurring in the latter part of August; this, however, is to be accounted for by the proximity of the mountains. A mountain or easterly wind invariably causes a great fall in the temperature; these winds are not frequent. During the summer of our operations, I found but *three days* noted of easterly winds.

The nights are cold, and affect the vegetation so far, that Indian corn will not ripen. Fruit-trees blossom early in April at Nisqually and Vancouver; and at the former place, on the 12th of May, peas were a foot high, strawberries in full blossom, and salad had already gone to seed.

The mean height of the barometer, during our stay at Nisqually, was 30,046 inches, and of the thermometer 66° 58 Fahrenheit. The thermometer at 4 A. M. on the 4th of July, way at 50° Fahrenheit, and on the same day, at 2 P. M., 90° Fahrenheit. The lowest degree was 39° at 4 A. M., May 22d, and at 5 P. M. of the same day, the temperature was 72° of Fahrenheit.

From June to September at Vancouver the mean height of the barometer was 30.32 inches, and of the thermometer 66° 33′ of Fahrenheit. Out of one hundred and six days, seventy-six were fair, nineteen cloudy, and eleven rainy. The rains are light; this is evident from the hills *not being washed*, and having a sward to their tops, *although of great declivity.*

The second, or middle section, is subject to droughts. During the summer the atmosphere is much drier and warmer, and the winter much colder than in the western section. Its extremes of heat and cold are more frequent and greater, the mercury at times falling as low as minus 18° of

Fahrenheit in the winter, and rising to 180° in the shade in summer ; the daily difference of temperature is about 40° Fahrenheit. It has, however, been found extremely salubrious, possessing a pure and healthy air.

The stations of the missionaries and posts of the Hudson's Bay Company, have afforded me the means of obtaining information relative to the climate. Although full data have not been kept, yet these observations afford a tolerably good knowledge of the weather.

In summer the atmosphere is cooled by the strong westerly breezes, which replace the vacuum produced by the heated prairie grounds. No dews fall in this section.

The climate of the third, or eastern section, is extremely variable. The temperature during the day, differing from 50° to 60°, renders it unfit for agriculture, and there are but few places in its northern part where the climate would not effectually put a stop to its ever becoming settled.

In each day, from the best accounts, all the changes are experienced incident to spring, summer, autumn, and winter. There are places where small farms might be located, but they are few in number.

Soil.—That of the first, or western section varies in the northern parts from a light brown loam to a thin vegetable earth, with gravel and sand as a sub-soil: in the middle parts, from a rich heavy loam and unctuous clay to a deep heavy black loam on a trap rock ; and in the southern, the soil is generally good, varying from a black vegetable loam to decomposed basalt, with stiff clay, and portions of loose gravel soil. The hills are generally basalt, and stone, and slate.

Between the Umpqua and the boundary, the rocks are primitive, consisting of talcon slate, hornblende, and granite, which produce a gritty and poor soil ; some places of rich prairie however, occur covered with oaks.

The soil of the second, or middle section, is for the most part a light sandy loam, in the valleys rich alluvial, and the hills are generally barren.

The third, or eastern section, is a rocky, broken, and barren country. Stupendous mountain spurs traverse it in all directions, affording little level ground ; snow lies on the mountains nearly, if not quite, the year through.

Agriculture, Productions, &c.—The

first section, for the most part, is a well-timbered country ; it is intersected with the spurs, or offsets, from the Cascade mountains, which render its surface much broken : these are covered with a dense forest. It is well-watered, and communication between the northern, southern, and middle parts is difficult, on account of the various rivers, spurs of mountains, &c.

The timber consists of pines, firs, spruce, oaks, (red and white), ash, arbutus, arbor vitæ, cedar, poplar, maple, willow, cherry, and tew, with a close undergrowth of hazel, rubus, roses, &c. The richest and best soil is found on the second or middle prairie, and is best adapted for agriculture, the high and low being excellent for pasture land.

The line woods run on the east side, and near the foot of the Cascade range. The climate and soil are admirably adapted for all kinds of grain, wheat, rye, oats, barley, peas, &c. Indian corn does not thrive in any part of this territory where it has been tried. Many fruits appear to succeed well, particularly the apple and pear. Vegetables grow exceedingly well, and yield most abundantly.

The surface of the middle section is about one thousand feet above the level of the first

or western section, and is generally a rolling
prairie country. That part lying to the
north of the parallel of 48° is very much
broken with mountain chains and rivers,
consequently barren and very rugged.
From the great and frequent changes in its
temperature, it is totally unfit for agriculture, but is well supplied with game of all
the kinds which are found in the country.

The mountain chains on the parallel of
48° are cut off by the Columbia, as before
stated, leaving an extensive rolling country
in the centre of the Territory, which is well
adapted for grazing.

The southern part of this section is destitute of timber or wood, unless the wormwood (artimesia) may be so called. To the
northward of the parallel of 49° it is covered
with forests. Wheat and other grains grow
well in the bottoms, where they can be irrigated. The soil in such places is rich, and
capable of producing almost any thing.

The missionaries have succeeded in raising good crops. Stock succeeds here even
better than in the lower country. Notwithstanding the severe cold, the cattle are not
housed, nor is provender laid in for them,
the country being sufficiently supplied with
fodder in the natural hay that is abundant

everywhere in the prairie, which is preferred by the cattle to the fresh grass at the bottoms.

No attempts at agriculture have been made in the third section, except at Fort Hall. The small grains thrive tolerably well, together with vegetables, and a sufficient quantity has been obtained to supply the wants of the post. The ground is well adapted for grazing in the prairies, and, despite its changeable climate, stock is found to thrive well and endure the severity of the winter without protection.

This section is exceedingly dry and arid, rains seldom falling, and but little snow. The country is partially timbered, and the soil much impregnated with salts. The missionary station on the Koos-koos-ke, near the western line of this section, is thought by the missionaries to be a *wet climate*.

The soil along the river bottoms is generally alluvial, and would yield good crops, were it not for the overflowing of the rivers, which check and kill the grain. Some of the finest portions of the land are thus unfit for cultivation; they are generally covered with water before the banks are overflown, in consequence of the quicksands which exist in them, and through which the water percolates.

The rivers of this Territory afford no fertilizing properties to the soil, but, on the contrary, are destitute of all substances. The temperature of the Columbia in the latter part of May was 42°, and in September 68°.

The rise of the streams flowing from the Cascade mountains takes place twice a-year, in February and November, from the rains ; that of the Columbia in May and June, from the melting of the snows. Sometimes the rise of the latter is very sudden, if heavy rains occur at that period ; but usually it is gradual, and reaches its greatest height from the 6th to the 15th of June. Its perpendicular rise is from eighteen to twenty feet at Vancouver, where a line of embankment has been thrown up to protect the lower prairie ; but it has been generally flooded, and the crops in most cases destroyed. It is the intention to abandon its cultivation, and devote it to pasturage.

The greatest rise in the Willamette takes place in February ; and I was informed that it rose sometimes twenty to twenty-five feet, and quite suddenly, but soon subsides. It occasionally causes much damage.

Both the Willamette and the Cowelitz are much swollen by the backing of their waters during the height of the Columbia, and all their lower grounds submerged. This puts an effectual bar to their prairies being used for any thing but pasturage, which is fine throughout the year, excepting in the season of the floods, when the cattle are driven to the high grounds.

My knowledge of the agriculture of this Territory, it will be well to mention, is derived from visits made to the various settlements, except Fort Langley and Fort Hall.

The Indians on the different islands in Puget's Sound and Admiralty Inlet cultivate potatoes principally, which are extremely fine, and raised in great abundance, and now constitute a large portion of their food.

At Nisqually the Hudson's Bay Company had fine crops of wheat, oats, peas, potatoes, &c. The wheat, it was supposed, would yield fifteen bushels to the acre. The farm has been two years under cultivation, and is principally intended for a grazing and dairy farm. They have now seventy milch cows, and make butter, &c., to supply their contract with the Russians.

The Cowelitz farm is also in the western section. The produce of wheat is good — about twenty bushels to the acre. The ground, however, has just been brought under cultivation. The Company have here six hundred acres, which are situated on the Cowelitz river, about thirty miles from the Columbia, and on the former are erecting a saw and grist mill. The farm is finely situated, and the harvest of 1841 produced seven thousand bushels of wheat.

Several Canadians are also established here, who told me that they succeeded well with but little work. They have erected buildings, live comfortably, and work small farms of fifty acres.

I was told that the stock on these farms did not thrive so well as elsewhere. There are no low prairie grounds on the river in this vicinity, and it is too far for them to resort to the Kamas plains, a fine grazing country, but a few miles distant. The wolves make sad depredations with the increase of their flock, if not well watched.

The hilly portion of the country, although its soil in many places is very good, is yet so heavily timbered as to make it, in the present state of the country, valueless : this is also the case with many fine portions of level ground. There are, however, large tracts of fine prairie, suitable for cultivation, and ready for the plough.

The Willamette valley is supposed to be the finest portion of the country, though I am of opinion that many parts of the southern portion of the territory will be found far superior to it. The largest settlement is in the northern part of the valley, some fifteen miles above the falls. About sixty families are settled there, the industrious of whom appear to be thriving. They are composed of American missionaries, trappers, and Canadians, who were formerly servants of the Hudson's Bay Company. All of them appeared to be doing well; but I was on the whole disappointed, from the reports that had been made to me, not to find the settlement in a state of greater forwardness, considering the advantages the missionaries have had.

In comparison with our own country, I would say that the labour necessary in this territory to acquire wealth or subsistence is in the proportion of one to three; or in other words, a man must work through the year three times as much in the United States, to gain the like competency. The care of stock, which occupies so much time with us, requires no attention there, and on the increase only a man might find support.

The wheat of this valley yields thirty-five to forty bushels for one sown, or twenty to thirty bushels to the acre ; its quality is superior to that grown in the United States, and its weight nearly four pounds to the bushel heavier. The above is the yield of new land ; but it is believed it will greatly exceed this after the third crop, when the land has been broken up and well tilled.

After passing into the middle section, the climate undergoes a decided change ; in place of the cool and moist atmosphere, one that is dry and arid is entered, and the crops suffer from drought.

The only wood or bush seen, is the wormwood, (artimesia,) and this only in places. All cultivation has to be more or less carried on by irrigation.

The country bordering the Columbia, above the Dalles, to the north and south of the river, is the poorest in the territory, and has no doubt led many to look upon the middle section as perfectly useless to man. Twenty or thirty miles on either side of the river are so ; but beyond that a fine grazing country exists, and in very many places there are portions of it that might be advantageously farmed. On the banks of the Wallawalla, a small stream emptying into the Columbia, about twenty-five miles from the Company's post, a missionary is established, who raises very fine wheat on the low bottoms, by using its waters for the purpose of irrigation. This is also the case at the mission station at Lapwai, on the Kooskoos-ke, where fine crops are raised ; grains, vegetables and some fruits thrive remarkably well. In the northern part of this section, at Chimekaine, there is another missionary station. Near the Spokan, and at Colville, the country is well adapted for agriculture, and it is successfully carried on. Colville supplies all the northern posts, and the missionaries in its vicinity are doing well. The northern part of this section will be able to supply the whole southern part with wood. At Colville the changes of temperature are great during the twenty-four hours, but are not injurious to the small grain. The cultivation of fruit has been successful.

FISHERIES.—It will be almost impossible to give an idea of the extensive fisheries in the rivers and on the coast. They all abound in salmon of the finest flavour, which run twice a year, beginning in May and October, and appear inexhaustible ; the whole population live upon them. The Columbia produces the largest, and probably affords the greatest numbers. There are some few of the branches of the Columbia that the spring fish do not enter, but they are plentifully supplied in the fall.

The great fishery of the Columbia is at the Dalles ; but all the rivers are well supplied. The last one on the northern branch of the Columbia is near Colville, at the Kettle falls ; but salmon are found above this in the river and its tributaries.

In Frazer's river the salmon are said to be very numerous, but not large ; they are unable to get above the falls some eighty miles from the sea.

In the rivers and sounds are found several kinds of salmon, salmon-trout, sturgeon, cod, carp, sole, flounders, ray, perch, herring, lamprey eels, and a kind of smelt, called " *shrow*," in great abundance ; also large quantities of shell fish, viz : crabs, clams, oysters, muscles, &c., which are all used by the natives, and constitute the greater proportion of their food.

Whales in numbers are found along the coast, and are frequently captured by the

Indians in and at the mouth of the straits of Juan de Fuca.

GAME.—Abundance of game exists, such as elk, deer, antelope, bears, wolves, foxes, musk-rats, martins, bears and siffleurs, which are eaten by the Canadians. In the middle section, or that designated as the rolling prairie, no game is found. The fur-bearing animals are decreasing in numbers yearly, particularly south of the parallel of 48°; indeed it is very doubtful whether they are sufficiently numerous to repay the expense of hunting them.

The Hudson's Bay Company have almost the exclusive monopoly of this business. They have decreased, owing to being hunted without regard to season. This is not, however, the case to the north; there the Company have been left to exercise their own rule, and prevent the indiscriminate slaughter of either old or young, out of the proper season.

In the spring and fall, the rivers are literally covered with geese, ducks, and other water fowl.

In the eastern section, the buffalo abound, and are hunted by the Oregon Indians, as well as the Blackfeet. Wolves are troublesome to the settlers, but they are not so numerous as formerly. From the advantages this country possesses, it bids fair to have an extensive commerce on advantageous terms with most ports of the Pacific. It is well calculated to produce the following which, in a few years after its settlement, would become its staples, viz: furs, salted beef and pork, fish, grain, flour, wool, hides, tallow, lumber, and perhaps coal. A ready market for all these is now to be found in the Pacific; and in return for them sugars, coffee and other tropical productions, may be had at the Sandwich Islands—advantages that few new countries possess, viz: the facility of a market, and one that in time must become of immense extent.

Manufacturing power.—This country, it is believed, affords as many sites for water power as any other, and in many places within reach of navigable waters. The timber of the western section, to the south of 49°, is not so good as that of the north. This is imputed to the climate being milder and more changeable. A great difference is found between the north and south sides of the trees, the one being of a hard and close grain, while the other is open and spongy.

To the north of the parallel 49°, on Frazer's River, an abundance of fine timber for spars of any dimensions is easily obtained.

There will always be a demand for the timber of this country at high prices throughout the Pacific. The oak is well adapted for ship timber, and abundance of ash, cedar, cypress and arbor vitæ, may be had for fuel, fencing, &c.; and, although the southern part of the middle section is destitute of timber, it may be supplied from the eastern or northern sections by water carriage.

Intercommunication would at first appear to be difficult between the different parts of the country, but I take a different view of it.

Stock of all kinds thrive exceedingly well, and they will in consequence always abound in the territory. The soil affords every advantage for making good roads, and, in process of time, transportation must become comparatively cheap.

SETTLEMENTS —They consist principally of those belonging to the Hudson's Bay Company, and where the missionaries have established themselves. They are as follows : In the western section, Fort Simpson, Fort McLaughlin, Fort Langley, Nisqually, Cowelitz, Fort George, Vancouver, and Umpqua ; Fort St. James, Barbine, Alexandria, Chilcothin, Kamloop's, (on Thompson's River) ; Okanagan, Colville and Wallawalla, in the middle ; and in the eastern, Kootanie and Fort Hall. Fort Boise has been abandoned, as has also Kaima, a missionary settlement on the Koos-koos-ke.

These are all small settlements, surrounded by palisades, with bastions at their corners, enclosing the houses and stores of the Company, sufficient to protect them against the Indians, but in no way to be considered as forts. A few Indians reside near them, who are dependant for their food and employment on them.

These forts being situated for the most part near the great fisheries, are frequented by the Indians, who bring their furs to trade for blankets, &c., at the same time they come to lay in their yearly supply of salmon.

Vancouver is the principal depot from which all supplies are furnished, and to which returns are made.

At Vancouver, the village is separated from the fort, and nearer the river. In addition to its being the depot of the Hudson's Bay Company, there is now attached to it the largest farm of the Puget Sound Company, the stockholders of which are generally the officers and servants of the Hudson's Bay Company. They have now farms in successful operation at Vancouver, Cowelitz, Nisqually, Colville, Fort Langley, and the Fualtine plains, about ten miles from Vancouver, all of which are well stocked, and supply the Russian post at Sitka, under contract, with a variety of articles raised on them. They have introduced large herds and flocks into the territory from California, and during our stay there several thousand head were imported. They are thus doing incalculable good to the territory, and rendering it more valuable for future settlers. At the same time, this exerts an influence in domesticating the Indians, not only by changing their habits, but food, and attaching them to a locality.

The Indians of the Territory are not a wandering race, as some have asserted, but change for food only, and each successive season will generally find them in their old haunts, seeking it.

The settlements established by the missionaries, are at the Willamette falls and valley, Nisqually and Clatsop, in the western section, and at the Dalles, Wallawalla, Lapwai, and Chimekaine, on the Spokan, in the middle.

Those of the middle section are succeeding well; and although little progress has been made in the conversion of the Indians to Christianity, yet they have done much good in reforming some of the vices and teaching some of the useful arts, particularly that of agriculture, and the construction of houses, which has had the effect, in a measure, to attach them to the soil. The men now rear and tend their cattle, plant their potatoes and corn, which latter they exchange for buffalo meat with those who hunt. The squaws attend to their household, and employ themselves in knitting and weaving, which they have been taught. They raise on their small patches, corn, potatoes, melons, &c., irrigating the land for that purpose. There are many villages of Indians still existing, though greatly reduced in numbers from former estimates.

Population.—It is extremely difficult to ascertain, with accuracy, the amount of population in the Territory. The Indians change to their different abodes as the fishing seasons come round, which circumstance, if not attended to, would produce very erroneous results.

The following is believed to be very nearly the truth; if any thing, it is overrated :

Vancouver or Washington Island	5,000
From the parallel of 50° to 54° north	2,000
Penn's Cove, Whidby's Island, mainland (Shatchet tribe) . .	650
Hood's canal, (Suquamish and Toando tribe) . . .	500
At and about Okanagan . . .	300
About Colville, Spokan, &c . .	450
Willamette falls and valley . .	275
Pillar rock, Oak Point, and Columbia River	300
Port Discovery . 150 ⎤	
Fort Townsend . 70 ⎬ Chalams .	420
New Dungeness . 200 ⎦	
Wallawalla, including the Nez-percés, Snakes, &c . . .	1,100
Killamouks, north of Umpqua .	400
Cape Flattery and Queen Hythe to Point Granville, (Classet tribe)	1,250
Blackfeet tribes that make incursions west of the Rocky Mountains .	1,000
Birch Bay	300
Frazer's River (Neamitch tribe) .	500
Chenooks	209
Clatstops	220
At the Cascades	105
At the Dalles	250
Y'Akama River	100

De Chute River 125
Umpquas 400
Roger's River . . . 500
Klamets 300
Shastys 500
Kallapugus 600
Nisqually 200
Chikelis and Puget's Sound . . 700
Cowelits or Klakatacks . . 350
Port Orchard 150

_____

19,154

The whole Territory may be estimated as containing twenty thousand. Of whites, Canadians, and half-breeds, there are between seven hundred and eight hundred, of whom about one hundred and fifty are Americans; the rest are settlers, and the officers and servants of the Company. The Indians are rapidly decreasing in all parts of the country; the causes are supposed to be their rude treatment of diseases, and the dissipated lives they lead.

The white American population, as far as I have been able to judge of them, are orderly, and generally industrious; although they are, with the exception of the missionaries, men who have led, for the most part, dissolute lives.

The absence of spirits, as long as it continues, will probably secure them from excesses. Very much to their credit, they have abandoned the use of spirituous liquors, by consent of the whole community.

I cannot but view this Territory as peculiarly liable to the vice of drunkenness. The ease with which the wants of man are obtained, the little labour required, and consequent opportunities for idleness, will render it so. The settlers of the Willamette valley have, with a praiseworthy spirit, engaged to prevent the establishment of distilleries, and there are, as yet, no places where spirits can be bought (to my knowledge) in the Territory.

It is highly creditable to the Hudson's Bay Company, that on a vessel arriving on the coast with some spirits on board, in order to prevent its introduction, they have purchased the whole cargo, while, at the same time, their storehouses were filled with rum. They have, with praiseworthy zeal, interdicted its being an article of trade, being well satisfied that it is contrary to their interest, and demoralizing in its effects on all the tribes and people with whom they have to deal, rendering them difficult to manage, quarrelsome among themselves, and preventing their success in hunting. Endeavours have likewise been made by the officers of the Company to induce the Russians, on their side, to adopt this example, and do away with it as an article of trade, but hitherto without success. This no doubt has been one of the causes affecting the decrease of tribes, as it was formerly almost the only article of trade.

In the event of the territory being taken possession of, the necessity of circumscribing the use and sale of spirits cannot be too strongly insisted upon by legal enactment, both to preserve order and avoid expense.

As far as the Indians have come under my notice, they are an inoffensive race, except those in the northern parts. The depredations committed on the whites may be traced to injuries received, or arise from superstitious motives.

MISSIONARIES.—Little has yet been effected by them in christianizing the natives. They are principally engaged in the cultivation of the mission farms, and in the care of their own stock, in order to obtain flocks and herds for themselves, most of them having selected lands. As far as my personal observation went, in the part of the country where the missionaries reside, there are very few Indians to engage their attention ; and they seemed more occupied with the settlement of the country and in agricultural pursuits than in missionary labours.

When there, I made particular inquiries whether laws were necessary for their protection, and I feel fully satisfied that they require none at present, besides the moral code it is their duty to inculcate.

The Catholic portion of the settlement, who form a large majority, are kept under good control by their priest, who is disposed to act in unison with the other missionaries in the proper punishment of all bad conduct.

I cannot close this report without doing justice to the officers of the Hudson's Bay Company's service for their kind and gentlemanly treatment to us while in the territory, and bearing testimony that, during all my intercourse, and in their dealings with others, they seemed to be guided by one rule of conduct highly creditable to them, not only as business men, but gentlemen.

They afforded us every assistance that was in their power both in supplies and in means to accomplish our duties. There are many persons in the country who bear testimony to the aid and kindness rendered them in their outset ; and of their hospitality it is needless to speak, for it has become proverbial.

To conclude, few portions of the globe, in my opinion, are to be found so rich in soil, so diversified in surface, or so capable of being rendered the happy abode of an industrious and civilized community. For beauty of scenery and salubrity of climate, it is not surpassed. It is peculiarly adapted for an agricultural and pastoral people, and no portion of the world beyond the tropics can be found that will yield so readily with moderate labour, to the wants of man.

THE END.

LONDON:
PRINTED BY SCHULZE AND CO., 13, POLAND STREET.